MW01269102

Garland Library of Music Ethnology

James Porter, *Series Editor*

Ethnomusicology Research
*A Select Annotated
Bibliography*
by Ann Briegleb Schuursma

Jazz Research and
Performance Materials
*A Select Annotated
Bibliography
Second Edition*
by Eddie S. Meadows

Traditional Anglo-
American Folk Music
*An Annotated Discography
of Published Sound Recordings*
by Norm Cohen

Central European
Folk Music
*An Annotated Bibliography
of Sources in German*
by Philip V. Bohlman

CENTRAL EUROPEAN FOLK MUSIC

AN ANNOTATED BIBLIOGRAPHY OF SOURCES IN GERMAN

PHILIP V. BOHLMAN

Routledge
Taylor & Francis Group

LONDON AND NEW YORK

First published 1996 Garland Publishing, Inc.

2 Park Square, Milton Park, Abingdon, Oxon OX14 4RN
711 Third Avenue, New York, NY 10017, USA

First issued in paperback 2016

Routledge is an imprint of the Taylor & Francis Group, an informa business

Notices
Practitioners and researchers must always rely on their own experience and
knowledge in evaluating and using any information, methods, compounds, or
experiments described herein. In using such information or methods they should
be mindful of their own safety and the safety of others, including parties for whom
they have a professional responsibility.

Product or corporate names may be trademarks or registered trademarks, and are
used only for identification and explanation without intent to infringe.

Library of Congress Cataloging-in-Publication Data

Bohlman, Philip Vilas.
    Central European folk music : an annotated bibliography of sources in
German / by Philip Bohlman.
        p.   cm. — (Garland library of music ethnology ; v. 3) (Garland
reference library of the humanities ; v. 1448)
        ISBN-13: 978-0-8153-0304-6 (hbk)
        ISBN-13: 978-1-1389-7001-4 (pbk)

        1. Folk music—Europe, Central—Bibliography.   2. Germans—Europe,
Central—Music—Bibliography.   I. Title.   II. Series: Garland library of
music ethnology ; 3.   III. Series: Garland reference library of the humanities ; vol. 1448.
ML128.F74B64   1996
016.78162 31—dc20   96-14970
                                                        CIP
                                                        MN

For Otto Holzapfel,
who opened the doors of the Deutsches Volksliedarchiv for me
and refused to turn away from the contradictions
at the borders of Central Europe

Contents

SERIES EDITOR'S FOREWORD

The Garland Library of Music Ethnology comprises mainly reference works in ethnomusicology, dance ethnology, music anthropology, and related fields. The series seeks to fill some gaps in reference and research: in specific, music areas such as Native American, Arab, Southeast Asian, Latin American, European, and North American, and through works of a more general methodological kind. Further contributions to the series will be in dance ethnology, discography, and filmography. In addition, some important works in translation, as well as the occasional monograph, will form part of the series.

The term "music ethnology" was chosen for a practical reason: to differentiate the series from The Garland Library of Readings in Ethnomusicology (7 vols., 1990). There are less obvious reasons for using "music ethnology": "ethnomusicology," though it has flourished in scholarly circles since its invention by Jaap Kunst in 1950, is a cumbersome term for the lay person; a certain ambiguity is built into it through the "ethno" prefix, with its connotations of "other," "different," or "ethnic" (e.g., Western vs. non-Western); and the nominal amalgam appears to emphasize the musicology component over the ethnological (or anthropological) rather than the interaction of musicology and ethnology on equal terms. While no single term is entirely satisfactory, "music ethnology" (like "dance ethnology") at least has the virtue of clarity as well as suggesting a more equable balance between the disciplines.

This fourth volume in the series, following Ann Briegleb Schuursma's *Ethnomusicology Research* (1992), Norm Cohen's *Traditional Anglo-American Folk Music* (1994), and Eddie S. Meadow's *Jazz Research and Performance Materials* (1995), supplies a fundamental resource for ethnomusicologists and students of folk music who do not read German. There is no question that German-language scholarship is of major importance for the ideas and methods that are presented in published works, especially since World War II. Philip V. Bohlman's bibliography is a much-needed reference work in this area: *Central European Folk Music: An Annotated Bibliography of Sources in German* presents the essential core of German-language scholarship, and even includes key works from before World War II.

Professor Bohlman's credentials in the field of European and North American folk music are impeccable. Currently Associate Professor of Music at the University of Chicago, he obtained his doctorate from the University of Illinois as a student of Bruno Nettl there (1984). He has also taught at the University of California, Berkeley (1984) and the University of Illinois at Chicago (1985–87) and has been a Guest Professor at the Albert-Ludwigs University of Freiburg im Breisgau,

Germany (1990–91). In 1995–96, he was Fulbright Guest Professor at the University of Vienna. In addition to his teaching posts, Professor Bohlman has held a number of research awards, including those from Fulbright-Hays (1981–82) and the Alexander von Humboldt Foundation (1990–91, 1993–96).

Among Professor Bohlman's many publications are *The Study of Folk Music in the Modern World* (1988), *"The Land Where Two Streams Flow": Music in the German-Jewish Community of Israel* (1989), and *Comparative Musicology and Anthropology of Music: Essays on the History of Ethnomusicology* (co-edited with Bruno Nettl, 1991). As well as being noted for his published work on German-language scholarship, Professor Bohlman is known for his studies of Jewish and particularly German-Jewish musical life. His attention to the special nature of German-Jewish culture, and its relationship to European culture as a whole, is an indication of his sensitivity to the central tragedy of Europe in this century.

The usefulness of the present work lies in its authoritative coverage of the scholarly material, and the inclusion of Austrian and Swiss-German sources makes for a vital supplement to sources from Germany itself. The logical arrangement of the parts and subsections makes it easy for the reader to follow the kinds of categories that European scholars have devised for the study of folk music. The annotations are concise, yet do not stint on providing full information regarding the author, origin, and nature of the work in question. Professor Bohlman's valuable introduction to each part of the work helps to place the section in its proper scholarly context. With this reference work, a positive and collegial step has been taken to the understanding, not only of folk music as an evaluative and indeed ideological category of culture, but of the intellectual course, or courses, of German-language scholarship in the twentieth century.

James Porter, *Editor*
The Garland Library
of Music Ethnology

PREFACE

I take as my point of departure for the concept and organization of this book my own engagement with the traditions and scholarship of Central European folk music. Admittedly, this approach suggests an unusual, if not somewhat self-centered, strategy to deal with the dilemma faced by all who prepare annotated bibliographies. More often, annotated bibliographies seek to be inclusive, to cover as much ground as possible, and to launch themselves with the slightly uncomfortabe disclaimer that no book could do justice to everything written on a given field, making it necessary to choose what to include and exclude. My engagement with the traditional music of German-speaking Europe and of those cultures to which German-speaking Europeans have immigrated, however, has resulted from activist motivations. I turned to German-language scholarship because in my own work I was confronted by problems of ethnicity and nationalism, the politics of identity and religion, the histories of mass migration and modernity. Such motivations have guided my choices in preparing this book and placing it in the discourses of contemporary ethnomusicological and folkloristic scholarship.

The point of departure that I have described here is, clearly, very American. It is not, however, the product of what some have called the tradition of Anglo-American musical scholarship. If there is a special set of problems articulated in an intellectual history of Anglo-American scholarship, this book owes relatively little to it. Again, let me underscore my activist engagement with German-language scholarship, whereby I mean that I have turned to that scholarship because of the common ground it sometimes shares with American ethnomusicology, and because of the contested domains that open up when American and Central European approaches clash. Both the common ground and the contested domains hold the potential of stimulating more widespread engagement among English- and German-speaking scholars. The present book, therefore, is not simply an effort to "make available" German-language scholarship to those who do not read German, but rather to sketch the possibility of recognizing and entering into a common intellectual history.

In order to realize this potential, it has become necessary to initiate a process of disciplinary translation with this book. The concept for the book as a whole and for the individual entries has taken shape as the result of this consideration. The entries are, in most cases, longer and more detailed than those normally found in an annotated bibliography. I decided to write more extensive entries for several reasons. First of all, I assumed, quite pragmatically, that most readers who use this book are not able to read the original German works. The entries here, then, are not simply bibliographical suggestions that the reader can pursue. I translate the title of each article or book, moreover, in the assumption that the title would not often be helpful without a translation. Second, I believe it important for an entry to convey something substantive about the German work, whether that be a central thesis, an ideological framework, or a body of particularly valuable evidence. I address these substantive issues with an introduction to each chapter, which, furthermore, places the issues in individual entries in a broader context of scholarship. Third, I consider the other meanings of "entry" to be at least as important as the one that aims primarily to locate an annotation on a list. I hope that these "entries" might present some access to different traditions of scholarship, debates and discourses, and ways of thinking about music in its social and cultural contexts. Classical works and ideas appear in this book, as do new and occasionally radical approaches. If the reader can gain entry into these aspects, the processes of disciplinary engagement and translation can begin.

German-language scholarship on folk music has both benefited and suffered from its complex disciplinary depth. Folk music and its study have been inseparable from the rich traditions of Central European musical and folkloristic scholarship, as well as from linguistics, ethnology, and history. In this sense, German-language scholarship traditionally exhibits a more interdisciplinary approach than English-language scholarship, in which, to put it bluntly, art-music and folk-music scholars have rarely known each other to exist. In Central European traditions, however, there have long existed areas of convergence, for example concerning questions of nationalism in music. It is on the level of theory and method, nonetheless, that the interdisciplinary potential of Central European scholarship has foundered. The boundaries between disciplines are too often impermeable, in part because of the extensive institutionalization of the university or academy of science, and in part because of the sometimes oppressive weight of scholarly tradition, that is, the need perceived by many to reproduce the ideas of those who came before.

The organizational choices I have made in this book reflect the interdisciplinary qualities of both Central European scholarship and my own experiences as an American ethnomusicologist. The choice of chapters, for example, is my own, and I suspect that no European would concur with all of them, perhaps not even with most of them. Whereas opening with a chapter on genre, about which there is a surfeit of scholarship, would be objectionable to virtually no Central European scholar, concluding with a chapter on religious and ethnic minorities, which from my American perspective has received shockingly little attention, would probably seem perplexing. The balance of chapters, no doubt, also has an American flavor to it, for I have not been shy about bolstering those themes that have been underrepresented, though again my motivation for doing so was to provide what I believed to be a point of entry for English-speaking readers who use this book. That categories overlap and that some entries might appear in several chapters goes without saying. There are no doubt decisions I have made that the authors of certain works would fail to comprehend, and I can admit myself to moving more than a few entries from chapter to chapter, eventually failing to convince even myself that there was a single place for the themes of those entries. One of my goals will have been achieved if my organizational concept and the inevitable overlapping of categories have served to problematize disciplinary borders and emblematize the complexity of the field as a whole.

In laying the groundwork for this annotated bibliography, there are certain decisions about inclusivity that I was forced to make from the beginning and to hold to them throughout the writing of the book. Even though dissertations play a role in German scholarship distinctively different from that in American scholarship—German scholars are required to publish their dissertations more or less as they are and to finance the publication themselves, but often in extremely small print runs—I have deliberately not included them, unless they appeared in a revised form at an important scholarly press. I have also restricted my choices to works published entirely or mostly in the German language. English-language scholarship on Central European folk music does not, therefore, appear in this book. Most of this literature, however, has been published in North America or England, in other words, outside the German-language scholarly tradition. As this book began to take shape, I increasingly saw the ways in which Central European folk-music scholarship was fundamentally concerned with the problems of European culture and history. With this in mind I further recognized the efficacy of focusing on scholarship devoted primarily to Europe, and by extension to folk-music practices and the other cultural practices with which folk music intersected. In short, the research of those Central European ethnomusicologists who have worked primarily on non-European traditions—outstanding scholars such as Veit Erlmann, Gerhard Kubik, and Artur Simon—does not appear here. I trust that these colleagues will understand the basis of this decision and will wait patiently until I reflect on their important work in another venue.

The personal nature of my own engagement with Central European scholarship has also meant that I have included works here that might not appear in a German-language equivalent. My own interests in Jewish music and in German-American traditional music have led me to emphasize these areas far more than Central European scholars, though I believe strongly that increased attention to areas such as these, as well as to the music of ethnic and religious groups in Europe itself, should occupy a much more important position than it has heretofore; such attention would urge European scholars to rethink the very foundations of their field. For somewhat different reasons, I have included a substantial number of entries created by and for *Volksmusikpfleger* (lit., cultivators of folk music), which is to say, for the practicing folk musician. The exchange between folk-music scholar and musician, particularly in southern Germany and Austria, continues to be one of the most distinctive traits of folk music's presence. This scholarly and practical discourse is virtually unknown in English-speaking traditions, and for that reason that I felt especially compelled to treat it fully here.

For still different reasons, I have chosen to include in this book works whose ideological content I personally find reprehensible. In chapters devoted to theoretical schools and to regionalism and nationalism, for example, there are entries of works by scholars who contributed to the racist ideologies of the Nazis and whose methods are, by extension, implicated in the human destruction wrought by the Holocaust. It is important to include such works here because they were not isolated aberrations; in fact, they cannot and should not be separated from a larger, more complex intellectual history. Accordingly, such works are not only products of a single historical moment but exhibit continuity with an intellectual history that still fails, on the eve of the next millenium, to give very little space to the study of ethnic and religious groups in Central Europe, the growing population of Turkish residents, or the many Roma and Sinti groups that seek refuge in this area.

This annotated bibliography, quite clearly, is not just a source for the assessment of the past. Even though it draws extensively on historical perspectives that have long given impetus to Central European folk-music research, it recognizes the dynamic quality that such perspectives necessarily afford. The histories of German- and English-language folk-music scholarship have long followed parallel paths uneasily, at times narrowing the gap between them, at other times widening it, but never quite losing sight of each other. At the end of the twentieth century, the reasons for narrowing the gap, however, are, in my opinion, greater than ever. Many of the issues fundamental to recent American folk-music scholarship and ethnomusicology—immigration, ethnicity, urbanization, gender, and race—cry out for more attention in German-language scholarship. Themes such as nationalism and the historicization of culture and language, which in turn have driven German folk-music theory, now have a more pressing presence than ever, not least because of the critical path along which Europe passes in its attempts to redefine itself. Such critical issues do not exist apart from the need for scholarly rapprochement and engagement beyond our own traditions of scholarship. This book is conceived in full recognition that American scholars have much to learn from European scholars, and they from us.

Acknowledgments

This book has been possible because I have been privileged to travel between the United States and Central Europe for many years. My journeys have been cultural, intellectual, and personal, with the boundaries between these more often than not difficult to determine. My journeys began when I wrote a master's thesis and Ph.D. dissertation on the music cultures of German-speaking ethnic communities, the first in the American Midwest, the second in Israel. It was Bruno Nettl who showed me from the start that the first guidebook to any scholarly journey was the literature of the field. That meant, in short, that I sat down and started to read German folk-music scholarship.

It soon became evident that the journey would be incomplete without a sojourn at the Deutsches Volksliedarchiv in Freiburg im Breisgau. The impact of that first of many stays there will be evident chapter after chapter in this book. More important to point out at the start is that it was the community of scholars in Freiburg, far more than an old mansion and its many books and transcriptions, that has influenced the present book. Every colleague in Freiburg deserves thanks, but I must instead save space and single out for special thanks Jürgen Dittmar, Barbara James, and Otto Holzapfel. For years, Otto has accompanied me on more than a few of my journeys, and it is because I have learned so much from him during the course of these travels that I dedicate this book to him.

The dedication is even more appropriate because the book owes its existence to financial support from a Trans-Atlantic Cooperation Grant from the Alexander von Humboldt Foundation, a grant held jointly by Otto and myself during 1993–96. For its continued support of scholars who travel to Germany, I should like to express my thanks to the Humboldt Foundation. Final preparation of the manuscript was made possible with funding from the Wieboldt-Rosenwald Collection of German Folk Songs at the University of Chicago, and I should like to express special thanks to Anita S. Darrow for her enthusiasm and generosity, which have made the recent revitalization of that collection possible.

My journeys to and from Austria were all the more meaningful because of my traveling companion, Rudolf Pietsch, of the Institut für Volksmusikforschung in Vienna. Rudi has always epitomized the Austrian folk-music researcher for me: musician, scholar, and, above all, human being. During the autumn quarter of 1994, a group of University of Chicago students asked me to give a special reading course on folk-music scholarship. I seized the opportunity, not just to present material that I was preparing for this book, but also to benefit from their feedback and perspectives. I did gain enormously from the perspectives of Cathy Cole, Robert Fried, and Petra Lehmann. Jerry Cadden, who also joined us, helped with the final stages in the publication of this book, making those stages learning experiences as well.

James Porter invited me to contribute this book to his series on music ethnology at Garland Publishing, but I originally declined the invitation. Jim persisted, I finally agreed, and I have long since known that Jim was right to persist. Leo Balk at Garland prodded me to keep at work on the manuscript by showing that he was interested in what ethnomusicologists do; there are few better ways to prod a scholar.

As I was putting the final touches on this book, two family members passed away, Ruth Bohlman and Gretchen Schroder, unexpectedly and tragically. The sense of loss I feel upon their deaths is bound up with this book because both were so much a part of my first journeys into the study of German traditional music in northern Wisconsin. Our families should know that this book, in some small measure, memorializes their lives.

I try never to make any scholarly journey without my immediate family. It is not just a matter of learning from them when they share perspectives on music with me, though I could not ask for three finer musicians as companions. Instead, we share in the journey because we do not always react in the same ways to the exploration of Central European folk music and because we perceive the contradictions of the journey in different ways. I could not and would not do it without Andrea, Benjamin, and Christine.

INTRODUCTION

If asked on the street about what "folk music" and "folk song" meant to them, most Germans today would be hard pressed to answer. Many would respond to the question with a question: "Is there any folk music in Germany today?" Implicit, of course, is that the respondents themselves have no personal connection to folk music. Some others would make the connection between the ambiguous notion of folk music in the question and a series of popular Saturday-evening television programs called "Musikantenstadel," literally, "the Musicians' Shed." "Musikantenstadel" is filmed on an auditorium stage made to look rustic, filled with a fairly elderly group from the local region in which the program is being filmed, who look on, often with beer in hand, as diverse ensembles from around Central Europe perform pieces from repertories ranging from traditional to folklike to popular. There would be still other Germans on the street who would answer almost repugnantly to the query about folk music. For them, folk music conjures up the conservative side of German history, the conscious cultivation of *Heimat*, the imaginary, even dangerous "homeland" toward which countless heroes and heroines in German folk songs have striven.

Were one to pose these same questions about folk music to contemporary Swiss or Austrians, one would be greeted by vaguely similar answers, perhaps even more ambiguous in the case of the Swiss, surely less ambiguous in the case of the Austrians. Austrians, at the very least, would respond that folk-music practices do persist, particularly in Styria, though also in the wine gardens (*Heurigen*) around Vienna, and that there are many fine ensembles, who appear in concerts and competitions and produce CDs. Whereas they are conscious of such practices, most of the Austrian respondents would probably confess to knowing few folk songs themselves. Folk music, after all, is the domain of the professionals.

These responses suggest that folk music in modern Central Europe is, at best, someone else's music or, at worst, a vestige of the past. To sing folk songs means to sing in dialect, and dialects belong to the residents of rural areas or regions other than one's own. The subjects of folk songs come from another era, a past that one would want to reclaim only cautiously as one's own. And yet, folk music persists, if staged for popular television programs and promulgated by professional ensembles. Even for those who distance themselves the most from folk music, it is full of contradictions. Perhaps those contradictions arise because folk music refuses to go away, to die out in a modern world in which it has ambiguous meanings. Maybe those contradictions result from the visibility of politically liberal singer-songwriters, who turn to folk song, its questionable past notwithstanding, to voice some of the most pressing concerns of post-reunification German society. Indeed, the voices of a new multiculturalism and an ethnically pluralistic society completely unlike the Romantic *Heimat* are heard most publicly in the musics of Turkish residents of Germany or Roma and Sinti (Gypsy) residents of Austria. These contradictions problematize the answers to questions about what folk music means to Central Europeans in the 1990s.

These contradictions have spilled over to the scholarship on folk song and folk music for centuries. To a large degree, moreover, it is the persistence of contradictions that have formed the many distinctive strands in the intellectual history of folk-music scholarship. Fundamental to the contradictions has always been a sort of gut feeling, which we witness in Herder and Goethe, no less than in the most cutting-edge writings two centuries later, that folk music is about something simple and basic, so simple and so basic, in fact, that definitions cannot truly do it justice. This being the case, Herder combined two nouns in 1778, *Volk* (people) and *Lied* (song), but failed to make it clear to anyone who the *Volk* were and what they actually sang. It has been unclear ever since, try as scholars would, to find the language to represent the simple and basic.

The ideological contradictions that surround folk music are no less evident in the scholarship devoted to it. Again, it has been the simple and basic issues that have historically plagued scholars the most. Were the *Volk* emblems of the past, or did they respond to the present by mobilizing their concerns through song? Were they a single people, as is the German noun, which is used in the plural only to refer to the many "peoples" (*Völker*) of the world, or did the people admit differentiation and advocate diversity? Depending on the branch of scholarship to which one turns, one can find just about any conceivable answer to such questions. The terms, however, remain vital to the answering of these questions. In the nineteenth century scholars increasingly interpreted *Volk* as nation, also in the singular, which meant that *Lied* needed to bear witness to national unity in some way. By devising methods of classification and analysis, and by laying the groundwork for different genres, folk-song scholars were able to forge links between *Volkslied* and German nation. The narrative genre of the ballad provides striking evidence for these links in works annotated throughout this book. Again, the simple and basic, once discovered, left little doubt about what was German in ballads: no matter who sang them or where they were sung, their texts were in High German. Austrian scholars were less willing to go along with such claims, and so they tended to relegate ballads to a less important position; at the very least, they did not mount massive ballad collecting and classification projects, such as that done by the German Folk-Song Archive in 1935.

Language itself, as well as the diverse ways of interpreting it, has been guilty for many of the contradictions in Central European folk-music scholarship. The clumsiness with which I have coupled folk song and folk music in the present introduction is but a symptom of a complex domain of linguistic uncertainty. At a surface level, folk song is distinct from folk music because the former has a text, explicitly a German text. It is the text, moreover, that gives the song its identity and allows the song to ascribe identity to those who sing it. Folk songs, therefore, anchor identity to people and place, and if a scholar gathers folk songs in anthologies and classifies them according to textual themes and poetic typologies, songs acquire the power to bound the nation, that is to become synonymous with Germany. Scholars can extend the potential of folk song to bound and be bounded literally and metaphorically, creating methodologies that place songs on maps, on the *Volksliedlandschaften* (folk-song landscapes) that, in early twentieth-century scholarship, extended across Europe, well into Eastern Europe, in fact at least to the shores of the Volga River. That other folk songs in other languages might also be common in these regions simply did not matter for scholarly geography, for they were not relevant to the argument being made. Folk song, in addition to being in a German language or dialect, was also not like many other types of music, which, whether traditional songs of rural Eastern Europe or popular song of Central European cities, existed beyond the borders.

Folk music, in contrast, was much harder to pin down. First of all, traditional folk-music practices contained the seeds of their own contradictory nature. Folk dances frequently bear the names of other places, *Schottisch* (lit., "Scottish"), for example, one of the most common dances in Central Europe. Also common are dances such as the czardas and the polka, both of which openly bespeak their Hungarian and Czech heritages. Second, as folk-music scholars began more extensively to classify and analyze the melodic components of folk music, it became increasingly evident that songs in one part of Europe turned up elsewhere, in fact places where they were not supposed to belong. Whereas language bounded folk song, melody freed folk music. In one of the most influential studies of the late nineteenth century, Wilhelm Tappert's *Wandernde Melodien* (1890), melodies literally "wandered about" Europe, ignoring the landscapes charted by folk-song scholars and wantonly breaking through linguistic and national borders. Third, although there is some evidence that connects language to musical style, there is considerably more that suggests that folk-song texts and musical styles create identity in very different ways and therefore follow divergent historical paths. Musical style has the potential to respond to the demands of changing instrumentation, even to lend itself to popular hits or to provide the vehicle for nationalism in art music. The same malleability may mean that folk music has the power to hold on to the most atavistic of styles from the past. Folk music undoes the boundaries of history in ways that folk song cannot.

The contradictions in Central European folk-music research have played themselves out in a variety of ways throughout the intellectual history of the field. National and regional approaches to the study of folk music are one of the most obvious, as I frequently note in assessments of the works included in this book. German and Austrian scholars, for example, maintain very different scholarly agendas, often in the course of openly contradistinguishing one national approach from the other. The national differences emerge even in the choices for interdisciplinary cooperation. Austrian folk-music scholars ally themselves rather closely with Austrian ethnomusicology; in certain areas, particularly in the choice of analytical methods, the two are inseparable. In contrast, German folk-song scholars have long incorporated the methods of folkloristics. In previous generations the chief influence from folkloristics was the philological rigor of textual studies, but in recent generations the more significant influence has come from the ethnological, community-based approaches of modern German folkloristics.

Throughout this book I interpret the contradictions within Central European folk-music scholarship as one of its most distinctive traits, indeed as the most compelling reason this scholarship deserves our attention. Clearly, the concerns and interests I bring to this scholarship, as I point out in the Preface, differ considerably from those a German, Austrian, or Swiss scholar might bring. Whereas I embrace the contradictions, there are surely those European scholars who would prefer that they finally be resolved. My organizational decisions, moreover, also reveal my American ethnomusicological biases and, I hope, my own set of very diverse perspectives. My own perspectives, then, enter into a sort of counterpoint with those in the German-language scholarship. That counterpoint will be apparent on the surface as well as in the deeper structures of the book. The choice of chapter topics, for example, reflects both European concepts and my own. Opening with a chapter on genre would seem a very natural choice to most German scholars, who have historically devoted a great deal of attention to the definition of genre. Closing with a chapter on religious and ethnic minorities, in contrast, would seem very unnatural to most German scholars, who have, in fact, devoted scant attention to this topic.

There are other chapters in which the counterpoint rattles away in the chapters themselves. In chapter 11 I open with a survey of classical studies on speech islands but then conclude with not-yet-classical studies on emigrant music cultures, again an area of research that has not penetrated the boundaries of the Central European scholarly canon. In both parts of the chapter, however, I annotate works about German music outside Germany, with the difference being that one has the sanction of intellectual history, while the other does not. In somewhat different ways I pair nationalism and regionalism in chapter 12, postulating that these two staples of the scholarly canon really conflict, for they reveal diametrically opposed processes of creating and ascribing identity.

The underlying reasons for the contradictions in the intellectual history that this book sketches are not only the products of scholars and their individual or national agendas. Folk-music scholarship has not existed in isolation from political and ideological movements, but rather has frequently intersected with them. The ways in which scholars have chosen sides in ideological and political debates have varied, some collaborating with those in power, others resisting the misuse and abuse of folk music toward social ends. There is no point in this book at which I try to sidestep the ideological and political, and in this sense, too, the book bears witness to my American ethnomusicological perspective. In particular, I include many works from the 1930s and 1940s in which the racism and prejudice of Nazism fully envelops the thinking of folk-music scholars. For the most part, these works and the trends they represent are unknown and forgotten, even in Central Europe; it is also the case, all too often, that they have been ignored. By including them, I do not only mean to bring them to the reader's attention and ask that we not forget them, but I mean also to argue that they belong in the larger intellectual history of the field. Many of them result from uses of evidence and processes of analysis that stretch throughout that history. Many of them rest on theories of *Volk* and nation that would be familiar in works from any moment during the past two centuries. Traces from many of them, moreover, are all-too-present in some of the ways ethnic and religious groups in Central Europe are or are not integrated into the folk-music scholarship of the 1990s.

The contradictions in Central European folk-music scholarship have often resulted from an uncertainty about the subject matter and methods of the field. In this book I also take this uncertainty to be a positive factor and one of the reasons that this body of scholarship deserves the critical scrutiny for which an annotated bibliography often provides the initial step. One has to read only a few pages in most of the works annotated here to realize that their authors are inspired, passionate scholars, whose interest in folk music is fired by the uncertainty of a subject that is hard to pin down and filled with meanings and identities that are nigh impossible to extract from the music itself. That same uncertainty becomes grounds for extensive experimentation. New forms of evidence and new processes of comparison emerge at every stage in the intellectual history that unfolds in the following chapters. One melodic typology supplants another, but only with the disclaimer by the scholars forging the new typology that theirs, too, will be supplanted in the near future because more advanced technologies will make it possible to examine even more repertories in greater depth. The uncertainty that was already apparent in Herder's writings has motivated scholars for over two centuries, making us ask just how many disciplines can, in fact, claim such longevity for their intellectual histories.

Folk music exists in Central Europe today, if indeed its contexts are no less contradictory than those attracting the attention of Herder and Goethe. Folk song for Herder was not, as the various entries under his name make abundantly clear, German, rural, or isolated from modernity. To find what he called *Volkslieder*, Herder looked about Europe, including songs in many languages and from many genres. There is no canon in Herder's approaches, or in those of his successors, but rather far too much contradiction to allow a canon to form. To Herder, folk song meant diversity, a Europe with permeable boundaries. That the concept of *Volkslied* could embrace such diversity was reason enough to establish the discipline that this annotated bibliography takes as its subject. That such diversity must become the basis for the study of music in the new Europe that is taking shape in the final decade of the twentieth century compels us to look critically at the ways in which folk-music scholarship has woven uncertain and contradictory images of Central European identity into the fabric of its distinctive and complex intellectual history.

I

APPROACHING THE SUBJECT

1

GENRE

Central European ontologies of folk music depend on the boundaries and regions, repertories and canons created by concepts of genre. Determining the genre to which a piece belongs provides a way of identifying its most salient internal structures and the connections or lack thereof that it has with contexts external to itself. It is through concepts of genre that Central European folk-music scholarship has constructed the identities of individual pieces, for example the ways in which different versions of a single ballad cohere and demonstrate the traits that give meaning to that ballad. It has also been through the disciplinary potential of genre that Central European folk-music scholarship has demarcated social and cultural differences, thereby bounding folk music from other types of music and using it to represent the boundedness of community, class, and national differences. Identifying genre and ascribing it to folk music has so preoccupied folk-music scholars that it would be impossible to understand what folk music means in Central European thought and history without using genre as a point of departure.

There is no single way in which categories of genre emerge and then develop the criteria that distinguish one genre from all others. The first two categories of genre in this chapter, narrative songs and regional and dialect songs, both depend on text, but with text functioning in different ways. The texts of narrative folk songs "tell a story," and it is this overriding trait, whether inherent in the strophic form of ballads or mediated through the modes of production necessary for broadsides, that provides the narrative scholar with an object to collect, study, and classify. The texts of regional or dialect songs, in contrast, function geographically and linguistically to anchor a genre to a specific place and the unique qualities displayed by dialect. Genre also derives from function and context, for example when the boundaries of folk song overlap with political song or religious folk music. With these categories, history and text transmission reinforce notions of genre, the ways in which political song is even specific and has the potential to mobilize "the folk" to political action.

As the identity of folk song depends less on internal structures and more on contextual influences, Central European concepts of genre similarly begin to fail in their capacity to account for the traits that distinguish one repertory from another. The final sections in this chapter, it follows, might not represent valid generic concepts for many

3

European folk-music scholars. Composed songs that enter oral traditions or the practices of singing societies, for example, might also enter into different genres—narrative, regional, or political—but it might seem foreign to many scholars to claim that they constitute a separate genre. I introduce such categories in this chapter not to suggest that new categories are needed, but rather to claim that these generic categories represent the processes that are at work when pieces enter certain repertories and repertories become bounded as canons. As a whole, then, this chapter proceeds from concepts of genre determined by text and its specification of genre to concepts resulting from processes of change and variability, the movement across the boundaries of genre, which nonetheless depends on the delimitation of genre.

Genre enjoys such central importance in the thought and intellectual history of Central European folk-music scholarship because it both includes and excludes. The most privileged of all genres, the ballad, has historically acquired its status because of its putative provenance and distribution among all Germanic peoples, within and without the German nation-states of Central Europe. It includes these peoples, whether they are residents of Alsace-Lorraine or Yiddish-speaking Jews in Eastern Europe, because ballad texts are in High German, despite the vernacular of the singer or region of origin. Linguistically, ballads are inclusive because they figuratively represent a centripetal pull toward Central Europe and the historical and literary language that unifies that region. By defining the German ballad as a narrative folk song in High German and according to a certain canon of narrative themes, one also excludes those communities and regions in which ballads are not found or exist only in contaminated versions (*Kontamination* is, in fact, a real theoretical construct of ballad scholarship). The criteria of the ballad, therefore, throw up boundaries separating us from them, those transmitting the privileged genre and those with no entrée to it.

The boundaries between genres are nonetheless fluid, and individual pieces do move between genres as social, historical, and stylistic changes occur. This generic mobility is abundantly evident in several of the sections in this chapter, for example *volkstümliche Musik* ("folklike music") and popular music, and composed folk music. Throughout the nineteenth century, in particular, poets, composers, and collectors created new repertories and contributed new works to old ones. During the seventeenth and eighteenth centuries, songs that appeared first (or at least first in a printed version) as broadsides frequently found their way into oral tradition. Art song and folk song continue to influence each other, and folklike and popular songs mediated by recordings, television, and radio find their way into genres with seemingly traditional boundaries. These processes of invention, composition, and mediation remain embedded in the ways genre continues to influence contemporary thought and modern folk-music scholarship. The contents of many genres continue to grow, whereas others seem fixed and bound to anachronistic practices. The persistent concern for genre, whether determined by rigid or flexible criteria, bears continued witness to the importance of folk and popular song as sites for the bounding and transmission of identity in Central Europe.

The Concept of Genre

1. Röhrich, Lutz. "Die Textgattungen des popularen Liedes." ("The Textual Genres of Popular Song"). In Rolf Wilhelm Brednich, Lutz Röhrich, and Wolfgang Suppan, eds., *Handbuch des Volkliedes.* Vol. 1: *Die Gattungen des Volksliedes.* Munich: Wilhelm Fink, 1973. Pp. 19–35.

   A survey of different ways of distinguishing and naming the genres of folk song. Serving as a sort of introductory chapter to an entire volume devoted to genre, the article begins by admitting to recent attempts to dismantle the larger generic notion of *Volkslied* (e.g., through Ernst Klusen's notion of "group song") but concludes that, despite alternative proposals and historical dissatisfaction with the concept (e.g., already from Herder and Goethe), "folk song" is the term that is most inclusive. Röhrich schematically presents seven different conditions determining the generic designations of folk song: terms referring to content; terms resulting from form; groups of songs resulting from those who sing and transmit them (*"Liedträger"*); occasion at which a song is sung; time and place of performance; function; and the degree to which a song is "folklorized," that is, has entered a written tradition or has become part of a popular tradition. In each of the sections devoted to these generic designations, Röhrich provides an extensive catalogue of examples, making the article a valuable source for German folk-song terminology.

2. Wiora, Walter. "'Gattungen des Volksliedes' und 'Gattungen der Musik.'" ("'Genres of Folk Song' and 'Genres of Music'"). In Max Peter Baumann, Rudolf Maria Brandl, and Kurt Reinhard, eds., *Neue ethnomusikologische Forschungen: Festschrift Felix Hoerburger.* Laaber: Laaber-Verlag, 1977. Pp. 37–44.

   Compares the ways in which concepts of genre in folk song relate to those in "music" in general, whereby Wiora usually means art music, though sometimes also sacred music, but always Western music. Wiora bases his comparisons on points of similarity or overlap, for example between *geistliches Volkslied* ("sacred folk song") and *kirchliches Gemeindelied* ("congregational song"). Folk song also turns up in art-music genres, for example in opera as peasant or pilgrim choruses, which nevertheless demonstrate quite specific narrative and dramatic functions.

Ballads, too, exist as genres in folk and art song. Wiora examines the processes of exchange between different "levels," when art song enters into folk-song repertories (cf. John Meier's *Kunstlied im Volksmunde* [1906] ["Art Song in the Mouths of the People"]). Most striking about this reflective piece is that it illustrates specific cases of the ways in which classification of one type of music influences other classificatory concepts.

⁂

Narrative Genres

3. Bartels, Hildegard. *Epos—die Gattung in der Geschichte: Eine Begriffsbestimmung vor dem Hintergrund der Hegelschen "Ästhetik" anhand von "Nibelungenlied" und "Chanson de Roland."* ("Epic—the Genre in History: Determination of the Concept Prior to the Background of the Hegelian Aesthetic According to the 'Nibelungenlied' and the 'Chanson de Roland'"). Heidelberg: Winter, 1982. (Frankfurter Beiträge zur Germanistik, 22).

    Mustering new research on the epic and bringing earlier research into new comparative perspectives, this book challenges many of the assumptions about the epic that developed within Hegelian historiography and aesthetics. Most significantly, Bartels calls for interpretation of the epic both as a written and oral tradition, thereby extending its transmission to a culture predating the first manuscripts and to the interaction of epic with other narrative traditions after the distribution of manuscripts. The epic, therefore, can greatly expand our ability to understand the culture and *mentalité* of the Middle Ages. It also complements theories of oral transmission, for example those that Ramón Menéndez Pidal developed for the *chanson de geste*. The volume contributes significantly to the literature on narrative genres, particularly on the German ballad, illumining the life and culture of the late Middle Ages, when these genres began to coalesce into their modern forms.

4. Beitl, Klaus. "Schnaderhüpfel." ("Alpine Narrative Quatrain"). In Rolf Wilhelm Brednich, Lutz Röhrich, and Wolfgang Suppan, eds., *Handbuch des Volksliedes.* Vol. 1: *Gattungen des Volksliedes.* Munich: Wilhelm Fink, 1973. Pp. 617–77.

    A thorough and well-documented treatment of the *Schnaderhüpfel*, which places it in many different historical, cultural, and generic contexts. Taking the central area of the *Schnaderhüpfel*, Bavaria and the Austrian Alps as his point of departure and archetype, Beitl argues for the great thematic and

musical variety made possible within the limited structures of the
genre itself. The *Schnaderhüpfel* (the most common name in the
central area of distribution, its etymology coming from
Schnitterhüpflein) is distributed in many areas of German-speaking
Europe; in his bibliography (pp. 666–77) Beitl documents the
sources and collections of the genre by region and approach.
Usually consisting of four lines, hence referred to often as
Vierzeiler ("quatrains"), the *Schnaderhüpfel* text improvises
concisely on a specific theme, ranging from love to political
songs. The tightness of the form itself makes it possible for the
genre to convey its messages in pointed fashion, and it offers the
singer the chance to improvise and compose new songs from pre-
existing themes and patterns. *Schnaderhüpfel* are often in the
dialect of a region, or even of a relatively small area within a
much larger speech area. The local qualities of the text and
music, as well as the opportunity for individual creativity in the
Schnaderhüpfel, lead Beitl to argue that the genre represents a
kind of "pure" folk song, one which lends itself to little
contamination from the outside, yet nonetheless influences other
forms and genres, for example dance genres and *Ländler.*

5.　Braungart, Wolfgang. *Bänkelsang: Texte--Bilder--Kommentare.*
　　　("Bänkelsang [lit., 'Songs Sold from Benches']: Texts,
　　　Illustrations, Commentaries"). Stuttgart: Reclam, 1985. (Antho-
　　　logien aus der deutschen Literatur).

　　　Detailed study of the *Bänkelsang*, a narrative form employing
posters and printed pamphlets or other broadsides. T h e
Bänkelsang usually told the story of a disaster or complex human
drama, which nevertheless resolved in such a way that a moral
lesson was obvious to those who bought them. So-called because
hawkers brought them to fairs and other public gatherings, and
then performed and sold them from a stand or bench (Ger. *Bank;
Bänkel* = "little bench"). Braungart frames the contents of the
book with a preface and an afterword, which provide a thorough
survey of the practices of creating the *Bänkelsang* and the
manipulation of texts and visual symbols characteristic of their
publication. A *Bänkelsang* and its accompanying printed story
were reports of presumably true events, although exaggeration
and enhancement of the tragic elements were often the rule.
Because the songs were printed and illustrated by large screens
with scenes from the narrative, the genre became a complex
representation of several different art forms. The body of the
book contains thirty-six songs, most of them with a facsimile of
the original title page and the narrative text that accompanied
the song texts. The section devoted to commentaries on each
song provides an historical background, lists melodic sources and
reproduces some melodies, and includes excellent bibliographical
references. The bibliography of secondary sources and detailed

footnotes make the book one of the best overall introductions to popular German narrative songs.

6. Brednich, Rolf Wilhelm. *Die Liedpublizistik im Flugblatt des 15. bis 17. Jahrhunderts.* ("Song in the Public Sphere in the Broadside of the Fifteenth through Seventeenth Centuries"). 2 vols. Baden-Baden: Valentin Koerner, 1974 and 1975. (Bibliotheca Bibliographica Aureliana, 55 and 60).

A study of folk song printed and disseminated on broadsides during the first three centuries of print technology. Focusing primarily on Central European traditions, but also briefly comparing German broadsides to non-German traditions from the same period (vol. 1, chap. 8), Brednich examines the broadside as a representation of the social and public milieu of a period of transition and turmoil in Central Europe (the Reformation, Counter-Reformation, Thirty Years War, and nascent German nationalism). Volume 1 is organized according to genre or medium of production for the broadside, with each chapter further broken down into more specific genres. Volume 2 contains extensive studies of the sources for early broadsides, and then reprints 143 examples, organized according to both genre or medium, and historical order. The volumes clearly illustrate the extensive network of media that produced and disseminated printed songs soon after printing developed. It was further characteristic of this network that boundaries between genre were regularly traversed, and that broadsides provided one of the most extensive means of contact and exchange between sacred and secular domains of society, as well as between different class and social levels. Few works in musical scholarship so effectively make it possible to rethink the position of music in early modern German culture. Non-German speakers will still find the illustrations and source materials in volume 2 very usable.

7. *Deutsche Volkslieder mit ihren Melodien.* ("German Folk Songs with Their Melodies"). Vol. 1. Ed. by John Meier, with Wilhelm Heiske, Fred Quellmalz, Harry Schewe, and Erich Seemann. Berlin and Leipzig: Walter de Gruyter, 1935.

The first volume of the so-called *Balladenwerk* ("ballad work"), a publishing project with which the Deutsches Volksliedarchiv (DVA) attempted scientifically to define a canon of German folk song and publish the musical evidence for that canon. First conceived in the early decades of the DVA (founded in 1914), the *Balladenwerk* will appear in its tenth and final volume in the mid-1990s. The ten-volume publication project represents an intellectual history of the presence of Germanness in folk song and its history. In the foreword to the first volume, John Meier speaks already of the need to catch up with Scandinavian (e.g., Svend Grundtvig) and Anglo-American (e.g., Frances James Child) ballad projects, and to do so by publishing ballads from the entire German-speaking area of Europe. As in other DVA projects in the early history of this institution, the *Balladenwerk* depended on the submission of examples from local archives and institutions throughout Europe, to which DVA researchers added collections from other libraries and archives. When establishing the principles for the ballad collections, Meier notes that the DVA had to confront the problem that the archive initially possessed few sources prior to 1700. The *Balladenwerk* first took shape only after sufficient sources were located to use ballads as a means of connecting the Middle Ages to the present, one of the fundamental criteria for this canon. Already at this time, language was another fundamental criterion, namely the fact that German ballads, though in oral tradition, were largely sung in High German, which served as evidence for connecting regional practices, not least among them the practices in politically contested areas (e.g., Alsace and Silesia) to a central narrative of German history. In this first volume, thirty-one individual ballads appear, among them well-known ballads such as "Graf von Rom" (no. 14), "Der Tannhäuser" (no. 15), "Die Königskinder" (no. 20), and "Schloß in Österreich" (no. 24). Each ballad appears with numerous text variants and a representative sample of melodies. The analytical notes that follow each song discuss the sources for the song and examine the different characteristics of the ballad in different political and dialect regions. Typologies are used to compare the different variants, for the most part based on the texts themselves. Comparison often reveals the ideological motivations that informed the *Balladenwerk*, for example when "contamination" between the beginning of "Die Königskinder" and another ballad, "Die Jüdin" ("The Jewish Woman," presented in vol. 9 of the project) is clarified (p. 209). Melodic analysis is largely comparative, revealing approaches to common melodic shapes that would serve later musicological research at the DVA. Remarkably thorough and already anchored to the canonic tradition the project would document, the *Balladenwerk* retained the general shape established in 1935 throughout its subsequent volumes.

8. Holzapfel, Otto. "Milieuschilderung im Schnaderhüpfel." ("Images of the Surroundings in the Alpine Narrative Quatrain"). *Jahrbuch des österreichischen Volksliedwerkes* 41 (1992): 100–104.

Examines some of the themes common to the *Schnaderhüpfel* (also *Vierzeiler* or quatrain), four-line songs that concentrate social conditions and interrelations, often through satirical and parodistic language. Holzapfel argues that the imagery of the *Schnaderhüpfel* provides a means of understanding better the local conditions of their composition and transmission, in other words, that the imagery is specific and possesses *Zielgerichtigkeit* ("intentionally direct focus"). Many focus on problems inherent in relations between the sexes, and class and economic differences often complicating them. The local nature of the *Schnaderhüpfel* means, moreover, that most employ dialects. Because many collections contain songs originally from German-speaking areas of Eastern Europe, they also reflect political and ethnic differences prior to World War II. The article summarizes many of the thematic considerations developed in the author's five-volume *Vierzeiler Lexikon* (see below) and serves as an excellent introduction to them.

9.   Laade, Wolfgang. *Musik und Musiker in Märchen, Sagen und Anekdoten der Völker Europas: Eine Quellensammlung zum Problemkreis "Musik als Kultur".* ("Music and Musicians in Fairy Tales, Tales and Anecdotes of European Peoples: A Source Collection for the Problematic 'Music as Culture'"). Volume 1: *Mitteleuropa.* Baden-Baden: Valentin Koerner, 1988. (Sammlung musik-wissenschaftlicher Abhandlungen, 78).

Culls references to music from the narrative folklore of the German-speaking areas of Europe. The examples and sources are very diverse: character-types in fairy tales; symbolic powers of music and musical instruments; and genres in which music possesses unusual folkloristic presence, e.g., in Alpine yodeling and songs used in cowherding (*Kühreihen*). The volume contains a wide spectrum of texts, but no musical notation; Laade comments briefly on each example, with references to secondary literature. The book represents, though does not argue strongly for, a thesis that folkloristic genres reveal a Central European belief in music's magical powers, and that this belief, articulated through folklore, provides an underlying unity in the music of the German-speaking regions. Valuable source for surveying the different ways in which music serves as metaphor in folk belief and literature.

10.   Laufhütte, Hartmut, ed. *Deutsche Balladen.* ("German Ballads"). Stuttgart: Reclam, 1991.

An anthology of German ballads, with critical commentary and an extensive afterword on the nature and history of the genre. The anthology contains exclusively "art ballads," that is those written by poets or others (e.g., philosophers or singer-songwriters such as Wolf Biermann). While gathering the anthology, Laufhütte concerned himself explicitly with the problem of canon and genre: just how do traditional notions and collections of ballads historiographically constitute the canon? Laufhütte regards this ballad canon as fundamentally German, and yet he seeks to rethink it in such ways that it more directly reflects the specific generic conditions of ballad, which many examples in the canon do not (e.g., Heine's "Die Lorelei," a standard member of the canon, but not a ballad). The anthology also eliminates the previous category of "folk ballads," restricting itself to a historical chronology of consciously composed ballads. Music and the images of music are standard tropes in these ballads. Some of the earliest ballads, for example, were written as variants of folk songs (e.g., Johann Gottfried Herder's "Edward," based on the Child ballad and later a model for compositions by Schubert and Brahms). The relation between German ballads and the history of German *Lied* is particularly striking, with poets such as Joseph von Eichendorff and Friedrich Rückert well represented. The anthology illustrates many of the processes of exchange between oral and written traditions in folk song and folklore, as well as the wealth of shared imagery in German folk- and art-song traditions.

11. Lüthi, Max. "Familienballade." ("Ballads about Families"). In Rolf Wilhelm Brednich, Lutz Röhrich, and Wolfgang Suppan, ed., *Handbuch des Volksliedes*. Vol. 1. *Die Gattungen des Volksliedes*. Munich: Wilhelm Fink, 1973. Pp. 89–100.

More than any other theme, family relations are found as themes in European ballads. Families appear in various forms, which Lüthi surveys in this article. One family member may offer counsel to another, who faces a particularly difficult decision; successive family members may serve to organize strophes through enumeration, for example as successive answers to the same theme (cf. "Edward" in the Child ballads); and ballads may be about the ways in which families interact, for instance when a member must react to a challenge from the outside. Whereas family relations are significant in other folklore genres (e.g., fairy tales), they undergird certain structural functions in the ballad and are therefore significant to the genre itself. The tight, integrated relations of the family, according to Lüthi, lend themselves particularly well to the strophic narrative of the ballad, itself tight and integrated. The article investigates the role of family relations in comparative fashion, drawing upon ballad traditions throughout Europe.

12. Petzoldt, Leander. *Bänkellieder und Moritaten aus drei Jahrhunderten* ("Bänkellieder ['Songs Sold from Benches'] and Moritaten ['Moralistic Songs'] from Three Centuries"). Frankfurt am Main: Fischer Taschenbuch Verlag, 1982.

Historical presentation of broadsides, with discussion and illustration of each example. *Bänkellieder* and *Moritaten* developed as an important and widespread genre in many parts of Europe during the seventeenth century, and closely related forms of song production and dissemination remained popular well into the twentieth century. Petzoldt concerns himself with the many ways in which these songs were interrelated with other genres and forms of vocal production. On one hand, *Bänkellieder* entered oral traditions, becoming folk songs; on the other, they frequently took up themes from folk tradition, serving as catalysts for their transformation into popular and art traditions, as in the case of "Der Hauptmann von Köpenick" ("The Captain from Köpenick"), a true event from 1906 that was disseminated in myriad broadsides before becoming the subject of a play of the same name by Carl Zuckmayer (1931), which employed scenes much as a hawker of *Bänkellieder* does. *Bänkellieder* and *Moritaten* are narrative genres, often relying on large canvases for the portrayal of individual scenes. The fifty songs in this volume are presented as melodies with texts and guitar accompaniments, as well as a visual depiction relevant for the song. The introduction and bibliography enhance the book's usefulness by scholars.

13. Seemann, Erich. "Die europäische Volksballade." ("The European Folk Ballad"). In Rolf Wilhelm Brednich, Lutz Röhrich, and Wolfgang Suppan, eds., *Handbuch des Volksliedes.* Vol. 1: *Die Gattungen des Volksliedes.* Munich: Wilhlem Fink, 1973. Pp. 37–56.

A concise and schematic examination of narrative song, in particular ballads, in a pan-European geographic context. The folk ballad is one of the genres that most clearly distinguishes Europe, not only forming internal regions and repertories, but transforming itself into different forms at the continent's peripheries, particularly in the southeast and east of Europe. Seemann understands ballads as beginning locally and regionally, and then spreading outward. Each "landscape," therefore, forms first at its center, with ballad creators taking local narratives and dialects into account. Variants result through oral tradition, and ballad repertories grow outward, sometimes spilling over regional boundaries and influencing other ballad traditions. Europe contains two large areas of folk ballads, determined by the formal domination of strophic structures in the center, north, and west, and of stichic (line-by-line) composition in the southeast and east. By considering all these "folk ballads," Seemann further unifies a European song landscape, without, however, considering the ways in which stichic compositional procedures may connect the Balkans and certain Slavic repertories with Asian musical styles and forms. Particularly valuable is the discussion of the largest folk-ballad regions: Scandinavia; English-speaking areas (including North America); Germany; and the Romance-language repertories. The most significant theoretical point in the article is Seemann's discussions of the ways in which the primary function of ballads was—at least originally—dance. Most theories rest upon the etymology of the term "ballad" (*ballare*, e.g., means "to dance" in Italian), but Seemann cites recent and modern settings in which ballads continue to be performed primarily with dance, for example on the Faroe Islands. Perhaps the best, article-length introduction to European folk ballads.

14. Würzbach, Natascha. "Figuren, Raum, Zeit in der klassischen Volksballade." ("Characterization, Place, Time in the Classical Folk Ballad"). *Jahrbuch für Volksliedforschung* 30 (1985): 43–53.

Examines the use of deictic references as means of orientation in ballads. Würzbach suggests that the possibility of generalizing with such references also allows them to be understood as having specific meanings for specific audiences. She applies this theory to all cultures in which ballads have a classical status, with special reference to the Child ballads and the ballad traditions of Central Europe and Denmark (*folkeviser*). As evidence, Würzbach notes that the landscapes in each ballad tradition are specific to the climate and geography in which their narratives are situated. The deictic qualities of characterization, place, and time differ, however. Time is the most specific when it refers to "moments in time" as opposed to long periods of time. Characterization functions by occupying a fairly "empty stage," giving the individual listener the opportunity to interpret the ballad's narrative with specificity. The theory extends several areas of ballad scholarship by claiming that ballads do not only present stereotypic characters acting out stereotypic roles, but rather narratives that audiences at different times and in different places can adapt to relevant conditions.

Regional and Dialect Genres

15. Etz, Albrecht. "Zur Mundart im Wienerlied" ("On Dialect in Viennese Song"). *Jahrbuch des österreichischen Volksliedwerkes* 18 (1969): 47–60.

Viennese dialect has functioned historically as one of the determining characteristics of the genre known as *Wienerlied*, which, though usually composed in the manner of popular music, often enters oral tradition and fundamentally influences the folk traditions of Vienna. Viennese dialect, though containing many of the same structures as other alpine German dialects, has been distinct for some seven centuries because of external influences, particularly from Slavic and Hungarian languages, as well as Yiddish. Viennese song not only contains dialect idiosyncracies but also has transformed and even canonized many of these. The article makes an important contribution through its detailed examination of elements from oral tradition (dialect) that enter written tradition (composed Viennese songs) only to be returned to oral tradition (dialect). Numerous song texts with examples; footnotes make possible further examination of Viennese popular music.

16. Müns, Heike. "Plattdeutsches Lied heute in Mecklenburg—ein Abgesang?" ("Low German Song in Mecklenburg Today: A Swan Song?"). *Jahrbuch für Volksliedforschung* 37 (1992): 65–85.

Assesses the situation of Low German dialect song in eastern Germany after the dissolution of the German Democratic Republic (1989). During the forty-year history of the GDR, dialect song passed through several transitions. First, such songs were tolerated as the true expression of the local and regional. In the next generation, however, singer-songwriters (*Liedermacher*) increasingly took up dialect songs, investing them with political meaning, often directed against the state. This article, written soon after the fall of the GDR, solicits responses from those who performed in Low German, receiving contrasting predictions about the future of dialect song, though primarily negative beliefs that the political function buttressing the songs had now disappeared. Numerous song texts illustrate the article. Concise history of one genre of folk song in the GDR.

17. Schepping, Wilhelm. "Zur Situation des Dialektliedes heute: Belege aus dem Niederrheinraum." ("On the Situation of Dialect Song Today: Evidence from the Lower Rhine Region"). *Jahrbuch für Volksliedforschung* 36 (1991): 29–47.

Written from the historical perspective of scholars raised in the Lower Rhine Region, whose Institut für Musikalische Volkskunde in Cologne (previously in Neuß) devoted much of its attention to dialect song, this article surveys the status of songs using the Cologne dialect in the late twentieth century. Various claims for the strength of dialect among current residents suggest that dialect has failed to disappear, and indeed there are numerous claims supporting the notion of a renaissance or revival of dialect. Schepping is cautious about such claims, observing that they rely on the notion that dialect had somehow died out, a notion he does not support. Schepping examines many different types of song, ranging from cultivated folk song to rock music, all of which consciously use dialect. Singing practices, moreover, have provided various opportunities for learning and using dialect, hence serving as a "dialect school." Competing forms of dialect have emerged in the vocal music culture of Cologne and its surrounding region, some stressing an upper middle-class dialect, others (e.g., rock bands) a street dialect, which does not aim at correctness. Schepping is careful to remind the reader of misuses of dialect song in the past (e.g., during the Third Reich). H e stresses, instead, a continuity with the history of the region, which lends dialect song the power to express identity in many different ways.

18. Schneider, Manfred, ed. *Jodler aus Tirol.* ("Yodels in Tyrol"). Innsbruck: Eigenverlag des Tiroler Volksliedwerkes, 1982. (Volksmusik in Tirol: Quellen, Dokumente und Studien, 1).

   A collection of 190 yodels, previously published in diverse sources, but gathered here and classified for the first time. Yodeling, particularly in Austria, is polyphonic as well as monophonic, requiring close singing, usually of textless yodels (only three in this edition have texts). Schneider has sought to classify the yodels in the edition according to the opening melodic gesture, and he determines eleven groups according to this principle. The edition further draws upon the collections in the German Folk-Song Archive and the Austrian Volksliedwerk ("Folk-Song Work"), thus making this volume representative of the efforts of diverse collectors and projects throughout the alpine region of Central Europe. The emphasis on textless yodels causes the editor to exclude modernized and popular genres, and to some extent also yodels from areas in which yodeling makes more extensive use of text. The edition stands, nonetheless, as a core repertory of the Austrian Tyrol, a region where yodeling continues to have extraordinary significance as a genre of folk music.

19. Wolkan, Rudolf. *Wiener Volkslieder aus fünf Jahrhunderten.* ("Viennese Folk Songs from Five Centuries"). 2 vols. Vienna: Wiener Bibliophilen-Gesellschaft, 1926 and 1920 [volume 2 appeared first].

   Historical examination of the evolution of the Viennese folk song, beginning in the late fifteenth century and culminating with the early twentieth century. Wolkan claims that folk song in Vienna formed from the confluence of numerous traditions, and it therefore is distinct not as an isolated genre, but rather as a genre that juxtaposes many of the different textual and musical influences on Vienna as the capital of the Habsburg Monarchy. Viennese folk song developed together with print technology, which by its nature gathered differences and placed them in the same song or collection. Print technology also determined the processes of dissemination for Viennese folk song, and Wolkan discusses the spread of different traditions in relation to particular modes and moments of technology (e.g., the use of broadsides already in the sixteenth century). The first volume opens with an extensive history of Viennese folk song and is illustrated by reproductions of the printed forms of many songs. The remainder of the two volumes consists of texts from Viennese folk songs, chronologically ordered, but also specified according to genre. Wolkan concerns himself primarily with German or German-dialect texts, but there are some songs with non-German parts. The volumes are exemplary studies of the city as a site for folk-music traditions. Wolkan recognizes not only the close relation between oral and written traditions, but also the ways in which urban folk song represents cultural particularity and difference. Although most texts are standardized, dialect and linguistic distinctiveness remains in the songs of this anthology.

⚜

Volkstümliche Musik and **Popular Music**

20. Bausinger, Hermann. "Schlager und Volkslied." ("Hit Song and Folk Song"). In Rolf Wilhelm Brednich, Lutz Röhrich, and Wolfgang Suppan, eds., *Handbuch des Volksliedes*. Vol. 1: *Die Gattungen des Volksliedes*. Munich: Wilhelm Fink, 1973. Pp. 679–90.

By restoring the *Schlager* to a field of study previously occupied only by folk song, Bausinger critiques some of the basic categories and assumptions in folk-song research. He argues that the *Schlager* has been neglected because it is not sufficiently anchored in local culture, transmitted orally, or maintained over a long period of time. Rather than being produced by the folk, the *Schlager* is consumed by them. Bausinger makes his critique even more pointed, however, by demonstrating that the relation between hit song and folk song has been constructed as an ideological distinction between the "pure" (*echt*) and "impure" (*unecht*), in other words that the folk song's presumed purity makes it appropriate for scholarly study, whereas the hybridity and contamination that reside in the *Schlager* render it inappropriate. Bausinger assails the ideological claims that relegate the *Schlager* to this position, many, but not all, of them stemming from the nationalistic ideologies about Germanness influencing the National Socialists; his interpretation of Frankfurt School theories on popular music (e.g., those of Adorno) is equally trenchant. Bausinger also argues eloquently that the conditions and materials that produce the *Schlager* are not substantially different from those that have always shaped folk songs. A brilliantly argued review of German popular music, whose footnote references to studies of Germanness in folk song are very valuable.

21.   Egger, Margarethe. *Die Schrammeln in ihrer Zeit.* ("The Schrammel [Brothers Quartet] in Their Time"). Vienna: Österreichischer Bundesverlag, 1989.

The first major study of the Schrammel Quartet, the ensemble responsible for transforming Austrian folk and *volkstümliche* styles into an urban popular music at the end of the nineteenth century. Egger has carefully culled reviews and anecdotes from the press of the period to reconstruct the lives of the quartet (Johann [Hanns] Schrammel, Josef Schrammel, Anton Strohmayer, and Georg Dänzer) and situated their musical tradition within the urbanization of Vienna's periphery and the rise of an urban, ethnically mixed Viennese working class. The book takes the form of a biography of the quartet itself, as well as the family members and other musicians associated with the Schrammels. As a social history, the book also reveals the ways in which diverse folk-music traditions undergo a transformation to crystallize into a popular-music tradition reflecting the social context. During the century since the deaths of the Schrammel musicians, the tradition has been canonized and continuously historicized, thereby influencing the interrelation among the numerous traditions that constitute a dynamic folk-music history in Austria. An excellent afterword by Walter Deutsch outlines the very palpable contributions of the Schrammel Quartet to the instrumentarium of Austrian folk and popular music.

22.   Wicke, Peter. *Rockmusik: Zur Ästhetik und Soziologie eines Massenmedium.* ("Rock Music: Toward the Aesthetic and Sociology of a Mass Medium"). Leipzig: Reclam, 1987.

Argues that rock music provides the younger generation with a cultural domain in which to respond actively to the industrialization and homogenization of modernity. Following Simon Frith, particularly in the privileging of the Anglo-American rock scene, Wicke seeks an alternative interpretation of rock music, not as a mass medium in which no differentiation exists, but rather as a culturally creative set of activities that make close and varied readings of a complex world possible. Of greatest importance in Wicke's analysis of the musical dimensions of rock music is the rhythm and other sonic aspects that can be realized only collectively. Published only two years before the *Wende* ("change") (1989) in the German Democratic Republic, the book does not offer a particularly thorough reading of GDR rock music or the distinctive ways in which rock music functions in the socialist economy of Eastern Europe. Theory, rather than practice, is the contribution of this economy to the study of rock as a form of popular culture. This theory, nonetheless, remains historically very significant, not least as a component of intellectual history in a nation that took the production of popular culture and the popular in music very seriously.

❦

Political Song

23. Eisel, Stephan. *Politik und Musik: Musik zwischen Zensur und politischen Mißbrauch.* ("Politics and Music: Music between Censor and Political Misuse"). Munich: Verlag Bonn Aktuell, 1990.

An ideological work arguing that music is largely misused during moments of authoritarianism, notably fascism and communism. Eisel bases the book on a thesis that music flourishes during periods of freedom, whereby he explicitly means the conditions of post-World War II democracy in the West, especially in Germany. During periods of political repression, according to the author, music must succumb to the politicization of those in power. The book does not really concern itself, then, with the political in music, but rather with what happens to music when certain types of politics recognize the potential for public use of music. In short, this work calls for a type of free-market approach to the political potential of music. Relatively little attention is given to theoretical and methodological approaches to music and politics, but the book looks at music during the Third Reich thoroughly.

24. Freitag, Thomas. "Alles singt oder Das Ende vom Lied? Liederbe und Singekultur der ehemaligen DDR" ("Everybody Sings, or The End of Song? The Heritage of Song and Song Culture in the Former German Democratic Republic"). *Jahrbuch für Volksliedforschung* 38 (1993): 50–63.

Introduction to the vast amount of singing that accompanied the history of the German Democratic Republic. On one hand, song in the GDR narrated post-World War II reconstruction of the country and the consolidation of its ideological agendas, reworking the texts of well-known folk songs and disseminating the songs of famous composers and poets (e.g., Hanns Eisler and Bertold Brecht). On the other hand, songs from individuals, some well known (e.g., Wolf Biermann) and others not, served as a counterforce to official politics. Motivating Freitag is the paradox of a country saturated with song, which nevertheless essentially abandons its song culture when its history ends, in this case with the reunification with the rest of Germany in 1990. GDR rock music, for example, was one of the only national traditions in Central Europe to make extensive use of the German language, thereby becoming archaic even before it might interact with rock music elsewhere in Central or Eastern Europe or on the international scene. Freitag introduces a history of song with much variety and complexity yet wonders how scholars can assess such a history now that it has come to an end; despite the extensive repertories, Freitag argues, only a few songs survive in the 1990s. Illustrated with songs from GDR youth and worker movements, the article reveals enormous possibilities for the study of the GDR and of the interaction between song and politics.

25.   Hahn, Kurt. "Das Lied im österreichischen Widerstand gegen den Nationalsozialismus 1938-1945." ("Song in the Austrian Resistance against National Socialism, 1938–1945"). *Jahrbuch des österreichischen Volksliedwerkes* 32/33 (1984): 219–37.

A selective overview of songs created by and associated with different aspects of Austrian resistance against National Socialism, from the annexation of Austria in 1938 until the end of World War II. Hahn's concept of resistance describes attempts to undermine the German presence in Austria. This resistance took several forms, from organized groups of workers and armed resistance to the voicing of resistance through songs created in concentration camps, especially in Dachau. The article includes transcriptions of several songs, many of them recorded from survivors or others who heard or sang these repertories. Hahn examines the ways in which songs were created and then transmitted within resistance circles, demonstrating the properties of folk song, especially those beginning in a broadside-like tradition. It is notable that the concept of resistance presented here fails to take into consideration that Austria itself was an ally of Germany and indeed was culpable politically and militarily in World War II. Resistance against National Socialism, therefore, was not simply an anti-German movement, but rather a much more complex phenomenon. No attempt in the article is made, for example, to discuss forms of Jewish resistance, or repertories from other groups persecuted and victimized by the Nazis in Germany and Austria.

26.   James, Barbara, and Walter Moßmann. *Glasbruch 1848: Flugblattlieder und Dokumente einer zerbrochenen Revolution.* ("Broken Glass 1848: Broadsides and Documents of a Shattered Revolution"). Darmstadt and Neuwied: Luchterhand, 1983.

The title of this book announces from the beginning that its documents present the more tragic side of the 1848 revolution in Central Europe, in which intellectuals and workers unsuccessfully attempted to overthrow the old monarchies. More commonly, political songs from the period are chosen as emblematic of heroism and the triumph of great ideas; in German-American history, the songs of the Forty-Eighters, moreover, provide the basis for one of the first important secular repertories. James and Moßmann, however, have assembled the songs of the everyday, the struggle for survival in the home and in the industrialized workplace. These songs have a different political function, namely that of voicing the concerns of the lower classes and the workers of Europe. The history that they document is subaltern, and its trajectory is not directed toward a culmination in the revolutions of the late nineteenth century, but rather toward the securing of adequate food and the alleviation of deplorable working conditions. James and Moßmann have turned quite different eyes and ears toward collections of political songs, and in so doing they have allowed the songs in this volume to tell a very different and powerful history of nineteenth-century Central Europe.

27. Juhasz, Christiane. *Kritische Lieder und Politrock in Österreich: Eine analytische Studie.* ("Critical Songs and Political Rock in Austria: An Analytical Study"). Frankfurt am Main: Peter Lang, 1994. (Vergleichende Musikwissenschaft, 1).

Distinguishing the approach in this book from more common approaches to the political contents of popular music, Juhasz develops a theoretical perspective using "musical-hermeneutic analysis." With primary emphasis on political song in Austria during the 1970s and 1980s, she examines different stylistic elements and the ways these express the political intent and content of popular songs. The volume begins with chapters devoted to the history of politically-engaged music, contextualizing that history within specific moments of socio-political responses. Juhasz then concerns herself with questions of genre, particularly with the different genres that most often serve as sites for social-critical song, ranging from more international genres (e.g., the blues) to genres more common to Austria (e.g., *volkstümliche Musik* ["folklike music"]), which are usually not associated with political criticism. Extensive musical analysis yields clear examples of the ways in which Juhasz's theoretical approach can identify how musical style enhances the political critique of popular music.

28. Klusen, Ernst. "Das sozialkritische Lied." ("The Social-Critical Song"). In Rolf Wilhelm Brednich, Lutz Röhrich, and Wolfgang

Suppan, eds., *Handbuch des Volksliedes*. Vol. 1: *Die Gattungen des Volksliedes*. Munich: Wilhelm Fink, 1973. Pp. 737–60.

Focusing on the "primary group" as the locus of musical practice, Klusen suggests a framework for song as a means for articulating social criticism and action. This context of social-critical song is both broader and narrower than other theories, to which Klusen compares and contrasts his theories. The point of departure is socio-psychological, namely, that primary groups form because of the need to mobilize a contrastive ideological or social cause. The mobilization may take many forms, whether against unfair labor practices or the hegemonic domination of state ideology. For Klusen it is important that the group's song has more power than the individual's, and that the song represents the conditions that bring individuals together as a group, thereby giving their collective action meaning. The article examines different types of social criticism, demonstrating the ways in which structures of institutions connect the individual through the group to the process of social criticism. The variety of criticism that this chain of structures makes possible is important for Klusen, and he uses it to argue for a much more inclusive and variegated model of social-critical song than Wolfgang Steinitz and other GDR folk-song scholars, who, in the 1950s and 1960s, were arguing for the revolutionary potential of all social mobilization through song. By broadening genres such as the social-critical song, Klusen believes folk-song scholarship could creatively expand its own discursive boundaries.

29.   Kollektiv des Arbeiterliedarchivs, ed. *Bibliographie der deutschen Arbeiterliedblätter 1844–1945*. ("Bibliography of German Workers' Song Broadsides, 1844–1945"). Leipzig: VEB Deutscher Verlag für Musik, 1975.

Uses printed workers' songs, which were produced in large numbers and distributed, to document the German workers' movement, given the dates here of 1844–1945. A bibliographical project of the Music Section and Workers' Song Archive in the Academy of Arts in the German Democratic Republic, this book has listings for over two thousand songs and includes various means of cross-referencing and illustration, including reprints of some broadsides and examples of sheet music. The political impetus of singing and song production in the workers' movement was that of mobilization, in other words, employing music to organize workers and articulate their causes. These songs are therefore often local and topical, and specific, for example, to a certain strike. As a whole, nonetheless, they show widespread connection at a more global level. The editors also include examples of songs related to the German workers' movement that appeared in songbooks or sources in other languages and outside Germany. As a bibliography the volume also documents the ways in which workers' songs negotiate issues of class in the spaces between different aesthetic levels, that is between folk, popular, and art song. Songs written by art-song composers (e.g., number 1324, the 1932 "Rotes Spartakalied" by Stefan Wolpe) appear in the same sources as those in local choral collections or published as popular "couplets" for cabaret. An important musical contribution to modern German intellectual history.

30. Lammel, Inge. *Das Arbeiterlied*. ("The Workers' Song"). Leipzig: Reclam, 1970.

Written by the director of the Arbeiterliedarchiv ("Workers' Song Archive") in the former German Democratic Republic, this volume contextualizes the workers' song historically as a means of struggling against the class oppression endemic in capitalist society. Born of that struggle, the workers' song empowers the working class to voice its own desires and to make history through the performance of song in mass demonstrations and in the activities of unions and other labor organizations. The volume contains sixty-one songs and their texts, with analytical discussions of both the textual and melodic components. Opening the book is a substantial discussion of the nature of workers' songs, the history of scholarship devoted to them, and the historical processes shaping and articulated by the songs themselves (e.g., the "Moorsoldatenlied," which began as a concentration-camp song but became the standard song of struggle for the workers' movement in the GDR). The anthology of songs, too, follows an historical trajectory, which provides musical documentation of the industrialization of European society, culminating in the modern GDR. The historical path of the workers' song has its origins in class struggle and resolution through the creation of a classless society. Its official language of GDR socialism notwithstanding, this volume provides a superb introduction to a Marxist aesthetics of music.

31. Maurer, Philipp. *Danke, man lebt: Kritische Lieder aus Wien, 1968–1983.* ("Thank You, One Gets Along: Critical Songs from Vienna, 1968–1983"). Vienna: Österreichischer Bundesverlag, 1987.

A survey and analysis of songs created and sung during the period of liberal popular politics in Vienna (and throughout Europe), beginning with the 1968 student movement. Playing the central role in the creation and mediation of this genre is the *Liedermacher* (singer-songwriter), many of whom flourished during the period. Maurer concentrates on the sites and settings in Vienna at which *Liedermacher* were particularly visible (e.g., the

Café Atlantis or in the successful protests against building nuclear power stations in Austria). Particularly important is the relation of critical songs to the mass media, which disseminated them widely but also provided the basis for a continued political impact. The study intentionally lends itself to comparative research by frequently raising questions about the role of political song in the shaping of the public sphere. Just why do songs that specifically address one event have the power to symbolize the philosophy and direction of an entire movement? Maurer sharpens his focus on Vienna, furthermore, by examining the presence of Viennese dialect in these critical songs, a conscious compositional technique whereby the composers localized meaning and yet broadened its contexts for different socio-economic and professional groups throughout Viennese society.

32. Mellacher, Karl. *Das Lied im österreichischen Widerstand: Funktionsanalyse eines nichtkommerziellen literarischen Systems.* ("Song in the Austrian Resistance: Analysis of the Function of a Non-Commercial Literary System"). Vienna: Europaverlag, 1986. (Ludwig Boltzmann Institut für Geschichte der Arbeiterbewegung: Materialien zur Arbeiterbewegung, 44).

Focuses on different types of song and contexts for singing that resisted Nazism in Austria. Mellacher identifies a surprisingly broad range of songs that openly or in a more or less coded language represented sentiments different from the official Nazi ideology of a new "people's society." Six "cases of resistance" organize the book's contents: workers' resistance; conservative opposition; individual resistance; cabaret; concentration camp and prison; and exile. The difficulty of creating a genre of resistance songs lies in the reliance on well-known tunes and text types, which therefore can be altered in such a way to mean different things to different listeners. That song is ideologically and textually malleable is essential to the author's argument. Mellacher takes seriously the distinction between "loud" resistance—in other words, resistance that is openly palpable—and "quiet" resistance, confined, that is, to the genre and those for whom it offers a special form of communication. It is particularly interesting to observe just how extensive the repertories of political songs were during the period of fascist domination in Austria.

33. Moßmann, Walter. *Flugblattlieder, Streitschriften.* ("Broadside Songs, Polemical Writings"). Berlin: Rotbuch Verlag, 1980.

A collection of political songs, created and performed by Walter Moßmann for demonstrations and political actions of the 1960s and 1970s. Dominating the collection are songs from the demonstrations against the construction of nuclear-power facilities in Wyhl, Alsace (France), just across the Rhine River from the Black Forest area of southwestern Germany. T h e s e demonstrations, joined by the student movement from the left and farmers and vintners alike, succeeded in stopping construction. The songs in this volume, therefore, reveal the persistent power of political broadsides to respond to the issues of modern Europe. Moßmann is one of the most distinguished political poets and singer-songwriters, whose scholarly prowess is also evident in the volume. He provides commentary to the individual songs, connecting them both to a longer history of political folk song and to the specific conditions for which these songs were created. Moßmann's discussions of his own creative processes and the autobiographical details about his career as a singer-songwriter in modern Germany, particularly during the period of most widespread student mobilization, make this a particularly interesting collection.

34. Schütz, Hans J. *Nun Brüder stehet wie ein Mann: Flugblätter, Lieder und Schriften deutscher Sozialisten 1833–1863: Im geschichtlichen Zusammenhang dargestellt.* ("Brothers Now Stand Like a Single Man: Broadsides, Songs, and Writings of German Socialists, 1833–1863: Presented in Historical Contexts"). Modautal-Neunkirchen: Anrich-Verlag, 1979.

Documentary study of the historical background, cultural activities, and literary and musical production of German socialists in the periods before, during, and after the failed 1848 Revolution. Schütz relies on two general types of documentary evidence. First, he presents and examines the writings of activist-intellectuals associated with mid-nineteenth-century socialism: Harro Harring, Wilhelm Wolff, Karl Marx, and Friedrich Engels, among others. Second, he examines the literature produced and consumed by the workers themselves, which includes numerous examples of broadsides and socialist songs. Song serves Schütz's history by documenting the conditions and struggles of German industrial workers in the mid-nineteenth century, but also by acting as a means of stimulating organization among the workers, for example the formation of the Allgemeiner Deutscher Arbeiterverein ("General German Workers' Organization") and the Internationale Arbeiter-Association ("International Workers' Association") in the 1860s. The political songs that were part of the socialist movement were both specific and general in the ways they articulated the workers' struggle. Many texts, for example, cluster around the figure of Friedrich Hecker, also known for his role in American exile, but other texts paint more general and romanticized pictures of workers' solidarity. An excellent example of the use of musical documents to present an historical narrative.

Religious Folk Music

35. Lieseberg, Ursula. *Studien zum Märtyrerlied der Täufer im 16. Jahrhundert.* ("Studies of Martyr Songs of the "Baptists" in the Sixteenth Century"). Frankfurt am Main: Peter Lang, 1991. (Europäische Hochschulschriften, Reihe I: Deutsche Sprache und Literatur, Vol. 1233)

Investigates the emergence of martyr songs as a genre during the sixteenth century, the beginning during the Reformation of the various sects known collectively as *Täufer* ("Baptists") in German, but variously as Hutterites, Amish, and Mennonites in English. Martyr songs have traditionally played an important role for these sects, both as a means of chronicling specific historical events and as a narrative genre constituting the canon for the distinctive hymnbooks for each group. The *Täufer* sects began to form during the sixteenth century, primarily in Germany, Switzerland, and Austria, but spread as they were forced to migrate because of persecution throughout Europe and eventually many to North America. Martyr songs chronicle the individual leaders and acts of faith that accompanied these migrations and settlement patterns. Lieseberg shows how two subgenres of martyr songs developed, one of them specific to the sects and individual martyrs, and the other largely accounts of martyrdom in the Bible. The genre itself, therefore, depends on the mixture of specific and general religious history, and furthermore remains encoded in a wide variety of hymnbooks, many of which remain in print and use after four centuries.

36. Markmiller, Fritz, ed. *Passionsmusik: Quellen, musikalische Elemente und Funktionen.* ("Music for the Passion: Sources, Musical Elements, and Funtions"). Dingolfing: BVS-Markmiller. (Niederbayerische Blätter für musikalische Volkskunde, 9).

Six essays devoted to historical and contemporary singing practices drawn from holidays and repertories related to the Passion, or final suffering, of Christ. The studies are both local and more generally devoted to the traditions that characterize the largely Catholic regions of South Germany and alpine Austria. The folk contexts for singing the music of the passion have often provided an alternative locus for the expression of religious faith, whether using texts in oral tradition that were more familiar to the faithful (dialect, as in Hermann Unterstöger's article, or, prior to Vatican II, German texts at all), or for voicing subaltern religious concerns. The music of the Passion in South Germany and Austria, it follows, has alternatively been supported and regarded with suspicion by the Catholic Church, and at times some of its practices were banned. One good example of the banning of such folk practices is the subject of Michael Bauer's article on mechanical models of the Mount of Olives in the Bavarian village of Reischach. In the Baroque encouraged as a means making Catholicism more vivid, the mechanical Mount of Olives was later alternatively banned and revived. When it was restored in 1980, Reischach's Mount of Olives served to stimulate new forms of worship, particularly the institution of Passion singing. Articles by Helmut Wagner and Ernst Schusser survey the literature on Passion singing and modern practices, respectively. Cesar Bresgan examines the creation of folk music for the Passion from the perspectives of a composer. As a whole, the volume documents the remarkable persistence, even against official sanction, of religious folk music in Catholic Central Europe.

37. Schroubek, Georg R. "Das Wallfahrts- und Prozessionslied." ("The Pilgrimage and Processional Song"). In Rolf Wilhelm Brednich, Lutz Röhrich, and Wolfgang Suppan, eds., *Handbuch des Volksliedes*. Vol. 1: *Die Gattungen des Volksliedes*. Munich: Wilhelm Fink, 1973. Pp. 445–62.

Survey of the development of folk-religious song for pilgrimage and processions, within the European context, hence in Catholicism. Schroubek takes as his point of departure the universality of music in ritual that involves movement. Pre-Christian Near Eastern religious processions required music, shaping it into repertories and genres. Judaism, for example, requires pilgrimage, and there are specific Psalms dedicated to the symbols of pilgrimage (Numbers 120–34). The importance of pilgrimage and processional songs developed throughout the early Middle Ages, with the significance of large-scale pilgrimage to Jerusalem receiving canonic status during the Crusades. Pilgrimage became one of the major forces mobilizing the Counter-Reformation (sixteenth century and following), and it is with the Counter-Reformation that the music for pilgrimage proliferated, disseminated by new forms of print technology, for example many new hymnbooks during the sixteenth and seventeenth centuries. Schroubek interprets pilgrimage songs structurally as a genre that lends itself to great popularity, for example because of its use of strophes and various rhyme schemes. As a genre pilgrimage songs can be both site and saint specific, or they can have a currency that cuts across cultural and linguistic boundaries, and includes political and social themes.

⚜

Composed Folk Music

38. Dahmen, Hermann Josef. *Friedrich Silcher: Komponist und Demokrat: Eine Biographie.* ("Friedrich Silcher: Composer and Democrat: A Biography"). Stuttgart: Edition Erdmann in Thienemanns Verlag, 1989.

A biography of Friedrich Silcher by the leading Silcher scholar and director of the Silcher Archive in Schnait, Germany. Friedrich Silcher (1789–1860) was the first composer to set folksong texts actively, as well as some non-German folk texts, in arrangements for chorus, small ensemble, and solo voice and piano. His 320 settings not only formed the basis for the standard repertory of singing societies and student groups in the nineteenth century, but his folklike compositions quickly entered oral tradition, spreading throughout Central Europe and to areas of German immigrant settlement, where they remain in standard repertories at the end of the twentieth century. The first university music director in Tübingen, Silcher was actively engaged in the role of song in the social and political foment within German liberal circles during the period prior to the aborted revolution in 1848. Dahmen focuses on this aspect of Silcher's life, attributing the dissemination of his folklike works to his concern for the musical activities at all levels and in all classes of German society. This biography examines the different choral institutions begun by Silcher, both in his university capacity in Tübingen and in his role as the founder of the Deutscher Sängerbund ("German Singers' Union"), in 1862. Dahmen uses archival evidence extensively to document Silcher's impact on German choral singing and folk-song repertories, and he does so also by taking Silcher's capacity as a composer very seriously. An outstanding study of the interrelations between folk, art, and folklike song in the early nineteenth century, when the boundaries between these genres were largely inchoate.

39. Schmid, Manfred Hermann, ed. *Friedrich Silcher 1789-1860: Studien zu Leben und Nachleben.* ("Friedrich Silcher 1789–1860: Studies on His Life and Its Legacy"). Stuttgart: Theiss, 1989. (Beiträge zur Tübinger Geschichte, 3).

Ten essays published on the occasion of the Tübingen exhibits celebrating the two hundredth anniversary of Friedrich Silcher's birth. Silcher held the position of university music director in Tübingen, therefore many of the articles, by Tübingen musicologists, assay his role in the musical life of nineteenth-century Swabia. The studies focus either on Silcher the composer or on Silcher the organizer of choral socities, both types of studies taking a fundamentally top-down approach. Rather little emphasis is placed on the processes whereby Silcher's folk- and art-song compositions entered oral tradition, becoming themselves well-known folk songs, as, for example, in the case of Silcher's setting of Goethe's "Heidenröslein." Essays by Susanne Johns and Maria Bieler concern themselves with sources of and influences on Silcher's compositions; Georg von Dadelson, Walther Dürr, and Jutta Schmoll-Barthel examine choral organizations in Tübingen and throughout Germany (notably, the Deutscher Sängerbund ["German Singing Union"], founded in 1862); a biographical sketch by the leading Silcher scholar, Hermann Josef Dahmen (see above), contributes added perspective. Friedrich Silcher played one of the most complex roles in the creation of romantic notions of folk song and folklike music, propagating these through the choral movements that penetrated all areas of German society during the nineteenth century. This volume contributes especially to an understanding of the musical sources from which Silcher drew and the institutionalization of composed folk song during the early and mid-nineteenth century.

✦✦✦

Genre as Social and Cultural Context

40. Baumann, Max Peter. "Zur Bedeutung des Betrufes in Uri." ("On the Meaning of the Prayer-Call in Canton Uri"). In Max Peter Baumann, Rudolf Maria Brandl, and Kurt Reinhard, eds., *Neue ethnomusikologische Forschungen: Festschrift Felix Hoerburger.* Laaber: Laaber-Verlag, 1977. Pp. 71–83.

The *Betruf* ("prayer-call") survives into the late twentieth century in Catholic cantons of Switzerland, such as Uri, where the phenomenon is investigated for this article. In the evening, alpine herdsman, with the help of a milk bucket formed into a megaphone, call across the meadows, invoking protection, usually from the Virgin Mary. Prayer-calls are patrilineally hereditary, which is to say that fathers pass them on to sons, albeit only after the father has performed prayer-calls during much of his life. There is some speculation that the phenomenon predates Christian meaning in Switzerland, although more dependable observations from the eighteenth and nineteenth centuries suggest firm association with Christian symbolism and meaning. Prayer-calls employ a melodic style similar to recitative, with extensive use of melodic and textual formulae. The survival of such folk-music practices offers considerable evidence of the connections between alpine occupations and the musical performance of these calls.

41. Pfeiffer, Karl, Michael Ottenschläger, and Wolfgang Wehap. "Die Geschichte von Schurl und Ferdl: Zwei Lebensentwürfe, dargestellt im Wiener Lied." ("The Story of Schurl and Ferdl: Two Life Sketches, Presented in the Viennese Song"). *Jahrbuch für Volksliedforschung* 37 (1992): 24–33.

Study of two Viennese songs recorded in 1967, but dating probably from the turn of the last century ("Der schönste Mann von Wien" ["The Most Handsome Man in Vienna"]) and the 1950s ("Da g'schupfte Ferdl" ["The Shoved Ferdl"]). The songs reflect the social conditions of their times, in the case of Schurl, the attempt of someone from outside Vienna to integrate himself into the social life of the cosmopolitan life of the capital, but in the case of Ferdl, the response of a post-World War II youth to the aspects of American culture influencing Austrian urban society. The authors hypothesize that the popularity of the songs has depended on their ability to provide texts and melodies that connected to the social and aesthetic expectations of the moment in which they came into existence; "Da g'schupfte Ferdl," for example, sounds like a "boogie-woogie," popular in Austria in the 1950s and representative of American popular culture. Each song, nevertheless, includes specific and local references and dialect, and has equally specific meaning as a reflection of social conditions. The essay is a valuable portrayal of the continued presence of Viennese song (*Wienerlied*) at the end of the twentieth century.

42. Schwab, Heinrich W. "Das Vereinslied des 19. Jahrhunderts." ("The Organizational Song of the Nineteenth Century"). In Rolf Wilhelm Brednich, Lutz Röhrich, and Wolfgang Suppan, eds., *Handbuch des Volksliedes*. Vol. 1: *Die Gattungen des Volksliedes*. Munich: Wilhelm Fink, 1973. Pp. 863–98.

Examines the songbooks employed by social organizations, which proliferated and became highly institutionalized during the nineteenth century. These social organizations were sometimes local and highly specialized according to profession, but they might also organize workers, students, religious groups, and professionals throughout Central Europe. Song was an important social component of the organizations, and the publication of songbooks became a necessary force in providing solidarity and purpose. On one hand, Schwab demonstrates that each organization assembled songs specific to its ideologies and goals. On the other, through statistical comparison of texts, variants, and melodic borrowings, he shows that *Vereinslieder* drew from existing repertories and canons. Particularly interesting is the way in which the songs of social organizations functioned to enhance the public transformation of many groups. As certain professions attempted to solidify and emblematize their social presence with songbooks, so too did religious groups, for example Jewish organizations, which became one of the largest producers and consumers of songbooks in the late nineteenth and early twentieth century, precisely at the moment of their greatest social and political emancipation. Schwab shows that thorough study of the *Vereinslied* provides one of the most significant ways to explore a vast domain between folk and popular music in German society.

43. Warneken, Bernd Jürgen, ed. *Massenmedium   Straße: Zur Kulturgeschichte der Demonstration*. ("Mass-Medium Street: Toward a Cultural History of the Demonstration"). Frankfurt am Main and Paris: Campus Verlag and Edition de la Maison des Sciences de l'Homme, 1991.

Thirteen essays by French and German authors, who concern themselves with the demonstration as a context for the expression of popular culture. Music appears only occasionally among the other subjects in these essays, but its presence reveals it to be one of the most significant forms of mobilizing the demonstration and then organizing it along ritual lines. The essays are deliberately historical, comparing demonstrations at several stages in their history (e.g., May Day demonstrations). The majority of essays concern themselves with demonstrations that arise from workers' movements or from workers' organizations, thus locating music in the demonstration as one of the media that allows a bottom-up performance of history. Among the essays that consider music more extensively, Jean-Pierre Bernard's looks at the ways in which Communist demonstrations in the twentieth century have organized themselves as quasi-liturgical. Jean-Claude Monet, in contrast, examines the use of pilgrimage as a means of mobilizing right-wing workers through urban pilgrimages, particularly in protests against foreigners in France. The essays in general reveal that more and different groups were mobilized through street demonstrations than historical accounts sometimes suggested. As a context for the public expression of culture, demonstrations have historically relied on music, both as a template for specific symbols and as a medium for their public performance.

Dance and Extra-Musical Determinants of Genre

44. Segler, Helmut. *Tänze der Kinder in Europa.* ("Dances of the Children of Europe"). 2 vols. Celle: Moeck, 1990 and 1992.

The magnum opus of Germany's leading scholar of children's dance. The concept of dance employed by Segler derives from social activities in which children use movement to express something specific about their relation with other children, as well as with adults. The emphasis, then, is not on dances in which children participate, but rather on the creativity with which children use movement as components of play, socialization, and the organization of their own social spaces. In the first volume Segler, with an excellent chapter also by Günther Batel, develops theoretical concepts and typologies that demonstrate the diverse settings and reasons for which children engage in dance. Segler musters a lifetime of statistics and individual dance types, and he derives his typology from comparative observation. The second volume contains documentation of dance forms, usually consisting of melodies, texts, and transcriptions. Although the volume titles refer specifically to "children in Europe," the comparative examples from non-Western cultures enhance the usefulness of the second volume. Children's dances, as theorized in these volumes, provide a lens for studying the initial stages of interaction in human societies. These volumes provide an equally valuable and stimulating starting point for the study of these social phenomena.

2

EDITIONS AND COLLECTIONS

It would be possible to construct the history of Central European folk-music scholarship using only editions and collections. The gathering and anthologizing of folk songs has preoccupied both amateurs and scholars in Central Europe, frequently providing them with common ground and shared goals. The compilation of an edition, moreover, often marks a distinctive moment, in which paradigms shift and the body of gathered pieces represents a recalibration of what folk music means in the past and present of a regional or national music culture. Seminal works in the history of German folk-music scholarship were, in fact, not infrequently editions or collections. Herder's *"Stimmen der Völker in Liedern"* and *Volkslieder* (1778–79) were collections of song texts, which in themselves symbolized the creative endeavors of the *Volk*; the critical preface for these volumes seems almost insignificant when compared to the collections themselves. Similarly, Arnim and Brentano's *Des Knaben Wunderhorn* (1806–08) is almost entirely a collection of folk poetry, with preface material far less critical than directed toward winning readership and patronage for the editors' project. This collection then passed through numerous editions during the course of the nineteenth century, around which various critical responses and a considerable reception history coalesced. Other collections (e.g., the *Lagerliederbuch* or Wolf Biermann's collections, discussed below) marked crucial moments in the political history of the twentieth century, further suggesting that folk songs, in themselves, possess an enormous power to represent the contexts that spurred collectors and editors to anthologize them.

Collections and editions, however, do not stand alone. Nor do they function as objective vessels into which artifacts are stuffed in order to be available to some maximized cross-section of the population. Collections signify far more than the objects they contain, and the transformation of collections into editions participates in the narration of history far more than simple processes of commoditization might imply. Collections and editions are the products of ideological motivations, and it is extremely rare that they do not promulgate political and cultural agendas. One might argue, moreover, that the German term, *Denkmal* ("monument"), sometimes given to editions, is even more telling than evident at first glance. The folk-song edition-as-monument not only remembers and recuperates the past, but it invests it with potentially powerful meanings in the present.

The collections and editions that I have chosen for this chapter have diverse historical and cultural functions. I have deliberately tried to include as many different types of collection as possible. By no means are these the only collections and editions to appear in the book, for there is no chapter in which I have not included them to illustrate another of the organizational themes. It follows that "collecting" is something that folk-music scholars do, whether as fieldworkers or as archivists. One of the primary motivations of collecting is simply to gather as many examples as possible and to make them accessible to a public that is as broad as possible.

The shared nature of this task notwithstanding, the actual mechanics and the implemented ideologies of collecting and editing differ considerably. The local collector, for example, is primarily concerned with gathering those traces of the world close at hand because they are ephemeral and because the local accrues value when communicated to others (see, e.g., Simrock 1851). The regional collection, perhaps reworked by a scholar, individualizes music-making practices but does so in order to convey a sense of the collective. Konrad Mautner, for example, edited seminal editions from Styria and the Styrian Salzkammergut region of Austria not because Styrian blood flowed through his veins—Mautner was, in fact, a distinguished Jewish collector—but rather to symbolize and romanticize the essence of folk song that he believed was distinctively Austrian. Editions, moreover, often result from a fundamental tension between songs as objects and songs as symbols invested with power. Wolf Biermann, negotiating the complex forces of socialism in the GDR, recognized the power of the song collection to thrust the debates of the German left into the public arena. Hans Breuer not only created a repertory for the youth movement of the early decades of the twentieth century, but his *Zupfgeigenhansl* (see below) and countless books imitating it transformed folk song into a framework for action by youth groups and movements throughout the entire century.

The folk-song collection achieves some measure of its power on pragmatic grounds. To greater or lesser degrees, the collection is designed for practice. Perhaps through the inclusion of guitar chords, perhaps through the beautifully executed etchings or illustrations, or, not to overlook the banal, perhaps because of the nails in the cover of the standard student songbook, the *Allgemeines Deutsches Kommersbuch*, which lift the book above the beer-drenched table, songbook editors intend that their collections should be used. The collection and edition, therefore, represent the processes of transmission, production, and consumption come full-circle. A collecting effort may begin among local practitioners, from which point a scholar transforms it into a body of pieces with national or political meaning. Further processes of editing and publishing make the collection available to those who can best utilize it, who then reintroduce it into practice again. For these reasons, collections and editions are inseparable from the history of folk music and folk-music scholarship in Central Europe. Indeed, they contribute substantially to its dynamic character in the past and continued significance in the present.

✦

45. Biermann, Wolf. *Alle Lieder*. ("All Songs"). Cologne: Kiepenheuer & Witsch, 1991.

The most complete collection of texts for songs written by the most influential and frequently controversial German singer-songwriter during the second half of the twentieth century, Wolf Biermann (b. 1936). The songs appear in the volume grouped according to different stages in Biermann's life, hence different patterns of engagement with German poets and musicians (e.g., Bertolt Brecht) and with German politics, especially the German Democratic Republic. The son of a Jewish father who was killed in Auschwitz, Biermann took up residence in the GDR in 1953, quickly following the aesthetic path created in the new German state by Brecht and Hanns Eisler. Restrictions were placed on his public activities in the early 1960s, and in 1976, his citizenship was revoked and he was forced to live in West Germany. In the 1980s and 1990s, Biermann became increasingly interested in Yiddish songs, especially those from the ghetto of Cracow. The texts in the volume reveal the diverse styles and themes of the singer-songwriter who coined the term *Liedermacher*. Parody is common, with most texts sprinkled liberally with dialect and colloquial terms. Many different song styles and genres are present, ranging from the social-critical to the blues to styles that respond to German multiculturalism. The songs are topical, often referring to a single event, yet as a whole they portray the complex intersection of ideology and public action in the GDR. A foreword and afterword frame this volume of influential political songs.

46. Biermann, Wolf. *Für meine Genossen: Hetzlieder, Gedichte, Balladen, mit Noten zu allen Liedern*. ("For My Comrades: Songs of Action, Poems, Ballads, with Music for All the Songs"). Berlin: Klaus Wagenbach, 1973.

One of the most important of a series of songbooks by Wolf Biermann, a political singer-songwriter, who had committed himself to socialism but was on the eve of being expelled from the GDR. The songs in this volume are sharply critical of the ways in which the state could thwart the positive achievements of socialism and its humanistic programs. The collection typifies Biermann's critique, full of satire and *double entendre*, creatively reworking traditional forms, such as the ballad, to sharpen his commentary on contemporary issues. Although musical notation accompanies the songs, most of the scores are transcriptions of an idealized or personalized version performed by Biermann himself. The themes, metaphors, and musical vocabulary of the collection are, therefore, very personal, but they are also specific to the historical moment. Biermann intends these songs to serve as a call to action, a goal he specifies in the title with the term *Hetzlieder.* The volume includes comments on how to interpret and use the songs, and a page inside the front cover even includes "instructions on how readers in capitalistic countries should use" the songs. Biermann employs this folk-song collection and others to demonstrate brilliantly the political potential of a published volume of songs to critique major public issues at the end of the twentieth century.

47. Böhme, Erdmann Werner, ed. *Deutsche Lieder—Heimat, Volk, Studentsein.* ("German Songs—Homeland, Folk, Being a Student"). Piano edition. 4th ed. Lahr/Schwarzwald: Moritz Schauenburg Verlag, 1978.

A volume containing piano accompaniments to the songs in the *Allgemeines Deutsches Kommersbuch,* the most widely used German student songbook, which was celebrating its 120th anniversary with its 160th edition in 1978. The piano versions are often traditional from the period in which a song entered the canon of German student songs, making this volume a valuable source for the intellectual history of German folk song. The contents and arrangements represent virtually all of the most important figures associated with the folk-song movement of the nineteenth century, for example Ludwig Erk and Friedrich Silcher.

48. Böhme, Franz M. *Altdeutsches Liederbuch: Volkslieder der Deutschen nach Wort und Weise aus dem 12. bis zum 17. Jahrhundert.* ("Old German Songbook: Folk Songs of the Germans from the Twelfth to the Seventeenth Century, According to Text and Melody"). Leipzig: Breitkopf und Härtel, 1877.

The most significant collection of premodern German folk songs, compiled to document both the long history of German folk song itself and the relation of a fundamentally German repertory to other traditions of music already in the Middle Ages. A total of 660 songs, with variants, constitute the edition itself, which Böhme introduces with a long analytical section. The age and canonic character of German folk song result both from musical traditions with which folk song melodies interacted and from the transmission of texts in oral and written tradition. The weight of evidence assembled here, therefore, provides Böhme

with a type of historical thick description that allows him to claim
that folk-song traditions in Germany have existed in essentially
unbroken transmission since the Middle Ages. Although there is
little cultural contextualization, many songs are identified
according to provenance. The research methodologies of the
volume derive from musicology and philology. Böhme presents
each melody in a stylized contemporaneous notation and then a
transcription of it; he provides the reader with a discussion of
early-music notation systems (e.g., neumes) in the introduction.
The textual variants demonstrate distinctive origins and yet fairly
wide distribution in Central and Northern Europe. Many of the
songs that appear in the volume passed from this collection into
other German folk-song canons, particularly into the ballad
tradition. This volume further contributes significantly to the
intellectual history of German folk-song scholarship because,
through its reliance on printed manuscripts, it literally documents
the connections between folk and court, secular and sacred, and
low and high traditions. A product of extraordinarily detailed
scholarship, the *Altdeutsches Liederbuch* is a classic in nineteenth-
and early twentieth-century folk-song research.

49.   Breuer, Hans, ed. *Der Zupfgeigenhansl*. (Lit.: "Little Hans, Player of
the Guitar"). Leipzig: Friedrich Hofmeister, 1908.

The songbook of the *Wandervogel* ("Wandering Bird") youth
group, the *Zupfgeiegenhansl* passed through many editions and
influenced other youth groups during the first half of the
twentieth century. The editor, Hans Breuer, assembled songs
from several different folk-song repertories: student songs,
ballads, soldiers' songs, and even stylized songs from the
Minnesingers. Individual folk songs demonstrate provenance
throughout Central Europe, with dialect songs mixed with those
in High German. Geographically, then, the repertory in the
Zupfgeigenhansl serves as a metonym for Germany—and to some
extent, German expansion—at the beginning of the twentieth
century. Images of nature and Romantic nationalism permeate
the collection, which symbolized for many German youth groups
the rite of passage from the family into the institutionalized life of
the nation. Standard collections provide the basic repertory for
the *Zupfgeigenhansl,* among those most frequently tapped being
Erk-Böhme (1893-96). Songs appear as easy-to-play melodies, with
guitar chords, taking the title's reference to that instrument
literally. These were songs that were meant for performance, and
the volume became the primary source from which young
Germans learned to sing folk songs. So effective were the
pedagogical and ideological functions of the *Zupfgeigenhansl* that
many youth groups (e.g., the German-Jewish Zionist *Blau-Weiß*)
adapted them to their production of songbooks and folk-song
repertories. This collection has contributed to songbooks until the

present, both to historicize the past and to undergird folk-song revival. The *Zupfgeigenhansl* is available in new and reprinted editions.

50. Buhmann, Heide, and Hanspeter Haeseler. *Das kleine dicke Liederbuch: Lieder und Tänze bis in unsere Zeit.* ("The Little, Fat Songbook: Songs and Dances up until Our Own Day"). 4th printing. Schlüchtern: Eigenverlag Heide Buhmann, Hanspeter Haeseler, 1986.

A standard and widely used songbook from the student movement of the 1970s and 1980s. Drawing upon many of the same sources used by other collections (e.g., broadsides and previous anthologies), the editors have anthologized some of the best-known songs from workers' movements and the left, combining these with new songs from the protests and causes of the student movement. The collection regards the spirit of Wolfgang Steinitz's collections from the GDR as standard, but they "go beyond Steinitz" by drawing on contemporary sources, including folk-music sources of all kinds in the Marburg University Library. The philosophy of the book is to provide songs that have meaning for and can be performed by the "simple people." In other words, the songbook should be practical, as exemplified by the illustrations and charts for dance steps and the pull-out pages for guitar accompaniment in the sleeve of the back cover. Many of the songs in this collection would never appear in standard folk-song anthologies. There are songs from concentration camps and new broadsides used to protest the building of nuclear power plants. Other songs fail to convey the symbols of Germanness or originate in popular culture. The volume uses the contexts and methods of the folk-song collection to criticize the very ideology that has supported this mode of folk-song production and transmission.

51. Deutsch, Walter. *Das alpenländische Liederbuch.* ("The Songbook from the Alpine Lands"). Vienna: Kreymayr & Scheriau, 1979.

A collection of 192 songs from the Alpine areas of Austria, Germany, Switzerland, and the German-speaking areas of northern Italy (Südtirol). Edited by one of Austria's foremost folk-music scholars during the second half of the twentieth century, Walter Deutsch, the volume is distinguished because of its superb commentary and its utility, that is its function as a *Gebrauchsliederbuch* ("utility songbook"), whose songs lend themselves to performance by musicians devoted to *Volksmusikpflege* ("the cultivation of folk music"). Deutsch draws on diverse collections from the different regions of the Alps for his collection, relying on extensive personal acquaintance through fieldwork, but also using historical as well as contemporary sources. The repertories therefore demonstrate regional unity through local function and dialect, here presented with orthographic conventions that are exceptionally singer-friendly, not least because the editor urges singers to adapt them to their own dialects. The argument for a larger alpine song style rests on stylistic and analytical arguments (e.g., the use of parallel polyphonic voices). The incorporation of folk songs from previous collections also strengthens the value of this work as a survey of the intellectual history of alpine, especially Austrian, folk-music studies.

52. Deutsch, Walter, Gerlinde Haid, and Herbert Zeman. *Das Volkslied in Österreich: Ein gattungsgeschichtliches Handbuch.* ("The Folk Song in Austria: A Genre-Historical Handbook"). Vienna: Holzhausen, 1993.

A collection assembled from traditional Austrian folk-song genres and therefore representative of the distinctive character and categories of folk music in Austria. Organized according to characteristic genres (e.g., *Schnaderhüpfel*, songs of the alpine meadow, or *Wienerlied*), the editors concern themselves with the historical development of the genre, by citing the earliest appearances in the literature, as well as contemporary scholarship addressing the genre. Conceptualizing folk song in its broadest sense, but also in a sense that distinguishes historical and regional traits in Austria, the volume expands the categories upon which it is built. Urban folk song and sacred song, in particular, play significant roles in expanding the notion of folk song found in this volume. The publications of couplet composers such as Carl Lorenz and the instrumental music of the Schrammel Quartet (see above) add considerable depth to an understanding of the vernacular and popular music culture of *fin-de-siècle* Vienna. In contrast, the editors do not abandon traditional Austrian categories, such as the connection to region and dialect. Also from the turn of the last century, the activities of scholars such as Josef Pommer and collectors such as Konrad Mautner serve to represent the diversity of dialect songs and to reveal some of the diverse and contrasting streams that constitute Austrian folk-music scholarship.

53. Deutsch, Walter, and Gerlinde Hofer. *Die Volksmusiksammlung der Gesellschaft der Musikfreunde in Wien (Sonnleithner-Sammlung).* ("The Folk-Music Collection of the Society of the Friends of Music, Vienna [Sonnleithner Collection]"). Part 1. With an introductory essay by Leopold Schmidt ("Zur Bedeutung der österreichischen Volksliedsammlung von 1819" ["On the

Significance of the Austrian Folk-Song Collection of 1819"]).
Vienna: A. Schendel, 1969. (Schriften zur Volksmusik, 2).

The first thorough attempt to assess and provide access to the
1819 collection of folk songs in the Gesellschaft der Musikfreunde
in Vienna, which, despite its ca. 1,500 songs, had remained almost
unknown and inaccessible since its inception. Regarded as the
"first major cross-section of folk songs" in Austria, the
Sonnleithner Collection also contains many songs from the lands
of the Habsburg Empire, particularly the former Czechoslovakia,
the Baltic nations, and Südtirol, now part of northern Italy. Many
different genres are represented and organized according to
function, as well as provenance and dialect group. Classificatory
principles predate the folk-music movement of the later
nineteenth century, but rather reflect a nascent Austrian
historicism seeking to distinguish an alpine folk culture from that
symbolized by a more hegemonic notion of German folk song
prevalent in the German states. Many songs and categories reveal
an awareness of recent historical events, some of which are
criticized. Diverse media of transmission are all present—
individual manuscripts, instrumental parts, texts with diacritics for
dialects—indicating little of a later-nineteenth-century notion that
folk song must be old and orally transmitted. Facsimiles and
printed versions of many texts make the volume valuable for
comparative research. Through an attempt to rehistoricize the
Sonnleithner Collection as the foundation for Austrian folk-music
research, the volume serves to document many of the distinctive
directions taken by Austrian scholars (e.g., Schmidt 1969).

54. Dreo, Harald, Walter Burian, and Sepp Gmasz, eds. *Ein
burgenländisches Volksliederbuch*. ("A Burgenland Folk-Song
Book"). Eisenstadt: Nentwich-Lattner, 1988.

A volume of 246 songs from the Austrian province of
Burgenland, which stretches along the western border of
Hungary. Burgenland has historically included the most
multicultural and diverse population in Austria, with large
communities of Romas and Sintis, Jews, Hungarians, Croats, and
Protestants, and this historical diversity, as well as its non-alpine
landscape, has produced a folk-song repertory distinct from that
of the rest of Austria. This volume conveys Burgenland's
distinctive diversity, not only because of the presence of non-
German songs, but also because of the ways in which the editors
have integrated these into the classificatory categories in the book
rather than setting them off by ethnic or religious groups. The
present volume and the collections from which it draws are the
product of an intellectual history that has stretched throughout
the twentieth century. Beginning with attempts to publish
regional and provincial song repertories in 1904 through the

project known as "Das Volkslied in Österreich" ("The Folk Song in Austria"), various commissions to collect and anthologize songs in Burgenland were established and then failed to complete their undertakings because of the world wars and the shifting of Burgenland's border in 1921. The current editors have incorporated materials from the older collections and relied on modern collectors and field research. Unlike the more complex polyphonic styles of folk song in alpine Austria, songs in Burgenland are characteristically in two voices. Transcribed to preserve continuity in oral tradition for contemporary singers, the volume is a model for regional collections.

55. Erk, Ludwig, with Franz M. Böhme. *Deutscher Liederhort.* ("Gathering of German Songs"). 3 vols. Leipzig: Breitkopf und Härtel, 1893–94.

The culmination of Ludwig Erk's collecting and editorial efforts, organized and completed by Franz Magnus Böhme. Erk was one of the most active folk-song collectors in the nineteenth century, who ceaselessly gathered and edited materials. He conceived of folk song in the broadest sense, concerning himself less with specific genres than with the connections between history and oral transmission. The folk songs in this edition, therefore, range from ballads and children's songs to student and sacred songs; historically, they date from as early as the Middle Ages and from the most recent anthologies of student songbooks and collections for singing society. Böhme worked primarily as a philologist and musicologist; therefore, many aspects of organization and documentation are due to his efforts to complete this project after Erk's death. The three volumes contain a total of 2,175 songs, many with melodies and accompanying variants. The editors surveyed an enormous number of sources in order to assemble the *Liederhort,* and extensive systems of bibliographical citation and cross-referencing make these volumes an invaluable guide to the publication and production of folk song in the nineteenth century. The *Liederhort* is frequently of great value for the research of historical musicologists, for Erk and Böhme integrate art-music sources into their methodology; in particular, sacred works from the Reformation and Counter-Reformation appear in the *Liederhort.* Although the portrait of German folk song is expansive, it also demonstrates clear boundaries and exclusivity. The *Liederhort* promulgates a nationalist vision of Germanness through folk music, anchored in a history that begins in the Middle Ages and is articulated in increasingly specific ways until the time of publication. An indispensable collection for understanding the construction of German folk song and the realization of its intellectual history.

56. Flechsig, Hartmut. *Revolution und Romantik in Deutschland: Politische und andere Lieder aus der Zeit von 1813 bis 1848.* ("Revolution and Romanticism in Germany: Political and Other Songs from the Period between 1813 and 1848"). Regensburg: Gustav Bosse Verlag, 1980. (Bosse Musik Paperback, 16)

A volume intended for educational uses, this book contains songs from the period known as *Vormärz* in Germany and the *Biedermeierzeit* in the Habsburg Empire. The importance of the book is twofold. First, no other volume devotes itself to the political songs of this period; instead, most focus on the early Romanticism of art song and on the closed salons and artistic circles of the time. Second, these songs represent the response of institutions and individuals to the oppressive political climate of pre-revolutionary Central Europe. Not only workers songs appear here, but also the first emigrant songs and what might be understood as alternative songs for men's singing societies. In short, the volume uses political songs to illuminate the early Romantic period in an alternative light. A cassette accompanies the text.

57. Friz, "Zupfgeigenhansel" Thomas, and Erich Schmeckenbecher, eds. *Es wollt ein Bauer früh aufstehn...: 222 Volkslieder.* ("A Farmer Wanted to Get Up Early...: 222 Folk Songs"). Dortmund: Verlag "pläne," 1978.

Collection of repressed folk songs from the sixteenth to the twentieth century, whose texts voiced protest and resistance to economic and political hegemony. These songs of "democratic character" reflect a post-World War II response to the elimination of songs from the German folk-song canon, in which political messages criticized the structures of German nationalism and the ideologies of power, notably fascism. With historical commentary for each song, the book intends also to be a source for performance and practice, particularly a revival of singing within politically active and leftist groups. Relatively few modern political songs are found in the book, but the authors intend the historical material to provide the basis for new variants and compositions by singer-songwriters of the post-1968 era. Valuable as a lens for understanding the symbolic importance of folk song for the socialist movements in both Germanies in the two decades prior to the *Wende* in 1989.

58. Goertz, Hartmann, and Gerlinde Haid. *Die schönsten Lieder Österreichs.* ("The Most Beautiful Songs of Austria"). Vienna: Ueberreuter, 1979.

A collection of folk songs from Austrian sources or those demonstrating specific connections to Austria. Organized by theme and genre ("folklike songs," "wandering and alpine meadow songs," "working songs," etc.), the volume aims to be inclusive in its selection of folk songs. In her contribution to the foreword, Gerlinde Haid observes that many of the songs, while originating outside Austria, entered into their current versions through Austrian practices, hence making them also *volkstümlich* ("folklike"). Some of the songs are well known, others only locally sung. As an edition, the volume uses certain fairly typical devices to aesthetic advantage, for example the inclusion of an earlier etching or illustration, most of them expressing nineteenth-century Romanticism. Songs appear without variants, but an overwhelming characteristic of the volume is the printing of songs in regional and local dialects. Accordingly, the volume is useful as a source for all Austrians, but it still places demands on performers to sing in dialects unfamiliar to them. The juxtaposition and *bricolage* of dialect songs has generally come to signify Austrianness in collections and repertories of Austrian folk songs. For the most part, transcriptions use two voices, with the melody harmonized at the third or sixth, often with parallel voicing. In some cases these evoke the sound of yodeling, but in general the arrangement of voices further works to ascribe an Austrian sound to the songs in this collection.

59.   Holzapfel, Otto. *Vierzeiler-Lexikon.* ("Lexicon of Quatrains"). 5 vols. Bern: Peter Lang, 1991–93. (Studien zur Volksliedforschung, 7–11).

An annotated lexicon of *Vierzeiler*, literally, "quatrains," and related forms of short, direct folk songs. The lexicon follows an alphabetical order based on typology, in which the concept "type" identifies the most salient subject in the text of the quatrain. *Vierzeiler* are most often treated as typically alpine, especially Bavarian and Austrian, but by expanding the genre to include related forms, ranging from dance verses to certain types of *Spottlieder* ("songs used to insult"), Holzapfel locates quatrains on the entire folk-song landscape of Central Europe. The sources for the examples and their variants in this lexicon are those of the German Folk-Song Archive in Freiburg im Breisgau, which has gathered quatrains from deposited examples from oral tradition and the several common forms of printing and disseminating quatrains. Each example appears in a representative form, regardless of whether it is in High German (e.g., from a printed source) or in dialect; variants and their distribution are notated together with the representative form. Many texts appear with a typical melody, again from either oral or printed tradition; unlike textual themes, however, there is no melodic typology or type employed in organizing the lexicon. Framing each volume is one or several essays that introduce certain aspects of the quatrain, its occurrence in German-speaking areas, and its study. Closing volume 2, for example, is an essay surveying the different names given to the quatrain, many of these dependent on the region or dialect; closing volume 3 is an essay describing typical textual structures. Walter Deutsch contributes the excellent final essay to volume 1, in which he discusses the characteristics of quatrain (especially the Austrian *Schnaderhüpfel*) melodies and the rhythms they ascribe to and derive from the texts. The annotations and commentaries that accompany individual examples are remarkably rich in detail, and each volume contains a number of fascinating illustrations from printed *Vierzeiler* texts. One of the most thorough studies of a single folk-song genre and the most authoritative study of the quatrain in any language.

60. Idelsohn, A.Z. *Hebräisch-orientalischer Melodienschatz.* ("Thesaurus of Hebrew-Oriental Melodies"). 10 vols. Berlin et al.: Benjamin Harz et al., 1914-32.

Vol. 1:   *Gesänge der jemenischen Juden.* ("Songs of the Yemenite Jews"). (1914)

Vol. 2:   *Gesänge der babylonischen Juden.* ("Songs of the Babylonian Jews"). (1922)

Vol. 3:   *Gesänge der persischen, bucharischen und daghestanischen Juden.* ("Songs of the Persian, Bukharan, and Daghestani Jews"). (1922)

Vol. 4:   *Gesänge der orientalischen Sefardim.* ("Songs of the Oriental Sephardic Jews"). (1923)

Vol. 5:   *Gesänge der marokkanischen Juden.* ("Songs of the Moroccan Jews"). (1929)

Vol. 6:   *Der Synagogengesang der deutschen Juden im 18. Jahrhundert.* ("The Synagogue Song of the German Jews in the Eighteenth Century"). (1932)

Vol. 7:   *Die traditionellen Gesänge der süddeutschen Juden.* ("The Traditional Songs of the South German Jews"). (1932)

Vol. 8:   *Der Synagogengesang der osteuropäischen Juden.* ("The Synagogue Song of the Eastern European Jews"). (1932)

Vol. 9:   *Der Volksgesang der osteuropäischen Juden.* ("The Folk Song of the Eastern European Jews"). (1932)

Vol. 10:   *Gesänge der Chassidim.* ("Songs of the Hassidic Jews"). (1932)

The ten-volume canon of Jewish traditional music, collected to depict the Jewish Diaspora, yet conceptualized and organized to represent the connection of Jews throughout the world to the musical traditions of the land of Israel. Idelsohn, a Latvian-born cantor, who undertook musicological training in Berlin and Leipzig, assembled this collection in several distinct stages. During the second decade of the twentieth century, he conducted fieldwork in Palestine with a wax-cylinder recorder, under commission from the Austrian Academy of Sciences. The first five volumes of the *Thesaurus* constitute the product of this fieldwork, and many of the examples are transcriptions of field recordings. To make these recordings, Idelsohn turned to the communities from the Middle East and North Africa, which had resettled in Palestine but still maintained distinctive ethnic traditions. The second five volumes result primarily from Idelsohn's study and compilations from written sources, both published collections of folk songs and manuscripts, particularly of synagogal and cantorial music. The written sources, too, stressed the role of oral tradition, and throughout his references to such sources, Idelsohn interprets manuscripts as evidence of the longevity and unbroken character of Jewish music traditions. The clear intent of the *Thesaurus* was to establish the integrity of Jewish music as a series of distinctive repertories that depended, nevertheless, on the histories of individual ethnic and regional communities. At the core of every repertory was a set of melodic and stylistic characteristics that outside influences might affect, but not to the extent that these negated the fundamental Jewish quality. In each volume of the *Thesaurus* Idelsohn systematically lays out a music theory for the repertory and community he anthologizes, clarifying how specific pieces demonstrate certain principles. The theoretical framework, maintained in part by musical professionals and in the specific context of the synagogue, also provides the necessary structures for a long history of transmission, extending ultimately to the core of Jewish musical traditions that existed in Israel prior to the destruction of the Temples and the Diaspora. The *Thesaurus* provides a model for the interpretation of collections based on differences in order to represent the musical unity of an ethnic or religious community. Compiled and published in the quarter century prior to the Holocaust, the virtual destruction of the Diaspora that the *Thesaurus* documented, Idelsohn's work remains unsurpassed in its breadth and detailed analysis of different Jewish musics.

61. Kaschuba, Wolfgang. "Volkslied and Volksmythos—Der 'Zupfgeigenhansl' als Lied- und Leitbuch der deutschen Jugendbewegung." ("Folk Song and Folk Myth—the 'Zupfgeigenhansl' as a Book of Song and Leadership for the German Youth Movement"). *Jahrbuch für Volksliedforschung* 34 (1989): 41–55.

Appearing in its first edition in 1909 (see above), the *Zupfgeigenhansl* quickly established itself not only as the songbook for the youth group known as the *Wandervögel* but became the most widespread songbook among all German youth groups during the years before, during, and after World War I. Kaschuba explores the reasons for this immense popularity, postulating that the book's elevation of the guitar (the "Zupfgeige") to an instrument that permitted youth groups symbolically to take charge of their own musico-social activities and the mixture of ideological and historical repertories endowed the book with enormous meaning and importance during the transformation from Imperial to Weimar Germany. Kaschuba concerns himself primarily with the second of these conditions, and he illustrates the ways in which the songs in the book historicized a Romantic German nationalism that supplanted the more critical challenge to nationalism characterizing youth organizations at the turn of the century. The mixed contents, therefore, invented a Germany that had never existed, yet whose existence was nonetheless threatened by World War I. Rather unconvincingly, the author concludes by connecting the ideology of the *Zupfgeigenhansl* to the rise of Nazism, claiming that its contents and the *Wandervögel* did "nothing to make the thousand-year consequences [of National Socialism] impossible."

62. Klusen, Ernst, comp. *Deutsche Lieder.* ("German Songs"). Frankfurt am Main: Insel Verlag, 1980.

A large (almost 900 pages) compilation of many of the best-known German songs, with an introduction and commentary by Ernst Klusen. The decision to designate these as "songs" instead of "folk songs" stems from the diverse functions and sources, which the editor notes do not always coincide with the characteristics established by J.G. Herder. The songs appear, nevertheless, in monophonic and normative versions, which make them a usable source for both scholars and general readers. The examples are consciously chosen from a period beginning with the tenth century and culminating with contemporary, twentieth-century songs. With history as one criterion for the "German song," Klusen classifies and organizes the volume according to themes that reflect different types of functions (e.g., "home and afar," or "God and the world"). Evident in the classification and commentaries about these songs is Klusen's theory that the primary function of song is social, in particular to undergird the interaction of "groups" (cf. the full theoretical articulation of *Gruppenlieder* in Klusen 1969). In addition to its excellent introduction and commentaries on individual songs, the volume serves as an excellent source for comparative study.

63. Latz, Inge. *Frauen-Lieder: Texte und Noten mit Begleit-Akkorden.* ("Women's Songs: Texts and Notes with Chords for

Accompaniment"). Frankfurt am Main: Fischer Taschenbuch
Verlag, 1980.

A collection of women's songs reflecting the issues and
musicians of the women's movement of the 1970s. A fairly small
number of historical songs and those from non-German traditions
(mostly American) complements songs from women's lives, as
well as those sung as responses to specific historical moments.
Folk songs and different types of popular song (e.g., cabaret,
broadside, and singer-songwriter repertories) make the collection
broadly representational; the guitar accompaniments and
illustrations increase its utility by contemporary singers and in
modern contexts. The strength of the collection is the way in
which the songs reflect the everyday lives and struggles of many
women, rather than the political agendas of a few.

64. *Das Lagerliederbuch: Lieder, gesungen, gesammelt und geschrieben im
Konzentrationslager Sachsenhausen bei Berlin 1942.* ("The
[Concentration] Camp Songbook: Songs, Sung, Collected and
Written in the Sachsenhausen Concentration Camp Near Berlin,
1942"). Reprint. Dortmund: Verlag "pläne," 1980.

Reprint of a handwritten songbook, assembled in a
concentration camp in which communists were the primary
internees. The texts are carefully written, many accompanied by a
drawing or illustration; musical notation is absent, indicating the
extent to which the texts represented an extensive oral tradition
in this camp, as well as in the contact with other work camps. This
songbook was the first reprinted musical product of the Nazi
concentration camps, and in 1980 it joined only a small number of
other works that documented musical life in the camps. Even by
1980, relatively little scholarly attention had been devoted to the
cultural life of concentration camps, making this volume a
pioneering publication. Songs come largely from other song
traditions, for example the German youth movement, both folk
and more contemporary popular songs. Songs such as the famous
workers' camp song, "Das Moorlied" ("The Song of the Moor"),
are also prominent. Song texts are remarkable for their
hopefulness, which served both as resistance to the conditions of
the camp and as a means of looking toward the future. There is
no comparison of these songs and themes with those of other
concentration camps, such as the death camps largely occupied by
Jews, Romas and Sintis, and others the Nazis wished to
exterminate, whose songs and musical activities expressed very
different responses to the reality they faced.

65. Mautner, Konrad. *Das steyerische Rasplwerk: Vierzeiler, Lieder, und
Gasslreime aus Gößl am Grundlsee.* ("The Styrian Rasplwerk:

Quatrains, Songs, and Street Rhymes from Gößl am Grundlsee").
Vienna: Stähelin & Lauenstein, 1910. With a supplementary
volume, also 1910.

The life work of a semi-professional folk-song collector (and
businessperson), who concentrated his efforts on the
mountainous province of Styria, in particular on the village of
Gößl and its environs. This collection functions as a thick
description, not only because of the detailed transcriptions of
songs that it contains, but also because of the presentation of the
publication itself. Transcriptions appear not only as texts and
musical notation, but colored drawings, marginalia, and
embellishing representations of all kinds enhance the
representational quality of the book. The entire book of 372
pages, then, is a product of Mautner's hand, executed in
remarkable detail. In every detail the book conveys a sense of
tradition. As songs appear in transcription, they are faced by a
drawing of performances, accompanying narratives, the
appropriate traditional clothing, or the common contexts of
family, community, custom, or nature. Mautner gives considerable
attention to dialect, and each song appears with carefully
transcribed Styrian orthography. Explanations of the dialect
markings, together with extensive glossaries and listings of
individuals sources and variants, appear in the supplementary
volume. Together, the two volumes combine the personal insight
of a *Heimatforscher* ("local researcher") with the expert knowledge
of a musical scholar, yielding one of the richest regional
collections in modern folk-music research.

66. Mautner, Konrad. *Alte Lieder und Weisen aus dem steyermärkischen
     Salzkammergut*. ("Old Songs and Tunes from the Styrian
     Salzkammergut"). Vienna: Staehelin und Lauenstein, 1918?.

A collection of folk songs and instrumental pieces from the
Salzkammergut region of the Austrian province of Styria. Using
nineteenth-century descriptions and collections, contemporary
linguistic and ethnographic studies, and his own extensive
participant-observation, Mautner represents a region whose
communities and culture are geographically and historically at the
greatest distance from urban Central European culture. Two
competing ideologies inform the collection. First, the pieces in
this volume should represent a disappearing past, a culture that
the twentieth century cannot entirely recover. Second, Mautner
makes it clear throughout that the Styrian Salzkammergut was not
entirely isolated from the urban and imperial culture of the
Austro-Hungarian Empire. Some songs, for example, are
preserved because their performers wrote them down in the
nineteenth century, situating them between oral and written
tradition. Others reflect a sense of *Heimat* ("homeland"), even

though they were sung by city dwellers and Styrians working in the lumbering projects in the eastern part of the monarchy. Each song or instrumental piece, nonetheless, demonstrates explicit connections to place, through dialect or stylistic nuances that Mautner elucidates in his fairly extensive footnotes for each piece. The richly-illustrated volume represents a superb collaboration between a self-trained folk-music collector, Mautner, and the institutions of scholarship in Vienna.

67.   Müns, Heike, and Burkhard Meier, eds. *Weiße Segel fliegen auf der blauen See: Pommern in Lied und Brauch.* ("White Sails Fly on the Blue Sea: Pomerania in Song and Custom"). Rostock: Reich, 1992.

Diverse collection of songs and folklore from Pomerania, the province in northeastern Germany and northwestern Poland. Published soon after the dismantling of communist governments in the German Democratic Republic and Poland, this collection presents the folk traditions that distinguish Pomerania both as a cultural area and as a region historically connected to north Germany. Organized according to the uses and functions of folklore, folk-song genres mix with other traditions, suggesting an integrated folklife, if even examples are drawn from different historical periods and sources. The analytical commentary for the collection is particularly valuable, and the editors have combined solid scholarship with their attempt to present a rich portrait of Pomerania. For those unfamiliar with Pomeranian *Plattdeutsch* ("Low German"), the collection introduces dialect traditions effectively and clearly. Modern songs, such as regional hymns and popular songs, are also found, although there is no attempt to integrate non-Germanic traditions, such as those of the predominantly Polish-speaking eastern part of the province. An excellent model for a late twentieth-century regional folk-song collection.

68.   Schade, Ernst. "Volkslied-Editionen zwischen Transkription, Manipulation, Rekonstruktion und Dokumentation." ("Folk-Song Editions between Transcription, Manipulation, Reconstruction, and Documentation"). *Jahrbuch für Volksliedforschung* 35 (1990): 44–63.

Traces the intellectual history of the nineteenth-century German folk-song canon by assessing the ways in which editors made their collections conform to the intellectual and cultural expectations of Romanticism. To frame this intellectual history Schade examines an initial stage, the publication of *Des Knaben Wunderhorn* in 1806 and 1808, and the mid-century culmination, the numerous editions and arrangements published by Ludwig Erk. The four processes of transcription, manipulation, reconstruction, and documentation, together and separately, characterize the editor's intent and editorial procedures. Briefly considers the ways in which these processes persisted into the twentieth century and continued to influence the creation of collections and the publication of editions in modern folk-song scholarship. Concludes by summarizing materials amassed by Ludwig Erk that nonetheless have only begun to attract scholarly attention and that would make it possible to reassess the formation of the nineteenth-century canon of German folk song.

69. Schmidt, Leopold. "1819: Zur Enstehungsgeschichte der Volksliedsammlung der Gesellschaft der Musikfreunde in Wien" ("On the History of the Origins of the Folk-Song Collection of the Society for the Friends of Music in Vienna"). *Jahrbuch des österreichischen Volksliedwerkes* 18 (1969): 1–9.

Description of the various scholarly and political factors influencing the origins and early history of the folk-song collection in one of the most significant organizations devoted to the support of music, music-making, and musical research in nineteenth-century Austria. Based on the private collections of Josef Sonnleithner, the collection reflects the philological scholarship of the early nineteenth century (e.g., the folklore collections of the Brothers Grimm and the Austrians Julius Maximilian Schottky and Franz Ziska), as well as the growing role folk song played in the representation of national and cultural identity, particularly in the contested regions now in northern Italy (Südtirol). Many contributions came from individuals, who sent their own collections and observations, establishing a long tradition of lay support of folk-music research in Austria, in the twentieth century associated with the concept *Volksmusikpflege* ("cultivation of folk music"). For a full assessment of the Sonnleithner Collections see Deutsch and Hofer 1969.

70. Simrock, Karl. *Die deutschen Volkslieder.* ("German Folk Songs"). Frankfurt am Main: Heinrich Ludwig Brönner, 1851.

One of the first attempts to collect songs exclusively in local oral tradition and to make the claim for these as representative of German folk songs. Simrock worked in and around Bonn and Honnef, transcribing the texts of songs performed for him by local singers. Friends and colleagues also provided a few examples from repertories with which they were familiar. Some of the songs are individual, connected to specific singers, but others are components of the emerging canon of German folk song. Simrock distinguishes his collection from previous efforts, such as Arnim and Brentano's *Des Knaben Wunderhorn*, which also include composed songs and *volkstümliche Lieder* ("folklike songs"). By doing fieldwork Simrock establishes new criteria for authenticity, for example through a claim that he took down the texts exactly as sung, without any editorial adjustments. None of the 379 songs in the collection includes a melody, although Simrock notes the importance of transcribing the melody with the text. The essence of a folk song, he argues nonetheless, lies in the text and its transmission, that is, its capacity to maintain tradition. The songs in the volume clearly demonstrate a local character. Many are connected to particular occupations, and others come from repertories that are part of the home, for example children's songs. Simrock's concept of German folk song, therefore, is primarily local, which stands in contradistinction to many of the other collecting endeavors in the nineteenth century.

71. Steinmetz, Horst, Otto Holzapfel, et al., eds. *Lieder aus dem Nachlaß von Stephan Ankenbrand*. ("Songs from the Legacy of Stephan Ankenbrand"). Simmershofen: Forschungsstelle für fränkische Volksmusik der Bezirke Mittel-, Ober- und Unterfranken, 1989.

Glimpse into the folk-song collection of a folk singer from Franconia (northeastern Bavaria) during the early decades of the twentieth century. The collection contains a surprisingly large number of ballads and songs from other narrative genres (46), drawn from various sources. This publication strikes a balance between presenting the material "as it was" during Ankenbrand's life and commenting on its meaning within other folk-song traditions in Franconia and in the German-speaking areas of Europe. Ankenbrand was himself an active collector and participant in folk-song traditions, publishing also on these aspects. This edition, then, presents him as a mediator and culture broker, who ranged widely in the sources he tapped in order to create a folk-song repertory appropriate for a region exhibiting extraordinary self-identity. Regionalism emerges more as a case of *bricolage* than as a geographically bounded and unique repertory.

72. Steinmetz, Horst, and Otto Holzapfel, eds. *Langensendelbacher Liederbuch: Eine fränkische Liedersammlung des 19. Jahrhunderts.* ("Songbook from Langensendelbach: A Nineteenth-Century Song Collection from Franconia"). Langensendelbach: Selisch, 1987.

A facsimile edition, with a modern publication, of a songbook from Franconia, which was probably first copied during the 1840s. Critical commentary by the editors places the book in contemporaneous practices and demonstrates the persistence of the songs in the 150 years since it was first used. Little is known of the circumstances of the songbook's origin, although it probably illustrates an individual's attempt to copy folk songs in oral tradition so that they might be used in a relatively small, intimate circle. The songs bear witness to mid-nineteenth century printed repertories, particularly the transformation of popular and semi-classical songs into oral variants (cf. John Meier's concept of *Kunstlied im Volksmunde* ["art song in the mouths of the people"]); more or less absent are narrative folk songs from earlier in the century. Contributes substantially to a deeper understanding of local folk-music practices in mid-nineteenth-century Franconia, a region in the northwestern part of Bavaria.

73.   Wallner, Norbert. *Deutsche Marienlieder der Enneberger Ladiner (Südtirol).* ("German Marian Songs of the Enneberger Ladiner [Southern Tyrol]"). Vienna: A. Schendl, 1970. (Schriften zur Volksmusik, 1).

Assimilates and anthologizes ten manuscripts from the Gader Valley in the high Dolomites of the Southern Tyrol region of Italy. From a multilingual (German, Italian, and an indigenous Latinate language) and multicultural area, the song traditions in these manuscripts, dating from 1777 to 1850, were entirely German. The manuscripts represent different forms of interaction between oral and written tradition. Some were probably compiled when their owners traveled to the larger market and religious centers of the Southern Tyrol, especially Brixen, where they came in contact with merchants, pilgrims, and other travelers. Others take account more closely of local oral traditions. The songs in the manuscripts, therefore, represent traditions from the peripheries of German-speaking Central Europe, particularly the repertories in pilgrimage centers, such as Einsiedeln in Switzerland and Mariazell in Austria. Pilgrimage plays a dominant role in the songs, consistent with the genre of Marian songs, as well as the common practice of pilgrimage in the Alps of Central Europe. Though from an isolated mountain valley, these songs not only document contact with a much larger area of European culture, but they do so in an historically contested region shared by Austria and Italy. Superb musical documentation of the interaction between oral and written, local and international.

3

MELODIC CLASSIFICATION AND ANALYSIS

The works annotated in this chapter raise the questions (1) why are order and classification necessary; and (2) why do the approaches to the analysis of melody fail to yield any consensus? These are serious queries, which preoccupy one of the most persistent domains of folk-music scholarship. The questions have become serious because they touch on some of the most contested issues in the study of folk music, indeed on the very capacity of folk music to possess and then ascribe identity. These are the questions, moreover, of the musicological and music-theoretical approaches to folk music, approaches that were seldom posed during the nineteenth century, when the study of folk song meant the study of texts, not melodies. In the earliest anthologies of folk song (e.g., *Des Knaben Wunderhorn* [1806/1808]), melodies were not included. The practice of including texts only (e.g., in the collections of Ludwig Uhland) continued throughout the nineteenth century and has not, indeed, completely disappeared at the end of the twentieth century. For philologists, and to some extent also for folklorists, the identity of a folk song lies in its text and its narrative. Melody, it would follow, tells a different story.

The impetus to study and analyze melody and musical structure arose at more or less the same moment as comparative musicology, that is, in the last decades of the nineteenth century. The first major proposal for a theory of melodic classification was Wilhelm Tappert's concept of "wandering melodies," which contained principles for melodic relationships that have influenced analytical thought until the present. The larger geographical framework for Tappert was Europe, which is to say, a culture area that could be melodically mapped out on the basis of unity. The unity, according to Tappert, resulted from the fact that melodic motifs were not bound to texts or to geography, but in fact had the power to move about rather freely. Melodic analysis, if true to this motivic mobility, must rely on criteria that are not limited to national repertories or bounded genres.

Subsequent attempts to determine analytical procedures struggled with two models of Europe. The first one, indebted to Tappert, took Europe to be a whole and European folk music to exhibit patterns of relatedness. In the 1950s, Walter Wiora took this model several stages farther, demonstrating that, in addition to motifs, melodic shape and formal structure demonstrated similarities throughout Europe (see Wiora 1953). Wiora argued that such similarities were possible because of parallel histories, specifically the gradual evolution of increasingly more complex forms, independent of national style and genre. The second model perceived Europe as a larger mosaic, with discrete and individual parts, which nonetheless shared common borders. These contrasting views are still evident, for example, in the diverse approaches of the Study Group of the Systematization of Folk Music, a part of the International Council for Traditional Music (see Stockmann and Stęszewski 1973).

The concepts of melodic structure itself have also coalesced around two different theoretical perspectives. From one perspective, the structure of a melody is internally determined: by characteristic motifs; through a shape resulting from the relation of ambitus to tonic; from archetypical formulae. From the other perspective, structure arises because of external influences. The narrative structures of a ballad mean that it will be strophic, and that each line will relate to the strophe in certain ways. Cultural and linguistic contexts will also play an external role, for example in providing the basis for the syllable patterns in the epics of southeastern Europe and Finland, or the markers of the "old style" in Hungarian melodies. These differences play out, furthermore, in theories about melodic stability. Internal structures provide stability over time, whereas external influences cause melodies to change over time.

Although these conflicting perspectives would seem to make consensus impossible, the study of melodic classification and analysis has, in the past two decades, turned increasingly to computer-assisted approaches to arbitrate its conflicts. Oskár Elschek and Alica Elscheková were among the first to turn to electronic tools for analysis, and these have now been adapted to entire repertories and collections, as Barbara Jesser's study (1991) of ballad melodies at the German Folk-Song Archive illustrates. As more technologies develop and as collections in Eastern Europe become increasingly accessible, it is likely that folk-music scholars will have the ability to look again at Europe as a whole, with parts related to the whole in far more complex ways.

The questions posed at the beginning of this introduction are important precisely because they arise from concerns about identity and authority, autonomy and ownership. In the political and national conflicts of the past centuries it has been important that a folk song or a genre of instrumental folk music belong to someone and to some place. In the politics of the 1990s, no less than in the 1880s and 1920s, it is no small issue that a melodic structure is Slovak rather than Czech, and that the Sami have melodic forms distinguishing them from the national cultures of Scandinavia. The theories developed for melodic classification and analysis will surely continue to be inseparable from some of the most trenchant issues in folk-music research.

74. Baud-Bovy, Samuel. "Ein 'lasisches' Lied." ("A 'Lasic' song"). In Christian Ahrens, Rudolf Maria Brandl, and Felix Hoerburger, eds., *"Weine, meine Laute..": Gedenkschrift Kurt Reinhard.* Laaber: Laaber Verlag, 1984. Pp. 47–56.

Examines transcriptional problems pertinent to songs from the Black Sea coastal area of Turkey. Using several well-known (both in Turkey and in the West) examples of Turkish folk song, Baud-Bovy demonstrates that different metric groupings are possible, depending on how the transcriber hears certain groupings and on the conditions of performance (e.g., tempo). Although Baud-Bovy discusses these differences largely in relation to the transcriptions, the article also serves as a representation of the actions of the ethnomusicologist as arbiter of the structures and meanings of musical style. By looking at different examples from the area and comparing them, Baud-Bovy also hypothesizes that meters do in fact change, and that different concepts of meter (e.g., a stretched final beat) must be considered. Serves as a brief survey of the ideas of ethnomusicologists who had worked with these repertories, including Béla Bartók and Kurt Reinhard.

75. Bielawski, Ludwik. "Zeit und Form." ("Time and Form"). In Hartmut Braun, ed., *Probleme der Volksmusikforschung.* Bern: Peter Lang, 1990. Pp. 15–21.

A sketch of the different ways complex structures of time relate to form. Two general hierarchies of time are present in most forms of music, one modeled according to "zones" (*Zeitzonen*) the other with "planes" (*Ebenen*). Each of these consists of low-level units, essentially so small as not to be temporally organized, and higher level units, which are so complex as to demonstrate unity in and of themselves. Form itself results from the interaction of the different levels in these different hierarchies. Time in any given piece is formed by small repetitive units, larger repetitive patterns, the overall structure of the piece, and temporal contexts residing in the moment and conditions of performance. Bielawski makes an extremely lucid argument, drawing from aesthetic theory and extending his concepts to all types of music. He bases his thesis of temporal and formal hierarchy on simple interactions within the different conditions of time in a piece or style, that is, the fairly straightforward interrelation between neighboring temporal zones or planes. Ultimately, temporal units come into existence because they are humanly grounded, thereby making form, too, a product of the human musical imagination.

76. Deutsch, Walter. "Anmerkungen zur Melodietypologie."
("Thoughts about Melodic Classification"). *Jahrbuch für
Volksliedforschung* 36 (1991): 18–28.

A critique of some of the fundamental principles in the four-
volume *Melodietypen des deutschen Volksgesanges* (ed. by Stief,
Suppan, and Braun; see the annotation in the present chapter).
These principles have been developed from various classificatory
systems, on one hand, the notion of harmonic movement
determined against a larger background (Heinrich Schenker),
and on the other, a system of pan-German and to some extent
pan-European melodic structures that stress the overall similarity
of melodic movement (Werner Danckert). These principles ipso
facto fail to take account of melodic traits that do not contribute
to systematicity, and therefore the melodic typology fails to
respond to those melodic forms that challenge the typology. In
particular, Deutsch demonstrates that not all traits necessarily
contribute to an overall harmonic profile. Polyphonic folk songs,
for example those in the alpine regions, contain voices that do not
provide harmonic movement. Deutsch concludes that, because of
its breadth, the melodic typology is extremely valuable, and that
its value will increase as the typology responds to exceptions in
addition to prescribing rules.

77. Elschek, Oskár, ed. *Methoden der Klassifikation von Volksweisen.*
("Classification Methods for Folk Melodies"). Bratislava: Verlag
der Slowakischen Akademie der Wissenschaften, 1969.

A collection of essays based on papers delivered at the first
meeting (1965) of the Study Group for Folk Music
Systematization of the International Folk Music Council, this
volume serves as a watershed for the approaches to melodic
classification and analysis. On one hand, mid-century concepts of
melodic relationships appear here as a point of departure, for
example in the contributions of Walter Wiora. Melodic
relationship resulted from internal structures and the ways in
which these anchored change and established processes of
variation. On the other hand, new approaches appear in this
volume, particularly those using growing computer technology
(e.g., the research in Slovakia by Oskár Elschek and Alica
Elscheková) and those arguing for the employment of different
classification systems because of the varying influences of cultural
context. This latter point is especially evident in the essays, written
at a time when the distinctive methodologies of the larger Central
and East-Central European schools of folk-music research were
seeking new prospects for cooperation. If, however, Czech, Polish,
Hungarian, German, and Austrian scholars were making strong
cases for the distinctive melodic systems of their own cultural
areas, the essays in this volume also stress the comparability of

those systems. Although it is not entirely systematized, there is an overall emphasis on structural properties of folk melodies, albeit with a focus on the ways in which each regional or linguistic repertory establishes the fundamental structures. Melodic shape and tonal parameters, for example, play a more important role in determining the structures of Germanic folk melodies, whereas temporal and metric structures predominate in Slavic melodies. All in all, this is a volume that breaks significant new ground for new approaches to melodic analysis during the last three decades of the twentieth century.

78. Elscheková, Alica. "Motiv-, Zeilen- und Strophenform: Begriffsklärung, Analyse und Klassifikation." ("Motive, Line, and Verse Form: Clarification of Concepts, Analysis, and Classification"). In Doris Stockmann and Jan Steszewski, eds., *Analyse und Klassifikation von Volksmelodien*. Cracow: Polskie Wydoawnictwo Muzyczne, 1973. Pp. 131–69.

   Because over ninety percent of all European folk-song forms are strophic, non-strophic forms and their classification have largely been neglected. Elscheková uses this article to redress that neglect and to suggest ways of approaching what she calls "pre-strophic" forms. She uses repertories of Slovak folk songs for her case study, noting that it is necessary for scholars working with other national and regional repertories to broaden the base of pre-strophic songs for comparison. Two large categories of pre-strophic songs are evident in Slovak repertories, with historical trajectory or lack thereof being the major criterion for identifying these categories. For many songs, aspects of form are already demonstrating a tendency toward strophic structures, and analysis and classification should proceed to identify these tendencies, thereby also constructing categories that contain possibilities for comparison to the dominant presence of strophic songs. The other group of songs contains structures that demonstrate no tendency toward strophic structure, hence require analysis of traits that are isolated and specific to the texts and contexts of individual songs or groups of songs. Elscheková makes extensive use of tables and charts, showing the many possible ways in which motives, line structures, and other processes of unity (e.g., close connection to linguistic structure) interact. Such interaction provides a diverse field for investigation and new possibilities for melodic analysis of European folk song.

79. Habenicht, Gottfried. "Melodien im zwischenvölkischen Umlauf: Über Gemeinsames im ungarischen, deutschen und slowakischen

Liedgut." ("Melodies in Interethnic Exchange: On Shared Characteristics in Hungarian, German, and Slovak Repertories"). *Jahrbuch des österreichischen Volksliedwerkes* 34 (1985): 68–93.

Comparing repertories from the German-, Hungarian-, and Slovak-speaking areas of eastern Slovakia and Hungary, and western Romania, this article argues for the historical development of interethnic traditions in the region. Habenicht observes that he discovered the interethnic folk-music traditions almost serendipitously, for the bulk of scholarship devoted to the region had previously focused on the distinctiveness of ethnic and linguistic repertories; Habenicht in his own studies of Banat German folk music in Romania had been able to determine very little evidence of exchange. To illustrate his case for the processes of interethnic traditions, Habenicht lays the melodies out on seven "melody tables," which order the melodies according to general shape and form. The seven melody groups reveal the predominance of certain characteristics, some of which are identifiably ethnic (e.g., the role of transposition in Hungarian melodies), and others that historically connect melodies to more international processes of musical change (e.g., the influence of folklike and popular compositions in the nineteenth century). Habenicht concludes that the overwhelming influence on these repertories was most likely the Hungarian popular song of the nineteenth century, but this, in turn, had responded to influences from Central Europe. The article illustrates that interethnic exchange is not just a process between two groups, but rather it takes place against an historical and international backdrop.

80. Jesser, Barbara. *Interaktive Melodienanalyse: Methodik und Anwendung computergestützter Analyseverfahren in Musikethnologie und Volks-liedforschung: Typologische Untersuchung der Balladensammlung des DVA.* ("Interactive Melodic Analysis: Methods and Applications of Computer-Supported Analytical Procedures in Ethnomusicology and Folk-Song Research: Typological Investigation of the Ballad Collection of the German Folk-Song Archive"). Bern: Peter Lang, 1991. (Studien zur Volksliedforschung, 12).

Using the melodies of the collections of ballads published by the German Folk-Song Archive (DVA) in Freiburg im Breisgau, Jesser expands upon techniques of computer analysis to examine the relatedness of melodies in both Western and non-Western folk musics. The opening chapters draw broadly upon studies in psychology and cognition to establish the different perspectives from which melodic similarity might be understood as fundamental to establishing the ways in which melodies can be comparatively classified. Jesser pursues the questions of similarity in two general ways. First, she concerns herself with similarity as a property of perception, that is, of human practice and decision-making. Second, she clarifies the decisions necessary for coding melodies with computer languages, recognizing that some aspects of a melody may be eliminated and others emphasized when translating into a computer representation. The middle chapters examine issues of linguistic analysis and computer modeling as they might be applied to melodic analysis. In the concluding chapters, Jesser turns to the corpus of melodies in the ballad collections, using these as one example of fruitful application of computer analysis. Central to the procedures followed throughout the book is the nature of "interactive analysis," namely the representation of melody with a sufficiently flexible computer language so that a broad range of analytical approaches can be applied to them by other ethnomusicologists and folk-music scholars. The book is one of the most comprehensive contributions to the understanding of computer-aided analysis and modeling in the late twentieth century.

81. Koller, Oswald. "Die beste Methode, volks- und volksmäßige Lieder nach ihrer melodischen Beschaffenheit lexikalisch zu ordnen." ("The Best Method Lexically to Order Folk and Folklike Songs According to Their Melodic Character"). *Sammelbände der internationalen Musikgesellschaft* 4 (1902–3): 1–15.

An early attempt to classify folk melodies in such ways that their melodies could be placed in a lexical order and accordingly compared. The need for such methods arose because of the growing repertories and collections, and the need to order these in such ways that they could contribute to the methods and findings of the new comparative musicology. Koller limits his sample to German folk songs and other German melodies that are connected to folk traditions in one way or another. He presumes, therefore, that the melodies have a tonic and that the structure of the melody owes something to the relation of other tones to that tonic. Koller assigns values to the notes above the tonic with Arabic numerals, those below with Roman numerals, the numerals themselves representing the distance in semitones from the tonic. In this way, numerical statistics could be applied, and distinctive patterns would emerge that could provide a dictionary of melodic types. Koller's method, restricted as it is to German repertories, has continued to provide the historical prototype for most attempts to order German folk-song melodies. Because of the same restriction, it has proved less valuable in comparing other repertories from other cultures, within Europe and without.

82. Krohn, Illmari. "Über das lexikalische Ordnen von Volksmelodien." ("On the Lexical Ordering of Folk Melodies").

Bericht über den zweiten Kongreß der internationalen Musikgesellschaft.
Leipzig: Breitkopf & Härtel, 1907. Pp. 66–75.

One of the contributions to the early twentieth-century debate
about how to order and compare the growing collections of folk-
music melodies. Using the diverse Scandinavian collections
available to him as a point of departure, Krohn argues that no
single method of ordering melodies can apply to all collections.
He illustrates by showing that Swedish folk-dance collections
require more attention to the influence of meter, whereas Finnish
epics must account for long melodies, whose identity changes
gradually but persistently during performance. Swedish chorale
melodies, bounded to harmonic structures, differ in extreme ways
from the Sami collections, which were not at all bounded to
chordal patterns. Krohn proposes that the melodies of each song,
nonetheless, might be reduced to a melodic motif, with the initial,
finalis, and midpoint of the melody positioned against the tonic
of the melody. This method, so Krohn argues, is abstract enough
to be independent of the different repertories and the distinctive
traditions from which they come, but it affords the opportunity of
crunching repertories with hundreds of pieces and comparing
these, at least abstractly, to other repertories.

83. *Melodientypen des deutschen Volksgesanges.* ("Melody Types of the
German Folk Song"). 4 vols. Tutzing: Hans Schneider, 1976-83.
   Vol. 1: *Zwei- und Dreizeiler.* ("Songs with Two and Three Lines").
      Ed. by Wolfgang Suppan and Wiegand Stief. 1976.
   Vol. 2: *Vierzeiler.* ("Quatrains"). Ed. by Hartmut Braun and
      Wiegand Stief. 1978.
   Vol. 3: *Fünf-, sechs- und achtzeilige Melodien.* ("Melodies with Five,
      Six, and Eight Lines"). Ed. by Hartmut Braun and Wiegand
      Stief. 1980.
   Vol. 4: *Register und Variantennachweis.* ("Index and Guide to
      Variants"). Ed. by Wiegand Stief. 1983.

Using the collections of the Deutsches Volksliedarchiv (DVA)
in Freiburg im Breisgau, these four volumes employ comparative
melodic classification to represent the melody types that
characterize German folk songs. The DVA contains the single
largest collection of German folk songs, with individual songs
collected from speech islands and other German-speaking areas
outside the borders of modern Germany. Comparison is not based
on region, dialect, genre, or age, but rather on only what the
editors have determined the shape and representative skeleton of
the melody to be. The criteria for ordering these melodies are (1)
form derived from the number of lines; (2) ambitus and position
of the tonic; and (3) melodic shape or *"Gestalt."* This approach
presumes the existence of a tonic, and that the melodic shape and
placement of cadential notes have a direct relation to the form.

There is a further assumption, moreover, that German folk song is fundamentally diatonic and that it tends toward shapes that suggest harmonic movement. The truly massive comparison in the first three volumes, nevertheless, suggests that German folk song statistically contains arch shapes, which give melodic form to the individual line and utilize melodic movement in which thirds predominate. Variants are ordered according to a development proceeding from simple to more complex melodic types, which results in turn from increasingly longer forms. These four volumes constitute the most thoroughly researched attempt to determine the musical basis for all German folk song, and to investigate this comparatively and statistically. In the 1990s, Wiegand Stief of the DVA began to subject these studies to further analysis utilizing complex computational models.

84. Nehlsen, Eberhard. "Von 'Est-ce Mars' zu 'Wer geht mit, juchhe.'" ("From 'Est-ce Mars' to 'Wer geht mit, juchhe'"). *Jahrbuch für Volksliedforschung* 35 (1990): 73–94.

The history of a melody that began as a seventeenth-century French composition but is best known in Germany today as a shanty, with no acknowledgement of its past. Using published sources, as well as accounts of the ways in which the melody both formed and resisted variants, Nehlsen documents the ways in which the song passed across national and generic borders. Originally a song addressing the glories of war, "Est-ce Mars" was set to many different kinds of texts in France and the Low Countries before disappearing from records in the eighteenth century. The melody served as the basis of a Dutch sea shanty, composed by A.D. Loman, which was one of the most popular songs in German songbooks in the period immediately after World War I. During its second life, the song represented a colonialist ideology, but by the end of the twentieth century these were understood largely in the context of a sailor's life. Reproductions of many songs based on the melody, as well as several of the texts set to it, make this article an exemplary history of a single melody and illustrate the ways in which a melody's history passes between oral and written traditions, as well as between art, folk, and popular genres.

85. Reinhard, Kurt. "Gedanken zur Statik in der Musik." ("Thoughts on Stasis in Music"). In Max Peter Baumann, Rudolf Maria Brandl, and Kurt Reinhard, eds., *Neue ethnomusikologische Forschungen: Festschrift Felix Hoerburger.* Laaber: Laaber-Verlag, 1977. Pp. 237–48.

Using a dialectic between the principles of "consonance" and "distance" established by Rudolf von Ficker as a point of departure, this article examines the musical phenomenon of stasis, that is, the sense that music is not moving with an internal dynamic. Reinhard suggests that musical stasis results from certain characteristics, for example alternating but repetitive patterns, a pedal tone, a secondary melody, or a tempo slow enough that no primary melody dominates a piece or style. As a primary example, Japanese *gagaku* is examined. At one level, *gagaku* possesses the characteristics of seemingly independent and non-teleological polyphony that is necessary for stasis. At another level, the scalar structures and chordal concepts in *gagaku* fail to give it a sense of directional dynamic. For example, absence of half steps in the pentatonic structures means that, according to Reinhard, there is no sense that one tone necessarily resolves dissonances by movement to another. Although the article demonstrates a sort of bias that Western music is more dynamic than non-Western, it is one of few to look at musical structure as a basis for immanent movement through time in music.

86. Schmitt, Ulrich. "Auswahlbibliographie zu Klassifikation von Volksliedmelodien und Melodieforschung." ("Selected Bibliography for the Classification of Folk-Song Melodies and Melody Research"). In Jürgen Dittmar, ed., *Dokumentationsprobleme heutiger Volksmusikforschung*. Bern: Peter Lang, 1987. Pp. 219–72.

An annotated bibliography of research devoted to the study of melodic classification, especially in folk song. The author surveys 184 individual works, by far the largest percentage in German-language sources, though some in other Western European languages, including English. The classification concepts derive from those used in the German Folk-Song Archive in Freiburg im Breisgau, although in the last two decades of the twentieth century these have benefited from some of the approaches to classification employed in the research surveyed by this bibliography. The three major areas of the bibliography are (1) ordering of folk-song melodies; (2) research on the nature of melody; and (3) text-melody relations. Within each of these sections there are further categories based on concepts from the intellectual history of folk-song scholarship, for example "wandering melodies" (pp. 268–69) and "comparative melodic research" (pp. 254–55). It is a strength of the bibliography that it cuts across the different disciplines that have theorized melodic classification, whether for folk-music research or not.

87. Steinbeck, Wolfram. *Struktur und Ähnlichkeit: Methoden automatisierter Melodienanalyse*. ("Structure and Similarity: Methods of Automated Melody Analysis"). Kassel: Bärenreiter, 1982. (Kieler Schriften zur Musikwissenschaft, 25).

Similarity in this volume refers to the ways in which scholars and their analytical methods (and machines) recognize and construct patterns in which some melodies cluster together as similar, while differing from others. Steinbeck utilizes computer hardware and programs that were widely used in Europe, though less well known in North America, but the method here is not to produce a universal method, but rather to bring together existing approaches, which will then lend themselves to further development in the computer revolution on whose eve the book was published. The source material for the studies of similarity consists almost entirely of German folk songs from nineteenth-century published collections. Using sections of these songs ("Liedabschnitte") for comparative analysis, Steinbeck determines certain groupings around similar traits, for example, rising or falling melodies, V-formed melodies, or melodies that level off in the "form of a roof." To counterbalance these groupings, Steinbeck also compares standard genres (e.g., hymns and wandering songs), whose criteria of similarity result more commonly from reception and performance practice. Although computer-assisted approaches here are now outmoded, the author's aesthetic concern for the properties and limitations of similarity in analysis makes this a thoughtful and engaging study.

88. Stockmann, Doris. "Formprinzipien samischer Joiken und ihre Zusammenhänge mit der Gattungsfunktion." ("Principles of Form in Sami Yoiking and Their Relation to the Functions of Genre"). In Hartmut Braun, ed., *Probleme der Volksmusikforschung*. Bern: Peter Lang, 1990. Pp. 22–46.

Attempts to lay the groundwork for general classificatory criteria for the yoiking (lit., singing in the manner of the Sami) of Samis, the circumpolar, semi-nomadic peoples in northern Scandinavia and the northwestern corner of Russia. Stockmann describes the general linguistic and cultural differences among the several groups of Sami, following the general geographic distinctions among East, South, and Central Sami. The repertories examined in this comparison come from both historical collections and from modern fieldwork, including that of the author during the 1980s. The article provides particular insight into the ways in which previous research efforts have led to the construction of Sami music and culture through putative relations to European folk music, whereas Stockmann maintains strongly that yoiking should not be investigated on the basis of such relations, but rather by considering internal formal structures and genres. These remain evident, she maintains, even in modern popular musics among the Samis. Central to Stockmann's argument is the role of yoiking as a specific form of musical communication. All Sami—male or female—use yoiking to achieve a specific goal, whether as part of reindeer herding or domestic activities. Yoiks primarily form, nonetheless, from strings of syllables without specific meaning. Meaning derives from the ways in which the singer forms these into individual pieces and genres. An excellent introduction to this distinctive practice of the Sami.

89. Stockmann, Doris, and Jan Stęszewski, eds. *Analyse und Klassifikation von Volksmelodien.* ("Analysis and Classification of Folk Melodies"). Cracow: Polskie Wydawnictwo Muzyczne, 1973.

Collected essays from several conferences of the Study Group of Folk Music Systematization of the International Folk Music Council, primarily the 1967 meeting in Radziejowice, Poland. The volume was to mark a watershed in the development of approaches to melodic classification and analysis, but the editors, admitting to their desire to come to some widespread methodological agreement, prefer to contextualize the volume as a point of departure for multifarious directions. The volume begins with three essays on possible approaches to a general theory of melodic analysis. Doris Stockmann considers the enormous range of material now available to scholars working in this area, Ludwik Bielawski concentrates on properties that lend themselves to ordering melodies, and Wolfgang Suppan addresses the ways in which overall melodic shape and form suggest analytical typologies. The middle section of the volume contains essays on individual national folk-song repertories (e.g., Bielawski on Polish verse structures, Jaromír Gelnar on Moravian melodies, and Benjamin Rajeczky on non-strophic forms in Hungary). Whereas these essays were originally intended to firm up the comparative basis for a general theory of melodic analysis, the editors conclude that they succeed instead in demonstrating that the extensive variety in Europe belies any truly general theory. A final group of essays adds Scandinavian studies to the geographical area covered by this volume. This volume remains one of the most important collections of analytical approaches to the study of folk melodies, not least because of its diverse array of essays from Eastern Europe from the heyday of support for research into national folk-music traditions from socialist governments.

90. Tappert, Wilhelm. *Wandernde Melodien.* ("Wandering Melodies"). 2nd ed., enlarged. Leipzig: List & Franke, 1890.

The first major attempt to theorize the similarity of melodies in different parts of Europe and in different genres of music. Tappert claims that the mobility of melodies lies in the motif, which retains its identity as it travels around Europe, from one culture and nation to the next. The motif, therefore, acts as the core of a melody's identity; it is the blueprint, so to speak, that makes the melody what it is. Tappert, who wrote about both folk and classical music, also extends his theory of wandering melodies to the relation between styles and repertories, and to the nature of composing melody. His theory rests on his ability to demonstrate the relation between two different compositions, the similar melodies of which could not have resulted from direct knowledge of the composers. Whereas some of Tappert's claims for identity today appear to be questionable, others do illustrate possible patterns of stylistic influence and perhaps even the transmission of melodic types by musicians and repertories that move from part of Europe to another. The similarity of motifs and melodies, nonetheless, owes no debt to context in Tappert's model, but rather resides entirely in the processes of diffusion within the closed culture area of Europe. So essential was the identity of the motif that the encumbrances of nature and movement between genres and styles had no effect on it. Comparison and classification of this sort influenced European melodic classification well into the twentieth century, lying also at the core of the comparative frameworks of Werner Danckert and, notably, Walter Wiora.

91.　Waldmann, Guido, ed. *Zur Tonalität des deutschen Volksliedes.* ("On the Tonality of the German Folk Song"). Wolfenbüttel and Berlin: Georg Kallmeyer, 1938.

An overt attempt to map Nazi racial theories on the analysis of German folk songs. The volume assembles essays by several notable folk-song scholars (e.g., Josef Müller-Blattau and Georg Schünemann) and less distinguished scholars (e.g., Fritz Metzler and Guido Waldmann), whose motivations were as opportunistic as ideological. The basic argument of these essays is that German folk song has a distinctive melodic structure that anchors folk melodies in major-minor tonality. In their foreword, Wolfgang Stumme and Guido Waldmann make it clear that the book will provide the younger generation with ways of distinguishing the tonal characteristics of German folk song from those of other "races," for example the Slavic peoples and those peoples whose heritages, hence musical traits, were not pure. The most brutal of the essays is Fritz Metzler's "Major, Minor, and 'Church Modes' as Musical Expressions of Race" (pp. 1–27). Metzler scientifically argues for the relation between interval size and cranial size, demonstrating that the "Nordic races" were the only ones capable of a so-called "principle of distance" (*Distanzprinzip*), which provided the connection between melody, as expressed in folk song, and the development of major-minor tonality. The authors then muster the entire range of German folk-song scholarship to argue for the fundamentally tonal character of German music. Guido Waldmann, for example, examines the ways in which the songs of "speech islands" succeed in preserving a prototonal stage of German folk songs that has disappeared from many songs in Central Europe (pp. 61–72). Gotthold Frotscher attempts to connect melodic movement in folk song to other forms of German music through typical pentatonic structures and their relation to the church modes. Throughout the book, comparative melodic analysis is used, and a map of racial differences is found on a fold-out page between pages 24 and 25. The racial scientism of the book does not succeed in masking an uncertain paranoia afflicting its authors, namely that analytical principles must be constructed to show that German melodies are as distinctive as Nazi racial theories wanted them to be.

92.   Wiora, Walter. *Europäischer Volksgesang: Gemeinsame Formen in charakteristischen Abwandlungen*. ("European Folk Song: Similar Forms in Characteristic Versions"). Cologne: Arno Volk Verlag, 1953. (Das Musikwerk, 4).

The classic comparative classification of common melodic patterns in European folk song. Drawing on examples of folk song from repertories throughout Europe, Wiora compares melodies from diverse traditions to demonstrate common structural principles. On one hand, the comparison of examples from different traditions suggests a certain objectivity, in which each music culture has the potential to develop many levels of complexity. On the other hand, complexity and the development toward complexity emerges as the overwhelming determinant of European folk song. The volume consists of three larger sections, determined according to growing melodic and formal complexity: "Melodies without Strophes," "Strophic Melodies," and "Polyphony." The principle of growing complexity also holds for the subsections; for example, in the part devoted to strophic melodies there is a progression from melodies with a single long line or two lines to those with more than four lines. Wiora also takes function and genre into consideration, mapping these onto the basic classification principles; for example, in the section devoted to melodies without strophes, he begins with "Archaic Ritual Songs," proceeds to "Calls," and then later to melodies that demonstrate harmonic possibilities, such as in yodeling. Wiora both assumes that European folk song demonstrates melodic unity and tries to show the ways in which the larger culture area of Europe emerges from the shared traits that melodies from different parts of the continent represent. This European melodic-cultural unity, moreover, resides in the music history of the continent, which well-chosen examples from sacred and art-music repertories underscore. If indeed late twentieth-century ethnomusicology admits considerably more complex processes into its consideration of musical change and music history, the model of classification that Wiora presents remains one of the most clearly articulated comparative approaches based on the assumption that it is unity that defines culture and that unity resides in the materials of music itself.

93. Wittrock, Wolfgang. *Die ältesten Melodietypen im ostdeutschen Volksgesang.* ("The Oldest Melody Types in East German Folk Song"). Marburg: N.G. Elwert, 1969. (Schriftenreihe der Kommission für ostdeutsche Volkskunde, 7).

With typological classification and comparison this book attempts to identify the oldest melodic forms in German folk music. Wittrock's approach relies on several assumptions about the relation of melody type to history. First, the simpler a melody's structure and form are, the older it is, or at least the older the historical moment is that it represents. Second, older melodies, because of their simple structures, are stabler within oral tradition. Third, cultures that are relatively isolated are more dependent on oral tradition and thus retain the oldest melodies longer. These conditions, then, obtained in the German-speaking culture areas of Eastern Europe, particularly those in Poland, Hungary, Romania, and the former Yugoslavia. Relying on earlier collections and some songs from former residents of these culture areas, Wittrock constructs a comparative framework using synoptic transcriptions in the tradition of Walter Wiora and other comparative melody analysts. Like Wiora, Wittrock establishes a history of growing complexity. The first groups consists of melodies with two, three, four, and finally five lines, followed by those with rhyme structures. The next developmental stage is the use of asymmetrical meters; the final stage is polyphony. Wittrock has plumbed a considerable body of literature and repertory collections, which is both a strength and weakness of this book. On one hand, the book serves to introduce the reader to the folk song of Eastern European German communities, but, on the other, the assumption that melodies relate to each other simply on the basis of their structures, that is, entirely out of social context, means that the book reveals very little about the use, function, and cultural history of the songs.

4

INSTRUMENTS AND INSTRUMENTAL MUSIC

Volkslied, Volksmusik; folk song, folk music. Throughout the history of folk-music scholarship, these two concepts have distinguished two distinctive domains of folk-music activity and the ways in which these were conceptualized and studied. Fundamental to such distinctions has been the mode of musical production, on one hand the human voice, and on the other musical instruments. For Herder in the late eighteenth century and for subsequent generations during the initial decades of the nineteenth century, instruments played no role in the development of theories and in the classification of song texts and their transmission. Instrumental music was, for all intents and purposes, silent. When folk-music instruments first begin to emerge in the history of the field, it was only as crude versions of art-music instruments. When Ludwig Erk and Friedrich Silcher arranged folk songs for singers and instruments in the mid-nineteenth century, the instrumental sound on which they relied came from Romanticism, the piano and the richly-textured ensemble. In this stage, it was the *folk-music instrument,* within the privileged folk music of the age, that was silent. The silence of folk-music instruments is perhaps most striking in modern ethnomusicological thought when one examines the systematic studies that Curt Sachs and Erich M. von Hornbostel eventually formulated as the classification system that remains standard until the present: they relied, indeed consciously so, largely on collections of European art-music instruments (see Sachs 1930, below).

The reasons folk-music instruments have played such an outsider role in the history of scholarship are not difficult to determine. Folk song represented a quality that was not only elevated but central to the expression of nationalism. It was vital to early folk-song scholars that, for example, German ballads were, at least in their imagination, sung in High German. The persistence of German folk song in speech islands beyond the borders of Germany, moreover, served as witness to some deeper historical level of German culture. Folk-music instruments did not contribute to these specific qualities of Germanness. On one hand, they were often locally built and distributed instruments, whose functions were not to elevate music but to connect it to diverse social activities. On the other, there were families of instruments that crossed borders and that appeared in German folk instrumentaria as witnesses to foreign contacts and influences that undermined clear-cut models of nationalism. Folk song and folk music, in short, often worked at cross purposes.

During the twentieth century, the study of folk-music instruments has developed an integrity of its own. Its history has run parallel to that of folk song, although there have been relatively few junctures at which they have intersected. Their theoretical methods and ends remain distinct, even at the end of the century. Still, there have been countercurrents to the tendency to separate folk song from folk music, notably new formulations of the study of folk-music instruments by Ernst Emsheimer and Erich Stockmann, through the Study Group on Folk Musical Instruments of the International Council for Traditional Music, and by the Austrian tradition at the Institute for Folk-Music Research in Vienna. Additionally, physical and acoustical study of instruments has fully demonstrated the fallacy of regarding folk-music instruments as simple. Since World War II, the study of instruments has occupied an increasingly important position in the study of folk music in general.

The study of folk-music instruments is distinguished by its multi- and interdisciplinary character. Using different approaches and relying on different methods, scholars working on instruments have succeeded in creating at least five distinctive areas of research, which the works in this chapter illustrate to varying degrees. The most general area is that which generally falls under the rubric of *systematic*. Canonized by the Sachs-Hornbostel classification, systematic research regards sound production and sounding materials as data, which can be measured and then compared. Oskár Elschek and Erich Stockmann have advocated a sweeping approach that relies on *typology*. More ethnomusicological in approach, any typology must take into consideration social use and function, as well as repertory and distribution. There are other approaches that focus on *single areas or music cultures*, providing thick descriptions of the instrumental musical life of those areas. The *history of instruments* influences several different approaches, ranging from those that examine the psychological motivations that cause musicians to craft an object into an instrument to those that employ early visual and literary sources for a broader understanding of folk music and its relation to other cultural activities. Finally, some scholars focus on *single instruments*, whether on their construction or their distribution in a particular music culture, or on their symbolic role in negotiating between complex social practices.

At the end of the twentieth century, these research areas are increasingly interdisciplinary, and it would be impossible to claim any more that instruments were the silent partners in the performance and transmission of folk music. The study of folk-music instruments, furthermore, integrates the methods of performing musicians, dance scholars, and even instrument makers. Indeed, instruments play an extraordinarily complex role in Central European music cultures, and perhaps because of this, their significance as a site for negotiating with modernity and global musical practices has contributed increasingly to a reformulation and redirection of folk-music theory in recent years.

Studies such as Christoph Wagner's in this chapter (Wagner 1993), which examines the ideological symbolism of the accordion, are moving the study of instruments toward ethnomusicology and cultural studies. Not only have instruments emerged from their silence, but they have come to represent some of the most salient processes of change in a postmodern age.

❦

94. Bachmann-Geiser, Brigitte. "'Schälleschötte', Schellenschütteln und Talerschwingen in der Schweiz." ("'Bells', Gongs, and Coin-Swirling in Switzerland"). In Walter Deutsch, ed., *Der Bordun in der europäischen Volksmusik*. Vienna: A. Schendel, 1981. Pp. 17–23.

The translations of the Swiss idiophones in the title of this article do little justice to their construction, meaning, and function in the folk-music traditions of Switzerland. These instrument types characterize three different techniques of producing drones in diverse folk-music practices. The *Schälleschötte* is a type of bell, modeled after and often overlapping with cowbells. *Schellenschütteln* describes the practice of striking differently tuned metallic slabs against each other, producing melodic patterns. *Talerschwingen* utilizes a milking pan, in which a coin is placed and swirled until it produces a distinct pitch. The importance of these instruments derives from their use with vocal practices, especially yodeling, hence showing that they connect folk music to agricultural labor, notably the seasonal alternation of alpine pastures for cows. Illustrated with pictures of these idiophones, the article emphasizes the importance of these styles in historical folk music and in the present, particularly as means of marking folk music as Swiss.

95. Brandl, Rudolf. "Der Bordun und seine Entwicklung in der Volksmusik des Dodekanes anhand eigener Feldaufnahmen 1965–1971." ("The Drone and Its Development in the Folk Music of the Greek Islands on the Basis of Field Recordings, 1965–1971"). In Walter Deutsch, ed., *Der Bordun in der europäischen Volksmusik*. Vienna: A. Schendl, 1981. Pp. 24–40.

Establishes theoretical breadth for the form and function of the drone in musical repertories throughout the world. In these different forms, the drone becomes the basis of melodic improvisation, distinguished from harmonically-generated forms and improvisation. Brandl observes that two larger categories of drone can be differentiated, the "real" drone and the "divergent" drone, the latter tending toward accompanimental and polyphonic functions. With this theoretical framework Brandl examines the changing presence of drones and drone instruments in the Greek islands, the instruments and musical styles of which have historically made diverse use of the drone. Various outside influences affected the function of the drone at different moments in this history. Under Middle Eastern, especially Turkish, influences drones lent themselves to melodic and improvisatory functions. With increasing Western influences, for example the growing importance of the guitar, drones increasingly accommodated harmonic movement, causing many genres to conform to more standardized forms. Brandl concludes, however, that the folk music of the Greek islands has not become Western, but rather has been able to rely on the drone as a means of adapting to Western influences.

96. Bröcker, Marianne. "Dokumentationsprobleme bei Volksmusik-instrumenten." ("Folk-Music Instruments and Their Documentation Problems"). In Jürgen Dittmar, ed., *Dokumentationsprobleme heutiger Volksmusikforschung*. Bern: Peter Lang, 1987. Pp. 201–9.

Bröcker's point of departure is that folk-music instruments today have functions quite different from those accounted for by existing classification systems and museum presentation. Simply accounting for an instrument's structure and evolution may tell little about how it functions in society, or even how it is played. Bröcker calls, instead, for new approaches to documenting the folk-music instruments and illustrates the potential for such approaches by discussing the burgeoning importance of drone-producing instruments in the folk-music revival of the late twentieth century. The European folk-music revival, which invented numerous traditions from a *bricolage* that borrowed from the international folk and popular scene, created a sudden need for instrument builders, whose musical backgrounds ranged from classical to jazz. Marking the folk-music revival, however, was the sound of the drone, which in turn led to a widespread proliferation of hurdy-gurdies and bagpipes. Instrument builders relied on diverse sources to create an amalgam of authenticity, but it was the reality of revival itself that gave new roles and realities to these instruments in the present. A fresh, uncomplicated look at the reconfiguration of organological studies for modern and postmodern uses.

97. Deutsch, Walter. "Geige und Geigenmusik in Europa: Einige Probleme ihrer Forschung." ("Violin and Violin Music in Europe:

Some Problems in Their Research"). In Walter Deutsch and
Gerlinde Haid, eds., *Die Geige in der europäischen Volksmusik*.
Vienna: A. Schendl, 1975. Pp. 10–15.

Introduction and overview for a volume containing revised
essays from a conference devoted to the violin in Europe.
Adapting the organological methods of Erich Stockmann,
Deutsch systematically lays out different approaches to studying
the violin. The violin poses methodological problems that differ
from those faced when studying other folk-music instruments, not
least among them the instrument's role in folk and art music, and
its multifarious forms throughout a long history of European
music. The violin is also distinctive because, when considering the
music associated with it, the scholar must take into account the
ways musicians integrate it, as an extraordinarily flexible
instrument, into sundry ensembles. Deutsch sketches some of the
earliest sources for studying the structure and music of the violin.
In addition to medieval and Renaissance visual and literary
depictions, the violin and its cultural uses appear in the records of
guilds, at least until the nineteenth century, when guilds declined
in importance. In folk music the violin is particularly bound to
dance, which makes it important for any systematic study of the
violin to consider the violin as a component of folk-dance
research. Study of the violin opens up a broad field of research,
which requires comparison throughout Europe, as well as with
music cultures worldwide.

98.   Deutsch, Walter, ed. *Der Bordun in der europäischen Volksmusik*.
("The Drone in European Folk Music"). Vienna: A. Schendel,
1981. (Schriften zur Volksmusik, 5).

Essays by a diverse and international group of European folk-
music scholars, all of whom examine the drone as a musical
phenomenon. Most essays focus on a region and its typical drone
instruments and styles. The drone has acquired a striking
importance, both historically, that is, in the earliest
instrumentarium of the European Middle Ages, and in the
present, when drone-producing instruments have considerable
importance in revivals and the marketing of folk music for tourist
consumption. Whereas many essays are organological, most relate
the phenomenon of the drone to vocal production,
demonstrating close relations and cross-relations between
instrumental and vocal styles. Taken as a whole, these essays
suggest that drone instruments consitute one of the most
European of all musical traits, for there is no region entirely
devoid of such instruments. This relation, moreover, is not
random, for drone instruments such as bagpipes often took part
in moments of musical exchange; the presence of other
instruments, such as the hurdy-gurdy, cut across the boundaries

between folk, art, and classical musics. The historical persistence and remarkable diversity of the drone in music instruments and styles, finally, resulted from the connections between local practices and more widespread—often continental—processes of musical change.

99. Dević, Dragoslav. "Typen serbischer Sackpfeifen." ("Types of Serbian Bagpipes"). In Walter Deutsch, ed., *Der Bordun in der europäischen Volksmusik.* Vienna: A. Schendl, 1981. Pp. 59–82.

The bagpipe, most commonly referred to as the *gajde* and utilizing drone pipes, is widespread in Serbia. Great variety exists, but the *gajde* assumes a central and important function in determining the Serbian quality of instrumental folk music. This article investigates the building, performance, and repertory of the *gajde* in meticulous detail. Charts, tuning patterns, pictures of instruments and their parts, photographs of performers, distribution maps, and transcriptions of individual performances make this a rich introduction to the Serbian bagpipe and the role it plays as a drone-producing instrument. The article further examines the peculiarities of the *gajde* in each region of Serbia, as well as in other areas of the former Yugoslavia with Serbian populations. The two-voice polyphony common for the *gajde* also characterizes vocal polyphony in Serbia, together with the predominance of one of these voices as a drone. Comparison with other bagpipe types in the surrounding nations and regions of the Balkans and southeastern Europe offers an unusually rich potential for identifying the regional history of musical style.

100. Ehlers, Tibor. "Formen und Möglichkeiten der Drehleier." ("Forms and Possibilities of the Hurdy-Gurdy"). In Walter Deutsch, ed., *Der Bordun in der europäischen Volksmusik.* Vienna: A. Schendel, 1981. Pp. 83–95.

An historical study of the hurdy-gurdy as an instrument found in different forms and with different functions in the music history of Europe. A contribution to a volume devoted to the concept of drone in European folk music, this article takes as its point of departure the hurdy-gurdy's accessibility, that is, its construction in such forms that musicians without special skills can perform on it. It is for this reason, according to Ehlers, that the instrument appeared early in the history of Western music and is an important instrument in various revivals at the end of the twentieth century (e.g., early-music and folk revivals). Ehlers divides the history of the hurdy-gurdy into four periods and documents the modification of its shape and functions in each of these periods. The first period is the Middle Ages (ca. the twelfth through fourteenth centuries), when the *organistrum* assumed a position as an instrument in the music of the monastic and religious traditions. In the late Middle Ages and early Renaissance, the hurdy-gurdy spread to folk musicians (peasants, according to Ehlers) and wandering musicians. In the seventeenth and eighteenth centuries, the instrument was increasingly associated with pastoral repertories. Finally, from the eighteenth century to the present, the hurdy-gurdy has become an important drone-producing instrument in folk music. The numerous illustrations of instruments document both the variety of hurdy-gurdies and the changing functions of the instrument throughout its history.

101. Elschek, Oskár. "Historische Quellentypen der Instrumentenkunde und die ihnen angemessenen quellenkritischen Methoden." ("Historical Source Types in Organology and the Appropriate Critical Methods for Utilizing Them"). *Studia instrumentorum musicae popularis* 4 (1976): 10–30.

An attempt to describe the types of source materials useful in historical organology studies. Elschek begins by surveying the growing importance of historical methods in the study of folk music in general, and then he calls for an extension and adaptation of these methods in the study of folk-music instruments. Such methods call into question issues of terminology and the boundaries usually applied to folk-music instruments. In premodern music cultures, for example, the difference between art- and folk-music instruments was rarely clear, as were the social venues in which musicians played such instruments. Folk musicians regularly performed in court settings, and art-music instruments were often adapted for more popular music-making. Three general source types lend themselves to the systematic study of historical materials: (1) surviving instruments, with various relations to earlier versions; (2) visual sources; and (3) written descriptions. Elschek examines the special problems and prospects that inhere in each of these areas, touching on important studies that have employed them. Written sources, for example, pose terminological problems, making it difficult to know just precisely what instrument is the subject of a depiction. Elschek provides practical solutions for dealing with these problems and calls for utilization of all three types of source material to flesh out the most meaningful histories of folk-music instruments.

102. Elschek, Oskár, and Erich Stockmann. "Zur Typologie der Volksmusikinstrumente." ("Toward a Typology of Folk-Music Instruments"). *Studia instrumentorum musicae popularis* 1 (1969): 11–22.

The lead article in the inaugural issue of the occasional publication of the Study Group on Folk Musical Instruments of the International Folk Music Council (later, the International Council for Traditional Music). The authors propose the concept of typology as the basis for a reformation of organology, especially as it pertains to folk-music instruments. A typological investigation of instruments would supplant the systematic classification of instruments by Sachs and Hornbostel. Rather than the static and statistical basis in the Sachs-Hornbostel system, a typological approach would permit the scholar (1) to account for the ways in which societies and individual musicians influence the uses and functions of an instrument; and (2) to recognize that instruments and their cultural meanings change in dynamic ways. The concept of a "type" is based on the ways in which instruments refer back to models, standard forms or shapes, interaction with other types (e.g., in an ensemble), and functions within society. Instruments respond to types in two general ways, some differentiating a basic type, and others conforming to basic type. The concept of type, furthermore, forms the core for a constellation of different traits that determine the uses and functions of an instrument. Some of these traits are specific to the materials used in the instrument, whereas others may pertain to musicians and still others to cultural or even cosmological meanings. Among the advantages of an instrumental typology are its flexibility and its ability to move organology out of the museum and into the field.

103. Emsheimer, Ernst. "Gedanken zur Welt der Kinderinstrumente und ihrer Beziehung zur Ewachsenenkultur." ("Thoughts on the World of Children's Instruments and Their Relation to the Culture of Adults"). *Studia instrumentorum musicae popularis* 7 (1985): 10–19.

Critiquing the common presumption that children's instruments are primitive versions of adult instruments, Emsheimer uses this essay to open a volume dedicated to research on children's instruments. Two issues lie at the center of this schematic presentation of the integrity of children's instruments. First, children create and use instruments for specific musical purposes, and they draw from a wide variety of materials to achieve their specific musical purposes. Second, the instruments of children are often "ephemeral," which here refers both to the specificity of function and the extent of practical use. In comparative fashion Emsheimer explores the different ways in which children create and acquire instruments. Also important to his thesis is the sheer abundance of children's instruments, which in many cultures demonstrate greater variety than the limited instrumentarium of adults. Both the creativity of children and the extensive distribution of musical activity—generally not the case among adults—explain this phenomenon. Depending on where they live and on the material objects readily available to them, children will turn to certain types of substances to create rhythm instruments or signal instruments. Emsheimer does not ignore the impact of modernity on the acquisition of instruments by children, for example when "toy instruments" or inexpensive tourist models are made available to children. The article opens a vast field for investigation, a field Emsheimer believes deserves far more attention, even as a means of studying the instruments of adults.

104. Frank, Karl. "Die neue Fidel, ein altes Volks-musikinstrument?" ("The New Fiddle: An Old Folk-Music Instrument?"). In Walter Deutsch and Gerlinde Haid, eds., *Die Geige in der europäischen Volksmusik*. Vienna: A. Schendl, 1975. Pp. 180–83.

The reflections of an instrument builder, this article considers the differences between violins that play with full volume, hence obviating the voice, and those that allow for vocal music, either from other members in the ensemble or by the violinist. Various structures in earlier fiddle-type instruments made it an instrument with softer volume and allowed it to be used more widely as a less dominating accompanimental instrument: stringing of the fiddle; gripping the bow from beneath rather than from above; tunings using fourths rather than fifths; and playing positions that allowed the musician to sing more easily. Surveying different folk-music cultures in Europe, Frank observes that the standard violin-playing practices associated with the modern instrument's use in art music constitute only one set of practices, which are relatively uncommon in the fiddle traditions of many areas, for example Poland and southeastern Europe. He calls for a rethinking of the diversity of the fiddle's repertory, historically and in modern European folk music, arguing that revival of the fiddle in its different forms would offer something to many different kinds of instrumental musician.

105. Graf, Walter. "Zur klanglichen Dokumentation von Volks-musikinstrumenten." ("Toward the Sound Documentation of Folk-Music Instruments"). In *Studia instrumentorum musicae popularis* 1 (1969): 159–64.

An historical survey of the development of different methods of sound measurement and comparison during the twenty years after World War II. Graf, the comparative-systematic musicologist at the University of Vienna during this period, examines the technology used for systematic study, demonstrating the ways in which each technology had certain limitations, which in turn led scholars to develop new technologies. Initial problems included the difficulty of measuring extreme overtones; similarly, technologies such as metal cylinders and wires could not capture changes that occurred rapidly. With the development of sonographs in the 1950s, new techniques followed quickly, and Graf demonstrates with photographs of tonal displays how these made it possible to engage in new forms of comparison. The general thesis of this article is that the specific characters of each instrument and sound quality from a specific place or music culture become increasingly more evident through the development of new technologies for electronically representing sound. This essay lends itself to comparison with other contemporaneous research, for example Charles Seeger's melograph studies at UCLA.

106. Hoerburger, Felix. "Bordunbildungen in der Volksmusik Griechenlands." ("Formations of the Drone in the Folk Music of Greece"). In Walter Deutsch, ed., *Der Bordun in der europäischen Volksmusik*. Vienna: A. Schendl, 1981. Pp. 129–40.

Taking the extensive presence of the drone and drone instruments as a point of departure, Hoerburger examines the diverse functions of the drone as evidence of diversity within a music culture. Whereas drones are present in both folk and art music, it is only in the former that diversity prevails, whereas in the latter drones become stylized and contribute to relatively similar functions. In Greece, both mainland and insular, the drone pervades virtually every type of folk and popular music. Hoerburger describes not only the different settings in which drone instruments are heard, but the ways in which the aesthetic functions of the drone may be reflected in ritual and performance. Drone instruments are by no means limited to repertories that are primarily Greek, but they enter the music culture through outside groups and repertories. Gypsy ensembles, for example, also make widespread use of drones and drone instruments, though in distinctive ways. The drone in folk music, it follows from the case of Greece, develops in the direction of greater differentiation.

107. Kaden, Christian. "Methoden der graphischen Modellierung sozialhistorischer Prozesse als Hilfsmittel bei der Erforschung instrumentaler Volksmusik." ("Methods of Graphic Modeling of Socio-Historical Processes as an Aid to Researching Instrumental Folk Music"). *Studia instrumentorum musicae popularis* 4 (1976): 39–45.

Proposes the use of visual models to depict the connections between different domains of music-making in a music culture. Drawing upon fieldwork in agricultural villages in the former GDR, Kaden makes the case that seemingly unrelated musical activities, for example, the signal instruments used by shepherds, the music in a tavern, or local folk musicians, are nonetheless part of a larger, complex web. By placing the different musicians, specialists and non-specialists alike, on a larger grid-like model, patterns of interaction emerge, sometimes because of social and economic connections, but at other times because of the use of instruments related because of their materials or structure. Such models allow the researcher to plot change over time, hence using the web in its different form as a means of constructing both synchronic and diachronic histories of a village. Kaden argues for the utility of models because of their capacity to communicate diverse information to readers with very different backgrounds, that is, to specialists and non-specialists alike. The article succeeds less in providing modeling procedures for others to use than in its presentation of instruments as evidence for the complex musical life of a relatively small and bounded social unit.

108. Michel, Andreas. "Zistern in der traditionellen Musik Sachsens und Thüringens." ("Cisterns in the Traditional Music of Saxony and Thuringia"). *Studia instrumentorum musicae popularis* 10 (1992): 81–90.

From the late Middle Ages to the present, the cistern has been a traditional instrument in Saxony and Thuringia, notably with constantly changing functions in a complex society. The culture of these areas in eastern Germany has been influenced by mining and industrialization, and already in the earliest accounts the cistern appears in ways associated with miners. Visual depictions and written accounts show not only that minstrels used the cistern as a central instrument in mining areas, but that amateur musicians, who were also miners, performed on the cistern. As the workers' culture of Saxony and Thuringia became more institutionalized, the cistern remained an essential component of public performances and large ensembles. In the nineteenth and twentieth centuries, the cistern passed through periods of historicization and folkloricization, and it continues to mark the history and folk culture of the region. Michel constructs his history through the use of illustrations—woodcuts, broadsides, and the like—and written accounts. He supports these further with studies of manuscripts and printed works of cistern music, which also reveal the transformations in the instrument, with its double courses of strings and possibility for extended range. The cistern emerges as an instrument that stands as a metonym not only for the industrialization of Saxony and Thuringia, but also for the interaction of different types and levels of music-making (e.g., between folk- and art-music practices) in eastern Germany.

109. Sachs, Curt. *Handbuch der Musikinstrumentenkunde.* ("Handbook of Organology"). 2nd ed. Leipzig: Breitkopf & Härtel, 1930. 1st ed. 1919. (Kleine Handbücher der Musikgeschichte nach Gattungen, 12).

The classic work on organology and the standard ethnomusicological classification system for instruments, which has yet to be supplanted. Sachs organizes this book systematically, dividing it into four sections according to the four classes of sound-producing instruments (idiophones, membranophones, chordophones, and aerophones) determined by Sachs and Erich M. von Hornbostel ("Systematik der Musikinstrumente," *Zeitschrift für Ethnologie* 4/5 [1914]); a fifth section on "the organ and its relatives" contains discussions of instruments that do not fit easily into one class or another. Within each class Sachs begins by discussing those instruments that, in relatively simple form, represent the basic characteristics of the class (e.g., clappers and rattles in the opening section on idiophones). The discussions take the form of concise essays, in which data is presented together with more extensive consideration of the most salient theoretical issues. The evidence Sachs musters for his discussions consists of material examples from instrument collections, descriptions from theoretical treatises and early accounts, and visual depictions of instruments. Whereas this evidence richly illustrates the volume, it also produces a certain European bias, for Sachs builds his arguments around the material most readily available to him in Berlin. Some of his discussions of non-Western instruments, particularly Middle Eastern and Asian instruments, reflect the thinking of the *Kulturkreis* school of anthropology, that is, the claim that cultural artifacts and practices that originated in Asia gradually made their way to Europe, where they reached more advanced or perfected forms. Whereas Sachs does not support such claims in any ideological way, he does not turn to non-Western instruments to problematize the characteristics of instruments that might lie outside the Sachs and Hornbostel system, but rather to the organ, which becomes exceptional because it contains characteristics from the main classes. Abundant footnotes and references to early organological works accompany this book, which has been sweepingly paradigmatic in the history of ethnomusicology.

110. Sárosi, Bálint. *Die Volksmusikinstrumente Ungarns.* ("The Folk-Music Instruments of Hungary"). Leipzig: VEB Deutscher Verlag für Musik, 1967. (Handbuch der europäischen Volksmusik-instrumente, Series 1, Vol. 1).

This is the first volume in the series *Handbuch der Volksmusikinstrumente* ("Handbook of Folk-Music Instruments"), edited by Ernst Emsheimer and Erich Stockmann. Devoted to Hungary, it rather strictly follows the organizational and conceptual plan for the series, which the series editors review in their foreword. The volume employs five sections, the first four following the Sachs-Hornbostel classification system of idiophones, membranophones, chordophones, and aerophones, and the last section a discussion of the structure of ensembles. Within each larger section, smaller sections present typical and important examples that conform to the subcategories of the Sachs-Hornbostel system. Sárosi contextualizes the volume's relation to previous Hungarian research, notably that of Bartók and Kodály, observing that this research, despite its systematic character, rarely considered folk-music instruments. The volume circumscribes the Hungarian quality of musical instruments in fairly restrictive fashion, not examining the instruments of non-Hungarian minorities in Hungary, but extending consideration to Hungarian communities elsewhere in Eastern Europe. Somewhat in contradiction to this principle, Gypsy ensembles occupy an extremely important position in the final section of the book devoted to ensemble structure. Extensive use of illustrations makes this book not only accessible to non-German speakers, but also expands its comparability. In addition to drawings and photographs of instruments, performers and scientific diagrams of instruments appear throughout the text. Sárosi's careful and extensive musical transcriptions assist the reader in connecting instruments to their sounds and characteristic repertories.

111. Stockmann, Erich. "Die europäischen Volksmusikinstrumente: Möglichkeiten und Probleme ihrer Darstellung in einem Handbuch." ("European Folk-Music Instruments: Possibilities and Problems of Their Presentation in a Handbook"). *Deutsches Jahrbuch für Volkskunde* 10, 2 (1964): 238–53.

An overall description of the planned six-volume *Handbuch der europäischen Volksmusikinstrumente* ("Handbook of European Folk-Music Instruments"), which Stockmann edited with Erich Emsheimer. This article describes the fundamental concepts used in the series and explains criteria for selection and organization in individual volumes. The concept of folk-music instrument is that of functionality within a given community or music culture. Accordingly, it is the individuals in the given culture who determine the qualities and structures of their instruments. This principle further allows the editors and authors of individual volumes to concentrate on issues such as technology and ergology, the concept that an instrument is conceived and used as a "tool," that is, to achieve a specific musical and social task. Further considerations will be performance practices, the ways in which instruments articulate musical characteristics, and performance repertories. Although there exist many possible ways of determining the contents and organization of each volume, the editors have determined to rely on the boundaries of modern European states, thereby accounting also for historical and contemporary practices. Instrument types will be discussed in relation to the Sachs-Hornbostel systematic classification. Stockmann closes by observing that the series will fill a scientific gap and spawn new research questions for all areas of musical research.

112. Stockmann, Erich. "Neue Beiträge zur Erforschung der europäischen Volksmusikinstrumente." ("New Contributions to the Study of European Folk-Music Instruments"). In Ludwig Finscher and Christoph-Hellmut Mahling, eds., *Festschrift für Walter Wiora*. Kassel: Bärenreiter, 1967. Pp. 512–19.

Survey of new areas of instrumental folk-music research at a time of increased scholarly systematization of that research. As coeditor (with Ernst Emsheimer) of the *Handbuch der europäischen Volksmusikinstrumente*, which was just beginning at the time of publication, Stockmann starts by surveying earlier organological scholarship (e.g., Sachs and Hornbostel) and the venues and methodologies of contemporary scholarship. The systematization provided folk-music scholars with another means of constructing the unity of a European folk music. Stockmann calls for widespread cooperation among nations and institutions in order to develop this area of research. The bibliography and annotations in the article are particularly helpful. The article also offers a valuable introduction to the state-sponsored and other organological museums and research projects in Eastern Europe at a time when these were flourishing.

113. Stockmann, Erich, ed. *Studia instrumentorum musicae popularis 9*. ("Studies of Folk-Music Instruments 9"). Stockholm: Musikmuseet, 1989.

The collected essays of a conference of the Study Group on Folk Musical Instruments of the International Council for

Traditional Music, devoted both to the theme "norm and individuality in the production of folk-music instruments" and to organological studies of Italian instruments. Despite the diverse treatments of the main theme and the several languages of the essays (German predominates, but essays appear also in English and French), a surprising unity and direction ties this volume together. Most of the essays recognize that norm and individuality are inseparable in the production of instruments and, moreover, that each aspect may influence the shape, sound, and function of instruments at any stage. The studies are not limited to the production of folk-music instruments, and several of the most interesting recognize the cross-influences of instrument production for several types of music-making. In some cases, furthermore, it is precisely the accommodation that results when folk-music instruments become stylized for popular or art music that allows for negotiations between norm and individuality. The symbolic role of instruments, too, provides a leitmotif lending unity to the volume. The volume begins with theoretical essays by Oskár Elschek, Ludwik Bielawski, and Christian Kaden, which introduce different aspects of the main theme. The essays on Polish instruments and on organological topics in Italy locate the theoretical principles of the volume in specific case studies. The essays on Italy (by Febo Guizzi, Nico Staiti, Roberto Leydi, Tullia Magrini, and others) constitute the single most important source for research on Italian folk-music instruments. One of the most valuable theoretical and reference works on the organology of modern Europe.

114. Stradner, Fritz. "Vom Scheitholz zur Kratz-Zither: Ein Beitrag zur Entwicklungsgeschichte der Zither." ("From Slab of Wood to Scratch-Zither: A Contribution to the Developmental History of the Zither"). *Jahrbuch des österreichischen Volksliedwerkes* 18 (1969): 66–80.

Using historical accounts of the construction of zither-like instruments, this article empirically traces the different ways in which such instruments might have developed from simple to more complex forms. Stradner refers to his approach as ergological, broadly meaning that form follows the materials and skills available to individual builders at various historical moments and places. The study focuses largely on evidence from rural alpine areas, in which individuals used materials available to them to construct zither-like instruments. Initially (the earliest source available to Stradner is from sixteenth-century Switzerland), this meant very basic slabs of wood, across which hair or gut was stretched. The development of specialized tools and construction techniques gradually made it possible for the zither to accommodate more complex musical demands. The developmental history—actually histories, for he always concerns himself with local developments—that Stradner re-creates experimentally remained, nonetheless, the practices of non-specialists, although awareness of instrument-building also brought about certain changes by the end of the nineteenth century. The article intentionally offers a perspective from the more global theories about zithers, namely, that they developed in Asia and spread over Europe prior to the modern era.

115. Suppan, Wolfgang. *Blasmusik in Baden: Geschichte und Gegenwart einer traditionsreichen Blasmusiklandschaft.* ("Wind Music in Baden: Past and Present of a Wind-Music Landscape Rich in Tradition"). Freiburg im Breisgau: Schulz, 1983.

Primarily a history of wind music in southwestern Germany, one of the most important regions for the development of wind and brass styles. Suppan begins by examining the earliest archeological evidence, which demonstrates widespread use of wind instruments even by the Germanic and Alemannisch tribal cultures of the region, and later by the Romans. Different historical strands developed in the Middle Ages, with musical professionals, such as Minnesingers and minstrels, making substantial use of wind instruments. In the modern era of Germany, increasing institutionalization led to the development of ensembles, both in art music (e.g., the Mannheim School of the eighteenth century, also in Baden) and the many folk-music ensembles in the nineteenth century. In recent years, wind music has flourished through the support of organizations, which have standardized repertories and social functions alike. Suppan argues that wind music has the capacity to unify a large cultural area because some aspects of it appeal to all social and class divisions. Extensive illustrations of ensembles and lists of performers, instrument builders, and organizational personnel.

116. Wagner, Christoph. *Das Akkordeon: Eine wilde Karriere.* ("The Accordion: A Wild Career"). Berlin: Transit, 1993.

A history of the social functions and cultural symbolism of the accordion. Beginning with the first appearance of button boxes in the music of European taverns as evidence of the transformation of the public sphere, Wagner interprets the accordion as an instrument for the common people, yet one that lends itself to folk, popular, and art musics. In the popular world music of the late twentieth century, the accordion has enjoyed a revival, but its role in this revival has nevertheless been to represent Europeanness, not least because the accordion was an instrument that was exported throughout the world through various forms of economic imperialism and colonialism. Contrasting histories and dialectical social functions shape the cultural presence of the accordion in Wagner's interpretation. European, especially German, histories contrast with those elsewhere in the world, particularly in the United States, where different ethnic groups gave individual meanings to the accordion. The social dialectic was shaped by uses in everyday practices, particularly the empowerment of the working class or women to make music and to engage in literate musical practices. Against this background, however, the accordion sometimes became an agent of public politics and nationalist ideologies, notably of the Nazis during the 1930s and 1940s. Wagner richly illustrates the book with advertisements, publicity photos from recordings, and postcards, all of which served as the icons of the accordion's dissemination and presence in the public sphere during the modern era.

5

EUROPEAN CONCEPTS AND CONSTRUCTS OF FOLK MUSIC

Two general questions inform the works annotated in the present chapter. First, is folk music a European construct? Second, to what extent does folk music contribute to constructs of Europe, its history, and its interaction with cultures beyond its borders? The concept of folk music, as we have witnessed throughout this book, particularly in those works and sections of the book devoted to intellectual history, crystallized during a specifically European moment in world history, the Enlightenment. Insofar as Herder's theorization of folk song and the growing interest in collecting and anthologizing folk song by Arnim and Brentano, the Brothers Grimm, Ludwig Erk, and others marked a transition from the Enlightenment to Romanticism, this historical moment also acquired a specifically German character. The European concept of folk music derived, furthermore, from the several centuries leading up to the Enlightenment, a period of intellectual foment unleashed by the Age of Discovery and the confrontation with the culture of "the other." Whereas the formulation of a concept of folk music depended on this fundamentally European historical framework, it owed much to the cultural contestation that formed at the borders of Europe and at the edges of its historical framework.

The works presented in the present chapter bring to the fore a number of basic issues, which, though raised elsewhere in the book, problematize the ways in which Europeans have used music to define their own culture area. One set of issues coalesces around the ways in which folk music maps out culture areas within Europe itself. Petra Farwick's three-volume charting of the folk-song landscape follows a long tradition of plotting folk songs according to the places they were sung or collected, as if they laid linguistic and cultural claim to those places. That the landscapes plotted by Farwick's studies differ from those bounded by the maps of nationalism is striking in the ways it suggests alternative borders and problematic histories. A.Z. Idelsohn used folk song to map culture and history in a different way, transforming the songs collected on wax cylinders in Palestine into a means of charting, if not musically inventing, the Jewish Diaspora. Idelsohn depended on the stability of oral tradition—one of the fundamental tenets of folk-music scholarship in the early twentieth century—to claim that present-day musical practices afforded the scholar the chance to perceive the past in each song and each version. Folk song itself not only embodied history but made it legible through performance and the interpretation of the map of the past that it contained.

Many of the works annotated in this chapter also reveal the tendency of Central European folk-music scholars to map their own methods and categories onto the folk musics of other cultures, within Europe and without. This has been particularly true in southeastern Europe, where folk-music scholarship followed on the heels of the political expansion of the Austro-Hungarian Empire (see, e.g., works by Walter Puchner, Hans Szklenar, and Susanne Ziegler). For different political reasons European scholars cultivated an intense interest in Turkish folk music. Long "the other" against which Central and Eastern Europeans measured their selfness, the Ottoman presence at the eastern borders of Europe became a common topos. During the nineteenth century Turkish music underwent processes of orientalizing in the European constructs of otherness. This orientalism, nonetheless, has proved inadequate to interpret the new presence of Turkish culture and music in Europe at the end of the twentieth century. Significant in these studies, however, is the very assumption that folk music exists in Turkey, that it lends itself to comparison with German folk music (see, e.g., the works by Ali Osman Öztürk), and that it participates in processes of translation along the borders between Europe and Asia.

Genre and repertory also provide concepts for translating across the borders within Europe. The centrality of narrative research in German folk-song scholarship has provided many scholars with a lens to focus on the processes of narration in folk-song repertories elsewhere. The Child ballads have been of special interest for German ballad scholars, not only because of the possibility for comparative textual study, but also because of the connections between oral and print traditions that the Child ballads exemplify in ways both similar to and different from the German ballads. It is interesting to observe that German scholars have devoted far more attention to English narrative traditions than have English scholars to German traditions, which suggests very different ways of bounding Europe in the two scholarly traditions. Indeed, whereas English-language scholarship turns more expansively toward the entire world, following the paths of empire, German-language scholarship continues to turn inward toward Europe, following different paths of empire.

At the end of the twentieth century, Central European folk-music scholarship is no less interested in the concepts and constructs of Europe than during the Enlightenment or the nineteenth century. There are, however, new concerns and new concepts of the boundaries and processes of translation that folk music can represent. New research has turned consciously toward the contested nature of cultural boundaries and has launched critical assaults on the privileging of "self" that much folk-music research has supported. As Europe changes at the end of the twentieth century, so, by necessity, is the folk-music research that charts its problematic path into the future.

※※⊕※※

Europe

117. Burkhart, Dagmar. *Kulturraum Balkan: Studien zur Volkskunde und Literatur Südosteuropas.* ("The Balkan Culture Area: Studies on Folklore and Literature in Southeast Europe"). Berlin: Erich Reimer, 1989. (Lebensformen: Veröffentlichungen des Instituts für Volkskunde der Universität Hamburg, 5).

A wide-ranging study of folkloristic and literary "complexes" in southeastern Europe, whereby the author focuses on the interrelations among genres and the culture and history from which they emerged. Although numerous areas of folklore are examined, considerable attention is given to folk song and other forms of oral literature. Central to Burkhart's approach is determining the nature of the interactions that constitute individual complexes. Lyric songs, for example, have been more responsive historically to change, particularly in the characters and events they represent. Epics, long one of the distinctive genres of southeastern Europe, also have responded to different historical conditions, sometimes undergoing a transformation from resistance against the Ottoman Empire to voicing individual paths toward nationalism in the nineteenth century. In contrast, Burkhart examines other genres (e.g., Haiduken songs), in which she believes the strict connection to historical events has been exaggerated. The complexes at which Burkhart looks do not primarily represent a single "Balkan area," but rather the interaction of processes that exist at the local level and are realized through folk song at regional levels.

118. Farwick, Petra. *Deutsche Volksliedlandschaften: Landschaftliches Register der Aufzeichnungen im Deutschen Volksliedarchiv.* ("German Folk-Song Landscapes: Indexed Landscapes of Transcriptions in the German Folk-Song Archive"). Part 1 (coauthored by Otto Holzapfel) and Part 2. Freiburg im Breisgau: Deutsches Volksliedarchiv, 1983 and 1984). Part 3. Bern: Peter Lang, 1986. (Studien zur Volksliedforschung, 1).

A three-volume catalog of the local origins of songs whose transcriptions make up the collections of the German Folk-Song Archive (DVA) in Freiburg im Breisgau. Retaining the cartographic areas of German-speaking Europe determined in 1871 and used at the DVA for numerous projects (e.g., the multivolume publication of German ballads), these publications plot the occurrences of songs on the maps of individual regions, according to the place where originally collected or in which singers lived. Each of the landscapes is introduced by two bibliographies, the first containing general folk-song publications from the area and the second listing the individual transcriptions and sources for the songs plotted on the landscape map. A third bibliography concludes each section with a listing of general works on folk music, folklore, and regional history for the area. The concept of German folk-song landscape arose at an historical moment in which Germany had gained political control over areas in Central and Eastern Europe that it claimed because of large (or sometimes very small) German-speaking minorities, for example Alsace-Lorraine, East Prussia, and Silesia. Speech islands and other Germanic-speaking areas also form their own landscapes, for example Belgium and Russia, in this latter case in part because of its Yiddish-speaking Jewish population. Otto Holzapfel introduces the volumes with an essay on reading the maps so that increasingly complex patterns and interrelations might emerge. Although the volumes provide a geographic representation of Europe based on a German historical perspective, there is no claim on Germanness for any of the landscapes outside Germany proper. Quite the contrary, there is considerable sensitivity to the ways in which the maps might contribute to a better understanding of the landscapes within Germany after World War II, when German-speaking residents of Eastern Europe returned to Germany.

119. Krauss, Friedrich S. "Guslarenlieder." ("Songs of the Guslar"). *Der Urquell: Eine Monatschrift für Volkskunde* (new series) 2 (1898): 5–26.

Analyzing the Bosnian epic called "The Milk Brothers," this article examines the religious, social, and legal interrelations of Christians and Muslims in Bosnia-Herzogovina. The text of the song, in a version with 621 lines, appears here in the original and in German translation; a transcription of a further description and interpretation of the epic by the singer accompanies the song in German translation. After introducing the history of Ottoman conquest in Bosnia and the cultural tensions that ensued, the author claims that the usual assumption that Muslims and Christians entirely failed to coexist is not borne out by the song. Indeed, examined from the standpoints of Bosnian and Muslim law, the song of two "milk brothers," whose cooperation turned out to serve the common good, portrays an historical picture that differs from that commonly held in the European imagination. The article is one of the first to look extensively at folk song in southeastern Europe as a means of rethinking the historiograpy of Europe, and it results from a new integration of folklore texts in general into the construction of European interaction with the Ottoman Empire. Not only does the text of this Guslar song provide a wealth of historical details, but its portrait of the Turkish and Muslim "other" reveals a far more complex process of representation than many twentieth-century scholars have imagined to be possible.

120. Mrytz, Barbara. *Das Verhältnis von Mündlichkeit und Schriftlichkeit in Textkonstitution und Tradierung der Balladen des Child-Korpus: Ein Beitrag zur Kompatibilität von Literaturwissenschaft und Volkskunde.* ("The Relation of Orality and Literacy in the Construction and Transmission of Texts in the Child Ballads: A Contribution to the Compatibility of Literary Theory and Folkloristics"). Frankfurt am Main: Peter Lang, 1989. (Europäische Hochschulschriften; Reihe 14: Angelsächsische Sprache und Literatur, 243).

A theoretical argument for the interrelatedness of oral and written traditions in the transmission of the Child ballads. Mrytz begins with a survey of previous scholarship (or lack thereof) devoted to the oral-written interrelation, and it is particularly evident that relatively little substantial work has come from German scholars or has addressed the problem in German folk song. Because of this Mrytz herself turns to the Child ballads and to the social and historical conditions in England and Scotland that shaped the interaction of oral and written transmission in the classic Anglo-Scottish canon. Central to her argument is the role of the street—or, rather, public sphere—in the creation and transmission of the Child ballads. Not only did the street create the printed genre necessary for the circulation of the ballads, the broadside, but it encompassed the social conditions favorable for oral transmission. In her analytical chapters Mrytz demonstrates how one can follow change in ballad tradition that occurred in both the printed versions and the oral variants. Her argument that these patterns of change depend on each other differs from most theories, which rest on notions that written versions arrest change, whereas oral transmission encourages it. A fascinating approach, which deserves to be applied more broadly to folk-song repertories throughout Europe.

121. Potthoff, Wilfried. *Vuk Karadžić im europäischen Kontext.* ("Vuk Karadžić in European Context"). Heidelberg: Winter, 1990.

Contributions to a 1987 symposium devoted to the Serbian national poet, Vuk Stefanović Karadžić, whose poetry and prose writings established a literary context for modern Serbian nationalism in the early nineteenth century. Vuk's influence spread far beyond Serbia, particularly to other Slavic-speaking areas of Eastern Europe. Music provided one of the most complex means for the dissemination of this influence. Writing Serbian poetry in the style of the early English and German Romantics, Vuk adapted Serbian genres, such as the epic, to a poetry that historicized the past in the present and created the foundation for a national lyricism. His poetry served as the basis for many settings by Serbian composers, and his epic style entered the repertories of Serbian epic singers. The essays in this volume examine the European contexts of Vuk's reception, examining the influences of Herder and Pushkin on Vuk and then the ways in which Vuk's influences were palpable in other traditions of European nationalism, for example in Poland. The most sweeping essay on the interaction between Vuk's poetry and music is that by Vera Bojić, who examines questions of textual setting in the poetry itself, particularly how these were solved when Vuk's works became international in character. One of the most accessible introductions to the widespread influence of a poet on folk- and art-music traditions throughout Europe in the nineteenth century.

122. Puchner, Walter. *Studien zum Kulturkontext der liturgischen Szene: Lazarus und Judas als religiöse Volksfiguren in Bild und Brauch, Lied und Legende Südosteuropa.* ("Studies of the Cultural Context of the Liturgical Scene: Lazarus and Judas as Religious Folk Figures in Image and Custom, Song and Legend of Southeastern Europe"). 2 vols. Vienna: Verlag der Österreichischen Akademie der Wissenschaften, 1991. (Österreichische Akademie der Wissenschaften, Philosophisch-historische Klasse. Denkschriften, 216).

A magisterial study of the complex contextualization of the Christian symbols, Lazarus and Judas, in the folk-religious expression of southeastern Europe. Puchner's approach is comparative, both in its examination of different Balkan traditions and its integration of different folk traditions. Accordingly, he rethinks the ways in which liturgy functions and results from the performance of folkloristic practices. The figures of Lazarus and Judas provide a framework because of the contrasting ways in which they are represented, on one hand as essential to the articulation of Christ's power to save and on the other as symbolic of his willingness to submit to betrayal and sacrifice. In the complex of traditions examined in this book, this imagery does not take the form of a single symbol (i.e., as a motif that repeatedly appears), but rather as varied forms of interpretation through performance. It is contextualization that brings about such variation. In Catholic areas, for example, the context of folk song is much more pronounced than in Orthodox areas; Lazarus songs are common in the first, but relatively rare in the second. Performance differs from area to area, and therefore the degree of ritualization within liturgy follows distinctive paths, if indeed these are locally determined. Volume 1 contains Puchner's interpretive text, volume 2 the data and primary materials he uses to theorize the liturgical relation between folk religion, folk theater, and folk music.

123. Rexroth, Dieter, ed. *Zwischen den Grenzen: Zum Aspekt des Nationalen in der Neuen Musik.* ("Between the Borders: On the 'National' in New Music"). Mainz: B. Schott's Söhne, 1979. (Frankfurter Studien, 3).

A wide-ranging collection of articles addressing the different meanings of the "national" in new music, in this case meaning twentieth-century classical compositions. The authors employ two general approaches that reflect two very different concepts of the national. One approach stresses the ways in which twentieth-century music expresses national characteristics, usually using a specific vocabulary, such as that derived from the folk music of a nation (e.g., essays by Kurt von Fischer and Peter Benary). The other approach emphasizes the influences of non-European music on the ideas and styles of modernist Western composers (e.g., the essay by Jürg Stenzl). In general, the authors interpret the national as fitting uncomfortably in most modernist concepts of classical music, which, according to the general consensus of the authors, strives to be international, even to break away from the influences of nationalism. Nationalism in music, nonetheless, has a particularly European history that composers have reinforced by turning with varied motivations toward folk music. The tension between the national and the international arises from other tensions, for example between vernacular and elite traditions, or between aesthetics that argue for music's representational capacity and those arguing against that capacity. Of particular interest are essays on the ways in which Eastern European nations encouraged and bolstered the express use of the national during the second half of the twentieth century. Essays by Hans Oesch and Everett Helm on the combinations of Western and non-Western vocabularies in new music balance the collection very well.

124. Schneider, Erich. "Türkische Musik in Vorarlberg." ("Turkish Music in Vorarlberg"). *Jahrbuch des österreichischen Volksliedwerkes* 32/33 (1984): 107–14.

Examines the history of ensembles performing "Turkish music" in Vorarlberg, the westernmost province of Austria. Turkish music was not the music of Turkey, but rather music emulating the janissary ensembles of the Ottoman Empire. Turkish music became popular in Vorarlberg and elsewhere in Central Europe in the eighteenth century, that is, after the retreat of the Ottoman Empire from lands then taken over by the Habsburg Monarchy. A typical Turkish-music ensemble might consist of several natural horns, oboes, bassoons, clarinets, a trumpet, piccolo, triangle, several drums, and a "Chinese bell tree." It became popular in Vorarlberg during a time of changing folk and popular music, in particular, Turkish-music ensembles accompanying outdoor processions, with many becoming semi-professional. Such ensembles also established themselves in the performance of some rituals of the Catholic church, notably in processions at the time of Corpus Christi in late spring. During the nineteenth century there was growing criticism of such sacred functions, and by the end of the century these had largely been eliminated from the church through the urgings of the St. Cecilia movement, which strove to re-create a pure, vocal sound in church music. The rise and fall of Turkish music provides a complex and unexpected case study for the examination of the relation between self and other, Christian and non-Christian, Occident and Orient, in the musical ensembles of rural western Austria in the eighteenth and nineteenth centuries.

125. Taylor, Archer. "Die gemeinsamen Themen der englischen und deutschen Balladen." ("The Common Themes of English and German Ballads"). In Rolf Wilhelm Brednich, Lutz Röhrich, and Wolfgang Suppan, eds., *Handbuch des Volksliedes.* Vol. 2: *Historisches und Systematisches—interethnische Beziehungen—Musikethnologie.* Munich: Wilhelm Fink, 1975. Pp. 271–83.

Establishes historical and motivic connections between English and German ballads by examining the different ways in which individual ballads demonstrate correspondences. Taylor argues from the standpoint that there are many similarities, and that these result from an earlier historical moment in the Middle Ages when the two repertories were closely connected. One of the connections was probably medieval minstrelsy, and Taylor shows how motivic connections might have traveled between the two traditions as motives, for example, the theme of Robin Hood. Less explicit are similarities that resulted from common responses to similar social and historical conditions, for example the relations between landowners and serfs in a feudal society; these correspondences resulted from the ways in which ballads articulated larger *mentalités.* There are also ballads that have similar origins, either in a tradition shared by German and English singers or in a tradition outside both, for example from French romances or *pastourelles.* Whereas Taylor does not consider music or musical contexts, his readings of literary motives reveal these to function in very complex ways. A good historical study of the larger folk-song landscape of Europe.

126. Voßschmidt, Liisa. *Das Kalevala und seine Rezeption im 19. Jahrhundert: Eine Analyse von Rezeptionsdokumenten aus dem deutschen Sprachraum.* ("The *Kalevala* and Its Reception in the Nineteenth Century: An Analysis Based on Reception Documents from the German-Speaking Countries"). Frankfurt am Main:

Peter Lang, 1989. (Bochumer Schriften zur deutschen Literatur, 9).

An intellectual history of the impact of the Finnish epic *Kalevala* on German thought and of German Romanticism and scholarship on the history of the *Kalevala*. Compiled from different fragments in and out of oral tradition by the Finnish physician Elias Lönnrot, the *Kalevala* influenced German concepts of the epic because it combined the qualities of both a nature epic and a folk epic. German philologists, caught up in the discovery of such an epic in the nineteenth century, not least because of its presumably deep historical roots, contributed significantly to the transformation of the *Kalevala* into the Finnish national epic. German hands were considerable in this formation of a national and nationalist folk narrative. Translations into German were numerous and demonstrated very diverse ideologies and symbolic ends. In the twentieth century, for example, Martin Buber, one of the leading Jewish intellectuals of the early century and translator of the Bible, prepared a translation, as did Wolfgang Steinitz, the leading folk-song scholar during the first scholarly generation in the German Democratic Republic. The *Kalevala* became the focal point for an emerging German-Finnish nineteenth-century discourse on folklore and folk music, which has remained broadly influential throughout the twentieth century. This volume serves as a valuable guide and survey of this intellectual axis in European folk-music theory and history.

127. Würzbach, Natascha. "Theorie und Praxis des Motiv-Begriffs: Überlegungen bei der Erstellung eines Motiv-Index zum Child-Korpus." ("Theory and Practice of the Concept of Motif: Considerations in the Preparation of a Motif Index for the Child Ballads"). *Jahrbuch für Volksliedforschung* 38 (1993): 64–89.

A survey of different concepts of what a motif can be in the study of narrative folk song and other areas of folkloristics, with a broad proposal for using motifs to bring new perspectives to the content and structure of the Child ballads. Würzbach distinguishes motif from formula and plot by placing it in a middleground between them, where its effectiveness depends on textual connections (e.g., to the syntax of the narrative text) and contextual differentiation (i.e., psychological motifs, local events, or characterization). Central to the author's proposal is that a motif index could encompass a hierarchy, with a larger thematic motif branching into numerous, but linked submotifs. Each motif, then, has the possibility of representing the widest possible semantic and thematic field, hence linking the Child ballads not only within individual families but across the regional and historical domains from which the Child ballads come. Thus, a motif such as "murder" may actually allow for several different hierarchies, depending on the function of murder in different ballads. References to and integration of the literature on motifs and motif indexes also make the article an excellent bibliographic introduction to this area of folkloristic research.

◆◇◆◇◆

The Boundaries and Margins of Europe

128. Idelsohn, A.Z. *Phonographierte Gesänge und Aussprachsproben des Hebräischen der jemenitischen, persischen und syrischen Juden.* ("Recorded Songs and Pronunciation Experiments with the Hebrew of Yemenite, Persian, and Syrian Jews"). Vienna: Alfred Hölder, 1917. (Kaiserliche Akademie der Wissenschaften in Wien: Mitteilung der Phonogramm-Archivs-Kommission, 35).

A musical and linguistic examination of the Hebrew in song and speech of Jews from Yemen, Persia, and Syria, who had settled in Palestine by the beginning of the twentieth century. Idelsohn, with a commission from the Austrian Academy of Sciences, used wax-cylinder recordings to collect songs and to gather spoken texts, which he systematically analyzed for this study. Idelsohn's point of departure was his belief that the Hebrew language, maintained in oral tradition through song since the destruction of the Temples, provided the cultural cohesion of the Jewish Diaspora and could therefore demonstrate patterns of cultural unity. Idelsohn makes extensive use of transcriptions, identifying them precisely in relation to the recording cylinders deposited at the Academy of Sciences. By comparing different pronunciation patterns from the Middle Eastern communities with those of European communities (e.g., Ashkenazic and Italian communities), he provides a linguistic map of the Diaspora and its history. Because song is the shared locus for singing in Hebrew throughout the Diaspora, it serves also as a means of charting the history of Jewish culture throughout the past two millennia. This volume, examined together with the ten volumes of Idelsohn's *Hebräisch-orientalischer Melodienschatz* (1914–32), attempts scientifically to connect dispersed and diverse Jewish communities in the underlying culture of Palestine, where the songs analyzed here were collected from living traditions.

129. Öztürk, Ali Osman. "Eine türkische Parallele zur 'Schönen Jüdin'?" ("A Turkish Parallel to 'the Beautiful Jewish Girl'?"). *Jahrbuch für Volksliedforschung* 36 (1991): 98–105.

Compares the Turkish ballad "Armenian Girl" to the German ballad "Die schöne Jüdin" ("The Beautiful Jewish Girl"). Establishing a considerable number of parallels, Öztürk nonetheless does not argue for relationship through transmission. At the deepest level, the parallels stem from the dilemma of religious conflict, when the female "other" (Jewish or Armenian Christian) falls in love with the male "self" (Christian European or Muslim Turkish). The gulf of conversion is rarely crossed, but in the "Schöne Jüdin" the resolution most often takes the form of suicide. The social and professional characteristics of the male are similar in German and Turkish versions, often a minor aristocratic figure or a scribe. Öztürk's study provides excellent analyses of individual texts, allowing him to suggest possible dates for the ballad prior to the twentieth century, more or less in the same period when the German ballad versions were collected. Excellent analysis of the narrative structures in "Armenian Girl."

130. Öztürk, Ali Osman. *Das türkische Volkslied als sprachliches Kunstwerk*. ("The Turkish Folk Song as Oral Artwork"). Bern: Peter Lang, 1994. (Studien zur Volksliedforschung, 15).

Written by the founder and director of the Turkish Folk-Song Archive in Konya, Turkey, this book proposes approaches and categories that will include all genres of Turkish folk song within a unified field. Öztürk uses textural and poetic properties as his organizational principle. Form in all Turkish folk song results from strophic genres, which are distinguished by syllable count in individual lines. The subject matter in folk song necessarily arises from the reality of everyday Turkish life and the actions of historical figures. Pragmatically conceived, Turkish folk song also has enormous potential to provide the basis for a culture history of Turkey and Turkish culture. To illustrate this concept, Öztürk devotes the seventh chapter to the genre of ballad known as "Destan" songs, the first evidence for which appears in the thirteenth century, but which is still a common designation for certain ballads and other folk songs in the twentieth century. Distinguishing the history of the Destan ballads has been a responsiveness to changes, for example a transformation away from ballad structure with the major influence of print technology in the nineteenth century. The opening chapters survey the existing collections and collecting activities, most of them local or regional, but seldom compared as in this book. Throughout the history of Turkish folk-song scholarship, Europeans have played a major role, beginning with nineteenth-century Austrians and Hungarians, and continuing in this century with Béla Bartók, and Kurt and Ursula Reinhard. The conceptualization of Turkish folk song and its classification has for centuries depended on this discursive exchange with Europe.

131. Puchner, Walter. "Die Wiener Türkenbelagerung von 1683 im kretischen Volkslied und im rumänischen Bildungsschriftum." ("The 1683 Turkish Siege of Vienna in Cretan Folk Song and Romanian Educational Writings"). *Jahrbuch des österreichischen Volksliedwerkes* 29 (1980): 59–75.

The siege by and final defeat of the Ottoman Empire at the threshold of Vienna marked a turning point in the history of the contested regions between East and West, transforming the historical moment into one of the most common themes in late seventeenth- and eighteenth-century German-language broadsides. The songs examined here, however, were created on the island of Crete, from which they entered into a history of dissemination and translation that included important Romanian sources from the eighteenth and nineteenth centuries. Puchner argues that the versions of this song, called in Greek simply "Vienna," encode foreignness in the Habsburg Empire, transform it into a local foreignness, and then use song to recontextualize sociopolitical criticism and resistance. The Ottoman Empire had long held the lands of Romania by the time of the siege of Vienna, and Crete had been conquered by the Ottomans in 1669. "Vienna," which sources indicate had a substantial oral tradition, became both a lens and a mirror for representing the relation of "self" to "other," that is, European to Turkish culture. The song, even in Greek versions, contains very specific historical details, which, however, symbolize as a whole the very impossibility of Austrian victory against overwhelming odds. The song itself, also in later Romanian versions, came to represent a much longer history of cultural confrontation in the boundary regions of Europe.

132. Reinhard, Ursula, and Tiago de Oliveira Pinto. "Zwei Liedgattungen der Âsik/Ozan im Osten der Türkei." ("Two Song Genres of the Âsik/Ozan in Eastern Turkey"). In Hartmut Braun, ed., *Probleme der Volksmusikforschung*. Bern: Peter Lang, 1990. Pp. 250–63.

Identifies the distinguishing characteristics of song genres of the professional singer known as *âsik* (lit., lover) in Eastern Turkey. Unlike *âsik* repertories elsewhere in Turkey, those on the borders with Iran and the nations of the Caucasus bear strong witness to influences from classical Turkish music and from Azerbaijani music. The repertories contain a broad range of genres, revealing not only the diverse social and musical activities of the *âsik*, but also the possibility that the *âsik*'s musical world must subsume numerous art-music domains and religious dimensions in Eastern Turkey (e.g., epic songs and religious Alevi songs). Specific use of the Turkish modal system, *makam*, further

determines the classification of the songs. Reinhard and de
Oliveira Pinto analyze two important genres, one which contains
songs expressing a "philosophical worldview," and the other,
which borrows consciously from the traditions of Azerbaijan,
called the "Azeri type." The analytical approach focuses on the
unique characteristics of each genre, in other words, on those
traits that make one genre different from others. The concept of
genre, in this sense, is one that admits fairly rigid boundaries,
determined by difference rather than similarity.

133. Reinhard, Ursula, and Tiago de Oliveira Pinto. *Sänger und Poeten
mit der Laute: Türkische Âsik und Ozan.* ("Singers and Poets with
the Lute: Turkish *Âsik*s and *Ozan*s"). Berlin: Erich Reimer, 1990.

One of the works with which Ursula Reinhard has completed
the lifelong researches of her husband, Kurt Reinhard. Together
with de Oliveira Pinto, Ursula Reinhard focuses this study on the
professional poet-singer, the *âsik*, historically also called *ozan*. The
âsik (lit., lover) is one of the most important musicians in Turkish
folk music (as well as in other parts of the northern Middle East,
where *âsik*s are also found), particularly because of the enormous
repertory he or she commands, often songs in several languages
and dialects. The *âsik* has figured in other German studies of
Turkish folk music, but this is the first study to recognize that the
âsik is not simply a Turkish version of the medieval *Minnesinger*.
The book considers both the social and cultural contexts in which
the *âsik* performs, as well as the musical texts associated with the
poet-singers. Although *âsik*s perform different repertories—
individuals, in fact, often maintain different repertories—and
styles, the authors attempt to classify the musical activities and
genres of *âsik*s according to region in Turkey. Although there is
no convincing case here for specific connections between region
and style, this ethnomusicological approach succeeds in providing
an alternative to the common model of Turkish music as a single
monolithic system. Richly illustrated with photographs and
transcriptions, the volume is accompanied by two excellent
audiocassettes.

134. Szklenar, Hans. *Studien zum Bild des Orients in vorhöfischen
deutschen Epen.* ("Studies on the Image of the Orient in Pre-
Courtly German Epics"). Göttingen: Vandenhoeck & Ruprecht,
1966. (Palaestra, 243).

Influenced by the successive crusades of the twelfth century
and the contact with the Middle East, Asia, and Africa that the
crusades encouraged, German epics represented a wide range of
cultural and religious images of the non-European world. These
images became the basis not only for the creation of a repertory of

poetic epics and the musical performances and settings of these in the late Middle Ages, but they also spilled over into vernacular musical traditions, among them the broadside traditions that first took shape with the emergence of print technology in the fifteenth century. Szklenar writes a reception history of the contact with the Middle East, particularly those regarded in many epics as "pagan," and then closely examines several of the most influential epics that created the representational basis for the imagery of "the other" (e.g., the *Song of Roland*). These images were initially quite complex, often reflecting the historical and geographic particularities present at the moment of contact. Over time, the images differentiated, with certain stereotypes forming and the overall relation between Europe and the East developing specific patterns. The images of "the other" in early German epics contributed significantly not only to a cultural bounding of Europe but to the establishment of representational vocabularies in the arts to express and narrate the history of Europe's interpretation of itself and its "others."

135. Yakut, Attila. *Saz: Spielgrundkenntnisse der türkischen Langhalslaute und Einführung in die Volksmusik.* (*"Saz*: Basic Playing Knowledge of the Turkish Long-Necked Lute and Introduction to Folk Music"). Frankfurt am Main: Landeck, 1987.

An attempt to provide basic knowledge and instruction on the *saz* to Germans. Yakut presents the *saz* as a typical symbol of Turkish music, as well as the rules, music theory, and repertories that a European could use to demonstrate a basic performance capability in Turkish music. The small book begins with an introduction to Turkish folk music itself and then continues with discussions of the Turkish tuning system, the mechanics and structure of the *saz*, and a small selection of pieces. The initiate also has the opportunity to learn the Turkish alphabet and pronunciation rules. The book will probably also be of use to second- or third-generation Turkish-Germans, who will find the bibliography—virtually entirely in Turkish—a helpful connection to the music culture of Turkey itself. The volume represents one of the several new directions in publishing, recognizing that Turkish culture has become an important part of a multicultural German society in the late twentieth century, not just a closed world of guest workers who fail to interact with a monocultural version of that society.

136. Ziegler, Susanne. "Gattungsprobleme türkischer Volkslieder." ("Genre Problems of Turkish Folk Songs"). In Hartmut Braun,

ed., *Probleme der Volksmusikforschung.* Bern: Peter Lang, 1990. Pp. 264–78.

Takes as a point of departure that Turkish folk songs do not obey the same classificatory principles as European folk songs. European classifications would determine genres on the basis of textual content and form, or they would derive from patterns of melodic similarity (as in the case of Bartók's methods). In Turkish folk songs, in contrast, text and music often exist in contradictory relation to each other. The classificatory dilemma facing the European folk-song scholar is further complicated by the fact that there are indigenous concepts of classification in Turkey, which are internally consistent but often at odds with the European systems. Musicians recognize some genres on the basis of one set of criteria, other genres on the basis of contrasting criteria. In some cases, there seems to be no need to ascribe classificatory criteria at all. Ziegler devotes the core of the article to a discussion of indigenous concepts of genre in Turkey, providing the reader with a valuable and concise survey of Turkish folk music. A helpful chart at the end of the article clearly shows how different from each other individual genres really are. Still feeling the need to recognize order in the classification systems—European and Turkish—Ziegler concludes by stating that there probably is no resolution to the problems of incompatibility.

II

FIELDS OF FOLK-MUSIC SCHOLARSHIP

6

THEORY AND METHODS

Lying at the core of Central European theory and methods of folk-music scholarship is the problem of determining the objects of study themselves: folk music and folk song. The diversity that the different works present in this chapter document results from uncertainty and contestation, and from the changing perspectives that have accompanied the transformation of musical practices through history. I take that diversity, as well as the uncertainty and change that have produced it, as positive aspects of folk-music scholarship and the vitality that it continues to possess. Had folk music and folk song been fixed as objects of study, had there been no disagreement about their ontological status and context in culture, the theories and methods with which folk-music scholars approached their field would surely have reached a state of moribundity decades ago.

The problem of determining the object of study assumes distinctive forms in all the theories and methods that have dominated the field. The objective status of folk song is inevitably at issue in discussions of the appropriate processes of collecting and archiving folk music. The importance of the archive itself confirms this concern for objective status, suggesting that one of the most pressing problems faced by institutions is what to do with a folk song once it is collected. The concern for classification and archiving previously overwhelmed other issues raised by methods of collecting. For the most part, those who archived were different from those who collected; more than anything, both needed to share a sense of what type of material they were gathering and storing. With the influence of ethnomusicological methods on folk-music scholarship in the 1960s and 1970s, methodological attention has shifted toward collecting itself, and a new generation of scholars (e.g., Max Peter Baumann, Gerlinde Haid, and Wilhelm Schepping in this chapter) actively developed theories of fieldwork, which in turn transformed the nature of the field and the objective status of folk music itself.

The development of fieldwork theory has followed some very distinctive routes in Central European scholarship. The folk-music scholar rarely goes far afield in order to do fieldwork. Quite the contrary, the fieldworker not only knows the field well but generally has a more intimate relation with it. One of the challenges faced by the folk-music scholar in the field, then, is how to distance oneself from its social contexts. The critical methods of modern ethnography do not afford the folk-music scholar the convenience of writing oneself into or out of the field. Objectivity continues to plague many larger areas of research, especially those that are regionally or nationally based. Some projects, such as INFOLK (Informationssystem für Volksliedarchive in Österreich) in Austria and the computer-analytical methods of Emil Lubej and Helmut Schaffrath, have turned to electronic media, though not simply to store folk music. New methods of analysis are possible because of such projects, which rely less on the single song or piece of instrumental music as an object, but rather investigate the components of sound and performance that ascribe identity to folk music.

The concern for the objective status of folk music that dominated scholarship until the mid-twentieth century often overwhelmed any concerted attempts to develop methods that would account for the social, psychological, and historical influences on folk music. This situation has undergone considerable transformation during the past half century, not least because of the theories of Ernst Klusen and his colleagues in Neuß and the more socially-motivated theorizing that stemmed from Marxist scholarship in the German Democratic Republic and Eastern Europe. Klusen's theory of "group song," though on the surface not radically different from the widespread view that folk song was the "natural" result of human expression, located the impetus to sing in the social cohesion that caused individuals to form groups. Wilhelm Schepping extends these notions to modern social contexts, theorizing the persistent presence of singing on diverse occasions, often creating a larger mosaic of smaller musical groups. Max Peter Baumann takes the notion of modernity several steps farther by observing the ways in which recovered and constructed objects of folk music allow for revived performances of the past. To some extent, Baumann returns to the object of folk song itself (e.g., in his attention to the composed "yodel song"), but in fact he and other recent scholars have succeeded in integrating the context and object in their theories and methods.

As it does throughout this book, the "cultivation of folk music" (*Volksmusikpflege*) appears here in the theories and methods of Central European scholarship. Laypeople who actively learn folk songs and dances, and then create new contexts for their performance, participate in the objectification of folk music. They often publish and disseminate older music or, in fact, music that they, as fieldworkers, have located in their own regions. In many ways, forms of folk-music cultivation bear close resemblance to early collecting projects; occasionally, they may be modeled on the methods of these projects, especially in Bavaria and Austria. Folk music and folk song as objects have not disappeared from the practices of European folk musicians and scholars but have instead provided them with complex ways of connecting tradition to modernity, and of emblematizing the past in the present.

※

137. Baumann, Max Peter. *Musikfolklore und Musikfolklorismus: Eine ethnomusikologische Untersuchung zum Funktionswandel des Jodels.* ("Musical Folklore and Musical Folklorismus: An Ethnomusicological Study of the Transformation of Function in Yodeling"). Winterthur: Amadeus, 1976.

Using the diverse ways in which yodeling has served as a means of ascribing local and traditional, national and modern identities in Switzerland, this book sketches a theory of ethnomusicological study based on changing functions. Baumann divides the book into three sections, the first two devoted to a survey of ethnomusicological methods and the ways they can assist in constructing theories to examine the changing shapes of tradition, and the third section to a history of yodeling in Switzerland, past and present. Baumann understands the theoretical problem for modern ethnomusicology to reside in the dialectic represented by his main title. The musical practices of tradition (i.e., those connected to specific social functions) differ from those that are invented to place tradition on a stage, as if separated from their initial functions. Neither set of musical practices is more important than the other, but many ethnomusicologists and folk-music scholars have studied the latter as if they were really the former. The empirical example of yodeling in Switzerland vividly demonstrates the ways in which these two sets of musical practices are dependent on each other and interact to create the modern music history of Switzerland. The creation of a genre of *Jodellied* ("yodel song") through published compositions in the nineteenth century was no less powerful a means of ascribing Swiss identity—indeed, a national, rather than local, Swiss identity—even though yodeling in the *Jodellied* had functions completely different from rural and local practices. This book is extremely valuable both as a theoretical model for an ethnomusicology of Europe and as an ethnomusicological history of a nationalist identity.

138. Baumann, Max Peter. "Aspekte zum Problem der musikologischen Ethnographie." ("Aspects of the Problems in Musical Ethnography"). In Deutsche Gesellschaft für Musik des Orients, ed., *Musikologische Feldforschung—Aufgaben, Erfahrungen, Techniken.* Hamburg: Karl Dieter Wagner, 1981. Pp. 12–36.

A survey of fundamental concepts of ethnomusicological fieldwork and a sketch of the necessary components of successful field study. Baumann takes as his premise that fieldwork arises from the connections of ethnomusicology to ethnology and anthropology, and he therefore brings to the fore concepts from those fields. In particular, his discussions of objectivity provide the opportunity to examine European ethnographic literature on this topic. Visual models in the second part of the article suggest different relations between the observer and those being studied, with fairly systematic paths along which observations and recorded materials must pass when transformed from field data to interpretation. Baumann lays special emphasis on the processes involved with transcribing field observations (*protokollieren*), and he argues for several different forms of transcription to account for the numerous techniques of observation that the ethnomusicological fieldworker employs.

139. Deutsche Gesellschaft für Musik des Orients, ed. *Musikologische Feldforschung—Aufgaben, Erfahrungen, Techniken.* ("Musicological Field Research: Conditions, Experiences, Techniques"). Hamburg: Karl Dieter Wagner, 1981.

A volume of essays on different problems and techniques in ethnomusicological fieldwork. The authors are German and Austrian ethnomusicologists or folk-music researchers, but their essays offer case studies from many different cultures, within and outside Europe. The first set of essays addresses conceptual and methodological problems, ranging from the ethnographic and psychological concerns in the field and new venues for conducting fieldwork to the nature of archiving and documenting sound recordings. The second set of essays comprises individual field studies, for the most part brief, but usually valuable because of their concise discussions of special field conditions. The volume is a *Gedenkschrift* (memorial volume) for Kurt Reinhard (1914-1979), the teacher of many of the scholars writing here and the founder of the ethnomusicology program at the Free University of Berlin. The essays are valuable additionally as intellectual history, an introduction to European institutions for ethnomusicological study, and a survey of disciplines upon which Central Europeans draw in the construction of fieldwork methods.

140. Dietrich, Wolf. "Psychologische Einflußfaktoren bei der Feldaufnahme." ("Psychological Influences during Field Recording"). In Deutsche Gesellschaft für Musik des Orients, ed., *Musikologische Feldforschung—Aufgaben, Erfahrungen, Techniken.* Hamburg: Karl Dieter Wagner, 1981. Pp. 55–65.

Argues that a musician's response to the fieldworker and the making of field recordings necessarily differs from the normal conditions of performance. Using examples from his own field experiences in southeastern Europe, Dietrich observes that musicians are unable to create the feeling of *keyif* or *kéfi* (well-being or comfort) for the tape recorder. Other musicians, believing that they must perform in a certain way, for example, with virtuosity or in a style that is particularly representative of tradition, alter their performances accordingly for the fieldworker. Dietrich makes no claim for changing these psychological conditions, only for remaining always and acutely aware of them.

141. Dittmar, Jürgen, ed. *Dokumentationsprobleme heutiger Volksmusikforschung.* ("Documentation Problems in Contemporary Folk-Music Research"). Bern: Peter Lang, 1987. (Studien zur Volksliedforschung, 2).

Papers, printed reports, and discussion from a conference of the Commission for Song, Dance, and Music Research in the German Society for Folklore (DGV). An enormous range of "problems" with an even greater range of solutions appears in these essays and reports from individual archives and research centers. The volume begins with a call from Wilhelm Schepping for the identification of common problems and the need for concerted efforts to make documentation and analysis more comparable. Otto Holzapfel (Freiburg im Breisgau), Erich Wimmer (Würzburg), and Stefaan Top (Leuven, Belgium) follow with descriptions of the approaches to documentation that have developed in their archives during the twentieth century. Individual studies of and approaches to folk dance constitute a thematic area, with Norwegian, German, and Austrian dance research brought into comparison. The closing essays focus on the promise of computer and film documentation, presentations ranging from the schematic (Gerlinde Haid for Austrian archives) to the technical (Helmut Schaffrath). Ulrich Schmitt closes the volume with an annotated bibliography of works in numerous languages devoted to the classification of folk-song melody. The volume as a whole suggests that documentation of folk music and folk dance, as well as archival and analytical practices, had reached a watershed in the mid-1980s, when traditional methods were yielding rapidly to electronically-assisted methods.

142. Elsner, Jürgen, and Givi Ordžonikidze, ed. *Sozialistische Musikkultur: Traditionen–Probleme–Perspektiven.* ("Socialistic Music Culture: Traditions–Problems–Perspectives"). Vol. 2. Berlin: Verlag Neue Musik, 1983.

A collection of essays on "the contemporary song" by scholars and musicians in socialist nations. Contemporary song is interpreted in the broadest terms, though inevitably within a dialectical framework. The dialectic usually embodies historical processes, for example the social changes that transformed folk song into a song for the masses. Moments that undergird and mobilize the dialectic (e.g., the creation of resistance or anti-fascist songs before and during World War II) play a special role in the individual histories of the nations represented here, the socialist countries of Eastern Europe, the Soviet Union, and Vietnam. A copublication of the Soviet Union and the German Democratic Republic, this collection concerns itself with both national developments (see, e.g., essays by Leon Markiewicz on the "Polish Mass Song" and Tú Ngoc on "Songs about Revolutionary Fighters in Vietnam") or the universal and international trajectory of socialist songs (see, e.g., essays by János Márothy on "Traditions of Democratic Music-Making" and Inge Lammel on the "Relation between Workers' Song and Folk Song"). Because the articles cover such diverse topics and historical moments but share a common desire to unify socialist and Marxist approaches in order to rethink the history of folk and workers' music in the late twentieth century, the volume as a whole is one of the best examples of the range of Marxist theory and methods. The articles also serve to portray in ethnomusicological terms the music of that part of the world that was—and remains—largely unknown to English-speaking scholars.

143. Haid, Gerlinde. "Zur Methodologie volksmusikalischer Feldforschung in Österreich." ("On the Methodology of Folk-Music Field Research in Austria"). In Deutsche Gesellschaft für Musik des Orients, ed., *Musikologische Feldforschung—Aufgaben, Erfahrungen, Techniken.* Hamburg: Karl Dieter Wagner, 1981. Pp. 37–54.

Primarily historical study of the development of fieldwork in Austrian folk-music and folk-dance research. Beginning with the early initiatives to use field-recording mechanisms, and concluding with attempts by the Österreichisches Volksliedwerk (Austrian Folk-Song Works) to systematize collection and archiving of folk music collected by teams of scholars, the article introduces the reader to attitudes toward informants and transcription held by some of Austria's foremost scholars, for example Josef Pommer, Karl Magnus Klier, and Leopold Schmidt. Motivating principles of several leading institutions for folk- and popular-music research, notably the programs in music sociology at the Vienna Music Academy and the Institute for Folk-Music Research, also reveal interesting shifts in the conceptualization of fieldwork in Austria. The article closes with a systematic outline of proposed steps for contemporary folk-music fieldwork.

144. Haid, Gerlinde. "Tradition und Innovation als musikalische Phänomene der Volksmusik in Österreich in der zweiten Hälfte des 20. Jahrhunderts." ("Tradition and Innovation as Musical

Phenomena of Folk Music in Austria during the Second Half of the Twentieth Century"). In Walter Deutsch, ed., *Tradition und Innovation*. Vienna: A. Schendl, 1987. Pp. 14–23.

Examines the traditionalization of innovation in Austrian *Volksmusikpflege* (cultivation of folk music), arguing that folk music today results from an active concern for maintaining tradition by a small number of activists. Haid's thesis is optimistic, based on the theoretical perspectives of Walter Deutsch and Franz Eibner, who have viewed change as ongoing and diversification as constant. A few excellent case studies illustrate this thesis. From the music itself, Haid cites the ways in which polyphony, always a component of some genres of Austrian folk song, has become an identifying characteristic, spreading throughout numerous genres and increasing in complexity. The chromatic hammered dulcimer (*Hackbrett*) serves as another example, in which the instrument builder and musician Tobi Reiser (1907-1974) introduced an instrument that would make performing from different repertories easier, but which became an instrument common largely in the activities of folk-music cultivators. New settings for folk music were also cultivated, ranging from special competitions at mid-century to the inns and taverns that sponsored regular special gatherings. Although some aspects of this new folk scene may seem artificial, together the *Volksmusikpflege* innovations have created a healthy tradition of folk music in Austria at the end of the twentieth century.

145. Haid, Gerlinde. "Volksmusikalische Feldforschung in Salzburg (mit besonderer Berücksichtigung der Exkursionen seit 1975)." ("Folk-Music Fieldwork in Salzburg [with Special Emphasis on the Excursions since 1975]"). In Rudolf Pietsch, ed., *Die Volksmusik im Lande Salzburg*, Vol. 2. Vienna: A. Schendl, 1990. Pp. 13–27.

Reflexive consideration of team fieldwork efforts in the Austrian province of Salzburg. Undertaken by scholars from Vienna, as well as local practitioners and experts, these efforts began as an attempt to collect as much material as possible in the Austrian province with the smallest folk-music archive. Fieldwork took place through the investigations of teams that self-consciously adapted long-standing fieldwork methodologies to the conditions encountered in the late twentieth century. The questionnaires and other methodologies notwithstanding, individuals and teams followed different paths and encountered the music-making of the province in individualized ways. In particular, many fieldworkers found themselves actively engaged in music-making, that is, joining together with folk musicians. Through intensive and thick descriptions of local traditions and by revisiting villages, valleys, and many musicians, the excursions revealed a rich tradition of music-making, which folk-music

research stood to encourage through its encouragement of
traditional practices. A detailed look at concepts of fieldwork from
the Austrian perspective, which stresses fieldwork as the point of
departure for research.

146. Hoerburger, Felix, Erich Stockmann, and Wolfgang Suppan.
"Volksgesang, Volksmusik und Volkstanz." ("Folk Song, Folk
Music, and Folk Dance"). In Friedrich Blume, ed., *Die Musik in
Geschichte und Gegenwart*. Vol. 13. Kassel: Bärenreiter, 1966.
Columns 1923–56.

A survey of the basic definitions, history, and literature in the
study of European folk music, condensed as an entry in the first
edition of the major German-language encyclopedia of music.
The perspectives provided by the authors in their separate
subentries are distinctive because of the emphasis they place on
the musical aspects of folk music, hence even the distinctive use in
the title of the less common *Volksgesang* rather than *Volkslied*. The
article begins with a concise but inclusive survey of definitions,
which sets folk music apart from other types of music-making in
cultures where there is a discernible "level" that differs from, yet
exists in relation to, a "high culture." The following subentry
under *Volksgesang* examines different approaches to the analysis
and interpretation of European folk song, with particular
attention given to the methods of Hungarian scholarship and the
classification of German folk-song melodies. One of the most
important aspects of this article is its inclusion of instrumental
folk music together with the study of melody and dance, all of
which together evoke a comprehensive framework for folk music
in all its aspects. Hoerburger and Stockmann provide two
distinctive approaches to instrumental music and folk-music
instruments, the first drawn more from function, the second more
from material and structure. The article closes with a subentry on
folk dance in its social contexts and finally with extensive
bibliographies. Although it is necessarily limited to the space
available in an encyclopedia, this article nonetheless provides one
of the most useful introductions to European folk music. A new
edition of *Die Musik in Geschichte und Gegenwart* began to appear
in 1994, with individual volumes appearing according to their
order in the alphabet; the article that will supersede this entry in
the first edition will therefore not be published for many years.

147. *Infolk: Informationssystem für Volksliedarchive in Österreich.*
("INFOLK: Information System for Folk-Song Archives in
Austria"). Project Director: Gerlinde Haid; Editorial Direction:
Dorli Draxler, Walter Deutsch, et al. Vienna: Österreichisches
Volksliedwerk, 1991. Special edition of *Jahrbuch des Österreichischen
Volksliedwerks* 39/40.

The product of a ten-year project to gather and computerize all the relevant criteria for the classification and comparison of folk-music materials in all Austrian archives. The eventual goal of the project is a complete edition of Austrian folk song. Seven main areas of comparison have been established, which allow a general portrait of each song and also subsume larger fields of individual parameters applicable to the songs. These fields and parameters contain an enormous level of detail, so much so that 120 pages alone are necessary for a listing of the definitions and concepts used in determining the correct fields for each example and classification. Characteristic of Austrian approaches to classification, the project includes materials from an impressive number of resources, involving provincial and regional archives, as well as the activities and contributions of individual folk-music practitioners. It is also a significant contribution of the project that it integrates many more materials than just the transcriptions of individual songs; photographs, slides, and contextual materials contribute to the portrait of local and regional traditions. *INFOLK*'s gigantic dimensions require the input and continued cooperation of professional and amateur scholars and musicians throughout Austria, perhaps making it difficult for those without considerable computing skill, but those who contribute to it and employ it in their research will necessarily take part in the rich tradition of national, regional, and local research that has characterized Austrian scholarship for at least a century.

148. Kaden, Christian. *Hirtensignale—Musikalische Syntax und kommunikative Praxis*. ("Shepherds' Calls: Musical Syntax and Communicative Practice"). Leipzig: VEB Deutscher Verlag für Musik, 1977. (Beiträge zur musikwissenschaftlichen Forschung in der DDR, 9)

Conducting extensive fieldwork in the hilly regions of Thuringia and Saxony in the former German Democratic Republic, where sheepherding was still practiced in the 1970s, Kaden seeks to establish links between the communication systems used by shepherds with their herds and musical practices in the society where these forms of labor and economy survived. Kaden does not endeavor to make connections between all elements that might be shared between communicative and musical systems, but rather only some that demonstrate similar processes of constructing syntactic structures in the systems. On one hand, the methodology grows from Marxist concerns for the relation between social structures and the communicative syntaxes that connect human activities to society and history. On the other, the methodology synthesizes concepts from a remarkably diverse intellectual tradition, little known in the West during the separation of Europe from ca. 1950 to 1990. Kaden illustrates his arguments with numerous transcriptions and with extensive charts that demonstrate the paths of communication that create a syntax for shepherds' calls and for the musical practices of the region. Kaden concerns himself with the transformation of this syntax through history, recognizing that the diminishing need for communication with shepherds' calls paralleled the potential of musical practices to communicate in direct ways. Perhaps the most detailed study in any language to examine why and how linguistic and musical systems can reflect each other.

149. Karbusicky, Vladimir. *Kosmos—Mensch—Musik: Strukturalistische Anthropologie des Musikalischen*. ("Cosmos—Human Being—Music: Structural Anthropology of the Musical"). Hamburg: Krämer, 1990.

An interpretation of the metaphysics of music as a product and conjuncture of various structures, primarily utilizing the intellectual framework of Prague linguistics and structuralism, of which Karbusicky is the leading proponent in musical scholarship. Karbusicky argues that "the musical" resides in six basic forms of structure, and that these evolve along a path of increasing complexity to create music itself. This evolution is reifiable at different levels, and a principle of energy immanent in the musical transforms music from one of these levels to the next. Important is the identification of these structures, paths of evolution, and levels of complexity, which give the scholar the chance to investigate music's metaphysical stuff in different stages and forms. A major contribution of the book is the ways in which different structuralist discourses are woven together, as music theorists such as Heinrich Schenker and Ernst Kurth are compared to Claude Lévi-Strauss and Boris Assafiev. Also an excellent primer for music semiotics and linguistic structuralism. Finally, the reader will find the book to be an accessible intellectual history of theories concerning structuralism and music.

150. Klusen, Ernst. "Feldforschung bei Medienproduzenten und -konsumenten: Anmerkungen zu künftigen Forschungsansätzen." ("Fieldwork with the Media Producers and Consumers: Remarks on Future Research Approaches"). In Deutsche Gesellschaft für Musik des Orients, ed., *Musikologische Feldforschung—Aufgaben, Erfahrungen, Techniken*. Hamburg: Karl Dieter Wagner, 1981. Pp. 93–105.

Arguing that electronic media will soon be the most important sites of musical activity in the modern age, this article postulates ways in which ethnomusicological fieldwork can provide a conduit for studying modern music cultures. Klusen was the foremost proponent of studying folk music as the musical practices of groups (see other works by Klusen, annotated in the present volume), and this essay interprets fieldwork in the media as means of understanding the formation of group music cultures and the social conditions of modern music-making. In his speculative thesis Klusen argues that fieldwork would provide a means of understanding the links between the domains of producer and consumer. The fieldwork methods themselves, nevertheless, are fairly traditional, altered only to respond to the special conditions of working in the radio and recording industry, and in the consumption of mediated music.

151. Klusen, Ernst. *Singen: Materialien zu einer Theorie*. ("Singing: Materials toward a Theory"). Regensburg: Gustav Bosse, 1989. (Perspektiven zur Musikpädagogik und Musikwissenschaft, 11).

　　The final book by Ernst Klusen, at once a culmination of his earlier theories on the phenomenon of singing and an attempt to formulate these as an overarching theory. Klusen organizes the studies here around three major topics: song itself; thought; and social contexts. He draws upon the earlier areas of research, particularly *Gruppenlieder* (group songs) and the dialectic *Funktion--Interaktion* (function and [social] interaction). The major contribution of the book, nevertheless, is Klusen's investigation of song as a human *Grundsicht* (fundamental level), as a phenomenon of expression connected with other—to some extent, all other—human communicative activities. The earliest forms of song, for example, develop at the same moment as crying and melodies with vocables. From these forms of expression different forms of vocal music-making develop in evolutionary stages, for example through the gradual choice of certain intervals and textual forms. Enhancing the book's value are also the examples drawn from non-Western, especially Asian, musics and religions. Although there is no reason that fundamental forms of singing cannot be understood as developmental rather than evolutionary, Klusen musters a broad range of theories and concepts from psychology, philosophy, and social theory, situating this book and Klusen's own theoretical development within the complex intellectual history of research on song and music-making, a history that ranges from Nicolai Hartmann and Theodor Adorno to Klusen's own paradigmatic theories, which form the basis of *musikalische Volkskunde* (musical folklore) in the second half of the twentieth century.

152. Lenk, Carsten. "Gepflegte Volksmusik—mehr Erfindung als Fund? Aneignung und Vermittlung von Liedern am Beispiel eines ostbayerischen Volksmusikpflegers." ("Cultivated Folk

Music: More Invention Than Discovery? An East Bavarian Folk-Song Cultivator as Example of the Appropriation and Mediation of Songs"). *Jahrbuch für Volksliedforschung* 37 (1992): 34–64.

Examines the development of a concept of folk music in the post-World War II period by a resident of eastern Bavaria, Otto Peisl. For want of a suitable concept of folk music and a system of practices for the Upper Palatinate region in which he lived, Peisl turned to earlier writings on what folk music ideally should be, in particular through the theories of the Austrian Josef Pommer, who disseminated his writings on alpine folk song in the journal *Das deutsche Volkslied*. It was necessary for Peisl to use various media—print and broadcast—to popularize his concepts among folklore groups and musical organizations. Necessarily, some domains of folk-music cultivation were successful, whereas others were ignored. The article provides an excellent example of the processes and intellectual history of *Volksmusikpflege* (cultivation of folk music), in which folk music is in the hands of those who did not originally create it. *Volksmusikpflege* is particularly important in Bavaria and Austria, and it has contributed substantially to the vitality of folk music and scholarship during much of the twentieth century. The author makes a strong case for more scholarly attention to *Volksmusikpflege*, which has until now been largely neglected.

153. Lubej, Emil H. "Quantitative Methoden in der vergeleichend-systematischen Musikwissenschaft: Automatische Intonations-analyse über die multimodale Verteilung und deren statisch-geographische Auswertung am Beispiel der Gesänge der *tenores* aus Sardinien." ("Quantitative Methods in Comparative-Systematic Musicology: Automatic Intonation Analysis through Division into Different Modalities and Their Statistical-Geographic Evaluation as Exemplified by the Songs of the *Tenores* in Sardinia"). *Musicologica Austraica* 7 (1987): 129-55.

Using analytical methods he developed at the computer laboratory of the Musicology Department at the University of Vienna, Lubej distinguishes different styles in the four-part polyphonic style of close-singing practiced by the *tenores* of Sardinia. For the most part, this singing style is used for sacred occasions, but Lubej demonstrates connections to secular practices. By dividing the different voices of the *tenores* style into the constituent parts of various parameters (e.g., pitch, duration, overtones), Lubej is able to determine stylistic groupings, which in turn reflect local and regional groupings in Sardinia. Charts demonstrate the different results of dividing the different parameters, and two maps of Sardinia illustrate how the stylistic differences cluster in certain ways. The article painstakingly details the technological materials and procedures used in these experiments, and Lubej has described these in general terms, hence making this article useful for scholars throughout the world. A superb example of the Austrian comparative-systematic method in ethnomusicology, which combines fieldwork and the laboratory analysis of sound.

154. Meixner, Walter. "Der 'Alpenländische Volksmusikwettbewerb' in Innsbruck—Ein Indikator für Innovation und Tradition in der Volksmusikpflege?" ("The 'Alpine-Land Folk-Music Contest' in Innsbruck—An Indicator of Innovation and Tradition in Folk-Music Cultivation?"). In Walter Deutsch, ed., *Tradition und Innovation*. Vienna: A. Schendl, 1987. Pp. 196–217.

Close examination of the "cultivation of folk music" (*Volksmusikpflege*) in Tyrol, south Germany, and German-speaking Südtirol in northern Italy by looking at the records from the Alpine-Land Folk-Music Contest in Innsbruck, Austria. These statistics reveal the extensive cultivation within family ensembles in Tyrol, but considerably less so outside Tyrol. From the first contest in 1974, an increase in participation is evident, but so too is a diversification of ensembles and activities during the course of the festival. Meixner compiles responses and statistics from application forms and surveys used for the contest (and published here as appendices), thereby allowing the individual participants to offer their own thoughts about the cultivation of folk music. The article is broadly comparative, showing that contests and gatherings that bring folk musicians, enthusiasts, and scholars together have historically provided support for folk music in Austria, situating it in a larger public sphere. Developing the theme of the volume in which this article appears ("innovation and tradition"), Meixner argues that public cultivation of folk music employs innovation to strengthen tradition.

155. Probst-Effah, Gisela, ed. *Feldforschung heute*. ("Fieldwork Today"). Neuß: Institut für Musikalische Volkskunde der Universität Düsseldorf, 1983.

Papers and discussions from a conference of the Commission for Song, Dance, and Music Research of the German Society for Folklore (DGV), examining the changing materials and methods of fieldwork. The underlying theme of the conference was the need to confront modern settings in which humans make music. These mean a shift of attention from rural to urban settings, as well as to an inclusion of more from the social surroundings in which music is made. Fieldwork should also emphasize a flow of information in two directions, which, according to essays by Günther Noll and Wilhelm Schepping, is facilitated by electronic media. The new fieldwork must reconceptualize the music-maker, for example by including those who listen to the radio or otherwise consume music. Computers and other resources of technological advance are also discussed as means of bringing about extensive transformation of fieldwork techniques. Although new fieldwork methods may necessitate a redefinition of the field, the concluding essays (e.g., by Gerlinde Haid) stress that the human component will essentially remain the same in future methods of fieldwork.

156. Puchner, Walter, ed. *Tod und Jenseits im europäischen Volkslied.* ("Death and the Otherworld in European Folk Song"). Jannina [Crete]: University of Jannina, Faculty of Philosophy, Department of Folklore, 1988. (Publications of Folklore Museum and Archives, 6).

A collection of essays from an international ballad congress, this volume contains various attempts to thematize a motif from both traditional and modern methodological perspectives. Death motifs are not only common in European folk-song genres, but death provides the central context for entire genres in Europe (e.g., laments in Greece or northeastern Europe). The volume editor, Walter Puchner, suggests a typology that might allow scholars to seek similaralities among these different treatments of death. Hermann Strobach and David Buchan investigate motif clusters in the German and English ballad repertories, both demonstrating the ways in which the ballad as genre bounds these clusters. Klaus Roth and Johanna Roth examine the presence of gruesome acts in Bulgarian broadsides, Tom Cheesman in English broadsides. The section devoted to laments is fascinating because of the diverse traditions the authors examine and the resulting comparative possibilities. The essays on Italian and Sardinian lament traditions are important new contributions. Also integrated into the discussions accompanying this conference report are commentaries on fieldwork, which compare some of the special problems faced in studying the contexts of folk song and death. A multilingual volume, this book offers valuable new approaches to folk-song research.

157. Schaffrath, Helmut, ed. *Computer in der Musik: Über den Einsatz in Wissenschaft.* ("Computers in Music: On the Entry into Scholarship, Composition, and Pedagogy"). Stuttgart: Metzler, 1991.

Essays on the state of the art in various musical areas affected by computer technologies. The authors range across the disciplines of music and beyond into other disciplines. Several authors concern themselves specifically with uses of computer technology to develop new pedagogical approaches (e.g., Bernd Enders and Ulrich Bloman). Others look at compositional problems (Dirk Reith) and notational innovations for analysis (Ioannis Zannos). Artificial intelligence (Marc Leman) and the use of computers for innovative approaches to music perception (Helmut Schaffrath) further reveal the extent to which European scholars are employing computers to transform the areas of their scholarship. In at least one essay (Enders) there is considerable criticism of the lack of unifying computer languages available to the German layperson and professional, thereby hindering the real possibilities for further rapid development of computer technology in music. The research here derives primarily from the technology and research in European, especially German, ethnomusicology and music pedagogy, but this makes the book a valuable contribution to the intellectual history of the late twentieth century. The quality of its essays will assure it a position in comparative studies for years to come.

158. Schepping, Wilhelm. "Tradition und Innovation in aktueller Brauchmusik: Ausgewählte Beispiele." ("Tradition and Innovation in Contemporary Functional Music: Selected Examples"). In Walter Deutsch and Wilhelm Schepping, eds., *Musik im Brauch der Gegenwart*. Vienna: A. Schendl, 1988. Pp. 213–27.

Using newspaper articles and advertisements, as well as other public announcements concerning social and musical events in the Rhineland city Neuß for the weekend of July 12-13, 1986, Schepping examines the relation between music and its functions in negotiating between functionality and tradition in the past and present. From the beginning of this survey it is remarkable just how many public music events actually appear in the media and then how thoroughly the musical contents are described. Also striking is the extent to which it is evident that the events are not only well attended, but that many report growing participation in recent years. Such active use of music to accompany other events, moreover, occurs in religious realms (e.g., in a pilgrimage and in other processions) and popular realms (e.g., street celebrations with rock music). Schepping interprets these seeming extremes as part of a larger fabric, in which music provides a necessary vehicle for the performance and social meaningfulness of cultural practices. This interpretation contrasts with claims that music is separated from social functions in the modern world. Schepping also relates the categories and concepts he sketches here to research done by other Central European scholars, suggesting that some general conclusions about modern folk-music practices are possible. Excellent example of the ways to use newspapers and other media sources to study folk-music practices.

159. Schepping, Wilhelm. "Zur Problematik der Objektbestimmung heutiger Volksmusikforschung." ("On the Problematic of Determining the Object of Study in the Folk-Music Research of Today"). In Jürgen Dittmar, ed., *Dokumentationsprobleme heutiger Volksmusikforschung.* Bern: Peter Lang, 1987. Pp. 31–48.

The keynote lecture in a conference on modern folk-music research (see Dittmar 1987). Schepping avoids entering the debates on the appropriateness of the concept folk music, preferring instead to admit to the fruitfulness of its contested nature. He identifies six points of departure that folk-music research has employed, and that have been reformulated in the late twentieth century as folk-music research enters a new era. These are discussed schematically, with relevant literature cited for each. Schepping calls the first point of departure "sociological," whereby he refers to the many folk-music studies that depend on the individual or individuals who transmit music. The second has the name "essentialist-normative," whereby Schepping means the importance accorded to definitions and naming (e.g., Herder's coining of the term "Volkslied" or the persistent connection to "oral tradition"). The "phenomenological" point of departure privileges the actual conditions of folk music, not idealized transmission, but those who actually perform and consume it. The "functional-interactive" approach relies on an understanding of folk music's social contexts and cultural practices. The fifth point of departure, called "operational," shifts focus from folk music as object to subject, in other words, as a practice that acquires different and changing meanings and functions. Finally, the "empirical-statistical" results from a more fully quantitative study of the conditions and distribution of music-making phenomena. The modern study of folk music, Schepping concludes, is ever more inclusive, and therefore scholars should be optimistic about its capacity to contribute to the broadest possible understanding of music and culture.

160. Schötz, Franz, ed. *Volksmusik: Forschung und Pflege in Bayern: Alte und neue Formen "überlieferter Lieder".* ("Folk Music: Research and Cultivation in Bavaria: Old and New Singing Forms for 'Transmitted Songs'"). Munich: Bayerischer Landesverein für Heimatpflege, 1991.

Essays by scholars, practitioners, and regional researchers (*Heimatforscher*) into the current state of singing. Most essays report on practices in Bavaria, though other parts of southern Germany and Austria also receive attention. The overall claim of the authors is that individuals must sing, hence folk music survives in the modern world. Some authors (e.g., Wilhelm Schepping) address the psychological, even biological, reasons for singing, whereas others (e.g., Franz Schötz describing an evening of singing in a tavern) examine the social settings in which singing continues to play an important role. Additional approaches to the problem include those drawn from philosophy, music therapy, and feminist studies. As a whole, the essays document a larger region in which singing, both individual and group practices, plays an extraordinarily important cultural role, but the various approaches suggest that the reasons for this may be vastly different. If there is a larger "singing culture" of Bavaria, then, it results from the concerted efforts of individuals and the interactions of local groups.

161. Stockmann, Doris, ed. *Volks- und Popularmusik in Europa.* ("Folk and Popular Music in Europe"). With contributions by Philip Bohlman, Oskár Elschek, Alica Elscheková, Roberto Leydi, Jan Ling, Andreas Michel, James Porter, Reidar Sevåg, Erich Stockmann, and Peter Wicke. Laaber: Laaber-Verlag, 1992. (Neues Handbuch der Musikwissenschaft, 12).

The most comprehensive study of folk and popular music in Europe, the methods used to research that repertory, and the history of scholarship devoted to this study. The final volume in a series devoted to a comprehensive examination of music and musical scholarship, this book both uses folk music and folk-music scholarship to construct a field devoted to the study of the "other" within Europe—those whose music is folk, ethnic, or vernacular—and reformulates European folk-music scholarship in the late twentieth century as the product of a new ethnomusicology with a new Europe as its subject. Certain approaches in the volume treat Europe as a culturally-unified whole, for example the opening chapter devoted to intellectual history and research methods, and the second chapter, which focuses on folk music as a component inseparable from work and everyday life. Other approaches uncover the distinctive patterns of European folk music and the processes of change that have produced new repertories, uses, and functions of music, especially popular music, rock, and jazz, at the end of the twentieth century. The larger intellectual history of the book relies on a trajectory from local to international practices, and Europe takes on distinctively different forms along the historical continuum this trajectory produces. It is one of the major contributions of the book that it examines traditional approaches to folk music with more innovative theories and methods. Chapter 3, "Singing forms and vocal genres," divides Europe up according to regions, and then by linguistic, national, or repertory divisions within those regions. Although such divisions have perhaps the longest history in European folk-music scholarship, several assume new forms here, for example the extensive treatment of circumpolar traditions in Scandinavia (e.g., the Sami), Jewish popular music in

Central Europe, and interethnic contact in all the regions. Chapter 4, "Instrumentarium of folk music," and chapter 5, "Regional instrumental practices," serve as an excellent pairing of traditional (e.g., Sachs-Hornbostel classification) and innovative (e.g., practice-based concepts) organological methods. Chapter 6, "Folk and popular music as processes of history," examines the fundamental historicizing impulse that folk-music scholars have long associated with Europe, indeed with the bounding of folk music itself, but takes it also into the modern era, for example with the consideration of "second existence" and revival in the concluding section. The concluding chapter, "Jazz, rock, and pop music," does little to locate these popular musics in Europe or in the processes of history and practice that are examined elsewhere in the book but nonetheless makes an important gesture toward opening up European folk-music scholarship to the popular and the international, thereby expanding the conceptual basis for modern ethnomusicological studies of Europe. Doris Stockmann has taken great pains to include new scholarly voices and overviews of cutting-edge analytical technologies (e.g., computer analysis). The volume also provides the first major attempt to combine Western and Eastern European scholarship, which broadens its perspectives considerably. Extensive use of transcriptions (176), photographs (153), tables (20), and other forms of illustration richly contribute to the documentation in the book. The bibliographies that accompany individual chapters and the discography that appears at the end are the most extensive in any one work devoted to the study of folk music. An indispensable source for the study of Europe and its folk-music traditions.

162. Suppan, Wolfgang. *Der musizierende Mensch: Eine Anthropologie der Musik.* ("The Music-Making Human: An Anthropology of Music"). Mainz: Schott, 1984.

An introduction to the use of anthropological approaches to the study of music, in many ways attempting to serve as a German version of Alan P. Merriam's *The Anthropology of Music* (1964). Surveying the different Central European anthropological methods, Suppan nonetheless limits his theoretical models—the three theses around which he organizes the book—to the different ways in which music and other aspects of culture interact. The anthropology of music proposed in this book, therefore, relies extensively on historical observations of other scholars, as well as on the materialist concept that music is a tool that does cultural work when used by human beings. Suppan's three theses, summarized in Part B (pp. 26–31), are: (1) musical anthropology is not a product of music, but rather of music-making; (2) as a part of the human symbolic world, music functions to communicate; and (3) music is an object used by

humans. The book samples a wide range of European
scholarship, some of which (e.g., the relation of music to legal
actions) will be relatively new to the English-speaking reader. The
survey of historical literature on European vernacular musics
serves as a substantial source of information, if indeed the
anthropological theories treated by Suppan have largely been
supplanted by more critical methods in sociocultural
anthropology.

163. Suppan, Wolfgang, ed. *Schladminger Gespräche zum Thema Musik
und Tourismus.* ("Discussions at Schladming of the Theme, 'Music
and Tourism'"). Tutzing: Schneider, 1991. (Musikethnologische
Sammelbände, 12).

A collection of papers from the Thirtieth Congress of the
International Council for Traditional Music in Schladming,
Austria, one of whose themes was "The impact of tourism on
traditional musical life." Despite the claim of the title, perhaps
only one third of the articles actually examines tourism in any way
at all; another group concerns itself with music and modernity, for
example culture contact, while a final group has nothing whatever
to do with the theme of the volume. Several of the articles that do
examine the theme of tourism are the best in the volume (e.g.,
Lisbet Torb on the "Zorba dance," Melinda Russell on reggae,
Martin Ramstedt on Indonesian cultural politics, and Tatsuko
Takizawa on tourism and music in Japan and Singapore). The
historical studies of folk music (Rudolf Brandl, Helga Thiel, and
Ruth Davis) make a good case for understanding exchange
between producers and consumers of music as a condition that
has always been part of traditional music. Several articles,
including an introductory essay by the editor, assume the
unfortunate stance of bemoaning what their authors regard as the
negative impact of tourism. It is an important contribution of the
volume that it contains articles by two distinguished
ethnomusicologists written just before their deaths, John Blacking
and Ernst Emsheimer. Blemishing the volume is the inclusion by
the editor of a list of his own publications and his activities as an
academic at the Music Academy of Graz, none of which has
anything to do with the theme.

164. *Volksliedforschung heute.* ("Folk-Song Research Today"). Basel:
Schweizerische Gesellschaft für Volkskunde, 1983. (Beiträge zur
Volkskunde, 6).

Proceedings of a conference celebrating the seventy-fifth
anniversary of the Swiss Folk-Song Archive in Basel. A diverse
group of distinguished folk-music scholars, folklorists, and
ethnomusicologists used the occasion to voice their opinions on

the topic encapsulated in the title of the volume. These opinions are vastly different and sometimes at odds with each other, but together they offer an interesting cross-section of Central European approaches to folk-song research. Most of the papers recognize the shift from text-based studies to those that take as essential the influence of social and historical context. Whereas some papers call for a more intensive study of context within Europe (e.g., Rolf Wilhelm Brednich and Max Peter Baumann), others make a strong case for the geographic and theoretical breadth of cultural anthropology (e.g., Wolfgang Suppan). The need for recognizing a more complex field for "folk song" appears throughout (the best essay on the subject is that by Wilhelm Schepping), but there is little agreement as to whether that should mean classical or popular musics. The volume is one of the first to deal directly with the effects of National Socialism and twentieth-century politics on German song.

7

THEORETICAL SCHOOLS

The intellectual history of Central European folk-music scholarship comprises a collective biography that is legible from the top-down or from the bottom-up. Reading this collective biography from the bottom-up, one encounters the collectors and regional folklorists, whose intimate knowledge of an area, its inhabitants, and its musical traditions leads to the publication of editions and to public awareness of dialect and variant. The individuals contributing to this side of the collective appear in other chapters of this book, particularly in those concerning collections, regional folk music, and musicians. In the present chapter, I concern myself primarily with a collective biography of scholars, in fact of theorists. The theorists we encounter here are more often than not polemicists, whose belief in a particular model of folk music leads them to found institutions and to formulate their theories in journals, books, and theoretical schools, that is, colleagues and followers whose approaches to the field undergird and refine a core of basic theories. The historical importance of these theoretical schools cannot, I believe, be underestimated, for they heighten the visibility of folk music and folk-music scholarship in Central Europe and accordingly move the study of folk music into the public sphere, where, in the twentieth century, it has often been inseparable from the politics and ideologies of that sphere and the production of culture that such politics and ideologies often unleash.

The works surveyed and annotated in this chapter suggest that two different influences came to bear on the development of theoretical schools. The first of these was nation and nationalism, and it resides primarily in the cultural context with which folk music was interpreted. The second was production, that is, just who created and transmitted folk music. Both issues are evident in perhaps the major polemic in the early twentieth century, that between Josef Pommer and his colleagues in Austria, and John Meier and his colleagues in Germany. Meier's theoretical approach depended on a text-based conceptualization of folk song, in which songs and repertories themselves remained bound with a type of integrity that kept them intact as they passed from a written culture into oral tradition. Pommer, in contrast, argued for the constant creativity and inherent musicality of the individual musician. By privileging the text, Meier grounded his concepts in theory itself, further suggesting that oral tradition had an historical impetus of its own. Austrian scholars, most of whom were active musicians themselves, believed in the efficacy of cultivating the production of folk music and actively encouraging individuals and organizations supporting performance. Whereas the Pommer-Meier polemic emphasized the importance of music and musician in contrasting ways, Ernst Klusen developed another major theoretical school in the second half of the twentieth century. Developing a concept of "group song," Klusen shifted the production of folk song to the social collective.

The theoretical schools of Central European folk-song scholarhip provide very different ways of reading the political and intellectual history of Central Europe during the past two centuries. Pommer's notion of "German folk song" was inseparable in his theories from a larger cultural area in Central Europe, in which Germanness occupied a privileged position. The weight given by Meier to the dynamics of textual transmission seemingly distanced his theories from politics, which led to a virtual retreat from interaction with the ideological stances of other scholarly realms during the Nazi period. Nazi ideologies did, nonetheless, affect German folk-music scholarship profoundly, turning many scholars, such as Josef Müller-Blattau and Werner Danckert, toward racist and expansionist theories, and bringing other historical streams to an irreversible halt, as in the case of the Austrian scholars connected with the journal *Das deutsche Volkslied.*

The collective biography surveyed in this chapter, furthermore, sheds light on theories that have had surprisingly little impact and those that weave in and out of the intellectual history of Central European folk-music scholarship as persistent leitmotifs. Ethnology and anthropology, though evident in theories such as Ernst Klusen's concept of group song, Leopold Schmidt's complex concept of *Volksgesang* in context, or Christian Kaden's applications of music sociology, do not, in my view, influence the major theoretical schools in any substantive way. If the nature of creativity was at issue for Pommer and Meier, it had less to do with cultural context than with the formation and transmission of text. Anthropology has played a more important role in Austria, but in general the theories of modern ethnomusicology, indebted as they have been in the United States to anthropological thought, have exerted relatively little impact on folk-music scholarship. None of the major theoretical schools, for instance, critically examines fieldwork. Comparative research, in contrast, frequently lends itself to critical examination, as both Michael Weber and Walter Wiora argue in their intellectual histories of Central European scholarship.

This chapter places the major theoretical schools in historical frameworks. There are individual entries for many of the most influential monographs and for books that survey the issues of modern folk-music scholarship. These historical articles and books examine a span of slightly more than a century, and I have tried to leave no important time unrepresented. I have found it particularly important to consider the ways in which the ideologies of the Nazi period spawned certain theories, some of which are noticeably connected to theories before and after this period. Finally, I have sketched parallel histories of the polemic between Josef Pommer and John Meier by providing entries for the journals associated with their theoretical schools, *Das deutsche Volkslied* and the *Jahrbuch für Volksliedforschung*, examining volumes at intervals of approximately one decade. Theory has been important to the conceptualization and persistence of German folk music in the modern era, not least because of the visible ways in which the theoretical schools have forcefully placed folk music in public discourse and debate.

⚜

165. Baumann, Max Peter. "Methoden und Methodologie der Volksliedforschung: Eine Anmerkung zur Verstrickung des Subjekts im Objekt der Zeit" ("Methods and Methodology of Folk Song Research: Remarks on Linking the Subject to the Object of the Times"). *Jahrbuch für Volksliedforschung* 35 (1990): 26–32.

A philosophical and personally engaged reexamination of the object—the folk song—in folk-song research. Baumann probes the very usefulness of the concept of folk song, particularly in a late-twentieth-century society where complex political, moral, and ideological realities would seem to demand very different processes of perceiving the world from those on which most folk-song theories have been based. While arguing for theoretical approaches that more sensitively take account of the folk musician's perception of how her or his music-making responds to complex social realities, Baumann cautiously suggests that folk song could have a renewed usefulness if investigated in relation to those complex realities. Empirical illustrations come from team research by Baumann, his students, and his colleagues in Berlin (see Baumann, "The Musical Performing Group: Musical Norms, Traditions, and Identity," *The World of Music* 31/2 [1989]: 80-113), with theoretical illustrations coming from a wide range of recent research.

166. Braun, Hartmut. *Einführung in die musikalische Volkskunde.* ("Introduction to Musical Folklore"). Darmstadt: Wissenschaftliche Buchgesellschaft, 1985.

Without establishing a theoretical school in and for itself, this volume introduces an approach to folk music, in which neither the object itself (a special type of music) nor the means of tradition (folkloristic transmission from one culture bearer to another) is privileged. Instead, "musical folklore" here comprises the music of the "average human being," regardless of whether it is folk song, a popular hit, or specialized music for entertainment. Braun begins by introducing traditional concepts of folk song, starting with Johann Gottfried Herder and Bishop Thomas Percy, and proceeding through the nineteenth century by concentrating on collecting efforts. Braun then broadens his nets to include folk music in a more general sense, including instrumental music and the presence of music in dance and other social activities. The contexts of music-making constitute the second part of the book, with institutionalization of folk music leading to its professionalization and its use in various forms of revival, such as the youth movements of the first part of the twentieth century. The overarching context in the closing section is "ideological renewal," in which singer-songwriters (*Liedermacher*) such as Wolf Biermann are discussed. The bibliography of this introductory volume is not especially large, but its inclusion of works in somewhat untraditional categories, such as folk music used in school instruction, enhances its value, particularly for English-speaking readers unfamiliar with this literature.

167. Bücher, Karl. *Arbeit und Rhythmus.* ("Work and Rhythm"). 4th, rev. ed. Leipzig: B.G. Teubner, 1909. 1st publ. 1896.

Theorizes about both the origin of music in labor and the ways in which labor contextualizes music within culture. Bücher initially conceived of this book as a contribution to late nineteenth-century studies of the relation of culture to nature, and he drew upon new evolutionary and psychological theories of the day. As he revised the study in subsequent editions, he increasingly incorporated comparative ethnological research, which enabled him to transform the book into one of the fundamental works in the nascent field of *vergleichende Musikwissenschaft* (comparative musicology). Bücher argues that music originates in basic human movements and the patterns that they create. He distinguishes bodily movement that exists only for itself from work, in which physical movement functions to achieve specific tasks, that is, to express the human being's potential to transform the world. The book unfolds in an evolutionary fashion, with increasingly complex patterns and forms of work, and examination of the rhythmic content of music that accordingly increases in complexity. Work songs not only accompany labor but reflect the organization of labor to the degree that music actually has distinctive functions in the expression of the human capacity to communicate culture through labor. In the fourth chapter, Bücher examines specific types of music connected to specific types of labor. The fifth chapter compares work songs in different large culture areas, from Africa and Asia to the Middle East. The concluding chapters examine the relation of music and language, women and work, and the economic development spawned by increasingly complex forms of rhythm. An extremely influential work of comparative musicology, whose concern for the relation of music to the body was in many ways path-breaking.

168. Danckert, Werner. *Grundriß der Volksliedkunde.* ("Structures of Folk-Song Research"). Berlin: Bernhard Hahnefeld, 1939.

Published in 1939, this introduction to the fields devoted to the study of folk song clearly illustrates the influences of Nazi ideologies on German scholarship. While it surveys the development of folk song in Europe and sketches the theories and methods of folk-song research, the book persistently finds ways to highlight the importance of developments in Germany and northern Europe, and to argue for the general superiority of the historical forces that eventually converged on Germany. Central to Danckert's argument is that folk song exists in relation to other levels of music, particularly art and religious music. Folk song becomes a way for individuals to express regional and national identity, as opposed to other types of music, which absorb international influences. German folk song and by extension the history of art music in Central Europe had existed in such a close relation that foreign influences had been staved off or modified to conform to the complex forms that developed throughout German history. There are many interesting aspects in Danckert's arguments, particularly those that derive from the book's strong interdisciplinary tendencies and his examination of musical phenomena that are anchored in the body and movement. The National-Socialist ideology that permeates the book is not always heavy-handed, or even particularly evident, and the subtlety of Danckert's prejudices must always be kept in mind. The book serves as a vivid reminder of the misuse and abuse of scholarship.

169. Deutsch, Walter, ed. *Tradition und Innovation.* ("Tradition and Innovation"). Vienna: A. Schendl, 1987. (Schriften zur Volksmusik, 11).

Honoring the twentieth anniversary of the Institute for Folk-Music Research in Vienna, the authors in this volume survey the different regional traditions and the distinctive repertories of Austrian folk music, particularly its status at the end of the twentieth century. "Tradition" in the title refers primarily to the persistence of folk music, that is, the general well-being of its practices even against a background of modernity; "innovation" refers to the constant changes—most of them consciously creative—that have produced the well-being of folk music. Many of the articles interpret innovation as *Volksmusikpflege* (cultivation of folk music), the activities of semi-professionals and professionals to collect, perform, and research folk music. Together with the innovations of *Volksmusikpflege*, new forms of traditionalization have emerged, for example the contests and gatherings that are incessantly a part of the Austrian folk-music landscape. Such forms of innovation were essential to the theoretical school founded by Josef Pommer in the late nineteenth century and developed by Austrian scholars during the twentieth century, culminating in the activities of Walter Deutsch in Vienna and a complex network of regional and local centers for folk-music collection, study, and cultivation. The articles survey different genres, repertories, and, especially, regions, serving also to introduce the reader to the diversity of Austrian folk-music practices in the twentieth century.

170. *Das deutsche Volkslied.* ("The German Folk Song"). Ed. by Josef Pommer and Hans Fraungruber. Volume 1 (1899). Containing ten numbers, published as five double issues.

The first volume of *Das deutsche Volkslied* appeared after the Deutscher Volksgesang-Verein ("German Folk-Song Association") had existed for a decade, and the journal quickly became the organ representing the activities of the society and expressing the ideologies of the founders, Pommer and Fraungruber. The subtitle of *Das deutsche Volkslied, Kenntnis und Pflege* ("Journal for Awareness and Cultivation"), clarifies the sense of mission that informs every article and announcement in the journal. At the theoretical level, Pommer begins the first volume with the manifesto "Was wir wollen" ("What We Want"), in which he lays out the characteristics of the *echt* (real) folk song, the object of the journal's endeavors and cultivating intent, and a leitmotif throughout the first volume. Based on the German language, the "real" German folk song nonetheless included dialects of German, as well as other Germanic languages, and at the farthest extreme even English. By extension, folkloric activities dependent on the German language—legends, tales, the cultivation of costumes (*Trachten*)—belonged also to the domain surveyed in the journal. Music that imitated folk song, such as folklike songs or compositions using folk melodies, could not be considered *echt.* These distinctions formed the basis for Pommer's theoretical notion of *Productionslehre* ("theory of production"), whereby folk song was understood to arise from the folk, not to be reproduced and filtered from other sources.

At the practical level, the journal was meant to serve the cultivators of folk song, not just the folk-song societies, but also individuals who might learn the new songs and pieces published in abundance in the pages of the journal. Reports of local activities, as well as necrologies and other informational sections, constitute roughly one third of each published number. Certain regional biases emerge, particularly a sense of Styria's canonic importance, undoubtedly the result of Pommer's and Fraungruber's roots in Styria; the second article in volume 1, number 1 is "Wie der Steirer singt" ("How the Styrian Sings"), an essay on the use of folk song to overcome the severe working conditions of the mountainous province. The first volume of *Das deutsche Volkslied*, therefore, establishes connections between collecting efforts and ideological approaches centered in Vienna with the Austrian folk-song practitioners throughout the German-speaking lands of the monarchy. This connection between theory and practice has remained a distinguishing characteristic of Austrian folk-music scholarship until the present.

171. *Das deutsche Volkslied* 10 (1908). Ed. by Josef Pommer, Hans Fraungruber, and Karl Kronfuß.

By the publication of the tenth volume, *Das deutsche Volkslied* had acquired a much more scholarly (i.e., academic) aura. Whereas the previous emphasis on *Pflege* (cultivation) was still present, particularly in the articles and small reports on local and regional activities written by Josef Pommer, considerable attention now shifted toward articulating a more international scope. At one level, the conditions of "Austrian folk song" were now much clearer and far more exclusive than in the first volume. In an article devoted to collections from Upper Austria in the February number (pp. 21 ff.), Pommer develops the concept of "Austrian" as applying to the *Kernland* (core land) of the Habsburg Monarchy, the countryside of mountainous regions, rather than to the "multilingual Austrian imperial city," that is, Vienna. Similarly, individual numbers contain a description of organizational folk-song activities in provincial areas (e.g., Moravia and Silesia in the January issue, Bohemia in the February issue). In various ways, the journal's scholarly writing became more intensified, with much more attention to the character of dialect and melodic nuances in individual songs, which in turn specified the local nature of a given repertory. Each issue contained several reviews, usually written by Pommer, and international news about folk song and folk-song scholarship. Still, the connection to the choruses and folk-song unions in Austria remains clearly present, and it is clear from the subscription mechanisms that the primary readership for the journal remained these Austrian organizations.

172. *Das deutsche Volkslied* 21 (1919). Ed. by Josef Pommer, Karl Liebleitner, Hans Fraungruber, and Karl Kronfuß.

Volume 21 represents several rites of passage in the theoretical school associated with *Das deutsche Volkslied* and the cultivation of German folk song in Austria. The volume appeared during the year immediately following the defeat of the Austro-Hungarian Empire in World War I, and the journal's founder and ideological architect, Josef Pommer, died, a victim of his own hand, on 25 November 1918. Volume 21 concerns itself with both of these events, devoting numerous articles to the passing of Pommer and to the new historical conditions within which the German Folk-Song Society of Vienna and its sister organizations in Austria would cultivate German folk song. The first number (January 1919) opens with an announcement of Pommer's death; this number, nonetheless, had been edited largely by Pommer. It is with the second double number of the volume (February/March) that obituaries and remembrances of Pommer and his contribution to Austrian folk-song scholarship conflate the history of the monarchy and Pommer's life. These commentaries contain numerous comments about the Pommer's belief in an historical and cultural justification of the war and about his inability to accept the defeat of Germany and Austria (his death followed the surrender by exactly two weeks). Essays in volume 21 deal with the end of the empire in various ways, but none can entirely avoid the reality that the spirit of this journal was bound to the centralizing potential of German folk song in the monarchy and its lands. The articles and transcriptions, nonetheless, are not devoted to German folk song outside Austria, but in fact begin to treat Austria as the core for traditions that had previously charted the expansion of the empire. In the final numbers the extensive reports on the local and regional folk-song organizations stress the strength of their responses to defeat and, similarly, the symbolic strength of German folk song in these responses.

173. *Das deutsche Volkslied* 31 (1929). Ed. by Karl Liebleitner, Hans Fraungruber, Raimund Zoder, and Georg Kotek.

The journal transformed its contents and approaches with volume 31. It moved substantially away from addressing the practical needs of the constituent organizations of the German Folk-Song Society of Vienna, and it exhibited instead many of the characteristics of a self-consciously scholarly journal. Several numbers, for example, are devoted to special themes; the first two numbers concentrate on folk music in Corinthia, and the fifth examines issues and repertories of folk dance. Specialized themes also appear in different numbers, for example the genre known as *Zahlenlied* (counting song) or the Austrian *Wandervogel* (wandering bird) youth movement, treated by Karl Magnus Klier. A more bounded Austria is now the focus of the journal's researchers, and it follows that a new comparative framework has asserted itself, namely the comparison of genres and practices in each of the provinces. Non-Austrian regions also appear, although the repertories examined and transcribed in this volume are largely those that survive in oral tradition in Austria. The transcription of repertories, moreover, includes more extensive notes and ethnographic data, again demonstrating a growing presence of scholarly interests. Finally, there is a palpable refocusing of attention on "folk music" (including instrumental traditions), rather than on "German folk song," signaling a clear transformation toward one of the most distinctive aspects of Austrian folk-music scholarship in the second half of the twentieth century.

174. *Das deutsche Volkslied* 41 (1939). Ed. by Georg Kotek, Karl Leibleitner, Karl M. Klier, and Richard Wolfram.

Published in the year after the annexation of Austria to Germany, volume 41 already reflects a transformed ideological treatment of German folk song. This transformation is both explicit (e.g., the inclusion in two numbers of small advertisements for the Nazi Party) and implicit, notably in the substantially increased interest in German folk song outside Austria, especially in the Czech regions of the Sudetenland and the Egerland. The awareness of German folk-music researchers and projects in Germany and in Germany's border areas (e.g., Alsace-Lorraine and Silesia) is much stronger than in previous volumes. In this sense, the landscape covered by the volume more closely resembles that of the first twenty volumes, during the final decades of the Austro-Hungarian Empire, than of the immediately preceding twenty volumes. The scholarship and the audience of volume 41, nonetheless, is the result of the more recent changes. Not only are there more scholars (and fewer amateurs) contributing to the journal, but the subject matter is much greater, with folk dance fully a component of the journal's scope. The next generation of scholars—Karl Horak, Leopold Schmidt, Richard Wolfram, and others—is actively contributing to this volume, which therefore provides an excellent basis for comparing pre- and post-World War II ideologies and approaches to Austrian folk-music research. Although each number contains abundant transcriptions, these now bear the earmarks of scholarly comparison rather than appearing as new materials for the cultivation of amateur folk musicians.

175. *Das deutsche Volkslied* 46 (1944). Ed. by Georg Kotek, Karl M. Klier, and Richard Wolfram.

The last volume of *Das deutsche Volkslied*, which notifies its readers at the close of the final number that the "total war" would force the journal to suspend publication indefinitely. Although this volume from 1944 has in many ways reduced its scope, not least because many of the contributors from the younger generation were in the army and because long-time editor, Karl Liebleitner, passed away, the substance and breadth of the journal remain consistent with the intellectual history represented by *Das deutsche Volkslied* during a period of almost one-half century. The essays and reports generally fall into two extremes. At one extreme, there are studies of German-speaking groups or speech islands in the areas conquered by the Axis powers during the early years of World War II; the volume begins, for example, with Hans von der Au's essay on folk song in the Dobrudscha-German colonies, a nineteenth-century settlement in the border areas of modern Hungary, Slovakia, Romania, and Ukraine. At the other extreme, several articles reflect an intensified focus on urban traditions in Vienna. Raimund Zoder, for example, writes on the characteristics of music performed in the *Heurigen* (taverns, in which wine from the present year is served) of Vienna, historically sites for urban music-making. In many ways, the final volume of *Das deutsche Volkslied* marks the end of a history shaped by ideological tensions contesting the meanings embedded in the two main components of its title, "German" and "folk song." When Austrian folk-music scholarship reemerged after World War II, the first of these terms would be supplanted by "Austrian," and the second would be broadened considerably to "folk music," which embodied a complex array of musical and cultural practices.

176. Deutsches Volksliedarchiv, ed. *"Freut euch des Lebens..." 75 Jahre Deutsches Volksliedarchiv.* ("'Take Joy in Life...' 75 Years of the German Folk-Song Archive"). Freiburg im Breisgau: Deutsches Volksliedarchiv, 1989.

Exhibit catalogue to accompany the celebration of the seventy-five-year history of the German Folk-Song Archive (DVA). Founded by John Meier in 1914, the Freiburg archive is the most comprehensive in German-speaking Europe. This book contains brief introductory and historical essays by Lutz Röhrich and Otto Holzapfel and continues as a series of thirty-one topical essays by DVA staff members. These essays focus on specific folk-song genres (e.g., *Bänkelsang*), settings for folk music (e.g., Fasching), or on folk-music practices (e.g., the final essay on songs about taking up residence in unoccupied buildings). Accompanying each essay is an illustration and a brief bibliography; a bibliography of DVA publications concludes the book. The concise and topical nature of the essays makes this book an extremely valuable introduction to German folk song.

177. Emmrich, Brigitte, Otto Holzapfel, and Heike Müns. "Sammlung Franz Magnus Böhme in der Sächsischen Landesbibliothek in Dresden." ("The Franz Magnus Böhme Collection in the Saxon State Library of Dresden"). *Jahrbuch für Volksliedforschung* 38 (1993): 27–49.

178. Thomas, Kurt. "Bericht über einen Teilnachlaß von Franz Magnus Böhme im Institut für Volksmusikforschung Weimar." ("Report on Part of the Estate of Franz Magnus Böhme at the

Institute for Folk-Music Research in Weimar"). *Jahrbuch für Volksliedforschung* 38 (1993): 13–26.

These two companion pieces assess the literary and scientific estate of Franz Magnus Böhme (1827–98), whose activities as collector and editor in the late nineteenth century did much to focus and standardize the study of German folk song. Böhme is best known for expanding Ludwig Erk's original *Deutscher Liederhort* (1856) to a three-volume monument (first published beginning in 1893), which remains the standard anthology at the end of the twentieth century, and which influenced many approaches to folk-song scholarship throughout the century. The two articles here provide reports on the materials left after Böhme's death, some of them unpublished. Thomas's article describes the estate that found its way into the hands of the Böhme family, where it was largely untouched until Böhme's great grandson determined to donate it to the Weimar Institute for Folk-Music Research in 1989. The article by Emmrich, Holzapfel, and Müns inventories the bulk of Böhme's estate, including the fifty-eight volumes of a series of collected works that were deposited in the Saxon State Library at the time of Böhme's death. In both cases, the estates had received virtually no attention, and these articles reflect upon some of the research and editorial projects possible with reunification of Germany in 1990, hence with much greater access.

Böhme collected many different volumes containing folk songs and folklike music, particularly choral music, and in addition he gathered reviews and articles written about the nature of folk song. In general, the materials he assembled reveal a reflective and self-critical scholar, who was interested in broadening the concepts of folk song and music, particularly in demonstrating the interaction and exchange with composed traditions. The range of unpublished material is considerable, with several major works lying in manuscript or prepared even for the publisher at the time of Böhme's death (e.g., a manuscript of on "The Essence and History of German Folk Song"). The estates suggest not only opportunities to reevaluate nineteenth- and twentieth-century folk-song scholarship, the sources for much of which are found here, but also new publications that would shed additional light on the period around the turn of the century, that is, the transition from the influence of Ludwig Erk to the new theoretical directions forged by John Meier in Germany and Switzerland and by Josef Pommer in Austria. In particular, Emmrich, Holzapfel, and Müns endeavor to describe the Dresden holdings to make them accessible to other scholars who would wish to undertake such reevaluations of Franz Magnus Böhme and the intellectual history of folk-music scholarship.

179. Holzapfel, Otto. *Das Deutsche Volksliedarchiv Freiburg i. Br.* ("The German Folk-Song Archive, Freiburg i. Br."). Bern: Peter Lang, 1989. (Studien zur Volksliedforschung, 3).

A history of the major repository and research center for German folk song in Central Europe. Written for the seventy-fifth anniversary of the Deutsches Volksliedarchiv (DVA), this volume employs numerous perspectives, including opening chapters in which the DVA's founder, John Meier (1864-1945), and classification systems are discussed, documentary chapters with early correspondence and surveys of the earliest publication series, oral-historical reminiscences offered by scholars who had previously worked at the DVA, and finally indexes of the individuals and institutions with whom the DVA interacted during its first half-century. Holzapfel sketches a history of the institution that shows it to have developed as an extension of John Meier's orientation to folklore and German philology, but that in recent years international, as well as ethnographic and ethnomusicological, approaches have shaped the character of the DVA's research program. The discussion of the classification methods in chapter 2 not only introduces the reader to the conceptualization of folk song underlying much of German scholarship, but it also provides an important guide to reading and interpreting the DVA's numerous publications, for example the *Jahrbuch für Volksliedforschung* and the ballad series *Deutsche Volkslieder mit ihren Melodien.* Its thorough and positive assessment of the DVA notwithstanding, this history does not hesitate to make critical judgments, for example about John Meier's idiosyncratic and often autocratic style of leadership, or of the distance kept by the DVA in relation to racial policies maintained during the Third Reich.

180. Haid, Gerlinde. "Das Österreichische Volksliedwerk." ("The Austrian Folk-Music Works"). In Walter Deutsch, Harald Dreo, Gerlinde Haid, and Karl Horak, eds., *Volksmusik in Österreich.* Vienna: Österreichischer Bundesverlag, 1984. Pp. 117–26.

An intellectual history of the Austrian Volksliedwerk, and the institutions and scholars whose activities led to its founding. Beginning with the founder of Austrian folk-music studies, Josef Pommer (1845-1918), and the initial attempts to publish a comprehensive anthology of folk music in all lands of the Habsburg Empire during the first two decades of the twentieth century, Haid sketches a history resulting from individual and regional endeavors, but frequently punctuated by efforts necessarily aborted because of the world wars and the transformation of Austria from an empire stretching into Eastern Europe to a bounded nation within Central Europe. Complicating the history of Austrian folk-music scholarship was the further difficulty of determining just what role a central institution in Vienna would play in the coordination of regional and local archives. In 1974, the Austrian Volksliedwerk became the solution to this dilemma, serving as an umbrella organization in Vienna that was linked to similar organizations in each province. The Volksliedwerk not only collects individual pieces, recordings, and other relevant materials, but it edits a yearbook and other scholarly publications. It is, furthermore, an activist organization, providing music to young musicians, who therefore continue the tradition of cultivation that has distinguished the history of Austrian folk-music scholarship.

181. *Jahrbuch für Volksliedforschung.* ("Yearbook for Folk-Song Research"). Vol. 1. 1928.

The first volume of the yearbook edited by the Deutsches Volksliedarchiv (DVA) in Freiburg im Breisgau, which continues until the present. The fundamental areas of research in the first fourteen years of the DVA's history appear in the themes of the individual articles. The theoretical approaches evident here, moreover, would dominate the DVA throughout the tenure of its founder and director (and the editor of its *Jahrbuch*), John Meier. The primacy of text in the determination of folk song, for example, is evident in John Meier and Erich Seemann's article on folk song and the nineteenth-century poet Annette von Droste-Hülshoff. Connections between folk song and art song appear in several articles, one devoted to more evidence for John Meier's theory *Kunstlieder im Volksmunde* (lit., art songs in the mouths of the folk) and another to text-melody relations, written by the musicologist Hans Joachim Moser. German folk song in speech islands and other areas outside Central Europe appear in articles on ballad-singing in the German-speaking colonies on the Volga River (Viktor Schirmunski) and characteristic song of Upper Silesia (Alfred Wirth). Historical traditions and intellectual history provide further tropes, for example in articles on Jacob Grimm as a folk-song collector (Johannes Bolte) and an examination of melody in a song from 1641. As a concept German folk song demonstrates considerable breadth in this first volume, and its study demands an equivalent interdisciplinary breadth. Indeed, it is a sense of expanding the concept of German folk song that pervades the volume, its different articles, and even its book reviews. Not only should German folk song be an intellectual domain with a long history, but it should represent, both ideologically and musically, the presence of German culture in many areas of Europe and at many levels of European culture.

182. *Jahrbuch für Volksliedforschung* 7 (1941).

The final volume of the yearbook published, before World War II made further printing impossible. In his foreword to the volume, DVA Director John Meier acknowledges the difficulties posed by the war but uses the foreword to express his deep concern that the international cooperation fostered by the German Folk-Song Archive—and Meier names specific foreign colleagues, such as Åke Campbell in Uppsala and Charles Williams in Urbana, Illinois—not be broken by the war. The articles in the yearbook reflect this broader concern for the folk-song research as an international endeavor, and whereas it would be an exaggeration to suggest that volume 7 launched open resistance to the racist and militarist agendas of much German scholarship at the time, this volume does offer what might be regarded as alternative avenues of interpretation. First of all, the articles fully admit to the possibility that German folk song is not entirely separated from other traditions, even from the influence of Jewish thought (e.g., in Meier's article on the ballad, "Verwunderter Knabe" ["Wounded Boy"]). Second, whereas several articles concern themselves with relations between folk- and art-music traditions (e.g., Bruno Maerker's lengthy study of Gregorian chant and German folk song, and Meier's opening essay on Minnesang and folk song), the usual Nazi-prescribed teleology of the Germanic being transformed into specifically German treatments of melody or tonality is not present. Quite the contrary, the possibilities of foreign contributions to the German repertory (e.g., Meier's study of the ballad "Das Totenamt" ["The Office of Death"], which he concludes is actually Dutch) and the interpretation of variation through oral tradition producing possibilities of hybrid forms (e.g., Walter Wiora's substantial essay on *Umsingen* [lit., singing into variations]) are strikingly atypical of the ideological discourse prevalent in much folk-music scholarship from 1933-45. While still emphasizing traditional areas of focus at the German Folk-Song Archive (notably, ballad and speech-island scholarship), this volume reveals a great deal about the avenues of scholarship that were still open to different forms of interpretation, as well as those that were not.

183. *Jahrbuch für Volksliedforschung* 8 (1951).

The first volume of this yearbook to appear after World War II, it nonetheless contains articles and reviews written for a continuation of the yearbook during the war. In his foreword, John Meier notes that the volume should have appeared in 1943 but the proofs were destroyed at the publisher's during a bomb attack. This volume represents, then, a certain type of continuity, at the very least the conscious attempt of John Meier to suggest that the endeavors of the German Folk-Song Archive from the middle of the war could continue after it. The ideological conditions and contradictions of the Nazi period are both evident and quietly recontextualized in this volume. The articles overwhelmingly concern themselves with ballads, both the genre as a whole and individual ballads that were being researched in Freiburg im Breisgau for inclusion in the ballad edition initiated in 1935. Three other larger areas of research emerge in the volume. First, the relation between folk and art music characterizes Josef Müller-Blattau's study of Minnesang. Second, the interrelation between German and other folk-song traditions (e.g., Erich Seemann's essay on German-Lithuanian relations), while present as a leitmotif, more often takes the form of cross-fertilization than serving as evidence of German political or cultural presence. Finally, there are essays that stress the continuity of the intellectual history of folk-song scholarship. In general, volume 8, appearing six years after World War II and containing articles written nine years earlier, attempts to heal or reinterpret one of the most profound schisms and breaks in German intellectual history, as if this left many aspects of German folk-song research unscathed.

184. *Jahrbuch für Volksliedforschung* 9 (1964).

A *Festschrift* for the seventy-fifth birthday of Erich Seemann, volume 9 starts again the annual publication of the *Jahrbuch für Volksliedforschung*. This volume exhibits a Janus-faced quality, looking back on the themes and approaches of the German Folk-Song Archive's first half-century of activity and establishing a new range of activities for the future, many of which would characterize the DVA for the next quarter-century. Seemann was John Meier's assistant during the difficult years of the Depression, World War II, and the recovery after the war, and he assumed the directorship of the DVA upon Meier's death. It is hardly surprising, then, that many of the articles in this *Festschrift* are devoted to ballads in specific and narrative folk song in general. These include an opening article (in English) by Bertrand Bronson, which surveys folk-song scholarship in the United States from 1910 to 1960. Lajos Vargyas examines narrative songs, especially stemming from the German-language areas of Central Europe, on Hungarian song, and Zmaga Kumer looks at Gottscheer folk song in light of Slovenian contacts. As these articles already suggest, volume 9 exhibits a striking international character, surely reminiscent of the broad range of colleagues that John Meier and the DVA had cultivated prior to World War II, the loss of which Meier had mourned in his 1941 foreword. Two articles appear with explicit Jewish subject matter, still an extraordinary occurrence in Germany in 1964: Wilhelm Heiske's path-breaking article on the relation of German and Yiddish folk song, and Erik Dal's study of the Ahasver ("wandering Jew") theme in Denmark and the folk traditions shared by Germany and Denmark. Articles by Rolf Wilhelm Brednich, Bengt R. Jonsson, Leopold Schmidt, and Archer Taylor ("The Parallels between Ballads and Tales") reveal new directions in German folk-song research, not least among these a conscious move away from strict textual studies toward more broadly interdisciplinary approaches.

185. *Jahrbuch für Volksliedforschung* 19 (1974).

New methodologies and theoretical directions are immediately apparent in the articles in this volume. In particular, there is evidence of a change in European folkloristics and the potential for this to influence folk-music scholarship. Rather striking in a comparison of this volume to volume 9 from a decade earlier is the palpable shift away from "German folk song," even from German music in general. Gottfried Habenicht, for example, contributes a long essay on the Romanian bagpipe, which contains many illustrations and photographs but is not primarily concerned with the music of the German-speaking residents of Romania, Habenicht's primary area of research. Samuel G. Armistead and Joseph H. Silverman contribute a report on Judeo-Spanish wedding songs, another shift of attention toward a new area of Jewish-music research. Rolf Wilhelm Brednich's study of "Song as Trading Good" and Wilhelm Schepping's critique of nineteenth-century attempts to purify sacred song emblematize the new disciplinary formulations of what song, in general, and folk song, in particular, potentially can be. Traditional approaches have by no means exited from the *Jahrbuch für Volksliedforschung*, as demonstrated by Karl Horak's text-based study of song in the Kremnitz speech island. In 1974, nevertheless, the yearbook is clearly more international and more contextual in the approaches of its contributors.

186. *Jahrbuch für Volksliedforschung* 29 (1984).

A more extensive and more detailed picture of European folk song in general emerges in volume 29. Whereas many articles take genre as their focus, their authors are less concerned with underscoring the meaning of genre than with the functions of certain songs or processes that belong to certain genres. Thomas Pettitt, for example, uses the example of "Lass of Roch Royal" to illustrate the role of individual singers in a collective biography of the so-called "Golden Age" of Scottish balladry. Heinz Rölleke examines issues of the reception and reproduction of *Des Knaben Wunderhorn* rather than analyze the Arnim and Brentano collection itself. Context in its most complex forms shapes the essays by Natascha Würzbach, Krista Ruehs, and Bernhard

Bremberger and Stefanie Döll. Regional boundaries are entirely open in this volume, as exemplified by Walter Puchner's study of interethnic exchange of Balkan folk-song texts. Even though the general historical tendency of the *Jahrbuch für Volksliedforschung* toward greater theoretical diversity and more international subject matter is still underway at the end of the decade marked by this volume, no article takes a radically new direction, but rather the whole issue seems to characterize a period of consolidation and reflection on the directions the DVA's yearbook had been taking.

187. *Jahrbuch für Volksliedforschung* 39 (1994).

The final volume of the DVA's yearbook to appear before the publication of the present book seems, at first glance, radically different from the earliest volumes. None of the ten main articles, for example, concerns itself with ballads. Indeed, none of these articles addresses German folk song in a cultural or historical context that could be considered rural, authentic, or isolated within folk culture. Quite the contrary, these articles deal with German folk song in extraordinarily different and distinctive ways. The growing internationalism of the yearbook is very evident in 1994. There are articles by Ildikó Kriza on Hungary, Constantu Cristescu on Romania, and Kirill V. Cistov and B. Cistova on Russia. The theoretical articles range broadly through international scholarship, for example in the articles by Walter Salmen and Flemming G. Andersen. This volume clearly reveals an acute awareness of current political issues in Europe, particularly in the reunified Germany of the 1990s, and these political issues are addressed critically, for example in Manfred Seifert's essay on wind ensembles during the Nazi period and in Ernst Kiehl's biographical study of a singer-songwriter involved in youth movements in Weimar Germany and then in the German Democratic Republic. The musics of ethnic and religious groups in Europe occupy an important position in the contents of the volume, for example in András Borgó's short article on Yiddish music in Hungary. The *Jahrbuch für Volksliedforschung* in 1994 not only documents a changing theoretical orientation in German folk-song scholarship, but it demonstrates vividly the ways in which the German Folk-Song Archive has participated in the writing of that reorientation.

188. Kaden, Christian. *Des Lebens wilder Kreis: Musik im Zivilisationsprozeß*. ("The Natural Circle of Life: Music in the Process of Civilization"). Kassel: Bärenreiter, 1993.

A wide-ranging book that locates music's fundamental historical context in social parameters. A music sociologist equally at home intellectually in ethnomusicology and historical musicology, Kaden draws on situations of music's palpable presence in examples as diverse as Gothic architecture in the Latin Middle Ages, improvisation in cultures without musical literacy, Wagner's compositional physiognomy, and the punk scene in the German Democratic Republic. The approach is not so much comparative as it is an attempt to show that all humans use music culturally to map out history and society, and to create art. Social context not only affects the structure and meaning of music (see, e.g., the concluding chapter on "Cultural Identity as a Theme in Life"), but the social world is constructed using the patterns and structures of music. Music is, according to Kaden, a meaningful and powerful agent in bringing about what he calls the "process of civilization" (see, e.g., the introductory chapter, "The Power of Music and Its Mandate in Civilization"). The text of the book is rich in metaphor, and Kaden draws from his depth as a scholar with experiences in several intellectual traditions. Written during the transition from the GDR to German unity (individual essays bear specific dates during the *Wende*), the book also embodies one of the sweeping moments of historical change that serve as leitmotifs within the text itself. The rich (and sometimes complicated) language is complemented by equally rich, wry humor and illustrative material. A book that connects the humanities and social sciences—and the disciplines of music—in impressive and significant ways.

189. Klusen, Ernst. *Volkslied: Fund und Erfindung.* ("Folk Song: Discovery and Invention"). Cologne: Hans Gerig, 1969.

The most complete formulation of Ernst Klusen's theory of folk song as "group song." In the 1960s, this theory was consciously polemical, conceived as a means of redressing notions that folk song was a functionless expression of human emotion. Klusen argues, instead, that folk song functions as a humanly-designed tool, capable of forming and shaping culture. Fundamental to Klusen's concept is, therefore, human agency and the ways in which folk song serves as a means of mobilizing that agency. These theories concern themselves, at one level, with the very nature of creativity. Unlike other theories of the nineteenth and early twentieth century, which regarded folk song as texts, repertories, and practices that an amorphous folk inherits, Klusen examines the two processes in his subtitle, which I gloss as "discovery" (*Fund*) and "invention" (*Erfindung*). In both cases Klusen stresses the creativity that humans exercise when acquiring, learning, and using folk song in their lives. Klusen develops his concept of group song by examining anthropological and ethnomusicological theories that demonstrate the importance of performance (cultural or musical) in small groups. He surveys comparatively and rethinks a broad spectrum of musical examples to demonstrate the centrality of the group. In the final two chapters, he looks specifically at European musical practices of all kinds, resituating folk-song practices within them from an historical perspective. Song at every stage of Western music history, therefore, retains a certain historical agency by serving as a primary locus of musical performance and agency. In the final chapter, Klusen examines the persistent presence of groups in social music-making of twentieth-century Germany, first by looking at the *Wandervogel* youth movement, then at the use and accompanying misuse of song by the Nazis, and finally at late twentieth-century singing practices. Folk song, in Klusen's theory, is not just a means of undergirding human collectives, but also a means of empowering each collective to contribute substantially to the whole of society.

190. Meier, John. *Kunstlieder im Volksmunde: Materialien und Untersuchungen.* ("Art Songs in the Mouths of the Folk: Materials and Studies"). Halle: Max Niemeyer, 1906.

John Meier's central treatise on the authorship and dissemination of folk song. Meier postulates that folk song began as a composition, which then passed into oral tradition once it was experienced, learned, and sung by the folk as part of their own tradition. Although the creation of folk songs requires two levels in Meier's theory—essentially a written and then an oral tradition—these two traditions are objectively separate from each other. The folk singer who hears, sings, and then transmits a composed song is more or less oblivious of the composer or the written tradition. Oral tradition, it follows, unleashes its own processes of creativity, which result from the nature of the material itself and the cultural contexts that influence those who perform it. Meier also maintains a broad range of meanings for *Kunstlied*, including folklike songs and composed traditions of all kinds. On one hand, Meier's theory extends an extraordinary degree of integrity to the text of song itself (and, indeed, he concerns himself almost entirely with the texts), which acquire an organic ability to survive and undergo transformations during transmission. On the other, this theory broadens the social and historical frameworks within which folk music could be understood. By sketching processes of transmission that actually connect different social levels and different regions of Europe, Meier's theory, today simply referred to as KiV, inscribes folk song into a much larger history of Central European culture. The volume closes with a catalogue of 567 folk songs, whose composers are known. The KiV theory has continued to influence research and scholarship at the German Folk-Song Archive throughout the twentieth century, with several current research projects still focused on refining the histories of creativity and transmission that the KiV theory unveils.

191. Müller-Blattau, Josef. *Germanisches Erbe in deutscher Tonkunst.* ("Germanic Heritage in German Music"). Berlin-Lichterfelde: Chr. Friedrich Vieweg, 1938. (Musikalische Volksforschung, 2).

A contribution from musicology and folk-music research to Nazi ideologies within the German intellectual and academic establishment. The explicit aim of this volume is to identify a fundamentally Germanic basis for German music and to examine its influence on a distinctively German music history. Müller-Blattau locates the Germanic basis in language, specifically in the ways in which basic rhythmic and melodic patterns owe their forms to that language. The Germanic basis of music, therefore, predates the historical records of the Middle Ages, but it also emerges in the youthful repertories of German-speaking children in the present, where it can serve as contemporary evidence to explain the distant past. Having argued for these protohistorical conditions in language, Müller-Blattau makes the case for an historical trajectory from folk song to art song, a trajectory that can be found throughout the history of German music, constantly assuming different patterns. In the Middle Ages, for example, the Germanic heritage formed secular repertories, which were nonetheless transmitted through German sacred song. In post-medieval Europe, the Germanic heritage became dilluted, according to Müller-Blattau, through the internationalization of art music, even though there were composers, such as J.S. Bach, who perceived the character of the Germanic heritage in folk song and drew upon this for their compositions. The book closes with a discussion of the *Erneuerung* (renewal, the standard Nazi call for a return to the basic Aryan Germanness), which remains anchored and palpable in German folk song, and, when placed in the hands of German composers, can shape the music of the present. The ideological polemic of this book is based less on strictly racial theories than on Müller-Blattau's tendentious linguistic and historical claims.

192. Noll, Günther. "Zur Problematik der Musik in der Brauch-Reaktivierung—Aktuelle Beispiele aus dem Rheinland." ("On the Problematic of Music in the Revival of Function—Contemporary Examples from the Rhineland"). In Walter Deutsch and Wilhelm Schepping, eds., *Musik im Brauch der Gegenwart.* Vienna: A. Schendl, 1988. Pp. 21–56.

Examines the reintroduction of function into musical practices that previously have not depended on specific connections to holiday or ritual contexts. Noll provides close analyses of several examples from areas in and around Bonn and Cologne, employing theoretical concerns from the Institute for Musical Folklore in Neuß. Specifically, processions and secular practices associated with the spring holiday of Pentecost provide traditional contexts to which new musical practices are connected. Rather than sacred musical repertories, the wind ensembles and other musical groups accompanying processions and celebrations mix many different repertories. Traditional Pentecost songs may be performed with popular music and the repertories used for many different occasions. Music is nevertheless essential to the rebirth and expansion of these traditions, some of which have undergone a hiatus for many years. Function, it follows, requires new ways of integrating different musics into traditional practices that have assumed modern forms.

193. Noll, Günther, and Wilhelm Schepping, eds. *25 Jahre Institut für Musikalische Volkskunde 1964-1989.* ("Twenty-Five Years of the Institute for Musical Folklore, 1964-1989"). Cologne: n.p. (University of Cologne), 1989.

An assessment of the accomplishments of the Institute for Musical Folklore during its first quarter-century. Founded by Ernst Klusen at the Pädagogische Hochschule in Neuß, on the lower Rhine, this institute initially attempted to reevaluate the traditional presence of folk song in German school textbooks. The focus of its research activities reflected its choice of a name— not "folk music" but "musical folklore"—whereby the institute included popular and folklike music and employed broadly interdisciplinary approaches. Under Klusen's direction the institute was also associated with his influential theory of "group songs," which postulates that the conditions of singing lie in the communication and social functions inherent in small groups. Scholars associated with the institute contributed to the loosening of German folk-song theories from the traditional association with region, that is, a belief that folk-song repertories were shaped by the special cultural and linguistic traits of a political and geographic area. Research stemming from the Neuß institute also represents a more characteristic North German school, distinctive from South German (German Folk-Song Archive, Freiburg im Breisgau) and Austrian scholarly traditions.

194. Schmidt, Leopold. *Volksgesang und Volkslied: Proben und Probleme.* ("Folk Song [as Context] and Folk Song [as Text]: Vignettes and Problems"). Berlin: Erich Schmidt, 1970.

A volume containing the most significant articles by the most influential Austrian folk-song scholar in the generation following World War II. The title of this volume immediately signals the nature of Schmidt's contribution. The concept *Volksgesang* embraces a much broader range of cultural practices and social contexts than does *Volkslied*, the research of which had more traditionally focused on folk-song texts and their transmission. Schmidt concerns himself primarily with folk song and its contexts in Austria, and his studies here result from both historical and ethnographic approaches. Indeed, through examination of early manuscripts, the changing impact of dialect, and the constant exchange between folk song and other aesthetic practices, Schmidt succeeds in sketching very different outlines for a history of—or through—folk song. Characteristic of the approaches in this volume is a willingness to craft different methods for the study of different musical phenomena. By diversifying his methods, Schmidt also succeeds in creating new subject areas (e.g., in section four, in which folk song and the city combine as a subject, or in section seven, in which the interaction between folk song and theater reveals new contexts for oral tradition in modern, urban settings). Arguably, the book leaves no stone unturned, which is to say, it seemingly asserts that no cultural practice is irrelevant to the study of folk song. The depth of the individual essays, however, is no less than the breadth of the entire book, making the book an excellent basis for comparative study with other national traditions of folk song. The extensive notes, bibliographies, and appendices further strengthen the contribution of this volume to the intellectual history of folk-song scholarship in the second half of the twentieth century.

195. Suppan, Wolfgang. "Volksmusikforschung in Österreich." ("Folk-Music Research in Austria"). In Walter Deutsch, Harald Dreo, Gerlinde Haid, and Karl Horak, eds., *Volksmusik in Österreich.* Vienna: Österreichischer Bundesverlag, 1984. Pp. 112–16.

A brief survey of the major directions and schools in Austrian folk-music research, with folk music understood to include music-making of various kinds. Suppan concentrates on the names of leading scholars and the places in which they actively instituted their theoretical schools. Folk-song scholarship began early in the nineteenth century, with Joseph von Sonnleithner's collection for the Gesellschaft für Musikfreunde in 1819 serving as the initial landmark. Collecting and scholarship throughout the nineteenth century remained individual and focused on regions. With Josef Pommer's founding of the "Deutscher Volksgesang-Verein" and the journal *Das deutsche Volkslied* in the final decade of the century, two new trends developed. First, Vienna and its institutions assumed a more centralizing role; second, folk-music scholarship was combined with the revival and cultivation of folk music. Suppan portrays the intellectual history in the first half of the twentieth century as one of tension between those primarily interested in cultivation and those, mostly academics, most concerned with scholarship. After World War II, specific emphases developed at the Austrian universities, for example comparative-systematic musicology in Vienna under Walter Graf and Franz Födermayr, and anthropological approaches in Graz under Walther Wünsch and Wolfgang Suppan.

196. Weber, Michael. *Eine 'andere' Musikwissenschaft? Vorstudien zu Theorie und Methodologie* ("An 'Other' Musicology? Theoretical and Methodological Prolegomena"). Frankfurt am Main: Peter Lang, 1990. (Europäische Hochschulschriften, Reihe 36: Musikwissenschaft, 49)

A theoretical survey of major areas of ethnomusicological activity since World War II. Weber places special emphasis on the influences from the German concern with global music histories (e.g., in the work of Walter Wiora) and contrasts this with the emergence of anthropology as a major influence on North American ethnomusicology. After focusing on several scholars and the ideas associated with them (Alan Merriam, Wolfgang Suppan, Max Peter Baumann, Bruno Nettl, et al.), the author closes with a look toward the future by arguing for the synthesizing potential of Austrian *vergleichend-systematische Musikwissenschaft* (comparative-systematic musicology), the school founded by Robert Lach and now flourishing in Vienna under the leadership of Franz Födermayr. The "otherness" suggested in the title serves as a leitmotif throughout the book, representing both the musics and music cultures examined by ethnomusicologists and the challenge posed by the field of ethnomusicology to the disciplines of music. Extremely useful as a survey of major ideas for both beginning graduate students and more advanced scholars, particularly because of the thorough citations and extensive bibliography.

197. Wiora, Walter. *Ergebnisse und Aufgaben vergleichender Musikforschung.* ("Results and Tasks of Comparative Musical Research"). Darmstadt: Wissenschaftliche Buchgesellschaft, 1975. (Erträge der Forschung, 44).

Examines the history, areas of research, and new possibilities for comparative research in music. Comparison has the broadest possible meaning, by no means limited to *vergleichende Musikwissenschaft* (comparative musicology), the historical predecessor of modern ethnomusicology. Wiora sees in comparison a means of linking all areas of musical research and further relating the results of musical research to other disciplines in the social and human sciences. Beginning with an historical survey of comparative practices and musical disciplines traditionally employing these (e.g., folk-song scholarship and systematic musicology), Wiora moves on to observe areas in which considering music itself (*Musik für sich gesehen*) lends itself to comparison, for example improvisation, instruments, and polyphony. Larger chapters on comparative approaches to music in context and to music cultures themselves conclude the book. Throughout the work, which appears in a series devoted to introducing readers to scholarly disciplines, Wiora cites a wide range of literature, not only in German, but also in other European languages, making the book itself a means for comparing the excellent representation of American ethnomusicological sources with similar European studies. The thesis, if not mission, of the book is that comparative research, despite its faults and the ease with which inappropriate comparisons can be made, potentially broadens the interdisciplinary discourse with musical practices at its core.

8

RELATED DISCIPLINES

The study of folk song and folk music in Central Europe has always taken its approaches and methodologies from many disciplines. Identifying one field of folk-music research and ascribing to that field a single intellectual history would be quite impossible, indeed ridiculous, for it may well be that the most identifying characteristic of this intellectual history would be its negotiation and interaction with related disciplines. Folk-music scholars have historically been Germanists, philologists, musicologists, scholars of literature, sociologists, and music educators. Some of these related disciplines have played more important historical roles than others, and the particular role of each discipline has changed according to the shifting emphases and focuses within the field and its intellectual history.

It is also undeniable that related disciplines turn their attention toward folk song and folk music because of the contrasting notions of what those terms mean and identify. By no means do they mean "the study of music." Quite the contrary, they rarely fail to confuse the simple definitions of music as a sonic phenomenon. These related disciplines, instead, perceive folk music as embedded in other cultural practices. For many folk-song scholars, folk song is a complex of narrative practices that have historically delineated the cultural geography of Europe and the world. For folk-dance scholars, sound is itself secondary to the physical properties of music that dance expresses. It may well be because of the slipperiness with which folk music is regarded that it also appears frequently within studies from disciplines that are less closely related, for example cultural studies in this chapter. In the German-language intellectual traditions, music occupies a much more salient and visible position than in the disciplines of the English-language academy. Music's powers of signification are greater, its historical presence in, say, nationalism, more demanding of consideration.

I arrived at the sections organizing this chapter in much the same way I determined the organization of the entire book. On one hand, much of my own work has depended on the ways in which these disciplines have opened up certain fields of investigation. In particular, I have welcomed the emerging forms of reflexivity and criticism in the more sociologically-informed directions of German folkloristics. On the other hand, my perspective as an outsider has led me to inquire more about related disciplines that are far more significant in the German-language intellectual traditions than in the English-language, for example, folk-dance research, which for all intents and purposes does not exist as a scholarly field in North America. That I integrate it into the present chapter results from my own belief that such studies would contribute much to the growing concern for music and the body in American ethnomusicology. The sections in this chapter, then, contain disciplines that exhibit very different forms of relatedness.

While observing the interdisciplinary history of folk-music research, one is also struck by those disciplines that are poorly represented, if at all. The most striking examples of these non-related disciplines are historical musicology and anthropology, both of which contribute substantially to the interdisciplinary study of music in North America. At one level, the absence of these fields can be explained on institutional grounds: the music and anthropology departments at German universities have historically not created positions, that is, chairs, for folk-music scholars. Instead, the institutional home for these scholars has been the folklore department. German anthropology, having collaborated extensively with the aims of the Nazi period, has been slow to institute programs to broaden its field beyond the study of bounded cultures beyond the borders of Europe. Institutional explanations, however, tell only part of the story. German historical musicologists have for the most part ignored folk music because it lies outside their privileged canon. Those musicologists who have broken rank, for example Walter Wiora and Walter Salmen, have produced some of the most innovative and significant research, incorporating related disciplines to their fullest.

The related disciplines I examine here also represent the changes and transformations in the intellectual history of folk-music research in ways somewhat differently from the works I present in other chapters. Quite intentionally, I let these disciplines introduce different perspectives to the larger field of study represented by the entire book. These different perspectives are evident, for example, in the shift of importance from one related discipline to another. Within folkloristics that shift moves from a concentration on the object of folklore to the cultural context that concerns European ethnologists. Folk-dance research, too, moves away from the definition of specific genres and forms to the study of movement and its social significance. As these perspectives change, so too does the nature of folk music as a concept and construct. The related disciplines that concern themselves with folk music are barometers of such changes, as well as of the vitality and value that folk music signifies for scholars in many different disciplines.

Volkskunde—Folkloristik—Europäische Ethnologie

198. Brednich, Rolf W., ed. *Grundriß der Volkskunde: Einführung in die Forschungsfelder der Europäischen Ethnologie.* ("Foundations of

Folklore: Introduction to the Research Areas of European Ethnology"). Berlin: Dietrich Reimer, 1988.

An introduction to German folklore studies, the twenty-two essays of which survey the methodologies and intellectual histories of different research areas. Intended for use by advanced students and scholars, the essays are written by many of the leading scholars in each specific area (e.g., Utz Jeggle on folklore in the twentieth century, Lutz Röhrich on narrative research, and Rudolf Schenda on reading practices). Each essay examines fundamental methods and approaches and contains an excellent bibliography. The authors are largely concerned with situating German folklore at the forefront of contemporary scholarship, the "European ethnology" of the title, whereby these folklorists signal their concern more with contemporary social processes than folklore as the study of objects preserved from the past. Few of the essays concern themselves with methods and research areas other than those of Central Europe, indeed German-language scholarship. In some cases this offers the reader an advantage because of the unique discursive boundaries of the German research area (e.g., Andreas C. Bimmer on family research and Herbert Schempf on folklore and the law); in other cases the less desirable result of revealing insulation from international and interdisciplinary research is achieved (e.g., Annemie Schenk's essay on interethnic research, which takes little account of studies of ethnicity and multiculturalism, or Wilhelm Schepping's essay on song and music research, which virtually ignores ethnomusicology, while touching on basic concepts in music sociology). Valuable as a survey and view of European ethnology as a whole.

199. Chiva, Isac, and Utz Jeggle, eds. *Deutsche Volkskunde—Französische Ethnologie: Zwei Standortbestimmungen.* ("German Folklore—French Ethnology: Identifying Two Positions"). Frankfurt am Main: Campus Verlag; Paris: Editions de la Maison des Sciences de l'Homme, 1987.

A collection of essays looking at the state of research in German and French folklore studies. Themes consciously contrast the distinctive areas pursued by scholars in both countries, while exploring ways in which these areas might benefit from expanded dialogues. Because the essays emphasize ideological issues (e.g., why German scholars must situate tradition in relation to the Holocaust, or the meaning of regionalism in French scholarship), they raise many issues of relevance to ethnomusicologists and folk-music scholars. The volume as a whole provides a critical overview of post-World War II issues in European folklore scholarship and clearly lays these out for readers less familiar with the movement to rethink German folklore as "European ethnology," thereby extending its domain beyond Germany and

Central Europe. Includes essays by distinguished French and German folklorists: Peter Assion, Hermann Bausinger, Wolfgang Brückner, Isac Chiva, Elisabeth Claverie, Utz Jeggle, Alain Morel, and Rudolf Schenda.

200. Eberhart, Helmut, Edith Hörandner, and Burkhard Pöttler, eds. *Volksfrömmigkeit: Referate der Österreichischen Volkskundetagung 1989 in Graz.* ("Folk Religiosity: Papers from the 1989 Austrian Folklore Conference in Graz"). Vienna: Verein für Volkskunde, 1990. (Buchreihe der Österreichischen Zeitschrift für Volkskunde, 8).

Essays that address folk religiosity, particularly as it has persisted and assumed new forms in modern Europe during the second half of the twentieth century. Folk religiosity results from the practices of individuals, small socio-economic or regional groups, or rituals and other forms of expression, most of which differ from those of "high religion," in other words, organized forms and institutions of religion in Europe. The authors represent different areas of Europe; written just prior to the fall of Communist governments in Eastern Europe, several essays offer insights into the patterns of religious practices there (e.g., Gábor Barna on research into religious folk life after World War II). Throughout the book traditional genres of folk religiosity (e.g., pilgrimage or magic and religion) are juxtaposed with new genres (e.g., belief systems of convicted criminals). Musical themes occur frequently, indicating the degree to which musical practices become sites for the expression of folk religiosity.

201. Just, Gisela. *Magische Musik im Märchen: Untersuchungen zur Funktion magischen Singens und Spielens in Volkserzählungen.* ("Magical Music in Fairy Tales: Investigations into the Function of Magical Singing and Playing in Folk Narratives"). Frankfurt am Main: Peter Lang, 1991. (Artes Populares. Studia ethnographica et folkloristica, 20).

Examines the presence of music in the narrative genres of folklore. In addition to fairy tales, other narrative genres figure into this study, with most examples coming from nineteenth-century collections, which also means that "magic" takes on the shadings of Romantic thought and imagination. The author is most concerned with the question of function. What does music achieve when it assumes magical power? Which are the domains in which music and magic intersect in narrative folklore? How does magical music illuminate the world of symbolic understanding shared by narrator and audience? The study examines the presence of magical music historically, showing it to be present in European folklore at least since the Middle Ages and also to be an area of European folklore that has served as a

conduit to non-Western, particularly Middle Eastern, folklore. An
original and valuable study of a rarely examined area of folklore.

202. Naumann, Hans. *Deutsche Volkskunde in Grundzügen.*
("Fundamental Characteristics of German Folklore"). Leipzig:
Quelle & Meyer, 1935. 3rd printing; first printing in 1922.

Employing chapters that present the fundamental
characteristics of the different domains studied by folklorists,
Naumann situates the field in the intellectual history of growing
German nationalism in Germany beween the world wars.
Naumann's approach identifies relatively conservative areas of
folkloristic study. The objects of study, for example, include
traditional clothing (*Tracht*), the farmhouse (*Bauernhaus*), and
the riddle (*Rätsel*). The contexts established in the central
chapters also suggest a conservative construction of Germanness,
for example, by naming the fourth chapter "the spirit of primitive
society" (*primitiver Gemeinschaftsgeist*). In addition to appearing in
other contexts, folk music receives an entire chapter in the
volume. Naumann discusses many of the predominant theories of
folk song from the early twentieth century in this chapter, for
example, *Zersingen* (singing into many versions) and
Formelhaftigkeit (formulaic structure). The overarching thesis of
the chapter, nonetheless, is that folk song develops from
composed art song in the centers of higher culture, hence it
maintains a connection to the expression of Germanness at the
court and in the aristocratic culture from which Germany
maintains its identity. Naumann's concept of folk song owes a
great deal to that of John Meier's *Kunstlieder im Volksmunde* (art
songs in the mouths of the folk; see chapter 7 in the present
book). Folk song is also fundamentally historical, which is to say
that it arises with essentially German social structures and textual
forms in the Middle Ages and follows paths of continuous
transmission to the present. Ideologically conservative, the volume
illustrates the ways in which folk song became one of the
cornerstones in the construction of German nationalism and
fascism.

203. Petzoldt, Leander, and Stefaan Top, eds. *Dona Folcloristica:
Festgabe für Lutz Röhrich zu seiner Emeritierung.* ("Dona Folcloristica:
A Festive Gift to Lutz Röhrich on His Retirement"). Frankfurt am
Main: Peter Lang, 1990. (Beiträge zur Europäischen Ethnologie
und Folklore. Reihe B: Tagungsberichte, 3).

A *Festschrift* for Lutz Röhrich, head of the Folklore Department
at the University of Freiburg and Director of the Deutsches
Volksliedarchiv, also in Freiburg im Breisgau. Although the
contents of the volume are diverse from the standpoints of subject

and discipline (folklorists, ethnomusicologists, folk-song scholars, historical musicologists, and others contributed to the volume), the juxtaposition of themes and approaches is unusually revealing of discursive change at a moment of political and ideological change in German history, namely, the reunification of Germany. The volume, therefore, symbolizes folkloristics in change, for example in the article of GDR folklorist Hermann Strobach on structure and process, one of the final opportunities to write on such a topic from the perspectives of the German Democratic Republic. Musicologist Walter Salmen writes here one of his first articles on the history of *klezmer* music in Europe, establishing his thesis about the connection of Jewish instrumental folk music to dance practices in European Jewish society. The collection contains twenty-three essays, from authors throughout Europe, suggesting that folkloristics might provide one of the disciplines serving as a harbinger of the potential unity in the new Europe.

204. Röhrich, Lutz, and Erika Lindig, eds. *Volksdichtung zwischen Mündlichkeit und Schriftlichkeit.* ("Folk Poetry between Orality and Literacy"). Tübingen: Narr, 1989. (ScriptOralia, 9).

An anthology of papers from a 1987 conference devoted to the interrelation of orality and literacy in the narrative genres of folklore. The essayists take a fairly unified position about this interrelation, not only that orality and literacy do not parse into separate processes, but also that the dynamic field between them must become the object of study, particularly to shift the emphasis of folkloristics toward process. This approach assumes revisionist potential in some of the essays, especially those that recognize new historical potential in the areas they have examined. Peter Assion's study of motives in German immigrant texts and Christoph Daxelmüller's examination of narratives about ritual murder in Hungary provide exemplary studies of the ways in which process lends itself to broadening the base of historical fact. Both traditional tales from the nineteenth century (many from the Brothers Grimm) and from popular culture in the twentieth century (e.g., Linda Dégh's piece on letters to the dead) lend the volume considerable breadth. The essays specifically concerned with music (Otto Holzapfel, Eva Kimminich, Waltraud Linder-Beroud, and Ernst Schade) examine traditional texts, but from the perspective of the oral processes that have affected and effected their transmission. An important contribution to the study of the interdependence and inseparability of oral and written traditions.

205. Weber-Kellermann, Ingeborg, and Andreas C. Bimmer. *Einführung in die Volkskunde/Europäische Ethnologie: Eine Wissenschaftsgeschichte.* ("Introduction to Folklore/European

Ethnology: An Intellectual History"). 2d ed. Stuttgart: J.B. Metzler, 1985. (Realien zur Literatur, Abteilung A, Literaturwissenschaft und Geisteswissenschaft).

A survey of the history of folkloristics, primarily in German-speaking traditions. The authors regard the pair "folklore/European ethnology" as two directions or emphases, folklore addressing issues of text, European ethnology the contexts of European culture. They also argue for an historical shift of emphasis from text to context, and this book takes its shape from this shift. Individual chapters focus on important moments and paradigms in the history of folkloristics, beginning with premodern writings and concluding with the postmodern research, particularly that which addresses the many different areas of ethnological research necessary in an age of extensive industrialization. The book lends itself well to use as a reference work, with tightly written chapters and sections, each with a selected bibliography. The authors also employ extensive reflexivity and disciplinary criticism, for they do not fail to address the problems that developed when folklore and folkloristics were used to dangerous political and ideological ends (e.g., chapter 9, "Folklore in the age of National-Socialism"). Folk song and folk music are not specific subjects in the book, but rather the folklorists and folklore institutions that incorporated music into their research activities. In this sense, music generally receives treatment as one of several areas that many folklorists study. The overall perspective is that of a field at a moment of transition and shifting emphasis.

Historical Musicology—*Musikwissenschaft*

206. Baumann, Dorothea, and Kurt von Fischer, eds. *Religiöse Autoritäten und Musik*. ("Religious Authorities and Music"). Kassel: Johannes Stauda Verlag, 1984.

In essays expanded from a special session on religion and music at the 1982 meeting of the International Musicological Society, six musical scholars describe the positions of religious authorities toward music in six "world" religions: Walter Blankenburg on Protestantism; Helmut Hucke on Catholicism; Gidô Kataoka on Buddhism in Japan; Mohammad Taghi Massoudieh on Islam; Amnon Shiloah on Judaism; Dimitrije Stefanovic on Orthodox Christianity. Each scholar presents the history of authoritative positions toward music, providing a backdrop for modern or recent positions. The positions range from virtually complete tolerance of local decisions (e.g.,

Protestantism) to intense centralization (e.g., in Shiite Islam in Iran). The essays encourage comparison, and the volume concludes with a transcription of responses to questions at the original conference. Missing from the volume is extensive information about the responses to authority in local or individual practice. There is also a lack of awareness that these religions stand out as "world" religions only for Westerners, with the result that the volume is not only weighted toward Christianity (three of the six "world" religions discussed), but that certain religions are excluded because they putatively lack authoritative positions on music (e.g., Hinduism, according to the editor, von Fischer). The individual essays, however, provide considerable insight into religious-musical thought.

207. Dahlhaus, Carl, and Hans Heinrich Eggebrecht. *Was ist Musik?* ("What Is Music?"). Wilhelmshaven: Florian Noetzel Verlag, 1987. (Taschenbücher zur Musikwissenschaft, 100).

An investigation into fundamental ontologies of music by two leading German historical musicologists. Each author writes a chapter on the ten thematic domains of the book: the possibility of "the" music (" *die*" *Musik*); music in the European tradition; what is "extra-musical"?; good and bad music; old and new music; aesthetic meaning and symbolic conceptualization; musical worth; "on the beautiful in music"; music and time; and what is music? The authors virtually dismiss non-European and folk musics from their consideration, arguing instead from the privileged position of European history. Historical and aesthetic considerations of music result from dialectical relations, whereby the authors tautologically construct concepts of music by using European models, which exclude other musics. The book is nonetheless valuable because of the diverse literature it surveys, as well as the diverse theories that depend on European aesthetic constructs. For folk-music scholars and ethnomusicologists the book exposes the underlying presence of history in the European conceptualization of music. German folk-music scholars often use similar criteria, for example, by claiming that folk music is the product of "people with history" (*Geschichtsvölker*). Many of the concepts of music surveyed in this book, particularly earlier theories, do account for folk and popular musics, hence making this book a contribution to the intellectual history of folk-music scholarship.

208. Doflein, Erich. "Historismus und Historisierung in der Musik." ("Historical Consciousness and Historicism in Music"). In Ludwig Finscher and Christoph-Hellmut Mahling, eds., *Festschrift für Walter Wiora*. Kassel: Bärenreiter, 1967. Pp. 48–56.

A reflective survey of the impact of historical consciousness on the construction of modern musicological discourse. Doflein is particularly concerned with the ways in which concepts of tradition and interpretation arose in the seventeenth and eighteenth centuries to establish connections between contemporary practices and those of the past. The several possible connections between present and past receive very nuanced readings. Although Doflein focuses largely on Western art music, he also concentrates on the rise of musicological discourse during the same periods that folk-music discourse emerged in Central European thought, especially the late eighteenth century. In hommage to Walter Wiora, in whose *Festschrift* this article appears, Doflein also recognizes that historical thought and historicism provided connections between the domains of scholarship devoted to different types of music. A concise introduction to the importance of history in European musical thought.

209. Gradenwitz, Peter. *Literatur und Musik in geselligem Kreise: Geschmacksbildung, Gesprächsstoff und musikalische Unterhaltung in der bürgerlichen Salongesellschaft.* ("Literature and Music in Social Circles: The Education of Taste, Conversation Material, and Musical Conversation in the Bourgeois Salon"). Stuttgart: Steiner, 1991.

Uses primary documents, particularly from the early nineteenth century, to demonstrate the development and dissemination of musical taste in the rising middle class of Central Europe. This transformation of taste served as a backdrop for Romanticism, but also provided a domain for the entrance into bourgeois society for those previously excluded, particularly Jews, who play a specially marked role in Gradenwitz's history. The salon culture described in the book included musical life that brought together artists and intellectuals from throughout society. It therefore served as a social world constructed by the new bourgeois, in which they contributed substantially to the cultural life that spilled over to life outside the salon. Gradenwitz restricts his study historically, although it would have been appropriate to examine the private sphere of music making prior to the nineteenth century, as well as into the twentieth century, when it intersected with the public sphere in more complex ways, for example, when Jewish cultural and intellectual life entered the public sphere. Similarly, issues of class remain untouched. Of great interest is the introduction to literary genres, such as conversation books, and musical activities necessary for the emergence of a cultured bourgeois in the nineteenth century.

210. Walter, Michael, ed. *Text und Musik: Neue Perspektive der Theorie.*
("Text and Music: New Theoretical Perspectives"). Munich: Fink,
1992. (Materialität der Zeichen. Reihe A, 10).

Although the eight essays in this volume generally miss
opportunities to incorporate theoretical perspectives from folk-
song research, they illustrate the overall interdisciplinary realm in
which German historical musicology is attempting to wrestle with
the relation between text and music. "Text" in this work largely
refers to song text, and vocal genres ranging from medieval chant
(Michael Walter) to Baroque opera in Latin America (Jürgen
Maehder) provide case studies. The theoretical perspectives in
individual essays also vary, from communications theory (Claudia
Krülls-Hepermann) and notions of musico-poetic form as an
interactive space (Clemens Goldberg) to the interpretation of
different narrative levels (Herbert Lindenberger). For the most
part, the essayists retain the common view in historical musicology
that text and music are not the same and that they signify
meaning (or fail to signify it) in different ways. At their best, the
essays attempt to apply theories of textual analysis to musical
analysis, thereby suggesting interdisciplinary possibilities that
should also be of interest to folk-music scholars and
ethnomusicologists, for example, Fritz Reckow's application of
models from classical and Renaissance rhetoric to interpreting the
contents of musical form. Whatever they contribute to a better
understanding of music's relation to text, however, these essays
fail to learn from music's relation to context.

❧❦❧

Systematic Musicology

211. Dahlhaus, Carl, and Helga de la Motte-Haber, eds. *Systematische
Musikwissenschaft.* ("Systematic Musicology"). Vol. 10: *Neues
Handbuch der Musikwissenschaft*, ed. by Carl Dahlhaus. Wiesbaden:
Akademische Verlagsgesellschaft Athenaion, 1982.

Presents systematic musicology largely from the perspectives of
German musicologists interested in Western art music. The
"systematic" in this musicology results from the historical
tendency to organize ideas and theories about music as systems,
that is, as discursive domains in which relatedness prevails.
Central to the arguments made by the authors in the volume are
key concepts such as originality, autonomy, and individuality, as
well as the more abstract notions such as music as the language of
feelings and musical hermeneutics. Systematic musicology, it
follows, provides a field of research in which all of these can be
investigated in order to yield results that can be reproduced and

applied to any, if not all, musics. The musical phenomena the systematic musicologist investigates are, on one hand, aesthetic, but, on the other, they owe their existence to social conditions and contexts. For these reasons, systematic musicology overlaps with and to some degree depends on the fields of musical aesthetics and music sociology, again two disciplines that are arguably most extensively developed in Central Europe. Curiously absent from the theories in this book are the systematic questions raised by folk-music research and ethnomusicology, which very well might challenge the persistence of aesthetic categories through history and across cultures.

212. Födermayr, Franz, and Werner A. Deutsch. "Zur Akustik des 'tepsijanje.'" ("On the Acoustics of the *'Tepsijanje'*"). In Max Peter Baumann, Rudolf Maria Brandl, and Kurt Reinhard, eds., *Neue ethnomusikologische Forschungen: Festschrift Felix Hoerburger*. Laaber: Laaber-Verlag, 1977. Pp. 97–112.

Takes the problems of sound production and sound perception that arise from the spinning pan of southeastern Europe, the *tepsijanje*, as a set of laboratory conditions that systematic musicology can illuminate. The *tepsijanje* mediates the sound produced by a singer, who projects that sound across the spinning pan. By placing loudspeakers and microphones in different positions, the authors measure the vastly different sonic experiences that the *tepsijanje* mediates as an instrument. Listeners directly opposite the singer, for example, hear music quite different from listeners on the side. Articles placed in the pan, moreover, deflect and direct sound in very distinct ways. These experiments demonstrate not just the capacity of systematic methods to examine musical performance in very refined ways, but also the presence of unexpected acoustical phenomena, such as the Doppler effect, in seemingly simple instruments and sound mediators.

213. Graf, Walter. "Zum Einsatz moderner Signalverarbeitungsverfahren für musikwissenschaftliche Analysen." ("Employment of Modern Acoustical Displays for Musicological Analysis"). In Christian Ahrens, Rudolf Maria Brandl, and Felix Hoerburger, eds., *"Weine, meine Laute...": Gedenkschrift Kurt Reinhard*. Laaber: Laaber Verlag, 1984. Pp. 139 58.

By examining the inherent limitations of recording technologies vis-à-vis different musical elements, Graf argues that new means of computer processing and visual display of sound can reveal much more about recorded sound, especially early sound recordings in archives, than previously imagined.

Systematic analysis allows for a greater understanding of overtone structures, the relation of fundamental tones to polyphonic styles, the duration of individual tones, the characteristics of transition between notes, and the like. Graf illustrates these with spectral displays in an appendix. This article appeared at an early moment in the use of digital technologies but nonetheless serves to point to new directions in Austrian systematic musicology. Graf looks toward the future, noting that the new technologies would be unusually helpful in the recovery of information about the earliest recordings in ethnomusicology. The article also reveals just how extensive the weaknesses of traditional visual representation of music (i.e., notation) are when applied to complex recorded sound.

❧❧❧

Folk-Dance Research—Dance Ethnology

214. Bröcker, Marianne. *Tanz und Tanzmusik in Überlieferung und Gegenwart.* ("Dance and Dance Music, Traditional and Contemporary"). Bamberg: Universitätsbibliothek, 1992. (Schriften der Universitätsbibliothek Bamberg, 9).

A conference volume, with contributions from folk-music and folk-dance researchers, as well as from practitioners and cultivators (*Volkstanzpfleger*). Despite these different backgrounds, though perhaps also because of them, a remarkable degree of thematic unity binds this volume together. Central to this unity is the way in which folk dance is a medium for gathering and negotiating social and ethnic differences. The ethnic and national aspects of this theme permeate the essays on genre and form, which examine the ways in which dances from one part of Europe appear in other parts. The relation between professionalism (e.g., the emergence of dance teachers as a profession in the nineteenth century) and amateur practices focuses the theme on the social and economic contexts of dance. The volume also serves as significant proof that folk-dance research must be interdisciplinary (e.g., in Otto Holzapfel's study of the ways in which the song genre, *Vierzeiler* [quatrain], serves as a vehicle for dancers to parody and even to insult others). Choreographic essays, such as those by Ernst Schusser and Karl Horak, gain a much wider meaning when placed in this interdisciplinary context. Suggestive of fruitful new directions in folk-dance research.

215. Hoerburger, Felix. *Volkstanzkunde.* ("Folk-Dance Research"). 2 vols. Kassel: Bärenreiter Verlag, 1961 and 1964. (Mensch und Tanz, 3 and 4).

Systematically sketches the different motivations, methodologies, institutions, and interdisciplinary potentials of folk-dance research. Although the approaches are meant to have cross-cultural applications, they are derived from Central European research, and to a lesser extent from Eastern and southeastern European dance research. Fundamental to Hoerburger's discussion of folk-dance research are the necessary contributions from scholars in different fields. The use of film, for example, is essential, as is the use of diverse forms of recording. Hoerburger concerns himself largely with transcription and film documentation as means of representing folk dance, and these largely serve as means of enabling the scholar to conduct comparative research. It is an important contribution of this book that it not only includes those who cultivate and practice folk dance (*Volkstanzpfleger*) in modernity, but also illumines the ways in which practitioners and theorists must combine their efforts.

216. Hoerburger, Felix. *Die Zwiefachen: Gestaltung und Umgestaltung der Tanzmelodien im nördlichen Altbayern.* ("The Zwiefach: Form and Transformation of Dance Melodies in Northern Old-Bavaria"). 2nd ed. Laaber: Laaber-Verlag, 1991.

The classic (the first edition appeared in 1956) study of Central European dances with shifting meters. The Zwiefach generally results when duple and triple meters alternate according to different patterns. Hoerburger develops two theories to explain this phenomenon. The first explains the shifting meter according to the melodies of the dances themselves, hence the texts upon which Zwiefach dances rely. The second depends on patterns that develop within the form, for example the particular relation of tonic to dominant harmonies. In the most general sense, these theories explain the shift of meter as paralleling the relation to either music or dance; in more specific senses, other contexts symbolize and parallel the shift, for example local melodic traits versus overall form, or dance genre versus local variation. Hoerburger employs meticulous analysis and comparative tables throughout, in which each aspect of his theories is shown in relation to its position in a particular dance melody. The strength of the book is its musicological methods, which would shed even more light on the specifically Central European phenomenon of the Zwiefach if they were combined with research from the practical and performance sides of dance research.

217. Novák, Petr. "Zur Dokumentation der Veränderungen im volkstümlichen Tanzrepertoire." ("Toward the Documentation of Change in the Folklike Dance Repertory"). In Jürgen Dittmar, ed., *Dokumentationsprobleme heutiger Volksmusikforschung.* Bern: Peter Lang, 1987. Pp. 101–12.

A call for expanding documentation systems for dance research beyond the usual concentration on discrete steps and fundamental musical structures. Most dance in Europe at the end of the twentieth century does not adhere strictly to the usual structures of folk dance, particularly those that are determined by specific relations between musical structure and movement. Instead, folklike (*volkstümlich*) dance provides many more opportunities for dancers to improvise and to expand the usual restrictions of genre. Novák suggests that there is an overall tension experienced by dancers, in which there is a pull, on one side, toward the motivic structures of dance (Novák illustrates this largely with round dances) and, on the other, toward greater freedom of expression (in contrast with the round dance, a tendency to open the circle and break into new patterns). Novák suggests ways to consider more broadly all aspects that inform a dancer's decision to dance in certain ways, ranging from musical and choreographic motives to social and emotional influences. All these must be taken into account if folk, folklike, and vernacular dances are to be documented in meaningful ways.

218. Oetke, Herbert. *Der deutsche Volkstanz.* ("The German Folk Dance"). 2 vols. Berlin: Henschelverlag Kunst und Gesellschaft, 1982.

Organizes dance forms in Central Europe according to a loose set of genres, such as "line dances," "pair dances," "artisans' dances," and "wedding dances." Oetke concerns himself with locating a multitude of examples across considerable spans of time and place, history and geography in Central Europe (the meaning of "German" in the title). He cites individual examples from the earliest sources known to him and then brings each genre to the present with examples from additional primary and secondary sources. Historical links generally do not emerge from these methods, not least because there is frequently a tendency to generalize about the earliest sources and contemporary practices. The most important contribution of the historical volume is that it lends itself to comparison with the studies of other dance ethnologists. The second volume contains transcriptions, more or less literally taken from secondary sources. Prepared by Kurt Petermann, these transcriptions permit only limited comparison but do provide a reasonable survey of diverse forms and individual styles.

219. Peter, Ilka. *Tanzbeschreibungen, Tanzforschung: Gesammelte Volkstanzstudien.* ("Dance Descriptions, Dance Research: Collected Folk-Dance Studies"). Vienna: Österreichischer Bundesverlag, 1983.

Essays by one of the leading folk-dance researchers in Austria, covering a period from 1941 to 1981. Peter conducted her research with both the cultivation of folk dance and its research in mind, hence the two components of the main title. The strength of the approach is to provide close readings of local practices, which nonetheless lend themselves to comparison with folk-dance practices throughout Austria. The individual essays examine (1) a genre and its forms; (2) a genre in a specific place; and (3) a genre from the perspective of a particular moment in time. Peter covers many different regional and local practices during the post-World War II transformation resulting from the confrontation between tradition and intensive cultivation (*Pflege*), hence making the volume not only an overview of Austria's folk-dance landscape but also a history and historiography of folk dance in the twentieth century.

≈⊙⊛⊙≈

Music Education—Music Pedagogy

220. Hammel, Heide. *Die Schulmusik in der Weimarer Republik: Politische und gesellschaftliche Aspekte der Reformdiskussion in den 20er Jahren.* ("School Music in the Weimar Republic: Political and Social Aspects of Reform Discussions during the 1920s"). Stuttgart: Metzler, 1990.

Focuses primarily on the reform programs introduced by Leo Kestenberg, an official responsible for music in the Prussian Ministry for Education. The reform movement stressed the importance of music as a component of general education, drawing upon an inclusive and broad definition of music. Folk music won a place in the reform of music education, although it was understood in nationalistic terms. Music reform in the school gradually came to have broad political connotations, becoming a means of inculcating German youths with social and national values. To a large extent, the valuable aspects of reform in the 1920s were supplanted with agendas connected to the rise of Nazism in the 1930s and the exaggerated and perverse musical nationalism that marked it. This book is at its strongest as a collection of source materials and as an examination of specific policies and their implementation. The "political aspects" of its title, however, are treated more descriptively than analytically.

Larger historical questions are sometimes absent or remain unanswered (e.g., the impact of reform in this period on Jewish culture in Germany, for Kestenberg, a Jew, immigrated to Palestine in the 1930s). Joins other studies of the position of music in German society during the political transitions and tragedies of the twentieth century.

221. Lorenz, Karl. "Die Metamorphose der Volksmusik im Industriezeitalter: Versuch einer Darstellung anhand des Umgangs mit Elementen der Volksmusik in der Jugendmusikschule einer mittleren Großstadt." ("The Metamorphosis of Folk Music in the Industrial Age: An Attempt at a Presentation by Examining the Ways in Which Elements of Folk Music Are Used in a Youth Music School in a Mid-Sized City"). In Hans-Friedrich Meyer, ed., *Heutige Probleme der Volksmusik*. Cologne: Deutsche UNESCO-Kommission, 1973. Pp. 119–26.

Surveys the ways students at a music school respond, largely with movement, to the diverse aspects in different types of folk music. The author claims that the mid-sized city (Remscheid, Germany) in which these experiments were carried out was totally devoid of folk music in the traditional sense, meaning here rural, transmitted orally, and the like. Arguing that the basis of folk music lies in its ability to stimulate movement, Lorenz finds that the students responded quickly to those elements that produce a swinging movement and a sense of pulse. He speculates that the fundamental nature of folk music lies in these elements and that the responses of these students, therefore, represent a natural tendency to engage in the performance of folk music. The new folk music of the Industrial Age, it follows, is not that of traditional repertories, but rather that possessing the elemental traits, for example, some forms of international popular music derived from African music. The article closes optimistically, observing that the metamorphosis of folk music will survive the homogenization many claim for the Industrial Age.

⚜

Cultural Studies

222. Dohrn, Verena. *Reise nach Galizien: Grenzlandschaften des alten Europa.* ("A Trip to Galicia: Border Landscapes of the Old Europe"). Frankfurt am Main: S. Fischer, 1991.

On the eve of the collapse of socialist governments in East-Central Europe, the author travels to cities and administrative centers of the former Habsburg Empire. These were formerly located in the province of Galicia, which today includes land from Poland, Belarus, and Ukraine. While looking for the traces of former Habsburg culture—opera houses, synagogues, great cities of the nineteenth century, such as Lemberg (L'vov) and Tschernowitz (Czernowitz)—Dohrn discovers a surprising resilience, particularly among the few surviving Jews, whose memories of the past remain as maps of the "old Europe." Each "border landscape" takes shape through a portrait of one of its major political or artistic figures, many of whom grew up in Conservative or Orthodox Jewish homes but built their careers in Austria or Germany, for example Rosa Luxemburg and Joseph Roth. Not only does the author show that the old Europe has not disappeared from history, but she illustrates that its complexity was far greater than cultural historians who only examine the major cities and leading political movements of Central Europe have imagined. Frequent reference to the venues of music-making—opera houses, cinemas, religious and cultural centers, the family—occur, making the book also a contribution to understanding musical life in the old Europe.

223. Goettle, Gabriele. *Deutsche Sitten: Erkundungen in Ost und West.* ("German Customs: Investigations into East and West"). Frankfurt am Main: Eichborn Verlag, 1991.

Vignettes and sketches of the cultural moments that represent the German everyday around the historic moment of reunification. With a critical yet dispassionate eye Goettle discovers the unusual in what seems usual, the exceptional that emerges from the unexceptional. Her sources vary widely, ranging from newspaper accounts to interviews and personal experiences. Her explorations of what Germans throw away and place in their garbage, or of the records about an individual's life after an automobile accident, suggest that German customs exist in a complex dialectic between institutions and social patterns of the past, and the postmodern conditions of industrial society. Whereas music is not specifically addressed, it exists as a background text of Germanness, that is, as a marker of institutional and everyday life. It provides a source of evidence for the linking of East and West, the loose thesis in the book that German customs, though frequently imagined as splintering, nonetheless are driven by the centripetalizing pull of history. The musics of Germanness provide a powerful and legible text in that pull of history. The individual essays often possess wry humor and brilliant cynicism.

224. Habermas, Jürgen. *Strukturwandel der Öffentlichkeit: Untersuchungen zu einer Kategorie der bürgerlichen Gesellschaft.* ("Structural Change of the Public Sphere: Explorations of a Category of Bourgeois Society"). Neuwied: Hermann Luchterhand, 1962. (Politica, 4)

A seminal theorization of the public sphere, which has exerted an international influence on critical approaches to the positioning of culture. Habermas considers the public sphere as a domain to which everyone has access. He interrogates the conditions of public access historically, taking as a given that the public sphere exists in dialectic relation to the private sphere, that is, those places of cultural activity to which only a few have access. The relation between public and private is constantly in flux, but a fundamental inversion occurred in Europe during the eighteenth-century Enlightenment, when (1) the public sphere included many more cultural practices; and (2) a growing bourgeois class had access to the public sphere because of economic mobility. Habermas concerns himself relatively little with music and the arts, although his historicization of the public sphere lends itself to comparison with the changing conditions of concert life, as well as public access to the arts in general. It is not by chance, moreover, that his identification of a modern inversion of the relation between public and private spheres parallels the development of folk-music theory, also a concept concerning public culture that stems from Enlightenment thought. Throughout the book Habermas compares different theories and contrasting case studies from different cultures, but his book essentially remains focused on Europe and European history, as well as on a notion of "public" that does not extend to non-Western cultures very convincingly. The book, nonetheless, has substantially influenced much thinking on the relation of folk music to European culture.

225. Kittler, Friedrich A. *Aufschreibesysteme 1800/1900*. ("Discourse Networks 1800/1900"). 2nd expanded ed. Munich: Wilhelm Fink, 1987.

Examines the complex interaction between emerging technologies for the mediation of oral to written expression during the nineteenth century. In particular, Kittler examines the ways in which these technologies made it possible for new groups (the petit bourgeoisie, women, etc.) to engage in "literary" activity, which in turn rendered social transformations, both domestically and in the workplace. Accordingly, newly emerging social groups were bound together in new forms of intellectual activity and social exchange, usually referred to in English as "discourse networks," though better glossed from *Aufschreibesysteme* as "systems for writing out." Music appears in several places in the book, first in its position close to speech as Herder and Goethe imagined it at the beginning of the nineteenth century, and then interacting with new media, such as film, at the beginning of the twentieth century. There are other models and patterns of interaction between oral and written traditions in the book that would lend themselves to ethnomusicological consideration, for example by examining collection, classification, and notational systems that emerged in the nineteenth century or by investigating the ways in which folk and popular song were increasingly connected to organized social activities by the end of the century (e.g., singing societies or labor movements).

226. Latz, Inge. *Die Stille würde mich töten: Warum die Musik weiblich ist.* ("The Silence Would Kill Me: Why Music Is Feminine"). Bonn: Meussling, 1987.

A personal and impressionistic attempt to identify feminine qualities in music and to suggest that these qualities provide an appropriate context for salvaging humankind's survival in a troubled world. Latz employs different vignettes to suggest the ways in which music is both structurally and culturally feminine. The structures at which she looks include, for example, the predominance of perfect fourths in genres with which women are particularly closely associated (e.g., lullabies and Marian songs). These and other structures appear in folk songs as codes of the feminine presence in music. The feminine also provides a conduit between music and the cosmos, and Latz extends this argument to make a case for the nurturing qualities of women, immanent in music, to a process of healing the universe. Feminine qualities exhibit a purity that male qualities do not. The woman's voice, for example, is portrayed as the original musical instrument (*Ur-Instrument*). The feminine qualities of music further result from the hegemonic control of men. Whereas many claims in this book reflect the impressions of its author but are generalized as if they represent all women, the book represents an ambitious attempt to theorize the feminine in music. It may not prove its points (nor does it usually try to prove them), but it reminds one of the persistent interest in investigating the gendered character of music, especially within the historical context of the German women's movement.

227. Steinert, Heinz. *Adorno in Wien: Über die (Un-)Möglichkeit von Kunst, Kultur und Befreiung.* ("Adorno in Vienna: On the (Im-)Possibility of Art, Culture, and Liberation"). Vienna: Verlag für Gesellschaftskritik, 1989.

Focuses on Theodor W. Adorno's 1925 residence in Vienna and the impact of his musical experience in that year on the development of his own theories, as well as those of the Frankfurt School of Social Research in the decades after World War II.

Music was central to Adorno's reconceptualization of social theory after his experiences in Vienna, first because he expected to find "revolution" in the music of the New Viennese School (he had planned to study composition with Alban Berg) and second because Adorno encountered a social and ethnic diversity in the musical life of Vienna. The subject of Adorno's musical writings about Vienna was never folk music, but this book suggests that some of Adorno's initial ideas about popular music and music for a broad cross-section of society may have first developed in Vienna. Vienna was for Adorno the "ideal city," a laboratory in which musical and social change potentially intersected. The book serves as a valuable and readable introduction to Adorno's later writings on popular music and the sociology of music.

228. Theweleit, Klaus. *Orpheus (und) Eurydike*. ("Orpheus [and] Euridice"). Vol. 1: *Buch der Könige.* Basel: Stroemfeld/Roter Stern, 1988.

Taking the transformation and distortion of time and space in the musical metaphors in the myth of Orpheus and Euridice as a point of departure, Theweleit creates an historical parable for the disjuncture and conjunction of myth and history. The text of the book constantly moves between the description of historical moments, particularly those in music history, and postmodern simulacra. Music animates time and history, but it also confuses it by creating a field of ceaseless signification, where anything can create a framework for perceiving music in anything else. Illustrating the book are examples from myth and modernity, but their juxtaposition seemingly breaks down the boundaries between these. On one hand, the book is idiosyncratic and occasionally arbitrary, but on the other, it is extraordinarily suggestive of the power of music's capacity to embody and convey meaning. The role of the physical body as a space within which music happens and as a vehicle for the transformation of external spaces makes the book an important contribution to an emerging literature on music and the body. Because there are no distinctions between folk, art, popular, or any other kind of music in the volume, Theweleit also makes the book itself a metaphor for rethinking the ontology of music.

229. Wischenbart, Rüdiger. *Karpaten: Die dunkle Seite Europas*. ("The Carpathians: The Dark Side of Europe"). With additional essays by Monika Czernin, Renate Reilig, Peter Klein, Herta Müller, Peter Polanski, Martin Pollack, Michael Schrott, Tilman Spengler, and Jan Tabor. Vienna: Kremayr & Scheriau, 1992.

A collection of vignettes and reports from the multicultural region of the Carpathians, the range of low mountains stretching in an arch from Slovakia across Poland, Hungary, and Romania into Ukraine. The essays represent both a geographical and temporal journey, the first eastward through the Carpathians and the second into specific historical moments that ascribe identity to the mountains. The authors concern themselves frequently with the meaning of multiculturalism in the Carpathians, not only the ways in which this has formed historical processes but also the impact it continues to exert on the modern identity of this region. The Carpathians constantly form border regions, between the past and present, as well as between modern regions and nations. Particularly trenchant in most of the essays is the Jewish history of the region and the failure of modern residents either to eliminate the Jewish past or to reintegrate the memory of it into the unstable present. The essays on German-speaking areas, most of which no longer exist, are also among the best in this volume. Folk and popular music appears often in these essays, especially as a narrative voice that reconfigures the history of the Carpathians. Many essays vividly describe the competition of different musics and media within the multicultural public sphere. The musical life of the present, therefore, represents the contestation and richness of a region whose identities are historically multiple, shifting, and volatile.

III

SOCIAL CONTEXTS OF FOLK MUSIC

9

Musicians

The first word in folk-music research was *Volk*, "the people," the term with which Johann Gottfried Herder determined to delimit the music-making practices he designated as *Volkslieder*. Herder drew attention to those who produced song, but by no means did he or his immediate successors focus that attention on individual musicians. The *Volk* remained, in fact, ambiguous, amorphous, far less a collective of musicians than an abstract category of nameless individuals. During the nineteenth century musicians were virtually absent from the study of folk music; instead, it was music as an object that could acquire a life and identity of its own without musicians that became the central focus during the first century of folk-music research. In some ways, the situation has not changed that much even today, with musicians remaining invisible in some of the most visible areas of folk-music research. There are other approaches, of course, several of which have actively attempted to redress the absence of musicians from folk-music research. Studies of musicians, nonetheless, remain relatively scarce, with recent attempts to bring the musician into view more the exception than the rule. Most of the works annotated in the present chapter recognize the need to redress the historical invisibility of the musician as one of those designated by Herder as *Volk*.

Musicians first enter folk-music research as individuals who, in some way, stand out from the *Volk*. The musician, then, is not an "everyperson," but rather a specialist, an outsider, or even a professional. The exceptional status of musicians in twentieth-century studies is, of course, one of the explanations for the absence of musicians in nineteenth-century studies. If *"das Volk dichtet"* ("the people create poetry"), as Jacob Grimm forcefully claimed, individual personalities were not legible in folk song. Insofar as individuals did contribute to the process of creating folk song, say, as hawkers of broadsides or as instrumentalists who moved between court and tavern, they preceded the moment in which music became folk music. More recently, scholars have rethought the nature of the contexts in which folk musicians lived and were active. Indeed, it is the "active" nature of music-making that has been important to studies of musicians in the rural villages of Burgenland (see, e.g., Sepp Gmasz and Anton Reiterits) or in the "most remote" regions of the Styrian Alps (see Walter Deutsch's study of Cyprian Händler). The musician was mobile and accordingly participated in many different contexts, thereby acquiring a diverse repertory (see Karl Schnürl). The folk musician was not, then, different from other musicians, that is, those who performed art or popular music (see the studies by Walter Salmen and Heinrich Schwab), but rather the folk musician relied on different practices, not least among them those that afforded the folk musician an exceptional status.

The ways in which folk musicians developed and maintained their exceptional status were themselves markers of difference and diversity. Historical studies of ethnic music in Central Europe have begun to suggest, for example, that ethnic differences distinguished many musicians. Roma and Sinti musicians, as well as Jewish musicians, possessed a double status of "otherness." Jan Raupp's historical study of Sorbian musicians in eastern Germany, for example, reveals that Sorbian music acquired its distinctive qualities not primarily because of the style of Sorbian repertories, but because of the mobility and presence of Sorbian musicians in a society where there were complex musical practices. Other musicians acquired an exceptional status because they achieved control over the means of musical production, for example, the publication and sale of music in a specific region (see, e.g., the studies by Leander Petzoldt and Christian Rubi). The more these studies turn up about folk musicians in Central Europe, the more the figure of the musician emerges as a central force in the creation and transmission of folk music.

The ways in which German, Austrian, and Swiss scholars focus on the musician differ vastly from each other, and it may well be that these differences provide one of the chief ways of distinguishing the specific qualities of the national schools of scholarship. Especially in Austrian scholarship, the musician has come to play a far more visible role in the past half-century (see, e.g., studies by Hermann Hummer and Rudolf Pietsch), although Josef Pommer had already emphasized the musician by insisting on the importance of actively cultivating folk music. It is at the periphery of German scholarship that interest in musicians has been developing, and perhaps this is due to a deep-seated belief that folk musicians ply their existence along the peripheries of society (see Barbara James below). It may well be that the edges of German society prove to be the sites where social change occurs and where the contestation of political and racial issues is most visible, both in the past and in the future. The failure of Jewish musicians, such as Léon Jessel, to penetrate beyond the periphery in the 1930s may call attention to the inability of Turkish or Roma musicians to acquire full status among the *Volk* in Germany of the 1990s. It may well be the case that it is the exceptional status of musicians in any diverse society that empowers them to repesent the diversity of a multicultural, modern Europe.

❧❦❧

230. Dengg, Harald. "Zur Liedtradition im Pongau am Beispiel einer Goldegger Bauernfamilie." ("On the Song Tradition in Pongau, as Exemplified by a Farming Family from Goldegg"). In Rudolf Pietsch, ed., *Die Volksmusik im Lande Salzburg.* Vol. 2. Vienna: A. Schendl, 1990. Pp. 89–112.

Treats the Hochleitner family of Goldegg in rural Salzburg Province as paradigmatic for the transition of folk-music practices from the early twentieth century to the end of the century. In the article Harald Dengg asks a series of eight questions about stability and change in the song traditions of Salzburg Province. Early in the century singing within most farming families was quite rare, with the most common setting for song being the tavern. Performance and tradition fell into the hands of unusual families, such as the Hochleitners, whose contemporary repertory exceeds 250 pieces. Dengg argues that song tradition, if maintained by exceptional musicians, nonetheless depended on the listeners and active consumers of song in taverns and in other public settings. With the encouragement of regional culture organizations and organizations devoted to the cultivation of folk song (*Volksliedpflege*), however, the degree of interaction between active performers and committed consumers of folk music has increased. The portrait of this musician family is enhanced by transcriptions of their songs and examination of their repertory lists.

231. Deutsch, Walter. "Cyprian Händler oder das obersteirische Musikantentum." ("Cyprian Händler, or the Upper Styrian Musicians' Culture"). *Jahrbuch des österreichischen Volksliedwerkes* 31 (1982): 29–48.

Interprets the responses of an extraordinary musician from the upper Enns Valley of the Austrian province of Styria to Josef Pommer's 1902 call for information about the musical life of Styria. Händler's letters, descriptions of musical activities, and transcriptions, preserved in Pommer's papers, provide a remarkably detailed and complex portrait of music-making throughout the nineteenth century. The musical activities of professional musicians embodied considerable variety, not just in the diverse settings for performances, but also in the instrumentation and repertory used by these musicians. Whereas Händler speaks of a standard Styrian instrumentation of two violins, flute, cymbal, clarinet, and small bass, the performances and musicians he describes constantly vary these. Even though the Upper Styrian region was especially remote from Vienna and urban Central Europe, the repertory of its professional musicians, at least as documented by Händler, took full advantage of published collections of classical and more popular music. Styrian instrumental musicians also interacted with other instrumental specialists, for example, those from Roma communities. Deutsch documents this article skillfully with facsimiles and transcriptions from Händler's communications to Pommer and closes with two extensive descriptions of music-making at a wedding and at a ball during Fasching season 1853.

232. Deutsch, Walter. "Georg Windhofer und Tobi Reiser: Persönlichkeiten der Pongauer Volksmusik." ("Georg Windhofer and Tobi Reiser: Pesonalities in the Folk Music of Pongau"). In Rudolf Pietsch, ed., *Die Volksmusik im Lande Salzburg*. Vol. 2. Vienna: A. Schendl, 1990. Pp. 65–73.

By investigating the different ways in which two rural musicians in the province of Salzburg used innovation to transform Austrian folk-music traditions, Walter Deutsch questions the absence of research into the roles of individual musicians in the study of folk music. Briefly surveying the intellectual history of Austrian scholarship, Deutsch observes that, when mentioned at all, individual musicians seem disconnected from their cultural contexts and the influences they may have had on tradition. Windhofer and Reiser, in contrast, exerted palpable influences on the folk music of the province of Salzburg, and by extension on that of Austria and Bavaria. Windhofer, the teacher and organizer of numerous folk-music and folklore groups, constantly introduced new musical ideas, compositions, and, even, instruments, for example the chromatic dulcimer, or "Salzburger Hackbrett." Whereas Windhofer's influence was local and regional, Reiser's performance style and the complex polyphonic textures of his ensemble arrangements had resonance for the development of folk music throughout the second half of the twentieth century. The exceptional folk musician, Deutsch concludes, is an essential component of transformation and innovation in modern folk music.

233. Deutsch, Walter, and Ursula Hemetek. *Georg Windhofer (1887-1964): Sein Leben—Sein Wirken—Seine Zeit*. ("Georg Windhofer [1887-1964]: His Life—His Influence—His Times"). Vienna: A. Schendl, 1990. (Schriften zur Volksmusik, 14).

The biography of one of the most influential folk musicians in the Austrian province of Salzburg (see above entry). Windhofer was not only an active musician who composed many new melodies for local and regional repertories, but he was also an organizer and activist, who transformed his personal vision for the presence of folk culture into groups dedicated to the restoration of traditional clothing (*Trachtenvereine*) and institutions for the cultivation of folk music (*Volksmusikpflege*). On one hand, Windhofer was an exceptional musician, whose two-voice arrangements of folk dances were distinctive and influential on the increasingly complex textures of twentieth-century Austrian performance practices. On the other, Windhofer's biography is broadly representative of the changes through which rural, alpine Austria passed during the century. Windhofer's activities, therefore, illustrate the ways in which folk music empowers rural workers and farmers to mediate the confrontation between rural and urban cultures, between traditional forms of life and the impact of industrialization on alpine culture. Tradition is not so much a repertory of customs passed from generation to generation as the product of conscious decisions to establish various types of links between generations and between the past and present. The regional folk culture and folk music of the Salzburg province therefore developed as responses to modernity, but responses forged by the knowledge of the past that Georg Windhofer and other regional musicians actively cultivated. Walter Deutsch and Ursula Hemetek have gathered a rich store of musical examples (51) and illustrations (95) to make the folk-music culture of Salzburg extremely palpable. Their scholarly perspectives, moreover, combine to provide a sensitive and detailed portrait of Windhofer and the people of Salzburg.

234. Dümling, Albrecht. *Die verweigerte Heimat: Léon Jessel—der Komponist des "Schwarzwaldmädel".* ("The Denied Homeland: Léon Jessel—The Composer of the 'Schwarzwaldmädel'"). Düsseldorf: Der kleine Verlag, 1992.

Employing the format of a life-and-works volume, this study of Léon Jessel (1871–1942) interpellates the complex nature of the conflicts between committed nationalism in music and the racist National-Socialism of the Nazi period. Jessel was a Jewish operetta and popular-song composer, who discovered his métier in genres that glorified the regional and national, which in his eyes epitomized the German in music. Jessel's *Schwarzwaldmädel* ("Black Forest Girl") of 1917 became a tremendous hit, not least because of the ways in which it encapsulated the spirit of local color on a larger German palette at the height of World War I. This spirit continued to make *Schwarzwaldmädel* one of the most popular German operettas throughout Weimar Germany, into the Nazi period, during World War II, and then in the post-war era, on the stage and in filmed versions. Jessel remained committed to this spirit after the Nazi ascension to political power, and at the same time was oblivious to the sanctions against operettas by Jewish composers and the emigration of many already in 1933 and 1934. Quite the contrary, Jessel openly tried to join and participate in Nazi cultural organizations because he believed their philosophies consistent with his own conservative nationalism. Ultimately, Jessel failed to perceive the futility of these efforts, perhaps because of the popularity *Schwarzwaldmädel* continued to enjoy (it was not banned, unlike virtually all works by Jewish composers). Eventually, Jessel was arrested for "medical reasons" by the Nazis, and he died in 1942 while in Gestapo detention. Dümling closes this book by considering the popularity of *Schwarzwaldmädel* after World War II, which proceeded apace in total oblivion of the questions of nationalism and racism embedded in Germany's musical life and embodied in the life of the work's composer.

235. Gmasz, Sepp. "Katharina Hirschmann—eine Balladensängerin aus dem Burgenland." ("Katharina Hirschmann—a Ballad Singer from Burgenland"). *Jahrbuch des österreichischen Volksliedwerkes* 32/33 (1984): 90–97.

A study of the oldest layer of ballads in the repertory of Katharina Hirschmann (born 1906), who spent virtually her entire life in the village of St. Margarethen in the easternmost Austrian province, Burgenland. Not only was she counted among those Burgenländer with quite substantial ballad repertories, but many of the ballads bear witness to versions learned when she was a child, thus providing a window to ballad repertories flowing into Burgenland in the mid- and late nineteenth century. Burgenland is unique among the Austrian provinces because of the substantial presence of ballads in the folk-song landscape. Burgenland ballads, moreover, lend themselves to the distinctive vocal singing style of the province, a melodic voice supported by a lower, polyphonic voice. Gmasz analyzes several "Ritter," or knight, ballads comparatively, in which motifs from the earliest-known versions, from the early modern era (ca. seventeenth century) in the larger European tradition, mix together with regional motifs and dialect. The complex nature of Katharina Hirschmann's personal tradition serves to explain the distinctive persistence of ballads in Burgenland itself.

236. Hoffmann, Freia. *Instrument und Körper: Die musizierende Frau in der bürgerlichen Kultur*. ("Instrument and Body: The Music-Making Woman in Bourgeois Culture"). Frankfurt am Main: Insel, 1991.

Provocative historical examination of the presence of the female body as both object (instrument) and subject (body) in music. Hoffmann considers only Western art music and the ways in which women have been imagined in relation to Western musical instruments, and the psychological and sociological approaches the author musters also come exclusively from the West. The book organizes the relation between women's bodies and musical instruments into three general categories. First, women's bodies as essential to private spaces imagined and controlled by men served as a psychological context for music-making; women playing pianos and harps, for example, were imagined to connect themselves to the bodies upon which they were playing physically. The second examines the growing interest of concert publics in the late eighteenth and nineteenth centuries in seeing women musicians. Finally, Hoffmann explores different motivations for the music-making of women, ranging from accompanying a spouse's musical activities to rebellion and resistance against a male-dominated musical world. The book contains portraits of several relatively unknown women musicians, but Hoffmann brilliantly finds alternative ways of presenting them as creative individuals, rather than simply as those with minor careers that nonetheless deserve our attention. Drawing on theoretical concern for the body in music and performance, the book stands as a bold, innovative way of understanding gender in Western music history.

237. Hummer, Hermann. "Der singerische Nachlaß des Kaswurmbauern." ("The Singing Heritage of the Kaswurmbauer"). In Rudolf Pietsch, ed., *Die Volksmusik im Lande Salzburg*. Vol. 2. Vienna: A. Schendl, 1990. Pp. 157–61.

Brief examination of the songs maintained by a farmer in rural Salzburg province, Michl Mooslechner (a.k.a. Kaswurmbauer) (1871-1959). Kaswurmbauer's repertory consisted largely of songs from the beginning of the nineteenth century, for example, from the period of the Napoleonic wars and Christmas songs in Pongau dialect. Most interesting is the extent to which a farmer who lived an isolated life also maintained a fairly isolated tradition of folk song. Isolation, nevertheless, has a distinctive meaning, one that is personal and not necessarily representative of a region removed from the influences of the city or other forms of music-making. Kaswurmbauer's songs of war, in fact, were cosmopolitan and broadly historical in their content.

238. James, Barbara. "'Freiheit und Glück!' Straßenmusik heute. Ein Sänger und sein Repertoire." ("'Freedom and Good Fortune!' Street Music Today. A Singer and His Repertory.") *Jahrbuch für Volksliedforschung* 26 (1981): 75–99.

Focuses on the biography and repertory of a German street musician during the 1970s. "Robert K." gradually expanded his repertory by adding songs to the notebooks, which also documented his activities and his responses to the changing political issues of the 1960s and 1970s. His repertory drew from many sources, ranging from the American folk-music revival and anti-Vietnam songs to German folk and political songs. Repertoire lists are reproduced in full, with careful documentation and identification of the sources used by the singer. The street singer, unlike other folk singers who use the street as a stage for, say, the sale of broadsides, must be able constantly to capture the attention of passersby preoccupied with other activities. Barbara James examines the distinctive role of the street musician, particularly against the backdrop of the changing urban landscape of Germany, in which pedestrian zones cover many innercity streets.

239. Meier, John. "Lieder auf Friedrich Hecker." ("Songs on Friedrich Hecker"). In John Meier, *Volksliedstudien*. Strasbourg: Karl J. Trübner, 1917. Pp. 214–46.

Comparison of the different songs composed about the political liberal and revolutionary, Friedrich Hecker, as well as the variants from these popular songs of the nineteenth century. Hecker was active before, during, and after the 1848 Revolution in Baden, in southwestern Germany, where, at the time of Meier's article, he had achieved the status of a folk hero. This article traces the different processes through which Hecker's historical role in the regional and national imagination owes much to the ways in which songs memorialize, both positively and negatively, Hecker's various undertakings, relating these to larger issues of German nationalism and history. Hecker was also an interesting figure in German-American history, for he immigrated briefly to the United States and represents the impact of the so-called 48ers on antebellum American liberalism. Particularly interesting are the ways in which these songs interpenetrate different popular and folk traditions, as well as different genres, ranging from specifically political songs to children's songs. The entire song tradition, a case of "art song in the mouths of the folk" (*Kunstlieder im Volksmunde*), provides a fascinating example of the ways in which folk song narrates the biography of an individual against the historical backdrop of his or her day.

240. Petzoldt, Leander. "Der Niedergang eines fahrenden Gewerbes: Interview mit Ernst Becker, dem letzten Bänkelsänger, aufgenommen am 9. November 1970." ("The Decline of a Traveling Profession: Interview with Ernst Becker, the Last *Bänkelsänger*, Recorded on 9 November 1970"). *Schweizerisches Archiv für Volkskunde* 68/69 (1972–73): 521–33.

Reflections of the last active singer of *Bänkelsang*, a subgenre of broadsides that utilizes large panels with narrative scenes, usually sold at open markets. Commentary by the leading scholar of the genre, Leander Petzoldt, further interprets Ernst Becker's life. Becker was a self-styled *Bänkelsänger*, cultivating the profession as a form of folklorismus from the late 1930s until the 1970s. Becker sought, nevertheless, to construct connections among his repertory, *Drehorgel* (cranked organ), and illustrative narrative panels and the specific traditions of a family of

Bänkelsänger and a "master of the trade," Paul Damm. Illustrates the persistence of a traditional genre in confrontation with modernity.

241. Pietsch, Rudolf. "'Gelegenheitslieder' im Repertoire des Pongauer Sängers Hermann Kössner aus Goldegg Weng." ("'Songs for Significant Occurrences' in the Repertory of the Pongau Singer, Hermann Kössner, from Goldegg Weng"). In Rudolf Pietsch, ed., *Die Volksmusik im Lande Salzburg*. Vol. 2. Vienna: A. Schendl, 1990. Pp. 113–55.

Hermann Kössner (born 1914) is best known in rural Salzburg province for the performance of *Gelegenheitslieder*, literally "occasional songs," but more accurately classified as songs that refer to significant occurrences, both locally and beyond the Pongau region of Austria. *Gelegenheitslieder* draw from several other genres, broadsides and popular sheet music from the time, and hence they demonstrate a connection to urban print culture. In this article Rudolf Pietsch explores the individual repertory of a specialist in these urban traditions, who nevertheless spent his entire life working on the farms and in the mountain pastures of Salzburg. Kössner's earliest contact to these songs can be traced to the influences of specific individuals, for example the swimming teacher Hermine Erhart, who taught many local children between the world wars. Knowledge of these songs also demanded an interest in and respect for literate song traditions, not only by the singer Kössner but also by those in the taverns and singing festivals for which he performed. It was the singer himself, however, who transformed the cosmopolitan tradition into local practice and meaning. Pietsch analyzes three songs in remarkable detail, concerning himself especially with the presence of local linguistic and musical dialect. An extremely thoughtful and revelatory study of the relation between rural and urban folk-song practices.

242. Raupp, Jan. *Sorbische Volksmusikanten und Musikinstrumente.* ("Sorbian Folk Musicians and Musical Instruments"). Bautzen: VEB Domowina-Verlag, 1963. (Schriftenreihe des Instituts für sorbische Volksforschung, 17).

A critical examination of Sorbian folk music and its history in eastern Germany, through wide-ranging documentary and archeological studies. The Sorbs, one of the Slavic-speaking peoples along the Elbe River, have for centuries played an important role in the total musical life near Cottbus and Bautzen, particularly in rural areas and the small court cities. Rather than defining Sorbian folk music as a single set of unified practices and the repertories that have been produced by these, Raupp turns his attention toward Sorbian musicians and their changing roles through history. Sorbian culture was not isolated in eastern Germany, but rather it existed in constant exchange with neighboring German-speaking communities, and to a far lesser degree with other Slavic-speaking areas in lands presently in Poland and the Czech Republic. Sorbian musicians were extremely important in determining the conditions of this exchange, which meant that they contributed significantly to a larger cultural history at certain critical moments. During the late feudal period, for example, it was Sorbian musicians, because of their outsider status, who were most actively involved in the creation and performance of political songs. The tension between Sorbian and German culture interacted with the history of socio-economic change, again affording Sorbian musicians the possibilty of contributing significantly to many areas of a larger musical culture. Sorbian musicians, for example, became professionals in large numbers, not only in groups that played for dances and other events in the emerging public sphere of the eighteenth century, but also in the religious life of eastern Germany as cantors and organists. Illustrations, depictions of instruments, transcriptions, and comparative tables fill this volume, making its high theoretical level accessible to the reader. Richly integrating sophisticated Marxist theories at a moment in the intellectual history of the German Democratic Republic when ethnic and religious tolerance was broadly embraced, this book is an outstanding example of the impact of socialist thought on folk-music scholarship.

243. Reiterits, Anton. *Dörfl: Gebrauchsmusik in einem burgenländischen Ort.* ("Dörfl: Functional Music in a Town in Burgenland"). Ed. and expanded by Walter Deutsch and Helga Thiel. Eisenstadt: Burgenländisches Landesmuseum, 1988. (Wissenschaftliche Arbeiten aus dem Burgenland, 80).

Drawing from the extensive collections and sketches of Anton Reiterits (1909–80), Walter Deutsch and Helga Thiel portray the diversity of musical life in the village of Dörfl (population ca. 690 in 1970) in Burgenland. Historically, Dörfl had a mixed ethnic population, including Protestants, Hungarians, and Croats, as well as Catholic Austrians, and this diversity is mirrored in the musical life portrayed by this book. Reiterits was an exceptional musician, not only because of his various roles as a professional musician in Dörfl (band leader, music-store proprietor, etc.), but also because of the extent to which he reflected on music in his village. He collected thousands of folk songs and other musical artifacts, which he notated, and wrote out his own impressions of the musical events that formed from the social fabric of the village. Deutsch and Thiel allow Reiterits's own materials to speak for themselves (e.g., by employing transcriptions in Reiterits's own hand as often as possible), while at the same time integrating these into a scholarly text. The musical life that emerges is rich in detail, not only about the virtually daily events determined by musical activity, but also about the long-term transformations through which Dörfl passed during Reiterits's life. The 293 transcriptions are complemented by photographs, postcards, and other documents, which together evoke the ways in which the lives of individual musicians form the basis for the musical life of an entire village.

244. Rubi, Christian. "Liederdruckhändler und Liedersänger im alten Bernbiet." ("Salespeople for Printed Songs and Singers in the Early Bern Region"). *Jahrbuch für Volksliedforschung* 19 (1974): 151–54.

Comparing recently discovered personal collections of printed songs and court records involving broadside salespeople, primarily in the seventeenth and eighteenth centuries, Rubi assesses the singing habits and song repertories of the Bern region in Switzerland. A region extensively influenced by the spread of Protestantism, particularly Calvinism, after the Reformation, the Bern region officially succumbed to the pressures of political and religious leaders to restrict music-making as much as possible to sacred practices. The selling of broadsides was severely limited in many places, with restrictions put on the sites in which they could be sold. Court records reveal frequent attempts to violate these restrictions, while, at the same time, indicating just how seriously their enforcement was taken. In contrast, personal and family collections of printed songs from this period suggest that those buying printed songs invested as much in the purchase of secular, popular songs as in sacred ones. Such popular songs reveal not only conscious attempts to trade in traditions from outside the region, but also the extent to which such musical activities might be investigated as sites of resistance against political and religious authority in the early centuries of Protestantism.

245. Salmen, Walter. *Der Spielmann im Mittelalter.* ("The Minstrel in the Middle Ages"). Innsbruck: Edition Helbing, 1983. (Innsbrucker Beiträge zur Musikwissenschaft, 8).

New edition of Salmen's classic 1960 study of "wandering musicians," *Der fahrende Musiker im europäischen Mittelalter.* Salmen approaches his subject from the standpoints of music sociology and music iconography. He endeavors to show the several sides of the minstrel's role in medieval society. On one hand, the minstrel's outsider role—as a music specialist with extensive mobility—made him or her suspect. It is an important contribution of Salmen's researches that they convincingly document the importance of women minstrels. On the other, minstrels gained entrance into the highest echelons of the medieval socio-economic structure. Salmen argues for a more varied reading and understanding of the terms used to describe minstrels and their musical and social activities. Hence, minstrels might be found locally as participants in folk- and popular-music practices, or they might travel widely throughout Europe as international music professionals, participating in the secular music practices constituting the art music of the Middle Ages. Typical of Salmen's publications, extensive iconographic evidence is mustered to document his arguments.

246. Schneider, Manfred. "Der Teufel als Tänzer—zu einem Motiv der Volkssage." ("The Devil as Dancer—Concerning a Motif in Folk Tales"). In Manfred Schneider, ed., *Festschrift für Karl Horak*. Innsbruck: Eigenverlag des Institutes für Musikwissenschaft der Universität Innsbruck, 1980. Pp. 189–214.

Study of the figure of the devil in the folk imagination of dance. Beginning with early Christian writings that specifically locate the figure of the devil in dance, Schneider traces the ways in which different diabolical figures come to represent different social metaphors and values in dance. At one level, the figure of the devil represents "the other" or outsider, that which is excluded within a hierarchical system of values. At another level, the devil symbolizes social fears and uncertainty about the ways in which music is a site for the representation of sexual and moral practices. At still another level, the metaphorical devil represents the roles played by the musician, in which the musician is at once outsider and cultural specialist. Many of a given society's ambivalences and concerns about "the other" are reconfigured into musical practice through this centuries-long preoccupation with the diabolical in music. Schneider makes extensive use of religious writings and folk sayings, in which dance is described as something tantalizingly diabolical. The nine visual depictions of devils and dance, drawn from different genres, historical periods, and cultures, effectively illustrate the complex patterns of representation articulating this folk motif.

247. Schnürl, Karl. "Die 'Einnahmenverzeichnisse' eines nieder-österreichischen Dorfmusikanten." ("The 'Income Records' of a Lower Austrian Village Musician"). *Jahrbuch des österreichischen Volksliedwerkes* 18 (1969): 61–65.

Examining two large account books for the years 1836-47, containing financial and musical records, this article reconstructs the musical activities of Georg Böck (1811-1877), a village

musician in and around Abstetten in the province of Lower
Austria. Böck was a semi-professional musician, who grew up in a
farm family and returned in 1859 to take charge of the family
farm. His record books reveal that he earned a decent income by
playing at a variety of occasions, ranging from weddings to church
festivals to dances and balls. These income records document his
expenditures as well, particularly those he made to other
musicians who joined him for certain occasions. Georg Böck's
musical world was limited not only to nearby villages, for he often
traveled substantial distances for special performances. His
records contain references to repertory, and in rare instances have
notations and scores, particularly of Viennese folklike and
popular traditions, thereby suggesting that Böck aimed to keep
his repertory as up-to-date as possible. These records describe the
life of a local village musician, whose public mobility was
nonetheless considerable, as he negotiated the spaces between
urban and rural settings, oral and written traditions, and folk and
popular repertories.

248. Schwab, Heinrich W. *Die Anfänge des weltlichen Berufsmusikertums in
der mittelalterlichen Stadt: Studie zu einer Berufs- und Sozialgeschichte
des Stadtmusikantentums.* ("The Beginnings of Secular, Professional
Music Life in the Medieval City: A Social-Historical Study of Music
Professionalism"). Kassel: Bärenreiter, 1982. (Kieler Schriften zur
Musikwissenschaft, 24).

An historical study of the rise of musical professionalism,
focusing on the figure of the official city musician, an
instrumentalist, employed by the city government, or some related
financial institution, to perform at public functions. The city
musician first appeared in financial records and descriptions of
cultural events in the Middle Ages and became an increasingly
significant figure through the Renaissance and the period during
which the early modern city emerged, that is, as a politically and
financially independent entity. By examining the city musician
Schwab throws new light on the complex musical life of European
cities, especially those in Northern and Central Europe. In the
Middle Ages, the city musician arrived in the city initially as a
wandering musician, usually in search of a longer period of
employment. More and more professional opportunities opened
up for the musician, and musicians came to earn their livelihoods
in this way, as witnessed in the accretion of names such as
"Pfeiffer" (piper), "Geiger" (violinist), etc. The growth of city
musicians also took place within a public domain in which "folk"
and "art musics" overlapped. City musicians, therefore, provided a
sort of cultural conduit between different socio-economic classes.
Evidence for the official activities of city musicians, moreover, can
be extrapolated to allow interpretation of folk-music practices of
various kinds. Particularly valuable in this study are the extensive

commentaries on documents, many of them from public records, which suggest new avenues for researching the public roles of musicians in medieval and early modern Europe.

10

MUSICAL INSTITUTIONS

The folk music of Central Europe is frequently a component of institutions, that is, the organization of musical practices to serve the needs of a specific group and the social context of which it is a part. The musical institution is, on one hand, a social setting for the group, providing those in the group with the opportunity to share in common goals, usually separate from their everyday activities. In Central Europe the musical institution, on the other hand, has historically been the site for participation in and expression of shared ideals and ideologies. So important is the musical institution as a place for identity and ideology, that it often comes to consolidate and symbolize qualities of Germanness, Austrianness, or Swissness in immigrant cultures. The singing society, for example, lends itself to the mobility of immigrant groups, providing in the new culture the opportunity to maintain connections to the old country through institutional activities, for example, sister societies or occasional tours. Many of the most distinctive aspects of Central European folk music depend almost entirely on the structure of activities of institutions. *Volksmusikpflege*, the conscious cultivation of folk-music practices, inseparable from modern Austrian research, developed as the product of Josef Pommer and a collective of singing societies in Vienna.

The institutions supporting folk-music activities remain, for the most part, strong at the end of the twentieth century, and this is perhaps one of the most surprising facts to emerge from the works annotated in the present chapter. At first glance, the contemporary health of musical institutions is surprising because the activities of these institutions will seem atavistic to many observing Central Europe from the outside. Why should brass bands thrive in the villages of southwestern Germany? Why should shanty choruses spring up in places with little connection to the sea? At another level of interpretation, the relative strength of musical institutions is surprising because, as several of the works here reveal, the past history of many musical institutions has been politically suspect. Particularly during the Nazi period, musical institutions were vulnerable targets for government ideologues wishing to inculcate fascist values among German and Austrian youths (see, e.g., Helmut Brenner's study of a Nazi music academy in Styria). The susceptibility of some musical institutions notwithstanding, others, such as the "Grauer Orden," furnished sites for resistance, not least because of the institutional connections they provided. It would be a mistake, however, to claim that musical institutions themselves necessarily express one ideology or another, for, as Ernst Kiehl and Lutz Kirchenwitz argue in works annotated below, the singing activities of youth groups in the GDR also provided a framework for working out conflicting ideologies.

Distinguishing the musical institutions surveyed here is their considerable diversity. Similarly, music functions in very different ways in these institutions. At one extreme, there are those that come into existence because members of a group share a certain set of values. Cohesive because of these shared values, the musical activities of such groups may take the form of ritual, strengthening the group itself through the performance of music. At the opposite extreme, certain musical institutions serve a broader public, which is to say, they provide entertainment for those who do not necessarily belong to them. The large singing societies of the nineteenth century, for example, reached the point of virtual professionalization, touring and competing with other singing societies on the stage of German nationalism, and canonizing repertories such as that in the anthologies published by Max Friedländer. Between these extremes, there are musical institutions that move between ritual and entertainment, amateurism and professionalism. The musical institution's activities rarely do not possess a dynamic quality, which in turn is underscored by the connections between local group, regional organization, and national hierarchy.

The institutionalization of musical practices in Central Europe has also contributed to the historicism of folk music, the ways in which it connects the past to the present. In its rituals of performance, a singing society reaches into its past and musters the symbols of history, and then performs these as a public witness to its own genealogy. The connections of the musical institution are, therefore, not just to place but to time, and it is such connections that yield complex levels of identity. One of the most striking characteristics of many musical institutions is the reproduction of their own pasts, through anniversary celebrations, through their own anthologies, and through reflexive accounts of their own achievements through time. Many of the works in the present chapter touch on the literature produced by musical institutions about themselves, but the sheer quantity of such materials would demand at least a volume of its own. Still, the surfeit of such interpretations of the social cohesion that music-making provides serves as perhaps the best witness to the ineluctable processes of institutionalization that lend continuity to the presence of folk music in Central European history and society.

❧

Singing Societies and Instrumental Ensembles

249. Brandsch, Walter. "Das Jagdhornbläserkorps Murnau-Werdenfels: Der Kreisgruppe Garmisch-Partenkirchen im Landesjagdverband Bayern." ("The Hunting-Horn Corps Murnau-Werdenfels: The Regional Group from Garmisch-Partenkirchen in the Provincial Hunting Association of Bavaria"). In Walter Deutsch and Wilhelm Schepping, eds., *Musik im Brauch der Gegenwart*. Vienna: A. Schendl, 1988. Pp. 107–11.

A modest article by the director of a Bavarian hunting-horn ensemble, in which he describes its contemporary activities. In contemporary Bavaria this ensemble has no relation whatsoever to hunting, and its members are themselves not particularly engaged in this activity. Still, the ensemble thrives in the rural alpine area in which it is active, primarily because the ensemble has assumed an entirely new range of social functions. These range from participating in religious holidays and rituals to performances at events celebrating individuals in the community. The survival of the hunting-horn ensemble, whose members are of various ages, is therefore not anachronistic, and it also bears witness to the historical connections to hunting (e.g., through its performance in the local church to honor the patron saint of the hunt, St. Hubert). Musical examples and a discussion of the sources of hunting repertory make this article an excellent introduction to a folk-music tradition previously widespread in Central Europe.

250. Brusniak, Friedhelm. *Das große Buch des Fränkischen Sängerbundes.* ("The Great Book of the Franconian Singing Association"). 2 vols. Munich: Schwingenstein, 1991.

Both a history of the choral tradition in Franconia (the northern and northwestern parts of Bavaria) and a detailed examination of the local and regional choral organizations in the region. The two volumes together include almost two thousand pages, although the historical sections at the beginning of both (264 pp.) are virtually identical. Because the tone of the volumes is celebratory, the Sängerbund's history is sketched in largely positive strokes, with evidence for the first stirrings of the Franconian choral tradition connected to Minnesingers and Meistersingers (Nuremberg is part of Franconia) and for the region's regularly playing a leading role as choral singing in Germany developed and became increasingly organized. The strength of the volumes is the view they provide of this extensive organization of German choral societies and the ways in which this organization has interacted with German history. Choral societies sometimes served almost to mediate the production and reworking of folk song into styles that reflected historical moments and served political ideologies. The perspective on the present, evident in the essays on local societies and personalities, reveals a singing tradition still dependent on a connection to folk song yet consistent with the social patterns of Germany in the late twentieth century.

251. Dahmen, Hermann Josef. "Der dörfliche Musikverein, seine Funktion und sein Repertoire." ("The Village Music Society, Its Function, and Its Repertory"). In Walter Deutsch and Wilhelm Schepping, eds., *Music im Brauch der Gegenwart.* Vienna: A. Schendl, 1988. Pp. 85–93.

Based on a survey of village musical organizations commissioned by the German Musikrat in 1980, this study paints a surprisingly positive portrait of the music societies in the villages of the southwestern German province of Baden-Württemberg. The music society plays an active role through its musical offerings as well as the social functions it provides for a community (e.g., essential assistance in raising money for new village halls). The music society is a general organization, although its core in the late twentieth century consists of wind-ensemble music played in diverse settings. The statistics reported in the survey show widespread direct involvement in the music society (5% of all villagers were members in 1980), with considerable indirect involvement from other villagers. Dahmen speculates that the strength of the music society lies in its ability to provide an incredibly wide range of musical and social services. It is, for example, the primary source for instruction on musical instruments, usually free of charge when older members instruct the younger. The music society also provides a social context for community interaction in rural areas. Contemporary repertories are mixed, drawing from musicals, popular hits, and traditional sources, but Dahmen observes that this repertory has probably always been eclectic. Dahmen concludes by arguing that it is the social role of the music society, far more than its specific musical functions, that assures its position in the community.

252. Ehrenwerth, Manfrid. *Teufelsgeige und ländliche Musikkapellen in Westfalen.* ("'The Devil's Violin' and Rural Musical Ensembles in Westphalia"). Münster: F. Coppenrath Verlag, 1992. (Beiträge zur Volkskultur in Nordwestdeutschland, 79).

Focuses on the differences and similarities between the structures and functions of the *Teufelsgeige* (devil's violin, though not a violin at all) and the *Bumbaß* (ca. "walking bass," an instrument constructed from a resonating chamber and a string) in order to examine the changing musical activities of ensembles in rural Westphalia. The two instruments, both of which demonstrate enormous structural variations, are similar insofar as both provide a single musician the option of several types of percussion—drums, cymbals, and strings played for rhythmic accompaniment. The *Teufelsgeige* was more commonly made by the individual musician and used for rural festivals, such as Fasching. The *Bumbaß*, often the product of an amateur instrument maker, connoted more formal music-making, such as that sponsored by a local music society. The coexistence of such functions in related instrumental practices make it necessary to reconsider the ways in which such instruments contributed to the history of musical ensembles in rural practices. Previously, most have assumed that these instruments provided no more than a rhythmic accompaniment, which was eventually taken over by a complement of percussion instruments common in marching bands. Ehrenwerth, however, documents the common use of the *Teufelsgeige* and the *Bumbaß* well into the twentieth century and demonstrates, furthermore, that these instruments mirrored changing musical styles and social contexts. Richly illustrated with photographs and comparisons of similar instruments in other European regions and national cultures.

253. Gradwohl, Karl, and Anton Sattler, eds. *Die Entwicklung des burgenländischen Sängerwesens bis 1971.* ("The Development of the Song Culture of Burgenland, until 1971"). Eisenstadt: Burgenländisches Landesarchiv, 1971. (Burgenländische Forschungen, 62).

Historical sketch of music cultivated in singing societies in Burgenland, on the occasion of the fiftieth anniversary of its annexation to Austria in 1921. The editors examine the records of singing societies that maintained some connection to official organizations, but have included information about independent societies whenever available. Singing societies in Burgenland responded to the changing political and ethnic histories of the province, for example by establishing diverse political affiliations to nationalistic parties or workers' organizations. The *Sängerwesen* (roughly, singer culture) of Burgenland included German repertories, as well as those of the large Croatian and Hungarian ethnic groups, and the social history of this *Sängerwesen* unfolds as a tension among the different identities available in Burgenland. Repertories range from choral works by Burgenland composers, notably Franz Joseph Haydn and Franz Liszt, to works from the nineteenth-century German folk-song movement to workers' and religious songs. Absent from statistics presented in the book is evidence of the large and important Jewish communities in Burgenland. The book provides valuable insights into the musical institutions of a border region.

254. Kommission für das deutsche Volksliederbuch, ed. *Volksliederbuch für gemischten Chor.* ("Folk-Song Book for Mixed Chorus"). 2 vols. Leipzig: C.F. Peters, 1915.

The most influential and widely used collection of folk songs arranged for chorus during the first half of the twentieth century. "Folk song" in these volumes crosses into many different genres and musical practices. Settings of works from the Middle Ages and Renaissance, as well as by famous composers from later periods of music history (e.g., many by Bach and Mendelssohn), are combined with repertories from the singing-society movement of the nineteenth century, various folklike repertories, and sacred repertories. Each volume exceeds 800 pages, and their combined contents of 604 songs contain sufficient repertory for any kind of singing society. If the contents are plentiful, they are also consciously German. Published during World War I, the volumes served individuals and choruses alike in the German army. The volumes, therefore, mark the major transition from the imperial Germany of Kaiser Wilhelm to the Weimar Republic, and in so doing they came to symbolize a canonization of the German past that provided a basis for choral performance in a radically reshaped Germany. The reception history of these volumes, nonetheless, was marked by complex issues raised by the role of the chief editor, Max Friedländer, who was Jewish. Drawing upon the ideologies and collections of Rochus Freiherr von Liliencron (1820–1912), Friedländer connected choral arrangements of folk song to a long history of German culture, rooted in the Middle Ages and influenced by Goethe, the Brothers Grimm, and nineteenth-century folk-song arrangers. Liliencron and Friedländer greatly expanded the cultural space in which folk song could represent Germanness, and these volumes provided the basis for mass participation within this space. In his introduction to volume one Friedländer speaks of over 60,000 copies of the arrangements and over 200,000 copies of individual parts already in use. The choral performance of folk songs, therefore, became inclusive, inviting groups from different religions and ethnic groups to participate in German folk-song traditions. Many emigrants during the next half century, whether to North or South America, or to Israel, brought the *Volksliederbuch für gemischiten Chor* with them, establishing it as the major influence on choral movements elsewhere.

255. Leinweber, Alois, and Guntram Probst. "Shanty-Chöre in der Bundesrepublik Deutschland: Aspekte ihrer Entwicklung."

("Shanty Choruses in the Federal Republic of Germany: Aspects of Their Development"). *Jahrbuch für Volksliedforschung* 37 (1992): 110–12.

A summary of results from a 1990 survey of shanty choruses, conducted by the University of Bremen. The shanty chorus (an ensemble usually dressed as sailors and singing songs of the sea) is a twentieth-century invention, the first choruses forming in the 1920s, but the rapid proliferation of this popular choral activity took place after World War II, especially in the 1960s. This study dispels the common assumption that shanty choruses are connected to the cultural activities of German seaport cities. The repertory of shanty choruses comes primarily from foreign sources, especially English-language shanties, and this repertory constitutes only a small part of the music performed by many choruses. Most published collections were initially produced by choruses, usually for their own use. The shanty-chorus movement emerged from the choral activities at naval training stations, and about half of all choruses (Leinweber and Probst make the claim for about 150 organized groups in 1990) remain connected to these training stations. For this reason many shanty choruses thrive in parts of Germany with no historical connection to the sea; for similar reasons, the shanty-chorus movement never took hold in the GDR. Shanty choruses have increasingly become part of musical folklorismus in Germany, and their history has entered a new phase of expansion and repertory consolidation in the 1990s.

256. Seifert, Manfred. "Blaskapellen in der NS-Zeit: Annäherungen an den musikalischen Alltag im oberen bayerischen Inntal." ("Wind Ensembles in the Nazi Period: Approaches to Everyday Musical Life in the Upper Bavarian Inn Valley"). *Jahrbuch für Volksliedforschung* 39 (1994): 41–61.

With statistics, repertory analysis, and examination of contemporary accounts, this article examines the impact of the Nazi period on the wind-ensemble tradition of Upper Bavaria. Already prior to the Nazi seizure of power in 1933, ideological pressures had been placed on Bavarian bands to represent a regional authenticity. By the late 1930s, this pressure flowed from the institutions of the government, notably from the Reichsmusikkammer, the official government bureau monitoring musical activities, and within the programs of tourism fostered by the government agency responsible for organizing free time, *Kraft durch Freude* ("Power through joy" [KdF]). Wind ensembles performing for gatherings of tourists or other celebrations of local culture were increasingly forced to play repertories of Bavarian traditional music, with the express motivation of representing authentic Germanness within the larger context of Nazi ethnic and racial ideologies. The wind ensembles, however, had never cultivated an authentic repertory, but rather an eclectic and international one, which afforded it many different social functions. After World War II, new international pressures came to bear on the repertories of wind ensembles in Upper Bavaria, and their music has undergone persistent transformation to adapt to new functions, for example the frequent performances in beer tents at many different types of public gatherings. Although wind ensembles now play an international popular music together with German folk and folklike traditions, Seifert regards this eclecticism as more representative of the wind-ensemble prior to the Nazi period. Seifert frames this study as an approach to interpreting the pressures on everyday, local life during the Nazi era.

257. Troge, Thomas A. *Gesangvereine—ohne Zukunft? Eine empirische Untersuchung über die Nachwuchs-Situation der Gesangvereine am Beispiel des Enzkreises und seiner Umgebung.* ("Singing Societies— without a Future? An Empirical Consideration of the Next Generation in the Case of the Singing Societies of the Enz Region and Its Environs"). Karlsruhe: Zentrum für Musik- und Freizeitforschung, 1988.

Using questionnaires and individual interviews, this book records the responses of some 4,000 members of singing societies, as well as 7,000 high-school students, to the future of the singing society. Many assessments predictably reflect generational differences: older members want to hold on to the more traditional repertories, whereas younger members want a more international and popular repertory; members who have been in singing societies value its diversified social functions, whereas new singers focus their interests on the quality of musical experience. Although these generational differences have persisted in one form or another throughout the history of German singing societies, this survey reveals some fundamental changes underway at the end of the twentieth century. The ways in which singing societies have interacted with the media have intensified. In general, professionalization has increased, which means, for example, that choral directors, no longer only members of the community, expect a much higher commitment and level of performance. Finally, repertories have responded to the demands of the next generation, which has led to a departure from the traditional repertories of the previous 150 years. Viewed from an American perspective, this book reveals a healthy situation, for Germans continue to participate in singing societies in large numbers, and they have adapted their choruses to the changing musical conditions in a modernized society.

꧁❀꧂

Youth Groups and Movements

258. Kiehl, Ernst. "Der Flug des Falken: Nebst einigen Gedanken zur Geschichte der Menschen in der DDR." ("The Flight of the Falcon: With Some Thoughts on the History of the People in the GDR"). *Jahrbuch für Volksliedforschung* 39 (1994): 63–75.

A biographical portrait of Werner Hartbrecht (born 1916), which illustrates the social role of singing in the youth groups of the SPD (Social Democratic Party) during the course of German political and ideological changes in the twentieth century. Hartbrecht was one of the most important singer-songwriters in the German Democratic Republic, but he traces the most significant influences on his music and social engagement through music to the activities of the youth groups of the SPD, the "Roter Falke," or "Red Falcon." Youth activities passed through numerous stages in the SPD, and at each of these stages musical activities provided means of socializing and engagement with the ideologies of socialism. The Red Falcon fashioned some of its musical activities after those of the "Wandervogel" (wandering bird) movement, emphasizing the freedom of nature and the strength of working toward common goals, but further inflected these with repertories of workers' songs. The youth groups of the SPD, like the party itself, were disbanded by the Nazis, and youth activities existed in considerable tension with the Hitler Youth (HJ). After World War II, the Red Falcon quickly became one of the prototypes for the Free German Youth (FDJ) in the German Democratic Republic, and Hartbrecht argues that the FDJ absorbed many of the ideals and much of the musical repertory of the earlier SPD groups, forming a continuity to the workers' and youth movements of the early part of the century. The article concludes pessimistically, with both Hartbrecht and Kiehl observing that the values shored up by the musical activities of working-class youth groups have found no place in a reunified Germany.

259. Kirchenwitz, Lutz, ed. *Lieder und Leute: Die Singebewegung der FDJ.* ("Songs and People: The Singing Movement of the FDJ"). Berlin: Verlag Neues Leben, 1982.

A collection of fifty songs and eight essays that document the organized singing activities of the Freie Deutsche Jugend (FDJ), the "Free German Youth," the youth group of the German Democratic Republic. The singing movement of the FDJ emerged first in the late 1950s and early 1960s as a response to the need for organized musical activities among GDR youth, who had less access to and interest in Western popular and rock music than their counterparts elsewhere in Germany. The essays here document the growth of the singing movement from the bottom up, as local clubs formed, workshops were organized, and eventually the November festival of political song became a nationwide celebration. The FDJ singing movement remained firmly anchored in local hands during the history that led up to this book in 1982, and to a large degree this accounts for its power to sustain interest among GDR youth. The essays come from the pens of active and longtime members, and the selection of songs, virtually all of them political, is intended for use by local FDJ organizations.

260. Nate, Richard. "'Nachsehen, was mit der alten Linde wâr...': Zum Umgang mit dem Volkslied in der Folkbewegung der sechziger und siebziger Jahre." ("'Look Back to See How Things Are with the Old Linden Tree...': The Presence of Folk Song in the Folk Movement of the 1960s and 1970s"). *Jahrbuch für Volksliedforschung* 39 (1994): 76–95.

Reflections on the attitudes toward older folk-song repertories during the German folk movement of the 1960s and 1970s. As this movement took shape in the 1960s, particularly at the international festivals of folk musicians at Burg Waldeck, traditional German folk songs were largely eschewed because of associations with the misuse of consciously German folk music by the Nazis. The repertories in the first decade were, instead, international, fueled especially by the English-language songs of the American folk-music revival in the 1950s and during the Civil Rights Movement. In contrast, the singer-songwriters and folk musicians of the 1970s assumed a more reflective posture toward traditional German songs, reworking them and resituating them in their repertories because of the leftist themes many expressed. Nate analyzes two songs in particular, Franz-Josef Degenhardt's "Die alten Lieder" ("The Old Songs") and Dieter Sûverkrüp's "Lindenballade" ("The Ballad of the Linden Tree"), both of which associated the themes of older folk songs with the natural world being assaulted by the modern industrial world. Such songs helped the folk movement to coalesce around political themes more specific to Germany at the end of the twentieth century, especially the freedom movement that began to take shape in the 1980s. In a type of postscript, Nate observes that the reunification of Germany in the 1990s has problematized the Germanness of German folk song again, particularly as issues such as "Volk" and "Heimat" ("homeland") have been taken up as emblems of the Right.

261. Schlosser, Horst Dieter. "Das Mittelalter im Lied deutscher Jugendbewegungen: Vom 'Zupfgeigenhansl' zur 'Ougenweide.'" ("The Middle Ages in the Songs of German Youth Movements: From 'Zupfgeigenhansl' to 'Ougenweide'"). *Jahrbuch für Volksliedforschung* 30 (1985): 54–67.

Throughout the twentieth century, the Middle Ages provided symbols for numerous German youth movements. Schlosser frames the century by examining the presence and use of medieval symbols in the songs and songbooks used by youth movements, in particular the songbook *Zupfgeigenhansl* of the early twentieth-century youth movement, known as the Wandervogel (wandering bird) and the *Ougenweide-Lieder* during the student movement of the 1960s and 1970s. The songs of the Middle Ages, especially those of Minnesinger, such as Walther von der Vogelweide, served both nationalistic ends and those of alternative philosophies. Schlosser examines common metaphors, such as nature and the social bonding of youth, and argues that these were especially prevalent in the songs of the Middle Ages chosen by German youth movements. Medieval metaphors were sufficiently varied to serve the ends of small and large youth groups, for example the needs of student fraternities and youth groups of the Nazi period. Schlosser identifies the contributions of important organizers and the editorial policies of songbook editors. Fascinating study of the use of song to invent the culture of youth movements.

262. Schmidt, Martin. "Lieder, die nicht opportun waren: Der Graue Orden als Beispiel bündischen Widerstands im Dritten Reich." ("Songs at an Inopportune Moment: The 'Grauer Orden' as an Example of Organizational Resistance during the Third Reich"). *Jahrbuch für Volksliedforschung* 37 (1992): 105–10.

An overview of singing in the activities of a youth group that provided an alternative to the Hitler Youth (HJ). The "Grauer Orden" (Gray Order) first constituted itself as a leftist and Catholic youth group in 1929, when it already stood in opposition to the growing conservatism of other youth groups. With the ascension of the Nazis to power in 1933 and the consolidation of other groups under the umbrella of the Hitler Youth, the Grauer Orden entered a politically difficult stage, albeit not yet a stage in which its existence was threatened. Members generally met as reading circles and took extended excursions to foreign countries, where they deliberately exposed themselves to non-German traditions. The songs of the Grauer Orden survive in small booklets and manuscripts (some in the German Folk-Song Archive in Freiburg im Breisgau), and express the oppositional interests of the group, for example interest in the achievements of the Soviet Union. Although folk song was not as central to the

Grauer Orden as to groups such as the Wandervögel, it did serve as a vehicle for expressing some fundamental ideas about the importance of choral singing. Leaders from the Grauer Orden endured very different fates; some contributed to the formation of the "Freie Deutsche Bewegung" (Free German movement), which would be important after World War II in the formation of the youth movement in the German Democratic Republic, and others were executed because of participation in the "White Rose" student resistance against the Nazis.

263. Scholz, Wilhelm, and Waltraut Jonas-Corrieri, eds. *Die deutsche Jugendmusikbewegung in Dokumenten ihrer Zeit von den Anfängen bis 1933.* ("The German Youth-Music Movement in Documents from Its Origins until 1933"). Wolfenbüttel: Möseler Verlag, 1980.

The youth-music movement has served as one of the most far-reaching influences on the *mentalité* of Germans from the turn of the century to World War II and beyond. This book employs documents from the archive of the youth-music movement to illustrate its enormous diversity: contrasting repertories, from Bach to folk song; differing ideologies, from workers' groups to fascist groups; and distinctive charismatic figures. Hardly surprising is the emphasis on the positive influences of the movement, particularly on the growth of music education in schools. The positive message of the book is possible, moreover, because its documentation ceases with 1933, when its messages, activities, and repertories were adopted by Nazi organizations, which recognized the reasons for its successful use of music to persuade and control young people. For these reasons, there are gaps in the historical coverage (e.g., of Jewish groups in the youth movement, such as the *Blau-Weiß* ["Blue-White"] Zionist group) and in the critical assessment of the ideological dilemmas and contradictions that culminated in the 1930s. The documentation, nonetheless, is massive (1042 pages) and diverse, and provides an excellent source for examining music's role in the institutionalization of German cultural life.

Educational Organizations

264. Brenner, Helmut. *Musik als Waffe? Theorie und Praxis der politischen Musikverwendung, dargestellt am Beispiel der Steiermark 1938-1945.* ("Music as a Weapon? Theory and Practice of the Political Use of

Music: The Case of Styria, 1938-1945"). Graz: Herbert Weishaupt, 1992.

A history and documentation of music education in the Austrian province of Styria as an extension of Nazi propaganda and ideology. The volume begins by theorizing the relations between music and politics, developing a notion that music's capacity to be a "tool" permits it also to become an effective tool for achieving political ends. The history follows developments in Styria from the early 1930s until 1938, when Germany annexed Austria, and through the 1940s, during which time Austria, as a military ally and presumably cultural relative of Germany, became a site for the inculcation of German cultural ideologies. Brenner contextualizes Styria as an Austrian province whose conservative cultural values made it a perfect region for the development of institutions for Nazi ideals in music education. By 1940, a plan for a complex web of institutions had been put into place, with funding assured from both Vienna and Berlin. The "Staatliche Hochschule für Musikerziehung" in Graz ("State Academy for Music Education") served as what Brenner calls the "tip of a pyramid," focusing and canonizing a program of music education and then assisting in the extension of this program to institutions and events on regional and local levels. That these programs had direct political ramifications is most evident in the case of so-called "Lower Styria" ("Untersteiermark"), the Slovenian-speaking areas of southern Styria and of Slovenia proper, where the establishment of German forms of music education undergirded German political claims to these areas. Accompanying the plethora of documents reproduced in the book is the extensive use of statistics. Brenner closes, for example, with lists of students and teachers from the State Academy for Music Education, showing that most of them moved into influential teaching or policy-making positions in post-war Austria and Germany.

Labor and Workers' Organizations

265. Steegmann, Monica, ed. *Musik und Industrie: Beiträge zur Entwicklung der Werkschöre und Werksorchester.* ("Music and Industry: Contributions to the Development of Labor Choruses and Labor Orchestras"). Regensburg: Gustav Bosse Verlag, 1978. (Studien zur Musikgeschichte des 19. Jahrhunderts, 54).

Examines the organized musical activities of workers during the industrialization of the nineteenth century. The opening section of the book relies on a sociomusicological approach, examining the different types of musical organizations created by industry to provide its workers with musical activities during their free time. The genre of music suggested by this volume, *Werksmusik*, is therefore a top-down phenomenon, to be distinguished from the folk and popular song created and sung by workers. It is remarkable, nonetheless, to witness the diversity of the choruses and ensembles in which workers participated, institutions which, in turn, participated in industrialization itself. In the second section, the authors look at individual case studies and survey these musical organizations in different places, especially in the mining and steel areas of western Germany (e.g., the Ruhrgebiet). Many of the essays are informed by the anti-socialist ideology of the Cold War, which fails to observe the extent to which industry used music to control workers and to discipline them into becoming more effective, goods-producing machines. The great value of the book is its identification and discussion of areas of active music-making, which have often occupied and explored the borders between folk music and art music.

11

SPEECH ISLANDS AND EMIGRANT MUSIC CULTURES

Connecting the approaches in the books and articles surveyed in this chapter is the problem of German identity outside Central Europe. In the first section, concerned with "speech islands," German identity resides in the retention of Germanness, that is, the musical practices that closely resemble German music prior to immigration to Eastern and southeastern Europe. In the second section, some entries reveal a persistent concern for the retention of Germanness, but others borrow from American theories of ethnicity to focus instead on German-Americanness. These various ways of constructing German identity are not just the result of different notions of ethnicity, but rather of ideological concerns over the core of German identity itself. Must German identity somehow retain a pure core, an unpolluted essence that unequivocally binds the history of a community or settlement outside Germany to a shared German past? Or can German identity assume new forms when in contact with other cultures, forms that nonetheless narrate a history of hybridization and cultural interaction? The entries in this chapter problematize and respond to these two questions in vastly different ways.

The concept of speech island (*Sprachinsel*) leaves little doubt, even in its name, of the precise character of German identity it recognizes. Speech islands were a phenomenon of German settlement in Eastern and southeastern Europe. A speech island resulted from the decision, usually a political agreement, to settle German-speaking communities in areas in need of special labor skills available in Germany, often mining and forestry, but most often agricultural practices. The earliest speech islands were established in the late Middle Ages (the Siebenbürgen and Gottschee colonies), with another set implanted in the eighteenth century, when the Ottoman Empire finally retreated from Eastern and East Central Europe. First identified because of the retention of language or dialect, speech islands symbolized the persistence of German identity: despite the pressures of time and external influences, that identity continued to anchor the colony to its past. By the end of the nineteenth century, scholars turned to folk song as one of the strongest pieces of evidence justifying the core strength of German culture and history. Because repertories of German songs and German musical practices survived the centuries of separation from

Germany itself, the purity of German folk-song traditions had successfully exerted itself. The music of speech islands was important at various moments in the history of German scholarship, in the nineteenth and early twentieth century as means of claiming territory and cultural superiority, and after World War II as a means of providing an ideological framework for the return of Germans in Eastern Europe to Germany itself.

Although the concept of speech island was not applied to German settlements in the New World, many of the same ideological motivations came to frame the study of music in these settlements. Those settlements in which the oldest traditions survived the longest enjoyed special attention, not least because they had not yielded to the pressures of assimilation. In North America language, too, was essential to recognizing the connection to the past, an aspect clear in the scholarship on the Amish or Hutterites, which usually stresses the close resemblance of their contemporary dialects to specific dialect regions of Europe. The music of such stringent religious communities, moreover, presumably preserves the styles and repertories of the distant past, hence establishing such groups as examples of marginal survival. In contrast, German-American communities that have mixed German and English repertories—or, even, entirely English repertories—remain almost ignored in European scholarship because of the "abandonment" of German identity in such communities.

Approaches to both speech islands and emigrant music cultures have changed rapidly during the last quarter of the twentieth century. Encouraging this shift has been greater attention to instrumental practices, as well as secular practices, in which the rigid claim for language insulation is not necessary. The shift in perspective has also resulted from more extensive fieldwork, both in Eastern Europe (or within communities that have returned to Germany or Austria) and in North America. Ethnographic studies, such as those of Ingeborg Weber-Kellermann, reveal that musical traditions bear witness to exchange between German-speaking and non-German-speaking residents of Eastern Europe, exhibiting a process she labels as "interethnicity." In emigrant music cultures, exchange of musical styles, for example in the dance styles of the "ethnic mainstream" studied by Rudolf Pietsch, is not only normative, but explains the ways in which American folk-music identities cannot be properly understood without taking account of diverse Central European influences. The musical practices of speech islands and of German ethnic groups in North America, therefore, have become interesting again for modern scholars not so much because of the bounded model they provide for making ideological claims for German identity, but rather because of the complex histories of cultural change and exchange that they narrate.

Speech Islands

266. Braun, Hartmut. *Was die Pfälzer in der Welt singen: Eine Untersuchung des Volksliedbestandes der Batschka.* ("What Palatinate Germans Sing Elsewhere in the World: An Investigation into the Situation of Folk Song in Batschka"). Kaislerslautern: Heimatstelle Pfalz, 1969. (Pfälzer in der weiten Welt, 7).

Comparative study of folk songs in Palatinate communities in the Batschka, Slavonia, and Syrmia regions in the border areas of Hungary, Serbia, and Romania. Residents of the Palatinate (in German, "die Pfalz") immigrated in large numbers to the area in the late eighteenth century and established a predominantly Palatinate cultural presence in many villages. Methodologically, Braun compares standard Palatinate collections with examples collected from former Batschka residents who had returned to Germany after World War II. Although many songs and genres (e.g., ballads) had changed relatively little during the almost two centuries of Palatinate settlement in the area, no specifically Batschka-German repertory developed. Braun employs both musicological and philological approaches to songs and texts. He argues that taking account of Batschka-German repertories in communities throughout the world enriches the larger understanding of folk song in the Palatinate itself.

267. Brednich, Rolf Wilhelm, Zmaga Kumer, and Wolfgang Suppan, eds. *Gottscheer Volkslieder.* ("Folk Songs of Gottschee"). Vol. 1: *Volksballaden* ("Folk Ballads") (1969). Vol. 2: *Geistliche Lieder* ("Sacred Songs") (1972). Vol. 3: *Weltliche Lieder, Volkstänze, Nachträge zu Band I* ("Secular Songs, Folk Dances, Supplements to Vol. 1) (1984). Mainz: B. Schott's Söhne.

An edition of folk songs from the German-speaking speech island of Gottschee, located in the border area between Slovenia and Croatia. First established in the early fourteenth century, the "Gottschee Colony" survived intact until 1941, when German-speaking residents were removed because of World War II. The culture of the Gottschee area attracted considerable attention from folklorists and linguists, who argued for the retention of German (or Austrian, for the settlers were originally from eastern Tyrol and Corinthia) customs, folk songs, and dialect. Various acquisitions of folk-song collections and manuscripts from the Gottschee area by the Deutsches Volksliedarchiv in Freiburg im Breisgau serve as the basis for these volumes, which attempt to represent the entire region. Transcriptions of melody and text show the concern of the editors for connecting twentieth-century oral tradition to the earliest traditions of the Gottschee settlers, hence making a strong case for marginal survival in an area completely surrounded by Slavic-speaking communities. Although

Zmaga Kumer's contribution to the project shows the influence of
Slovenian traditions in these repertories, it is not clear from the
editions, which contain almost exclusively German-language
examples, how extensively the Gottschee residents participated in
folk-song traditions from the Slavic environment. A detailed study
of the *locus classicus* for speech-island research.

268. Habenicht, Gottfried. *Liedgut und Liedleben in einem Hauerländer
Dorf: Der Gewährsmann Anton Köppl aus Honneschau: Lieder,
Selbstzeugnis, Kommentare.* ("Song Repertory and Musical Life in a
Village in Hauerland: Songs, Oral History, and Commentary of
the Consultant Anton Köppl from Honneschau"). Freiburg im
Breisgau: Johannes-Künzig-Institut für ostdeutsche Volkskunde,
1987.

Using the extensive repertory (190 songs) of a single
consultant from the central Slovakian village of Honneschau as a
point of departure, this volume establishes complex connections
between the individual, the local, the European, and the historical
context, all of which reside in folk song itself. The songs and
interviews were collected from Anton Köppl between 1975 and
1984, and they represent a cross-section of the social and cultural
context of a German-speaking area, settled with miners and
laborers by the Habsburg Empire. The repertory itself contained a
fairly large number of ballads and religious songs, many from
songbooks used in Hauerland, and these are balanced by several
different kinds of dialect song, thus demonstrating the presence
of several different types of influence on a core repertory. The
songs are published so as to enable comparative research, and the
editor discusses variants and distribution of the songs.
Habenicht's introduction is especially valuable as a
contextualization of folk song in the life and history of an Eastern
European speech island.

269. Hauffen, Adolf. *Die deutsche Sprachinsel Gottschee: Geschichte und
Mundart, Lebensverhältnisse, Sitten und Gebräuche, Sagen, Märchen
und Lieder.* ("The German Speech Island, Gottschee: History and
Dialect, Social Life, Customs and Practices, Legends, Fairy Tales,
and Songs"). Graz: K.K Universitäts-Buchdruckerei und Verlags-
Buchhandlung 'Styria,' 1895. (Quellen und Forschungen zur
Geschichte, Literatur und Sprache Österreichs und seiner
Kronländer, 3).

The classic study of a speech island, which serves as a model
for folkloristic and ethnomusicological study of speech islands
until the present. The Gottschee colony was situated in an area on
the borders of Slovenia and Croatia, where German settlements
remained in a relatively isolated area from the early fourteenth

century until 1941, when German-speaking residents were moved from the region. Maintaining a dialect from eastern Tyrol and Corinthia, the area provided Hauffen with the possibility of observing a wide spectrum of folk practices that presumably survived from the late Middle Ages. These folk practices, moreover, constituted a cultural level in which largely German traditions undergirded the "insulation" of the speech island itself. The book also serves as an early example of the ways in which Central European folklorists perceived folk song to be integrated into other domains and genres of folklore.

270. Hollós, Ludwig, and Julius Schweighoffer, eds. *"Schönster Schatz...": Ungarndeutsche Volkslieder*. ("'Most Beautiful Treasury...': Hungarian-German Folk Song"). Budapest: 'Lehrbuch'— Tankönyvkiadó, 1979.

Songs of Hungarian German-speaking communities, collected particularly in the years immediately after World War II. Concentrated primarily in the Trans-Danube region, the collectors do not make the volume representative of the entirè range of German-speaking areas of Hungary; Batschka and the northern part of the Banat, for example, appear almost not at all. The strength of the volume is its use of methods adapted from Bartók and Kodály to analyze a German-language repertory. This approach opens up new possibilities for understanding the ways in which folk song represents the culture contact in the region. Transcriptions are attentive to dialect distinctions, which make the volume far more than an attempt to privilege the preservation of Germanness in a speech island. Although the volume would be stronger had it incorporated a greater range of communities and historical collections, it is a useful introduction to more recent approaches to German speech islands by scholars resident in them.

271. Rohr, Robert. *Unser klingendes Erbe: Beiträge zur Musikgeschichte der Deutschen und ihrer Nachbarn in und aus Südosteuropa unter besonderer Berücksichtigung der Donauschwaben*. ("Our Heritage in Sound: Contributions to the Music History of the Germans and Their Neighbors in and outside Southeastern Europe, with Special Consideration of the Danube Swabians"). Passau: Verlag Passavia, 1988.

An overview of the music culture of the Danube Swabians, Germans (and not only those from Swabia) settled by the Habsburg Monarchy in southeastern Europe after the retreat of the Ottoman Empire in the seventeenth and eighteenth centuries. The Danube Swabians transformed relatively unpopulated areas in eastern Hungary, Romania, and Serbia through intensive agricultural practices, retaining many aspects of their German heritage into the twentieth century. During the Cold War, most Danube Swabians were forced to leave southeastern Europe, from which they returned to Austria or Germany, or immigrated to North America. This volume maintains rather conservative shadings of the music history of the Danube Swabians, stressing that their music was (1) fundamentally German; and (2) inseparable from a larger music region determined by the Habsburg Monarchy. Numerous illustrations make the musical past of the Danube Swabians more vivid, and Rohr succeeds in constructing a collective musical biography by describing the musical activities of many different types of musicians. His sources are largely those—newspapers, books, printed material of all kinds—produced by the Danube Swabians, thereby providing considerable breadth to the documentation and context of the music history. If indeed the Germanness of the music history is stressed almost to the exclusion of other national and ethnic influences, this book offers the most extensive music history of one of the largest German-speaking speech islands in Eastern Europe.

272. Schaaf, Karlheinz. "Das Volkslied der Donauschwaben." ("The Folk Song of the Danube Swabians"). In Rolf Wilhelm Brednich, Lutz Röhrich, and Wolfgang Suppan, eds., *Handbuch des Volksliedes.* Vol. 2: *Historisches und Systematisches—interethnische Beziehungen—Musikethnologie.* Munich: Wilhelm Fink, 1975. Pp. 199–219.

Relying primarily on historical sources and research from the first half of the twentieth century, Schaaf sketches the general characteristics of folk song in the German-speaking communities of Slovakia, Hungary, Romania, and Serbia. The unifying historical conditions for German and Austrian settlement of these areas—the Habsburg Empire's attempt to reclaim the agricultural potential of its eastern regions after the Ottoman Empire evacuated the regions at the end of the seventeenth century— provides the basis for the comparative approach of the study. Schaaf notes that different patterns of settlement characterized each village and region, and he recognizes individual processes of acculturation or isolation. His concept of Danube Swabian folk song, nonetheless, is that which demonstrates connections to earlier German repertories rather than possible assimilation of non-Germanic traits. Of particular importance, for example, is that ballads form a distinctive part of the repertory, thereby serving as a link to the Middle Ages. He explicitly describes this area of research as historical, and there is little evidence here that folk-song scholars in the 1970s had begun to study the Danube Swabians upon their return to Central Europe and after the subsequent reorganization of their social institutions and cultural practices. The descriptions of music's social functions and its use in conjunction with other cultural activities are very good, as is the schematic breakdown of the different regions of Danube Swabian settlement into the subcultures formed by specific places of origin in Central Europe. A good summary of German traditions among the Danube Swabians prior to World War II.

273. Schaller, Anna Katharina. *Singgewohnheiten und Liedvortrag bei den Schwaben in Südungarn.* ("Characteristics of Singing and the Performance of Song among the Swabians in Southern Hungary"). Hamburg: Dietrich Wagner, 1988. (Beiträge zur Ethnomusikologie, 21).

Focuses on practices of song and performance in a region of southern Hungary (sometime called the "schwäbische Türkei" [Swabian Turkey]) with extensive German-language song repertories. Schaller draws broadly on collections and research from the 1960s to the early 1980s to sketch ten "singer portraits." On one level, these portray the vitality and persistence of song itself, serving as a means of cultural identity and history. On another level, one more fundamental to the author, the portraits illustrate the processes and "gesture" of performance. Folk song, then, provides a means of understanding how individuals construct identity using specific human practices, and why these serve as a larger portrait of everyday life in the villages and small cities of southern Hungary. German song and singing, then, do not serve to mark the exceptional nature of preservation in a speech island, but rather the contexts and communication that build community and other forms of identity. Extensive transcriptions and the discussions of individual songs provide further documentation for this approach. Schaller also examines the Hungarian songs in the repertories of the ten singers, observing that knowledge of non-German songs is a distinguishing characteristic of exceptional musical practice. A significant and paradigm-making contribution to research on German-language musical practices outside Central Europe.

274. Scheierling, Konrad. *Geistliche Lieder der Deutschen aus Südosteuropa.* ("Sacred Songs of the Germans from Southeastern Europe"). 2 vols. Kludenbach: Gehann, 1987.

The first two volumes of a six-volume series, edited by Gotthard Speer and devoted to the music of German-speaking areas of the entire region of southeastern Europe, not just the Balkan areas but also the regions bounded on the north by the Carpathians and on the east by the Volga. Historically, examples begin with the first settlements of Germans and Austrians in Eastern Europe, especially the communities founded in the eighteenth century. Recent collections, also those gathered from Eastern European Germans who have returned to Germany and Austria, complement the historical approach. Oral traditions, written traditions, and mixtures of the two (e.g., manuscripts with commentaries and variations noted on them) provide diverse source materials. The editorial principle derives from establishing text types and then includes textual and melodic variants. A total of 189 songs appear, organized according to 683 text types. This complex of texts and variants allows Scheierling to suggest a history of transmission that links the history of Eastern European communities to religious practices fundamental to the Central European musical area. Comparison of songs to the variants, however, does not always make the history of transmission clear, for some variants seem only arbitrarily related to original versions. Songs appear in the two volumes in categories derived from the progression of festivals during the church year. Only songs in German and Latin are included in the collection, with no discussion of repertories that might have songs in German and the vernacular of a surrounding region. Although many songs appear somewhat disembodied from their contexts, about which the reader can only speculate, the volumes serve as a rich source for understanding the music sung in German-speaking communities of Eastern Europe.

275. Schenk, Annemie. *Deutsche in Siebenbürgen: Ihre Geschichte und Kultur.* ("Germans in the Siebenbürgen Region of Romania: Their History and Culture"). Munich: C.H. Beck, 1992.

A comprehensive historical and ethnographic study of one of the most important speech islands in Romania, written from a contemporary folkloristic perspective. Rather than focusing on the preservation of German or Saxon culture in the Siebenbürgen— the usual approach—Schenk examines patterns of change and exchange. Accordingly, the history of the Siebenbürgen Germans, who settled in Romania to increase agricultural productivity, reflected responses to and interaction with other ethnic communities and cultural groups in Romania. This difference in method of investigation is reflected in Schenk's approach to folk music, which is not treated as isolated rural or village traditions, but as practices integrated into the cultural institutions of the Siebenbürgen (see Ingeborg Weber-Kellermann, below), for example artisans' groups (*Zünfte*) and the religious life of the village. The author considers recent history as one of decline with the deportations and expulsions of German-speaking residents in Romania during World War II and the second half of the twentieth century.

276. Schünemann, Georg. *Das Lied der deutschen Kolonisten in Russland.* ("Song among the German Colonists in Russia"). Vol. 3: *Sammelbände für vergleichende Musikwissenschaft* (ed. by Carl Stumpf and Erich M. von Hornbostel). Munich: Drei Masken Verlag, 1923.

The product of a systematic investigation of the vocal music and music culture of the German-speaking residents of Russia, based on studies conducted among the thousands of German-speaking Russian prisoners captured during World War I. Encouraged to settle in the agricultural regions of southern Russia from the mid-eighteenth throughout much of the nineteenth century, the German "colonists" lived in fairly closed communities, in which many traditions, at least according to Schünemann, remained intact. The author, nonetheless, interprets the colonial musical life as if it were changing under the impact of conscious Russification, especially in the schools, where the language of instruction was Russian; other political (e.g., required military service) and social pressures (e.g., intermingling of colonists with Russians) placed German and Russian customs in conflict. The book is remarkable because of the extensive field research upon which it was based, not only the field recording of 434 songs for the Berlin Phonogrammarchiv, but also the use of questionnaires and interviews, through which Schünemann was able to contextualize the musical life of these communities. Religious practices were the primary source for preservation, and an overwhelming number of the songs retained by the prisoners in oral tradition were from the church or from religious instruction. Performance practices, too, bore witness to the influence of the church, for many required the presence of a lead singer (*Vorsänger*). Schünemann engages in considerable comparative analysis of texts and melodies, measuring change against the presumed stability of songs in the standard German canons, for example the Erk-Böhme collections (see chapter 2 of the present book). As a whole, this volume provides a methodological model for German comparative musicology and a remarkable insight into the ways song contains and embodies the history of a German speech island.

277. Schwab, Alexander, ed. *Rußlanddeutsches Liederbuch.* ("Songbook of the Germans in Russia"). Edited from collections of Mathias Trausch, Johann Windholz, Oskar Geilfuß, Georg Dinges, Konrad Scheierling, Viktor Klein, and Georg Schünemann. Kludenbach: Gehann, 1991.

A collection of songs from former German "colonies" in Russia (see above entry), especially those on the Volga and Black Sea, as well as in the Caucasus. Published by an organization of former Germans in Russia, the collection is intended for use by such organizations. The songs represent both the retention of repertories from Germany and songs that result from different patterns of acculturation and accommodation in Russia. Historically, this is an important collection because of the sources it assembles, notably those of Georg Schünemann from the period after World War I. Songs are organized according to function and topic, and in some cases reflect a conservative political ideology. Issues such as *Heimat* become blurred, that is to say, confused as to whether Germany or the Russian colonies are really the cultural homeland for the Germans in (or from) Russia. One of the most complete anthologies of folk songs from an area of large and important speech islands.

278. Sulz, Josef, Johanna Blum, Gretl Brugger, and Stefan Demetz. *Kommt zum Singen: Liederbuch aus Südtirol.* ("Come and Sing: Songbook from South Tyrol"). 2nd, expanded ed. Bozen/Bolzano: Verlaganstalt Athesia, 1986.

A collection of songs from Südtirol (South Tyrol), a trilingual area of northern Italy, which was part of the Austro-Hungarian Empire until World War I. A region in which three language groups overlap—German, Italian, and a Retoromantic language called *ladino*—the cultural history of Südtirol has been and continues to be highly contested. Connected to northern Europe through the Brenner Pass, Südtirol has been in continuous contact with cultures on both sides of the Alps through trade routes for centuries. Not an isolated speech island in the strictest sense, the region has witnessed the constant mediation of musical repertories for political and cultural reasons. This songbook, for example, contains songs putatively rooted in the practice of the region, but this means that most are in German, either High German or in the Tyrolian vernacular. A section of songs in *ladino* is included because of the "common cultural cause" shared by German and *ladino* speakers. Songs in Italian are completely absent, despite the inclusion of a section of English songs from the American folk-music revival. Most songs include several voices and are arranged for choral ensemble. This songbook itself constructs the linguistic region that it self-consciously represents, a region claiming a musical genealogy to a modern nation-state of which it is not a part.

279. Weber-Kellermann, Ingeborg. "Probleme interethnischer Forschungen in Südosteuropa." ("Problems of Interethnic Research in Southeastern Europe"). In Rolf Wilhelm Brednich,

Lutz Röhrich, and Wolfgang Suppan, eds., *Handbuch des Volksliedes*. Vol. 2: *Historisches und Systematisches—Interethnische Beziehungen—Musikethnologie.* Munich: Wilhelm Fink, 1975. Pp. 185–98.

While assessing the major research trends in the study of speech islands, this article lays out broad new possibilities for the study of folk song in the areas of southeastern Europe with histories of German-speaking settlement. Weber-Kellermann rejects the label "speech islands," noting that it treats culture as materials whose meaning comes from bearing witness to a purely German past and from throwing up barriers between the community and surrounding cultures. Thus, when previous folk-song researchers collected in the speech islands, they gathered only those songs that were in German and gave preference to those that had presumably survived from the era of settlement. Modern research, instead, must account for mixed repertories, those from the surrounding nation, and popular music in the national language. Weber-Kellermann herself draws upon new approaches to ethnicity, particularly those that recognize ongoing processes of change and the tendency of cultures in contact to mix rather than remain isolated. She also argues for the efficacy of a structuralist interpretation of culture, in which all different cultural practices interact to contribute to the larger functioning of the entire cultural system. Weber-Kellermann rethinks the nature of folk song in speech islands, calling for a shifting of attention from song as an artifact to which the objects of the past adhere to song as a complex social and psychological phenomenon responding to the changing conditions of the present.

280. Weber-Kellermann, Ingeborg, ed. *Zur Interethnik: Donauschwaben, Siebenbürger Sachsen und ihre Nachbarn.* ("Toward Interethnicity: Danube Swabians, Siebenbürger Saxons and Their Neighbors"). Frankfurt am Main: Suhrkamp, 1978.

An anthology of historical descriptions and contemporary analyses of the German-speaking communities and cultures of East Central and southeastern Europe (see Robert Rohr, above). Weber-Kellermann uses these writings forcefully to argue against the theoretical model of the speech island. As opposed to the "insulated" culture this model suggests, and which it was created ideologically to represent, Weber-Kellermann makes the case that the German-speaking Eastern Europeans always interacted with their neighbors, fostering "interethnicity," cultures that were enriched through cross-influences. Interethnicity, however, is not the same as assimilation, for Weber-Kellermann also argues that there have been many customs that German-speaking communities maintained separately from those of their neighbors.

These communities, moreover, should be understood as vastly different from each other. Some (e.g., the Siebenbürger Saxons in the northern Carpathians, which were ruled in the Middle Ages by Hungarian kings) maintained political control in the areas of their settlement; others (e.g., the Banat groups settled after the departure of the Ottomans in the late seventeenth century) developed their distinctive cultures as components of the imperial policies of the Habsburg presence in Eastern Europe. Music and ritual appear in many of these articles as symbolic of both the distinctiveness of these communities and the domains in which interethnic culture developed. The two articles specifically devoted to folk music (Zmaga Kumer's essay on Slovenian variants of the German ballad "The Birth in the Forest," [pp. 226–29] and Weber-Kellermann's study of interethnic relations in the folk music of a village in Hungary [pp. 295–301]) document the processes of tradition and change in folk music, treating music as a significant text for cultural exchange on an extensive European scale. A very important work for the evaluation of the population shifts and movements realigning Eastern Europe's cultural and national allegiances in the final decade of the twentieth century.

281. Windholz, Johann. "Bäuerliche deutsche Mehrstimmigkeit in Kirowo/Karaganda um 1980." ("German Peasant Polyphony in Kirowo/Karaganda around 1980"). *Jahrbuch für Volksliedforschung* 36 (1991): 48–68.

Investigates four different styles of polyphony surviving in Russian-German villages in Kazakhstan, the easternmost region of intensive German settlement from the late eighteenth through the nineteenth century. The first style results from heterophonic practices, the second from two-voice, often parallel singing, the third style from quasi-competitive styles allowing individual singers the possibility of independent lines, and the fourth from octave duplication, albeit with high, male falsetto voices. On one hand, Windholz argues that these styles represent a very early stage in the development of German vocal practice, hence making the styles in the village, Kirowo, truly relics and survivals. On the other, certain aspects of these styles derive from polyphonic practices found in the cultures surrounding German colonies in Eastern Europe and the regions near the Caucasus. Windholz himself begins the article by observing that Russian-German and Russian song share the common trait of juxtaposing different aspects of time, almost in postmodern fashion. Particularly valuable for its transcriptions and careful analyses of a music culture whose context disappeared when Russian-Germans were repatriated in Germany in the 1980s and 1990s.

❦

Emigrant Religious Communities and Ethnic American Music

282. *Ausbund, das ist: Etliche schöne, christliche Lieder.* ("Ausbund, Which Is: Numerous Beautiful, Christian Songs"). Lancaster: Verlag von den Amischen Gemeinden in Lancaster County, Pa., 1980. 1st printing 1564. 13th printing 1949.

The *Ausbund* is the hymnbook of the Amish, a German-speaking religious community, which coalesced around doctrines of adult baptism in the sixteenth century, and then separated from other Anabaptists to follow the charismatic leader, Jakob Amman, at the end of the seventeenth and early eighteenth century. Persecuted for their beliefs and practices, the Amish pursued a path of exile from southern Germany through Switzerland and finally to the United States, where they live in largely isolated colonies, primarily in Pennsylvania and various Midwestern states. Shunning many aspects of modern culture, the Amish have maintained musical practices in relative isolation since the sixteenth century. For the most part, music is a part of social exchange among the younger Amish, and the community participates in non-liturgical sacred services in the homes of community members. Both traditions rely on songbooks—the more "social" of the two is simply called *Gesangbuch* (songbook)—which the community prints itself. The typefonts and printing errors from the earliest editions of the *Ausbund* have been maintained until the present. The hymns of the *Ausbund* are largely psalms and hymns narrating Amish history, particularly the tales of early martyrdom. There is no printed notation, but the heading of each hymn refers to one or several tunes, both sacred and secular, that would be suitable for performance. The singing style is unaccompanied, with a song leader initiating each phrase, then to be followed by the congregation. The slow melodic style lends itself to embellishment, though the appropriate patterns are transmitted through oral tradition, not left to free improvisation. Transmission of the Amish repertory depends on the intersection of both oral and written traditions, which together make it possible to anchor a German sacred repertory in North America, even though the practices with which that repertory is connected disappeared in Europe centuries ago.

283. Bachmann-Geiser, Brigitte, and Eugen Bachmann. *Amische: Die Lebensweise der Amischen in Berne, Indiana.* ("Amish: The Way of Life of the Amish in Berne, Indiana"). Bern, Switzerland: Benteli, 1988.

A sensitive portrayal of what it means to be Amish in northeastern Indiana, an area of intensive Amish settlement. The best known of the German-speaking religious sects in North America (see above entry), the Amish began their historical exodus as a charismatic sect in the Palatinate of western Germany but attracted their largest following in Switzerland, before further persecution drove them to North America. The authors organize their study through broad comparisons between the culture of Canton Bern in Switzerland and the area also designated as Berne in Indiana. Whereas the direct connections and parallels between these two areas are at times somewhat exaggerated—the notion that the Amish are an emigrant Swiss culture results from a modern, outsider's perspective—the comparison nevertheless provides a complex historical narrative. Because Bachmann-Geiser is an ethnomusicologist, the music of the Amish provides one of the primary ways of representing the meaning of Amishness, the eventual aim of the book. Not only does she reproduce sacred songs from the *Ausbund* and other printed traditions, but she transcribes contemporary songs, among these also songs that reveal contact with the surrounding American cultural environment and the mass media. Bachmann is a painter, and the book is filled with drawings and water colors depicting the details of Amish life recorded during periods when Bachmann and Bachmann-Geiser lived among these communities. In these and other ways, the authors are able to represent the culture of the Amish, who otherwise do not permit documentation by modern, electronic means (e.g., photography or tape recording). By far the best available study of the music and folk culture of the Amish in late twentieth-century North America.

284. Bohlman, Philip V. "Deutsch-Amerikanische Musik in Wisconsin—Überleben im 'Melting Pot.'" ("German-American Music in Wisconsin—Survival in the 'Melting Pot'"). *Jahrbuch für Volksliedforschung* 30 (1985): 99–116.

Based on fieldwork in the 1970s and 1980s, a study of musical practices in one of the areas of most intensive German-American settlement in the late nineteenth and early twentieth century. With most residents tracing their ancestry to northeastern Germany, especially to Pomerania, the music history of northern Wisconsin has been trilingual: Low German and dialect repertories, High German traditions, and English-language musical practices. Musical life centered around the religious institutions of the community, particularly the different German synods of the Lutheran church. Oral and literate musical traditions mixed with the underpinning of several published genres of German song: those for the church and school, for the home, and for German-American choral and instrumental ensembles. Utilizes theories of ethnicity and cultural pluralism, thereby situating German-American music among other American traditions that allow for several different musical repertories and practices. Illustrated with examples of the most widespread German-American musical publications in the Midwest.

285. Bohlman, Philip V. "Die 'Pennsylvanische Sammlung von Kirchen-Musik': Ein Lehrbuch zur Deutsch-Amerikanisierung." ("The *Pennsylvania Collection of Church Music*: A Textbook for German-Americanization"). *Jahrbuch für Volksliedforschung* 38 (1993): 90–109.

A close textual analysis of a shaped-note hymnbook containing hymns and sacred songs in German, English, and a mixture of the two. Bohlman examines the book, published in 1840, in its performative context, as it would have been used in "singing schools" during the westward expansion of the Second Awakening. A non-liturgical hymnbook, the *Pennsylvania Collection* begins with primarily German hymns in traditional Bar-form, gradually mixes German and English texts and musical styles, and concludes with Protestant American hymns, for example by William Billings. Published in an area and at a time of heavy German immigration, the hymnbook was not just a metaphor for German-Americanization, but rather provided a musical text and a pedagogical method (shaped notes) for acquiring American musical practices and juxtaposing these with German musical practices.

286. Brednich, Rolf Wilhelm. "Beharrung und Wandel im Liedgut der hutterischen Brüder." ("Stability and Change in the Song Repertories of the Hutterites"). *Jahrbuch für Volksliedforschung* 26 (1981): 44–60.

Based on fieldwork in Saskatchewan during 1977, this article interprets the repertory of the Hutterites by examining the history of their songbooks in relation to their contemporary practices. The Hutterites are a communal Christian religious sect, which formed first during the early Reformation (first half of the sixteenth century), but then were forced to resettle in various parts of Europe because of religious intolerance. The Hutterites moved their "colonies" to Slovakia, Hungary, Ukraine, and Russia, picking up important charismatic figures from Corinthia (Kärnten) in Austria, whose dialect still dominates the German spoken by Hutterites. Hutterites fled to North America in the late nineteenth century and settled predominantly in Canada after World War I, where their numbers, according to Brednich, increased fortyfold. The article begins by criticizing European scholars for largely neglecting the Hutterites; North American scholarship, too, is greatly faulted for filiopietistic perspectives, in other words, interpreting Hutterite music from an internal perspective, as frozen through the intensive preservation enforced by the Hutterites (e.g., endogamous marriage). Brednich proposes an alternative hymnology, which identifies the entrance of new songs and hymns into the printed sources of the Hutterite repertories; he achieves this by demonstrating the specific sources of individual songs. Contemporary practices, therefore, represent the processes of change and response necessary throughout Hutterite history.

287. Holzach, Michael. *Das vergessene Volk: Ein Jahr bei den deutschen Hutterern in Kanada.* ("The Forgotten People: A Year with the Hutterites in Canada"). Hamburg: Hoffmann und Campe, 1982.

A personalized ethnography of life in a Hutterite colony of Alberta, including discussions of the function of hymnody as a means of remembering Hutterite history and performing it in the present. Holzach was a German journalist, whose year with the Hutterites began initially for personal and secular reasons, but gradually intersected with Hutterite values and worldviews. Although the book is organized around the passage of the author's year with the Hutterites, it also examines Hutterite history, folklife, and contemporary confrontation and negotiation with modernity. While respecting the centrality of Hutterite sacred song, Holzach also observes the ways in which music from the outside enters the colony, for example through the hidden radios to which young Hutterites listen, or the performance by Hutterite youths of country-western songs accompanied by harmonica. Several Hutterite song texts are included, with discussion of their meaning. A remarkably sensitive study of a communal German-speaking sect, written from the perspective of an individual negotiating both insider and outsider statuses.

288. Holzapfel, Otto. "Totenlieder deutscher Auswanderer in Kansas (USA)." ("Funeral Songs among German Emigrants to Kansas"). *Jahrbuch für Volksliedforschung* 31 (1986): 83–87.

Examination of the sources and genealogy of a manuscript of funeral songs from Fort Hays, Kansas. The songs bear a remarkably close resemblance to nineteenth-century funeral songs collected from German-speaking communities in the southern and western border areas of the current Czech Republic. The manuscript arrived with Russian-German immigrants in the late nineteenth century, although the manuscript itself probably had Austrian origins, perhaps in the hands of an individual named Alvin Polifka. In Europe, prior to emigration, these songs probably represented several different traditions, at the very least resulting from complex paths of migration and emigration. In the largely Russian-German area of western Kansas, however, the tradition consolidated, owing its transmission and stability to the manuscript. The tradition, therefore, could survive outside a German-American liturgical tradition and represented largely European, rather than American, musical and ritual practices. Transcriptions of the texts and one transcription of a song for four voices conclude the article.

289. Holzapfel, Otto, and Ernst Schusser, eds. *Auf den Spuren der Westpfälzer Wandermusikanten.* ("In Search of the Traces of Traveling Musicians from the Western Palatinate"). Munich: Volksmusikarchiv des Bezirks Oberbayern, 1995.

A collection of documents, essays, songs, photographs, and recollections about an area of small villages in the western Palatinate, from which musicians and musical ensembles have historically emigrated in extraordinarily large numbers. Already in the early seventeenth century, the emigrants from the Palatinate constituted one of the largest settlement groups in the American colonies. Early emigrant movements comprised religious communities, such as the Amish, and individuals unable to survive in the agricultural economy of the region. Economic motivations predominated in the nineteenth and early twentieth century, when several communities began to specialize in the training of musicians, particularly instrumental ensembles, which then could travel about Europe, performing at spas, at festivals, or simply in the public spaces of larger European cities. Systems for the training of young musicians developed, often producing adequate performers for professional ensembles in a matter of weeks. Several villagers produced so many traveling musicians that their names (e.g., "Mackenbacher") became almost synonyous with the trade itself. The documents in this volume consider the socio-economic and musical conditions that led to this specialized emigrant culture. They also demonstrate that the musical repertories of individual ensembles were both diverse and variable, resulting from the extreme adaptability of these traditional musicians. Folk-song collectors from the region (e.g., Georg Heeger [1856-1915] and Wilhelm Wüst [1868-1947]) anthologized emigrant songs, further transforming the songs of the western Palatinate into a symbol of music in emigrant cultures. Because many of the wandering musicians immigrated to the United States, there is a palpable Palatinate influence in American folk and popular music from the nineteenth and early twentieth century.

290. *Lieder-Perlen.* ("Pearls of Song"). St. Louis: Concordia Publishing House. Published in numerous editions from the mid-nineteenth to the early twentieth century.

The most widely used German songbook in the Protestant German communities of the Midwest. Published by the Concordia Publishing House, the press of the Missouri Synod of the Lutheran Church, *Lieder-Perlen* contains a core collection of hymns and other religious songs. Their arrangement is topical and seasonal, rather than liturgical. Following the initial sacred songs are sections of German folk songs, and then singing games for children. The volume concludes with a section of "English songs," many of which are decidedly patriotic. Like many other German-American religious song publications, *Lieder-Perlen* serves as a metaphor for acculturation and change in the German-American community. The editors specifically note that the book is to be used in "our schools," that is, Lutheran schools, especially in the predominantly rural and German areas of the Midwest; its chapbook format ensured its portability and thereby its use in the home and in other social contexts. The organization also narrates processes of Americanization, beginning with German songs in traditional harmonizations and forms, adding secular songs, many with added voices, and concluding with American songs. The *Lieder-Perlen* responded to changes in the German-American and Lutheran community, gradually expanding its English-language contents. The history of its publication and reception, therefore, symbolizes that of German-American culture in the Midwest, from its first settlements in the mid-nineteenth century, to its expansion with major waves of immigration later in the century, to the decline of its specifically German components after World War I.

291. Martens, Helen. "Die Lieder der Hutterer und ihre Verbindung zum Meistersang im 16. Jahrhundert." ("The Songs of the Hutterites and Their Connection to the Songs of the Meistersingers in the Sixteenth Century"). *Jahrbuch für Volksliedforschung* 26 (1981): 31–43.

By using textual evidence from the major collection of Hutterite songs, *Die Lieder der Hutterischen Brüder* (first published in Canada in 1914), Martens argues for possible connections between Hutterites and Meistersingers in southern Germany during the early Reformation. The Hutterites, a strictly observant, *Wiedertäufer* (Anabaptist, i.e., believing in adult baptism) sect, live in large communal settlements primarily in Canada, but also in the Upper Plains states of the United States. They settled in North America after centuries of moving their communities in response to persecution in Central and Eastern Europe. Not only do they continue to speak German, often in dialect, but they maintain German song traditions, in which both tune and text are orally transmitted. Some Hutterite songs designate Meistersingers as their composers, for example, Hans Sachs as the composer of

"Wach auf, in Gottes Namen." The author compares other songs from sixteenth-century songbooks with orally-transmitted versions she collected in Canadian communities. Though not conclusive, evidence is strong that the Hutterite repertory began to form because of early influences from the Meistersinger tradition.

292. Pietsch, Rudolf. "'Grȧd so wia dahoam draußt'... Steirer bei burgenländischen Amerikanern." ("'Just Like at Home Over There'... The Steirer among Burgenland-Americans"). *Der Vierzeiler* 14 (1/2): 8–11.

Compares the different ways of performing and understanding typically Styrian *Ländler* among the ethnic communities of Burgenland-Americans in eastern Pennsylvania. Pietsch argues that dance musicians can use Styrian dances to negotiate between Austrian styles and those that have developed in the United States, especially through the influence of the dance scene of the "ethnic mainstream." Close musical analysis of three different types illustrates this process of negotiation. At one extreme, *Ländler* follow closely the stereotypic form known to the musicians from their early youths; at the other extreme, Styrian style is employed only sporadically, even in exaggerated forms, to mark a more homogeneous sound as Burgenland-American. These dance forms serve as vehicles for the measured and meaningful acculturation of Burgenland-Americans, especially in those areas where they settled in large numbers during the 1920s and later in the 1950s, Chicago and the Lehigh Valley of Pennsylvania. Pietsch concludes that ethnic folk music does not necessarily disappear when combined with elements of popular dance music, particularly when each contributes to a cultural mix meaningful to the different generations of an ethnic community.

293. Pietsch, Rudolf. "Zu den Begriffen 'Ethnic Music' und 'Ethnic Mainstream.'" ("On the Concepts 'Ethnic Music' and 'Ethnic Mainstream'"). In Elisabeth Th. Hilscher and Theophil Antonicek, eds., *Vergleichend-systematische Musikwissenschaft: Beiträge zu Methode und Problematik der systematischen, ethnologischen und historischen Musikwissenschaft.* Tutzing: Hans Schneider, 1994. Pp. 451–74.

Taking field studies of Austrian-Americans originally from the province of Burgenland as a point of departure, this article examines the various meanings embedded in the concepts "ethnic music" and "ethnic mainstream." Fundamental to Pietsch's interpretation of these concepts is the understanding of many Burgenland-American musicians that the larger American context of their music is not a mainstream melting pot, but rather a context of European-American styles, repertories, and social settings for music-making. Pietsch examines the polka in North America as a case in point. Performed by dance bands from many different ethnic groups, the polka nonetheless lends itself to distinctive dialects, which may identify a band on a given night as "German-American," "Burgenland-American," or simply "ethnic." Pietsch analyzes the repertory of a dance band from northeastern Pennsylvania, "John Kositz and his Polkateers," providing a close reading of the different complex ethnic elements in a performance of "Good Morning Polka." Ethnic music, so argues Pietsch, provides the opportunity to adapt to a North American musical style, while providing a flexible store of symbols to assert individual and regional patterns of ethnicity.

294. Salmen, Walter. "'Tyrolese Favorite Songs' des 19. Jahrhunderts in der Neuen Welt." ("Nineteenth-Century 'Tyrolian Favorite Songs' in the New World"). In Manfred Schneider, ed., *Festschrift für Karl Horak*. Innsbruck: Eigenverlag des Institutes für Musikwissenschaft der Universität Innsbruck, 1980. Pp. 69–78.

Traces the development of the characteristic "Tirolerlied" ("Tyrolian song") and its subsequent spread within the United States as a genre of popular music. The Tyrolian song became popular as an outgrowth of eighteenth-century notions of a return to nature. The Tyrol Mountains symbolized the power of nature and the encounter with nature championed by Jean-Jacques Rousseau and others. Popular literature and the fashion of stylized clothing from the Tyrols accompanied the spread of popular songs in Tyrol style, which were set by composers such as Beethoven and Czerny, and which were performed in various stage genres by traveling "family groups" from the Tyrols. The Tyrolian song spread to the United States in the same way, both as a published popular genre and through the tours of family ensembles, notably the Zillertaler Rainers. In the United States, moreover, Tyrolian songs became immensely popular during the nineteenth century, not least because of the ways in which they dovetailed with several American popular phenomena. Salmen suggests that the popularity of American family groups, such as the Hutchinson Family Singers, may have been due in part to their origins in mountainous states. Tyrolian songs were also fitted into minstrel traditions, both implicitly and explicitly. As a genre, the Tyrolian song quickly absorbed American tropes, such as assimilation, and contained stereotyped markers of the mountain culture of Austria, which appealed to the growing waves of immigrants from Central Europe. Through careful study of printed collections Salmen examines the complex border between invented and experienced ethnicity in music.

295. Steinmetz, Horst, ed. *Die Coburger Liederhandschrift des J.L. Friedrich L. Briegleb.* ("The Coburg Song Manuscript of J.L. Friedrich L. Briegleb"). Hammelburg: Saaleck, 1984.

A facsimile edition of a folk-song manuscript, compiled by a German student activist on the eve of his emigration to the United States. Friedrich Briegleb was the son of a pastor and teacher from Thuringia, with family connections to the region around Coburg for several centuries. Briegleb wrote this manuscript by hand while briefly in prison because of charges of political agitation. One of the conditions for his release was that he emigrate from Germany as quickly as possible. The manuscript, therefore, provides several significant glimpses into the music culture of eastern Germany prior to the major waves of emigration from the mid-nineteenth century to the early twentieth century. As Otto Holzapfel points out in his commentary on the collection, Briegleb's intensive collection from a single area in 1835 was one of the first attempts to associate repertory with region, and it therefore occupies a very significant position in the intellectual history of German folk-song scholarship. Relatively little is known of Briegleb's life in America, but he settled in Missouri, near St. Louis, and his manuscripts, sketchbooks, and other song collections remained in the family estate until the late twentieth century. Briegleb provides scholars, therefore, with a sort of snapshot of the music culture and musical knowledge brought to the United States during emigration. In addition to the facsimile this edition includes transcriptions of the Coburg song manuscript according to the "A" classification category (songs from oral tradition) at the German Folk-Song Archive, and comparative analysis of the texts and melodies by Otto Holzapfel, with DVA musicologist Wiegand Stief.

296. Yoder, Don. "Die Volkslieder der Pennsylvanien-Deutschen." ("The Folk Songs of the Pennsylvania Dutch"). In Rolf Wilhelm Brednich, Lutz Röhrich, and Wolfgang Suppan, eds., *Handbuch des Volksliedes.* Vol. 2: *Historisches und Systematisches—Interethnische Beziehungen—Musikethnologie.* Munich: Wilhelm Fink, 1975. Pp. 221–70.

A survey of the folk songs of the different German-speaking groups subsumed under the larger rubric "Pennsylvania Dutch" or "Pennsylvania German." Yoder treats these groups as inclusively as possible, dividing them into several more groups, each with additional subgroups. The religious sects, for example, range from the Old Order Amish to the German Methodists, and their musical repertories, both sacred and secular, reflect the different histories and social organizations of the groups. Because of the different histories of German-speaking groups that converged in and dispersed from Pennsylvania, the folk songs of the Pennsylvania German demonstrate varying patterns and processes of isolation, change, and acculturation. Any given repertory with a certain Pennsylvania German group, therefore, might reveal contact with and influence from English-language repertories, whereas other repertories might retain an older form of song and related practices. Yoder also factors the conscious interaction with English-speaking traditions (e.g., in nineteenth-century religious revival movements, or twentieth-century folklore revivalist movements) into the processes that have yielded a diverse folk-song repertory. Even though a long history of dialect disappearance has characterized the Pennsylvania German, they have nonetheless maintained complex singing practices to express their distinctive identities. Yoder breaks down the folk-song repertories of the Pennsylvania Germans into sacred and secular categories, some of which reflect European German classifications (e.g., the detailed discussion of different types of broadsides from the nineteenth century), and others that document the distinctive singing practices of North America (e.g., the widespread influence of shaped-note hymnody on a Pennsylvania German spiritual tradition). Also conceived as a guide to the research on Pennsylvania German song, this article is indispensable reading for any scholar examining German musical traditions in the eastern United States.

12

REGIONALISM AND NATIONALISM

Regionalism and nationalism provide Central European folk-music scholars with two contrasting ways of using music to construct identity and the histories that narrate identity. Through its emphasis on the centrality of tradition—common language, shared repertory, unified practices—nationalism undergirds a framework of the whole, in which historical symbols may be claimed by and for all. Regionalism, in contrast, admits to the decentralizing forces of cultural history, in which the groups and communities at the periphery claim their own symbols as manifestations of difference and uniqueness. The tension between nationalism and regionalism in the history of German folk-music scholarship, however, is far more than a dialectic between center and periphery. Whereas it is a tension that has shaped collecting projects and provided guidelines for mapping the cultural landscape of Europe, it has also historically charted political and military undertakings that have scarred the landscape of Europe. Regionalism and nationalism embed essential questions about authority in the identity of folk music, that is, about how boundary regions are defined by the politics of modern nation-states.

In the different studies of regional and national folk music that this chapter surveys, the criteria for claiming authority and identity differ from one historical moment to another, and from one nation or region to the next. If there is a fundamental criterion for a connection to nation in German folk song, it is the recognition of a body of non-dialect folk song, that is, repertories in High German. Early in the history of German folk-song scholarship, such repertories were, in fact, a contradiction, or at least an idealized level of common creativity to which "the folk" could only aspire. The production of folk song was individual and local, providing a means of shared identity only insofar as folk song was known in oral tradition. The early Romantics, for example Ludwig Uhland, perceived that there was an historical trajectory between the local and the national, and they sought to consolidate that history by means of inscribing songs in regional dialect in such ways that their relation to an emergent nationalism was ensured. Nationalism in folk music ensued in large part from such processes of inscription, which then unleashed even more expansive and expansionist projects, such as the multi-volume attempt to anthologize and centralize *landschaftliche Volkslieder* ("folk songs in their landscapes"), organized and stewarded, in part, by the German Folk-Song Archive in Freiburg im Breisgau.

The different studies in this chapter from Germany, Austria, and Switzerland, as well as from the Czech Republic, Hungary, and France, make it abundantly evident that there is no single concept of nationalism in folk music. Each of these nations has historically pursued its own nationalist agenda, and it follows that each nation has mustered very different symbols toward this end. The national hymns of Germany and Austria, while utilizing the same melody by Haydn, have very different histories; the national hymns that Hermann Kurzke examines weave complex strands of ideology into numerous national histories, some of them real, others imaginary. Whereas German nationalism has depended more on the ways in which regions have bounded a central entity, with Alsace-Lorraine, Silesia, and the historical implantation of speech islands, Austrian folk song accounts for Austrianness by embracing dialect, in effect constructing nationalism out of the denseness of regional folk-music landscapes.

The distinctive forms of nationalism that we witness in these studies, moreover, spawn different forms of regionalism. At one extreme, regionalism resides in the traces of the past, the "disappearing melodies" of Louis Pinck's Lorraine, or the social contexts that Moravian dance styles evoke. At the other extreme, regional differences fiercely assert themselves to narrate long histories, for example, of the border areas shared by Germany and Denmark. The tension between regionalism and nationalism has also meant that not all regions are equal. Styria in Austria, historically a site for a distinctively Styrian regional music, has often been privileged as the benchmark against which it has been possible to construct Austrianness, whereas Vorarlberg and Corinthia have served as constituent elements in an Austrian folk-music landscape rich with diversity, albeit a sort of egalitarian diversity.

If the tension between regional and national practices of folk music has accompanied a complex, entangled history in Central Europe, that same tension seems no less evident in the new Europe emerging in the final decade of the twentieth century. Folk-music regions spill across national boundaries, suggesting alternative pasts and presents for the Pannonian region or the linguistic and religious areas of the Balkans. Folk-dance styles in Slovakia, as Oskár Elschek argues, are characterized by a unity that defies the ways in which Slovakia has been carved up throughout much of the twentieth century, and therefore it provides one model for Slovakia as a nation-state in the future. If and when national cultures may fail to yield the forms of identity they promise, regional cultures persist in the historical imagination as alternatives for the re-bounding of folk music and the many forms of identity that remain immanent in the social practices animated by folk music.

Nationalism

297. Düding, Dieter. *Organisierter gesellschaftlicher Nationalismus in Deutschland (1808–1847): Bedeutung und Funktion der Turner- und Sängervereine für die deutsche Nationalbewegung.* ("Institutionalized Nationalism in Germany, 1808–1847: Meaning and Function of Athletic and Singing Societies for the German Nationalist Movement"). Munich: Oldenbourg, 1984. (Studien zur Geschichte des neunzehnten Jahrhunderts, 13).

Using documents produced by the earliest singing and athletic societies, as well as by their individual members, this book provocatively and convincingly connects the earliest exercise of nationalism among the German bourgeois to the institutionalization of the organizations in which they participated. Both types of societies emerged first in the post-Napoleonic period, influenced by charismatic leaders and heightened senses of nationalism. The author argues forcefully that the organizations occupied the public sphere ("Öffentlichkeit" in the sense of Habermas 1962; see chapter 8), therefore providing a place where citizens from all parts of society could meet, including, later in the century, from emancipated Jewish circles and similar subcultures. Song was important to both types of organization, often ritualizing the meetings and excursions of athletic societies. Song was also a means of establishing and propagating sets of symbols (the oak tree, the Rhine, etc.), which later encoded the meanings of German nationalism. Düding makes fascinating new connections between institutionalized song and nationalism, for example, by documenting the extent to which folk song was considered masculine, hence the symbol for men's singing societies; women, in contrast, were more likely to sing in private spheres, and the feminine ideal in song was more Italianate. The fundamental argument of the book is that nationalism also signified social origins, and music secures nationalism an important position in fundamental social organization.

298. Deutsch, Walter, Harald Dreo, Gerlind Haid, and Karl Horak, eds. *Volksmusik in Österreich.* ("Folk Music in Austria"). Vienna: Österreichischer Bundesverlag, 1984.

A collection of essays by leading Austrian folk-music and folk-dance scholars and folklorists, each devoted to an area of folk-music activity or to the development of some area of folk-music research in Austria. Although the volume is not overtly nationalistic, individual essays often take pains to point out the unique qualities of Austrian folk music vis-à-vis that in neighboring lands, for example, Germany. Austrian folk music is at once varied, because of its historical connections to other nations in the Habsburg Empire, and more grounded in the activities of individual musicians, in what the first great scholar of Austrian folk music, Josef Pommer, thought of as *Produktionlehre* (theory of production; see the discussion of the journal *Das deutsche Volkslied* in chapter 7). Accordingly, Austrian folk music is less bound to the German language (hence, the more common distinction of "folk music"), but more tied to other genres of folklore, especially folk dance and instrumental music. Austrian scholarship, moreover, has traditionally interacted with and encouraged practice, taking part of its character from *Volksmusikpflege* (the cultivation of folk music). An historical dynamic, in which regional styles were individual yet related in certain ways to one another and to a centripetal pull toward Vienna, has therefore determined the intellectual history of Austrian folk-music scholarship, the subject of essays by Dietrich Schüller, Wolfgang Suppan, and Gerlinde Haid. With many photographs, transcriptions, and an excellent closing essay on genre and classification, this volume is a fine introduction to both Austrian folk music and its study.

299. Elschek, Oskár. "Volkstanzmusik heute und gestern." ("Folk-Dance Music in the Past and the Present"). In Walter Deutsch and Rudolf Pietsch, eds., *Dörfliche Tanzmusik im Westpannonischen Raum*. Vienna: A. Schendl, 1990. Pp. 171–87.

Employing recent studies of the cultural geography of Slovakia, Elschek argues that, despite changes in the style and function of folk-dance music, core Slovak elements survive up to the present. The major transformation in folk-dance music during the nineteenth and twentieth centuries was from music functioning in the village to accompany dance and the activities of which dance was a part to a stylized form, in which certain elements were deliberately marked to display nationalistic traits. In village forms, the music for folk dance depended both on the movement of the dancers and on the role played by instruments and vocal genres, hence making it impossible to separate folk-dance music from the complex music culture. Elschek plots the retention of these functions, styles, and instruments on the cultural landscape of Slovakia, showing that, when viewed as whole, these elements are still present and they intersect with each other. A superb article, not only because of the imagination of methodological approaches but also because of the clarity with which it identifies Slovakness in contemporary folk-music practices.

300. Holzapfel, Otto. *Das deutsche Gespenst: Wie Dänen die Deutschen und sich selbst sehen.* ("The German Ghost: How Danes See the Germans and Themselves"). Kiel: Wolfgang Butt, 1993.

Probes the construction of national prejudices and the ways in which these determine history and international relations between countries with a common, but sometimes contested border. Holzapfel focuses on issues that arose during moments of conflict between Germany and Denmark, wars over the placement of their common border in the nineteenth century and diplomatic struggles over growing German economic domination of the European Community at the end of the twentieth century. As a folklorist the author skillfully examines the ways these moments of crisis enter folklore and national cutural movements, for example that organized by N.F.S. Grundtvig in the mid-nineteenth century, which persists to shape Danish national identity up to the present. These images of Germans interpenetrate all domains of the arts in Denmark, novels and the stage, as well as models of historiography. As a folk-song scholar the author gives special attention to music as a medium for the production and transmission of national identity. A superb study of the ways in which national identity results from the interaction of images of both self and "other."

301. Knopp, Guido, and Ekkehard Kuhn. *Das Lied der Deutschen: Schicksal einer Hymne.* ("The Song of the Germans: Fate of an Anthem"). Frankfurt am Main: Ullstein, 1988.

A generally negative interrogation of the reception history of the so-called "Deutschlandlied" (lit., "Germany Song"), known best in the English-speaking countries as "Deutschland, Deutschland, über alles." The authors trace the song from the moment of its appearance as a mid-nineteenth-century text by Hoffmann von Fallersleben to the melody of Haydn's "Emperor Quartet" through its appearances in printed sources and its meanings in various moments of changing nationalism in German history, for the most part wars and revolutions. As reception history the book is valuable, for it demonstrates that what the "Deutschlandlied" is has depended on both official propagation and different forms of reception. It was also necessary for the "Deutschlandlied" to compete with other songs for the true bearer of national meaning (e.g., with "Die Wacht am Rhein" ["Watch on the Rhine"] during the second half of the nineteenth century). By concluding with a critical examination of the song in the rapidly changing political climate of the two Germanies on the eve of their reunification, the authors illustrate the great importance of song in the public debates about nationalism.

302. Kurzke, Hermann. *Hymnen und Lieder der Deutschen.* ("Anthems and Songs of the Germans"). Excerpta classica, 5. Mainz: Dieterich'sche Verlagsbuchhandlung, 1990.

Exegesis of the changing texts and meanings of anthems and songs associated with historical moments and movements in Germany. Among the songs and versions examined are "God Save the King," "Das Deutschlandlied," the "Marseillaise," the "Internationale," the "Horst-Wessel-Lied," and "Ein feste Burg." Whereas European nationalistic songs often contain specific textual ideas and melodic traits, these demonstrate remarkable flexibility, depending on the symbols and motivations of each group that reshapes a song for itself. The study is of special interest because Kurzke does not limit himself to "national anthems," but rather includes songs that come from diverse sources to function as anthems for specific groups and movements. Appearing at the time of the reunification of Germany, the book places the changing function of anthems in the GDR in historical perspective. In the concluding tenth chapter, "Wirkungsgeschichte" (lit., impact history) is systematically investigated as the framework that allows for change, yet also directs it.

❖

Regionalism

303. Deutsch, Walter, and Erich Schneider, eds. *Beiträge zur Volksmusik in Vorarlberg und im Bodenseeraum.* ("Contributions to Folk Music in Vorarlberg and the Lake Constance Region"). Vienna: A. Schendl, 1983. (Schriften zur Volksmusik, 7).

A model of regional folk-music research. Vorarlberg is the westernmost province of Austria, linguistically related to the region around Lake Constance, on which Vorarlberg borders. Because of its geographical location Vorarlberg has historically been multicultural, and it has been an important part of European trading routes between north and south, and between east and west. The contributors to this volume are both local researchers and scholars from national research institutions in Vienna. Folk music is treated in its broadest sense: as a set of complex musical practices shaped by the history and culture of the region. Some essayists consider historical practices (e.g., Erich Schneider's music history); others examine the findings available through modern fieldwork (e.g., Gerlinde Haid); individual musicians (Anton Martinelli in Walter Deutsch's contribution) and individual valleys or forested areas (in Artur Schwarz's article) are portrayed through intensive ethnographic study; folk dance has considerable prominence (in articles by Karl Horak and Richard Wolfram); and yodeling is subjected to melographic analysis (Helga Thiel). The folk music of Vorarlberg and the Lake Constance area is regional not because of its unity—of style or repertory—but rather because its differences have resulted from the many responses to the region's history and position in Europe. There are more than a few important observations in some of the articles (e.g., Karl Heinz Burmeister's discovery of the importance of Jews in the history of the "dance house" in rural Vorarlberg), which further illumine the complexity that produces regionalism in Vorarlberg.

304. Falvy, Zoltán, and Wolfgang Suppan, eds. *Musica Pannonica.* ("Music in the Pannonian Region"). Vol. 1. Oberschützen [Austria] and Budapest: Akaprint, 1991.

　　The region known to the Romans as "Pannonia" includes the broad plains on each side of the Danube as it stretches from Vienna to Belgrade. Not only does it occupy a region that includes both Central and Eastern Europe, but its diverse regional and ethnic cultures have profoundly shaped European politics, culture, and music. From largely historical perspectives this volume attempts to recover a regional meaning for the study of music in the region, accompanying the political changes that followed the dismantling of Communism in the nations of Eastern Europe. The essays examine a wide range of musical topics, including the composer and theorist Johann Joseph Fux, Hungarian brass-band music, military orchestras in Bosnia-Herzegovina during the last forty years of the Habsburg Empire (1878–1918), and the operetta as a genre produced by the history of the Pannonian region. The essays and the research concept suggested by the volume are by necessity interdisciplinary (folk-music research, ethnomusicology, music sociology, and historical musicology), and they lay the groundwork for widespread reformulation of regional music research.

305. Fleischer, Alexander. "Ein Weihnachtsspiel aus Südmähren: Das Schilterner Hirtenspiel." ("A Christmas Play from South Moravia: The Shepherd's Play of Schiltern"). *Jahrbuch des österreichischen Volksliedwerkes* 41 (1992): 49–62.

　　Reconstruction of the texts and melodies of a Christmas play from the previously German-speaking village of Schiltern in South Moravia, now part of the Czech Republic, but previously an area of mixed Moravian and German culture. The Christmas play first appeared in the mid-nineteenth century, but traditional performances ceased in 1921. Performed largely by men and boys who sang and acted the parts in the homes of important village officials (the mayor, priest, etc.), this Christmas play was a complex series of seven scenes, which mixed spoken and sung parts, as well as aspects of the Christmas story itself with local characters, thereby combining High German and local dialect. The complexity of the play, for example, the need to memorize parts and prepare elaborate costumes, accounts for the survival of the Christmas play in oral tradition and in the memories of former community members. The author bases his reconstruction on interviews with former residents of Schiltern, who had settled in Austria and Germany. Songs, texts, photographs, and schematic diagrams of the seven scenes accompany the reconstruction.

306. Holzapfel, Otto, Eva Bruckner, and Ernst Schusser, eds. *Pfarrer Louis Pinck (1873–1940): Leben und Werk.* ("Pastor Louis Pinck [1873–1940]: Life and Works"). Bruckmühl: Volksmusikarchiv des Bezirks Oberbayern, 1991. (Auf den Spuren von..., 5).

A collection of documents, remembrances, songs, and reprinted articles concerning Louis Pinck, whose *Verklingende Weisen* is the major twentieth-century source for German folk song from Lorraine in eastern France. This volume surveys the events and important places in the life of Pinck, who was not only a village pastor, but an extraordinarily active folk-song collector. The diverse documents in the volume also serve as an intellectual history of the cultural politics affecting this contested region, which both France and Germany have controlled during the past century, but which nevertheless maintains its own dialect of the Alsatian (*Elsäßisch*) language. Depending on the earlier collection from which the documents here were drawn, the folk songs in this volume are in dialect and High German, which is itself significant because of the extensive presence of German ballads, always in High German, in Lorraine. Other documents make it possible to examine Pinck's manuscripts and the methods he employed as a collector. The volume is the fifth in a series devoted to retracing the life and works of important folk-song collectors ("Auf den Spuren von...", or "In Search of..."), edited by the Deutsches Volksliedarchiv in Freiburg im Breisgau and the Volksmusikarchiv of Upper Bavaria.

307. Kiehl, Ernst. *Die Volksmusik im Harz und im Harzvorland.* ("Folk Music in the Harz and Its Adjoining Region"). Vol. 1: *Darstellungen und Übersichten.* ("Presentation and Overview"). Leipzig: Zentralhaus-Publikation and Edition Peters, 1987.

A compendium of studies and analyses of folk music in the Harz Mountains of eastern Germany by the leading scholar in the region from the time of the German Democratic Republic. The

materials assembled here contribute to the intellectual history of
the Harz region, examining sources since the fourteenth century
and culminating with those of the GDR, when the Harz region
was an important center for local and regional folklore study.
Kiehl demonstrates different analytical approaches to the folk
music with which he has worked, drawing upon and employing
different methodologies (e.g., those developed by Oskár Elschek
in Slovakia). The major contributions of the book are its attempts
to identify repertories and styles typical to the Harz region.
Whereas these are successful to varying degrees and Kiehl's
analytical categories are sometimes contradictory, the author's
concept has the advantage of being broadly inclusive, in other
words, of including musical genres from popular and *volkstümlich*
music, and even from repertories influenced by operetta and
light-classical music. The volume provides an excellent
opportunity to experience the ways in which GDR scientific
approaches opened up new ways of understanding the local and
regional.

308. Kiehl, Ernst. *Die Volksmusik im Harz und im Harzvorland.* ("Folk
Music in the Harz and Its Adjoining Region"). Vol. 2:
Volksmusikalischer Teil. ("Folk-Music Section"). Clausthal-
Zellerfeld: Pieper, 1992.

Provides the musical examples for the first volume (see Kiehl
1987, above) of an intensive study of the Harz region in the
former German Democratic Republic. A region of small
mountains, the Harz has supported diverse folk-music traditions,
including instrumental signal repertories as well as yodeling. The
repertories transcribed here reflect a sense of preservation, which
in part connects it to a GDR past, but in part distances it from
that past, because traditional GDR folk-music categories are
largely absent here. The categories in this volume draw almost
entirely from Harz collections, and in some cases comparison with
non-Harz collections would increase the analytical potential of
these transcriptions. The great strength of this project (i.e., both
volumes together) is the meticulous thick description of the Harz
undertaken by Ernst Kiehl as a magnum opus. These songs
represent the Harz in remarkable detail and therefore make it
possible to understand the historical change of the entire region
as a construction of nineteenth-century folk-music scholarship,
the politics of the GDR, and the historicism of a reunited
Germany.

309. Kunz, Ludvík. "Untersuchung zum szenischen Bild der
Tanzmusikunterhaltungen in Südmähren." ("Studies in the
Visualization of the Occasions of Dance Music in Southern

Moravia"). In Walter Deutsch and Rudolf Pietsch, eds., *Dörfliche Tanzmusik im westpannonischen Raum.* Vienna: A. Schendl, 1990. Pp. 37–50.

A profile of typical occasions for village dancing in southern Moravia. Although there is no specific historical framework for these occasions, the bibliographic sources and reminiscences upon which the article is based situate them in the nineteenth and early twentieth century, prior to the communalization of village life after World War II. Folk dance here is not cultivated or separable from other social activities, but rather woven into the fabric of village celebrations and gatherings. Dance generally took place in a large, outdoor space in the village, or in taverns and inns of various kinds. Extensive social and musical stratification characterized these occasions, and musical organization reflected this stratification. Still, dance was widespread in the village, and on many occasions it served as a means of uniting the village through performance. Southern Moravia's border position between Austria and the Bohemian region of the modern Czech Republic introduced a fairly extensive multicultural component into dance occasions. Although Jewish, Roma, and Sinti musicians are only obliquely mentioned (e.g., one standard type of tavern had the generic name, "Zum Juden" ["To the Jew"]), it is German musicians and musical styles that Kunz claims as most evident. Diagrams and line-drawings illustrate this article by one of the leading Moravian folk-music scholars of the twentieth century.

310. *Landschaftliche Volkslieder.* ("Folk Songs in Their Landscapes"). Ed. by Johannes Bolte, Max Friedländer, and John Meier. Various publishers, 1924–71.

A series of single-volume publications, each one devoted to a particular region or folk-song landscape. Originally commissioned by the Verband deutscher Vereine für Volkskunde (Union of German Societies for Folklore) and the Prussian Commission for Folk Song, the project fell under the aegis of the German Folk-Song Archive (DVA) in Freiburg im Breisgau, which supervised it through to completion, that is until the songs of all German-language regions had been published. Each volume contains ca. 100 pages, with folk songs, their melodies, and texts. Many also include arrangements for chorus, lute or guitar, or other settings. A large number of illustrations, usually in the form of etchings or woodcuts, accompanies most volumes. Though individual volumes were regional in focus, the entire project assumed an overtly nationalistic ideology from its inception. Many volumes, during but also before and after the Nazi period (1933–1945), came from landscapes outside Germany (e.g., vol. 1 from Silesia in Poland and vol. 25 from the Volga colonies), in addition to linguistic or cultural regions within Germany. By concentrating on both regional songs (e.g., in dialect) and those from a larger German repertory (e.g., ballads), the volumes equated the geographic space of the region with cultural space occupied only by German-language songs. By publishing the early volumes in the region they represented (vol. 1 appeared in Breslau/Wrocław), a further claim to the presence and reproduction of German culture through folk song is made evident. Even use of the volumes juxtaposes regional and national traditions. The project, nonetheless, remains an extremely important contribution to regional folk-music repertories and to the intellectual history of German folk-song research in the twentieth century.

311. Volume 1: *Schlesische Volkslieder mit Bildern und Weisen.* ("Silesian Folk Songs, with Illustrations and Tunes"). Ed. by Theodor Siebs and Max Schneider. Breslau: Bergstadtverlag, 1924.

Forty-one songs, all of them with German texts, from Silesia, today the southwestern area of Poland. Silesia historically had large populations of Germans, Poles, and Jews, but no songs from the latter two groups appear in the volume. The songbook opens with songs from a larger German repertory in High German; songs in the second half of the book are largely in dialect and more local in character. Relatively few refer specifically to places or events in Silesia, though some Silesian place names appear in some of the songs (e.g., no. 37, "Schlesischer Bauernhimmel" ["Silesian Farmer's Heaven"]). Overall, the songs here demonstrate their connection to the entire German folk-song landscape. They have lute accompaniments, which further place them in the tradition of wandering songs of German youth groups. The volume is richly illustrated.

312. Volume 10: *Niederdeutsche Volkslieder aus Schleswig-Holstein und den Hansestädten.* ("Low German Folk Songs from Schleswig-Holstein and the Hanseatic Cities"). Ed. by Hermann Tardel. Münster i.W.: Aschendorfsche Verlagsbuchhandlung, 1928.

A collection of songs from North Germany, entirely in dialect. The songs are topical, many of them revealing the connection of the region to the sea and to the distinctive imprint of the sea on rural and urban cultures. The folk-song landscape emerges from the distinguishing characteristics of the German land. These are firmly established, whereas the long history of border disputes between Schleswig-Holstein and Denmark and the extensive international contacts between the German Hanseatic cities and those elsewhere do not inform this collection. The illustrations confirm the local nature of the dialect songs, but the lute accompaniments for each song, many transcribed over several pages, connect the songs to other German traditions for those who do not speak Low German.

313. **Volume 25:** *Wolgadeutsche Volkslieder mit Bildern und Weisen.* ("Volga German Folk Songs, with Illustrations and Tunes"). Ed. by Georg Dinges. Berlin and Leipzig: Walter de Gruyter, 1932.

German colonies, primarily agricultural settlements, formed in the fertile Ukrainian lowlands of the Russian Empire in the nineteenth century. Contact with soldiers from these areas in World War I stimulated interest among folk-music scholars to investigate the maintenance of German culture. The songs in this volume come almost entirely from the major repertories of ballads and German lyrical songs, as if to confirm the Germanness of the Volga colonies. Local and dialect songs are absent, thereby offering further confirmation of the connection to Germany itself. Most songs have only two voices, which suggests that singing practices existed in the small group, the family, or the community. There is no foreword or introduction to contextualize the collection. The illustrations are in *Jugendstil* (art nouveau), but they tend to represent an agricultural society that was, in fact, in contact with its Ukrainian neighbors.

314. **Volume 31:** *Lothringer Volkslieder mit Bildern und Weisen.* ("Folk Songs from Lorraine, with Illustrations and Tunes"). Ed. by Louis Pinck. Kassel: Bärenreiter, 1937.

Edited by the most important folk-music collector in Lorraine, Louis Pinck, this volume reflects the aesthetic and conception of Pinck's *Verklingende Weisen* ("Disappearing Tunes," see below). The woodcuts in this small volume come from that multi-volume work, as do the fifty-five folk songs. The songs in this volume are largely in High German. In his preface, Josef Müller-Blattau reminds the reader that it was Goethe who first collected folk songs in Alsace-Lorraine (1770–71), thereby laying the cornerstone for the study of German folk song in the region as a classical canon. Many songs, though in High German, are regional and local (e.g., no. 7, "Odilienlied" ["Song to St. Odila"], a locally revered saint). The woodcuts, moreover, are folkloric and describe cultural practices from Lorraine. The political agenda, though subtle, of a volume of German folk songs from a contested region in France, published in 1937, is unquestionable.

315. **Volume 35:** *Deutsche Volkslieder aus Mittelpolen mit Bildern und Weisen.* ("German Folk Songs from Central Poland, with Illustrations and Tunes"). Ed. by Robert Klatt and Karl Horak. Kassel: Bärenreiter, 1940.

One of the most blatant attempts to use a volume from the folk-song-landscape project to lay claim to foreign soil by declaring its songs represented the "depth and purity of Germanness in central Poland." In his foreword, written from the

Eastern Front in World War II, Karl Horak lays the ideological groundwork for a history, actually only 100 to 150 years old, of a growing German presence. Drawing from the larger collections of Robert Klatt, Horak bases his choices on what reflects a truly German cultural and economic presence, for example songs that do not give an exaggerated sense of Protestant piety, even though religion was one motivation for settling in the area. The songs and the illustrations overwhelmingly connect the German folk culture to the soil, often possessing calendric subjects or deriving from rites of passage.

316. **Volume 38:** *Volkslieder aus Niederdonau mit Bildern und Weisen.* ("Folk Songs from the Lower Danube, with Illustrations and Tunes"). Ed. by Leopold Schmidt. Kassel: Bärenreiter, 1943.

Finished in 1939 but first published in the middle of World War II, this collection of songs from the "Ostmark," the Nazi designation for Austria, celebrates the lower Danube and its surrounding areas as a "classical" landscape for German folk song. Leopold Schmidt, one of the most distinguished Austrian scholars, drew upon historical collections and the canonical research in Austria to assemble the collection. Contents range from ballads and standard German folk songs with topical references to Austria to specifically Austrian traditions, such as yodeling and songs from the alpine meadow (*Almslieder*). The volume, therefore, portrays an historically specific folk-song landscape, distinctly Austrian yet bound to the politics and military might of Germany.

317. **Volume 43:** *Deutsche Volksweisen aus Südmähren.* ("German Folk Tunes from Southern Moravia"). Ed. by Wenzel Max. Kassel: Bärenreiter, 1971.

With the sporadic publication of a few remaining volumes after World War II, the folk-song-landscape project came to a close. This final volume, stripped in many ways of the wartime ideologies, nonetheless contains a manuscript collection that the editor assembled during the period 1929-1939 during "song weeks" in the southern part of Moravia, now in the Czech Republic. The songs in this volume differ from many earlier volumes, for they are local and individual, with reference to personal singing practices rather than to an overwhelming German canon. Texts, many still in dialect, are transcribed as accurately as possible, that is, from individual performances. Symbolically, these songs were connected, as were the rivers along which German-speaking settlements were found, to Lower Austria, the Danube, and Vienna, hence still to a notion of a Central European folk-song landscape.

318. Mauerhofer, Alois, ed. *Musikethnologisches Kolloquium zum 70. Geburtstag von Walther Wünsch (1978): Die südosteuropäische Volkskultur in der Gegenwart.* ("Music-Ethnological Colloquium for the Seventieth Birthday of Walther Wünsch [1978]: Southeastern European Folk Cultures in the Present"). Graz: Akademische Druck- u. Verlagsanstalt, 1983. (Musikethnologische Sammelbände, 6).

A volume with two thematic areas, each represented through outstanding essays. The first is evident in the subtitle, namely the studies of folk culture in southeastern Europe. Though focusing on different genres of folk culture, not only folk song but also narrative genres, these essays are outstanding and timely studies of this area in the 1970s, for example, in Rihtman's study of children's songs in Bosnia and Herzegovina. The methodological approaches unify this part of the volume, reflecting a centuries-long cooperative tradition between Austrian scholars and scholars from institutions in the southeastern regions of the Habsburg Empire. These emerge as a rich intellectual history, which had the capacity to unify the local, regional, and international. The second focus of the volume comprises methodological essays, again representing a tradition of Austrian scholarship that reached out to other regions of the Habsburg Empire. Franz Födermayr's essay on the comparative-systematic school of Austrian ethnomusicology in this volume remains the classic assessment of this school. Oskár Elschek's comparative study of the educational frameworks for contemporary ethnomusicology and music history in Europe has become a counterpart for the Eurocentric arguments of some German scholars, particularly Carl Dahlhaus. A cross-section of ethnomusicological approaches in Central and East Central Europe in the 1970s and 1980s.

319. Pinck, Louis. *Verklingende Weisen: Lothringer Volkslieder.* ("Disappearing Melodies: Folk Songs from Lorraine"). 5 vols.
Vol. 1—Metz: Lothringer Verlags- und Hilfsverein, 1926.
Vol. 2—Heidelberg: Carl Winters Universitätsbuchhandlung, 1928.
Vol. 3—Metz: Lothringer Verlags- und Hilfsverein, 1933.
Vol. 4—Kassel: Bärenreiter, 1962.
Vol. 5—Kassel: Bärenreiter, 1962.

A classic collection of German folk songs from the contested border region of Central Europe, Lorraine, in eastern France. Gathered throughout the lifetime of Louis Pinck (1873–1940), the parish priest of Hambach, these songs demonstrate strong connections to the central canons of German folk songs. Numerous examples of ballads in High German, for instance, anchor Pinck's collections to the core of secular German traditions; the large number of sacred songs, also in High

German, claim membership in a larger Central European history and cultural area. Relatively few examples come from dialect repertories; none comes from French repertories. The title of the collection, nonetheless, bespeaks Pinck's belief that these German folk-song traditions were disappearing from Lorraine, and that modern traditions, as well as French song traditions, were coming to dominate the region. Pinck, though motivated by a desire to rescue these songs from extinction, was an excellent collector, using wax-cylinder recorders and transcriptions. His collecting strategies depended on his knowledge of the people of Lorraine, which allowed him to contextualize individual songs in relation to the lives of individuals and specific communities. Extensive notes and essays providing cultural analysis appear in all the volumes. Texts and melodies are generally regularized, and the illustrations that appear throughout the volumes provide a romanticized interpretive framework. *Verklingende Weisen* constructs a collective biography of Lorraine, based on a folk-song repertory and those who sang from it, making it one of the outstanding regional studies of the twentieth century.

320. Rohr, Auguste. *Trilogie: Chansons et documents en français, allemand et dialecte. Dokumentarische Grenzlandlieder Französisch—Deutsch + Dialekt.* ("Trilogy: Songs and Documents in French, German, and Dialect. Documentary Border Songs, French—German and Dialect"). Freyming-Merlebach: Petits Chanteurs Lorrains, n.d. [1991].

An anthology and documentary study of folk and folklike composed songs from Lorraine, including songs in the three languages of the region: French, German, and Lorraine dialect. The volume serves as a musical biography of the collector, composer, and choral director, Auguste Rohr (1906–92), with many of these documents and songs produced during his career, which spanned both world wars and the contested nationalist politics that influenced Lorraine in the twentieth century. The volume as a whole serves as an introduction to a multicultural folk culture in Lorraine, albeit a folk culture that in this volume rather often appears as atavistic, a quaint past that needs to be recuperated. The more than 200 songs in the volume—one-third in French, the rest in German or Lorraine dialect—reflect the themes of Lorraine's folk culture. Figures important in the music and folk-music history of Lorraine (e.g., Louis Pinck) are treated in a section devoted to them. Although there is sometimes a sense that the folk music and the cultural identity of Lorraine must be protected from the threat of modernity, particularly from the overwhelming presence of both French and German mass media, the volume represents the culture of a border region in detailed and revealing ways.

321. Röhrich, Lutz. "'...und das ist Badens Glück': Heimatlieder und Regionalhymnen im deutschen Südwesten. Auf der Suche nach Identität" ("'...and That Is Baden's Fortune': Homeland Songs and Regional Anthems in Southwestern Germany. In Search of Identity"). *Jahrbuch für Volksliedforschung* 35 (1990): 13–32.

Examines the larger issues of regional identity in folk song by surveying the changing, and often ambivalent, meanings evident in repertories from southwestern Germany, particularly in Baden. Regional songs often cross the boundaries between genres, for example, the songs in the books of social organizations or on broadsides and postcards, and similarly acquire a remarkable degree of flexibility. As a case study the author recounts the regional songs composed by individuals for a contest in Baden, in which regional identity ranged from traditional themes to critical stances toward contemporary political issues. Documented with many texts and illustrated with four postcards that bore regional songs.

322. Schärmeli, Yvonne. *Königsbrauch und Dreikönigsspiele im welschen Teil des Kantons Freiburg.* ("Royal Function and Three-King Games in the French-Speaking Part of Canton Freiburg"). Freiburg, Switzerland: Universitätsverlag Freiburg Schweiz, 1988. (Germanistica Friburgensia, 11).

Examines Epiphany traditions in the Swiss canton of Freiburg, which embraces the speech (and to some degree religious) border between Swiss-German- and French-speaking parts of Switzerland. Traditionally, this border was seen as absolute, that is, as a separation of two larger cultural areas. Schärmeli's comparison of Three-King plays in the small towns of the canton, especially those closer to the French part of Switzerland, with those in Freiburg, reveal considerable continuity, indeed virtually no difference when the traditions are German or French; German texts, for example, predominate in some villages that have been French-speaking for centuries. Some characteristics of the tradition (e.g., the interweaving of military motives from Swiss history) differentiate Canton Freiburg's Three-King plays from those elsewhere in Central and Western Europe. The texts of the songs in these traditions illustrate unity within the speech border region, rather than forming the characteristic schism that folklorists and linguists generally assign to such borders.

323. Schramm, Franz-Josef, Otto Holzapfel, Eva Bruckner, and Ernst Schusser, eds. *Auf den Spuren von Peter Streck in der Rhön und in Unterfranken*. ("In Search of Peter Streck in the Rhön and Lower Franconia"). Munich: Volksmusikarchiv, Bezirk Oberbayern, 1993.

A volume in the series "Auf den Spuren von..." ("In Search of...", published by the Folk Music Archive of Upper Bavaria), which investigate the places and repertories of significant folk musicians and folk-music scholars. Peter Streck (1797–1864) made his career primarily as a military musician, directing military ensembles in Bavaria throughout his career. Streck's musical activities crossed the boundaries between genres, and the different repertories and musical practices to which he contributed crossed the boundaries between social groups and economic classes. Streck composed works for various types of musical ensembles, but also for religious choruses, as well as dance and popular ensembles. The volume is particularly interesting for the way it reveals the interdependence of music-making at various levels and among various groups within Central European society. His works remain significant evidence of the musical life of nineteenth-century Bavaria, and many were published during his lifetime (estimates run as high as 390 different works). Others entered oral tradition. The volume includes essays and reprinted articles about Streck and the region of the Rhön and Lower Franconia, which lies roughly between Würzburg and Frankfurt, including historical essays and discussions of folk-song repertories from the area, notably Otto Holzapfel's article about Veronika Reder (1883–1979). The volume is richly illustrated with maps, photographs, examples of Streck's pieces, and musical works composed by or associated with this extremely important composer of military and popular music from nineteenth-century Bavaria.

324. Schwarz, Rudolf, and Emil Seidel. *Steirische Volkslieder: 290 Lieder und 45 Jodler aus der Steiermark in Sätzen für drei Stimmen*. ("Styrian Folk Songs: 290 Songs and 45 Yodels from Styria, in Three-Voice Settings"). Graz: Verlag Leykam, 1981.

Drawing on the many historically important collections of Styrian folk songs from the past several centuries, this volume attempts to establish a canonic core repertory for modern use. In their introduction, the editors clarify the nature of Styrianness in folk song. On one hand, this feature is difficult to establish because not all folk songs in the Austrian province demonstrate provenience there. On the other, there are specific musical traits that contextualize a song as Styrian, for example, the predominance of three-voice performance practice. Age, too, becomes a factor for establishing the qualities of Styrianness, but it also provides a theoretical context for the volume's explicit attempt to encourage Styrians to sing from this canonic repertory. Just as the early-music revival relied on printed sources from the Renaissance and Baroque, so too do the songs in this volume, many of them from early sources, deserve to enter oral tradition as components of a modern Styrian folk-music revival. Each song or yodel appears in a transcribed version, with dialect spellings of its texts and careful documentation of the collections from which the editors took the printed version (e.g., Josef Pommer, Konrad Mautner, or Viktor Zack). The collection, therefore, also serves as an intellectual history of the attempts to represent Styria in folk song, a history lying at the core of Austrian folk-music scholarship itself. The songs range across various genres, including sacred songs and yodels specific to Styria.

325. Stockmann, Doris. *Der Volksgesang in der Altmark: Von der Mitte des 19. bis zur Mitte des 20. Jahrhunderts.* ("Folk Song in the Altmark: From the Mid-Nineteenth to the Mid-Twentieth Century"). Berlin: Akademie-Verlag, 1962.

An extraordinarily detailed study of folk song in the Altmark, the region around Magdeburg in the western part of the former German Democratic Republic. This study differs from other regional studies in the extent of its employment of ethnographic and historical examination of changing social contexts for song. Stockmann's methodology is therefore ethnomusicological rather than folkloristic, though she draws considerably on the collections and approaches employed by folklorists. The central thesis of the book holds that folk-singing practices in the present are related to those in the past but are the result of ongoing change and persistent influences from diverse external sources. To understand folk song in the Altmark in the present, it becomes necessary to construct a history that documents the patterns of change and explains them as products of society in transformation. Stockmann begins by presenting the different sources, ranging from Ludolf Parisius's collections in the mid-nineteenth century to her own field research in the mid-twentieth century. She proceeds in the second and third sections of the book to connect the various collections by (1) looking at singers and their profiles; and (2) examining the conditions and institutions of singing. The term *Volksgesang* (also glossed as "folk song" in English) in the title differs from *Volkslied* because of the extent to which it reflects the social and cultural contexts of folk song and singing. Numerous transcriptions and extensive use of comparative tables further make this study the outstanding regional musical ethnography in the GDR.

326. Strajnar, Julijan. "Zur Tanzmusik im slowenischen Raum." ("On Dance Music in the Slovenian Region"). In Walter Deutsch and

Rudolph Pietsch, eds., *Dörfliche Tanzmusik im westpannonischen Raum*. Vienna: A. Schendl, 1990. Pp. 231–35.

Begins by suggesting that classification of musical instruments should also consider the uses of instruments by ethnic groups and within regions. Strajnar proposes three overarching categories to complement the Sachs-Hornbostel system: first, a classification according to the materials from which instruments are built (wood, clay, etc.), particularly as these afford an indigenous quality; second, instruments that are specific to a group or region; third, instruments whose structures may be the same, but whose uses and sonic qualities differ vastly across regions (e.g., the violin and clarinet in East Central Europe). Strajnar applies these concepts to the instrumental music in the Slovenian region, whereby he means a culture area stretching from the Adriatic in the southwest and into the Austrian Alps in the northeast. Whereas instrument types are fairly similar throughout the region, their functions, particularly in the performance of dance genres, demonstrate extensive variety, often resulting from local and ethnic differences. It is the character of this functional and contextual variety, rather than distinctive instrument families, that distinguishes Slovenian instrumental music.

327. Wulz, Helmut. "Tradition und Neuschöpfung im Kärntner Volksgesang." ("Tradition and New Creativity in Corinthian Folk Song"). In Walter Deutsch, ed., *Tradition und Innovation*. Vienna: A. Schendl, 1987. Pp. 64–89.

Among the Austrian provinces, Corinthia is best known for its remarkable choral tradition, with some 500 official choruses alone in the provincial choral organization. Interpreting the choral tradition as a musical phenomenon of the center and the result of centripetalizing institutionalization in the twentieth century, Wulz uses this article and its numerous musical examples to examine the vocal traditions constituting the peripheries of Corinthia. As a province, Corinthia is marked both by contrasting dialects and locally bound practices and by the multiculturalism resulting from the Slovenian-speaking population and the common border with Slovenia. Wulz examines the gradual change in individual repertories, particularly a trajectory stretching from songs used specifically with folk customs (e.g., annual religious holidays) to those that are consciously cultivated by specialists and therefore yield some of the markers of local practice; there is a tendency, for example, for songs that mix German dialect and Slovenian texts to lose one language or the other. Most important, however, the strengthening of choral tradition in the center has meant that songs at the periphery have contributed to a changing and growing, if different, Corinthian folk-music repertory in the late twentieth century.

꧁꧂

Land and Locale

328. Brandl, Rudolf M., ed. *Lüneburg und Umgebung.* ("Lüneburg and Environs"). Göttingen: Edition Re, 1989. (Dokumentation des Musikleben in Niedersachsen, 2).

A project of ethnomusicology faculty and students at the University of Göttingen, aimed at observing the everyday musical life in Lüneburg, a small city in Lower Saxony. Originally part of a province-wide project to create a musical atlas of the area, the reports and fieldwork studies collected here paint a portrait in which musical activities are many and varied, with some distinctive of the local culture and others typical of the musical life in most small German cities. Several fieldwork projects are particularly interesting because they document the almost haphazard organization of musical activities, yet an organization that was normalized throughout its reception by Lüneburgers. The approach used by the volume stresses the objectivity achieved by straightforward observation and statistical tabulation. There is relatively little theory to back up this approach, which makes it difficult to compare much of the material here with studies of musical life in other small cities, in Germany and elsewhere in industrialized societies. One of the few studies of its kind in Germany undertaken by ethnomusicologists.

329. Härtel, Hermann. "Musikalische Gebrauchskultur auf der Alm (Warum singt es sich so leicht?)." ("Musical Functional Culture on the Alpine Meadow [Why Does One Break into Song So Easily?]"). *Jahrbuch des österreichischen Volksliedwerkes* 41 (1992): 143–49.

Relates folk song, particularly singing as a form of communication, to the culture of the alpine meadow. The meadow, located high in the mountains, is the site of pastures for the grazing of cattle, but also the services that are necessary for commerce and life in the mountains: a seasonal inn or tavern; facilities for cattle-trading; a church or chapel that embodies local narratives and history; and tourist services. A folk musician and folk-music scholar who frequently takes part in the cultural practices of the alpine meadow, Härtel investigates possible reasons that music plays such a distinctive role, not only through genres specific to the culture (e.g., the *Vierzeiler,* or quatrain; and the musical practices of cattle-trading), but also through the presence of music in more intimate communication (e.g., polyphonic yodeling). An excellent introduction to the music culture of a local site of music-making in Central Europe, especially the high mountains of Austria.

330. Klusen, Ernst, Hermann Stoffels, and Theo Zart. *Das Musikleben der Stadt Krefeld 1780-1945.* ("The Musical Life of the City of Krefeld, 1780-1945"). 2 vols. Cologne: Arno Volk, 1979 and 1980. (Beiträge zur rheinischen Musikgeschichte, 124).

A study of musical life in a small city in the Rhineland, researched and written from musicological, sociomusicological, and ethnomusicological perspectives. The concept of "musical life" grows from the ways in which music and music-making is connected to the institutions and practices of the residents of the city. No domain of music-making has a privileged status, but rather, music in homes and private gatherings, schools, industry, folk-music organizations, religious institutions, and art-music ensembles is presented here as an interdependent whole. The authors also focus on venues of musical performance and on publications of music that relate to the musical life of Krefeld. Individual musicians also appear in this history, but not as great composers or performers, rather as concert organizers, choral directors, music-store owners, and musicians contributing to the complex musical life. Brahms does receive a longer section in volume 2, but so too do religious and ethnic minorities, for example Mennonites and Jews in Krefeld. The volumes contain a great deal of information and statistical data, which add to the richness of this local music history. In particular, the contributions of Klusen, as the theorist known for his concept of "group song," and the sociological approaches of the book make this a model for investigating musical life in a modern urban setting.

331. Uhland, Ludwig. *Alte hoch- und niederdeutsche Volkslieder.* ("Old High and Low German Folk Songs"). 2 vols. Stuttgart and Tübingen: J.G. Cotta'scher Verlag, 1844 and 1845.

The landmark first attempt to gather folk songs in specific German dialects. Uhland, the leader of a circle of Swabian poets, drew upon regional dialects to broaden the basis for establishing Germanness in the arts and in history. The title of the volumes itself suggests several different types of space for representing Germanness through folk songs. First, these folk songs are "old," whereby Uhland explicitly establishes a connection to the Middle Ages. Second, they utilize both High and Low German, in other words, serve as an expressive connection between oral and literate cultures, country and court. The Germanness of the symbols brought to the fore by these collections notwithstanding, Uhland was himself a liberal and a polymath, who actively cultivated pan-

European cultural exchange, particularly with France, where he lived for several years. Active in the 1848 Revolution as a politician, Uhland also represented the cultural side of Romanticism at a national level. The two volumes contain a total of 357 folk-song texts, though without melodies. A thorough philological discussion of the sources for the songs appears at the end of the second volume. German folk-song scholarship and collections repeatedly refer to these two volumes and their role in establishing a place for dialect studies, establishing Uhland as one of the seminal figures in the history of German folk-song scholarship.

332. Walcher, Maria. "Ottakringer Sing- und Spieltradition im 20. Jahrhundert." ("The Song and Instrumental-Music Tradition of the Ottakring in the Twentieth Century"). In Walter Deutsch, ed., *Tradition und Innovation*. Vienna: A. Schendl. Pp. 184–95.

The Ottakring, Vienna's Sixteenth District, was incorporated into the greater metropolitan area in the late nineteenth century, when its culture of inns supporting music-making was fully developed. A distinctively Viennese music culture developed in Ottakring, benefiting from the position of the district on the periphery of the city. The musical life of Ottakring comprised a multicultural component, as well as the working class that flourished in the district. Musical performances in the inns were diversified, with *volkstümliche Musik* ("folklike," popular music) and stage acts of various kinds. Although an Ottakring musician had to know these different components of successful performance, distinctive repertories, many influenced by the Schrammel Quartet, which frequently performed in Ottakring in the second half of the nineteenth century, developed and were published on sheet music and in broadsides. Walcher interprets the special character of Ottakring music as a result of the combination of traditional Viennese popular styles and the need for accommodating Viennese audiences, rather than outsiders or tourists. At the end of the twentieth century, the district remains the urban site in which the most distinctively Viennese tradition (i.e., the most distinctively Viennese mixture) of folk and popular musics thrives, still responding to many new influences.

IV

Wozu Volksmusik?—Past, Present, and Future

13

HISTORICAL FOLK-MUSIC RESEARCH

The folk music of Central Europe has always existed in a web of historical moments and historical imaginations. A folk song's capacity to record specific events and retain them through the constant narrations of oral tradition has not been lost upon folk-music scholars, who accordingly began to theorize the historical aspects of folk music in the mid-nineteenth century. By the mid-twentieth century the study of folk music's historical basis had led to the formation of a subfield within folk-music scholarship and European ethnomusicology, one that supports its own study group in the International Council for Traditional Music and sponsors numerous publications, some of which appear in the annotations in the present chapter.

The historical study of folk music musters many different theoretical and methodological perspectives. The historical imagination of which folk song is a part, for example, contains elements of regionalism and nationalism. It has also taken on specifically European traits of distinguishing self from "other," and therefore folk songs with historical themes frequently document the politics of expansion or the settlement of emigrant groups. The "history" that folk music inscribes, moreover, may assume abstract forms, as in Bartók's three style periods, or it may be specific, as in the repertories that Rochus Freiherr von Liliencron and Leopold Schmidt compiled in their studies discussed below. Through historical folk-music research scholars have determined the ways in which folk song reifies the past for the present.

History intersects with folk music in many different ways, thereby making it possible to maintain very complex processes and forms of narration. The texts of historical songs, when performed or read in the present, produce the impression that one is in the position of an observer in the past. One witnesses events in the texts of songs as if they were unfolding according to the structure of the song itself. The scholarship employing historical folk-music research suggests roughly four different directions in the works included in this chapter. In the first, scholars are largely interested in reconstructing the music culture of the past through the observations of travelers or others encountering music-making. Through the historical potential of folk song or the musical activities of others that have caught the attention of an observer (e.g., the seventeenth-century Adam Olearius, whom Hartmut Braun discusses in a work below), the modern scholar acquires the potential to extend and refine music history itself. In the second direction, folk song lends itself to analysis because it is a medium for the narration of history. Thus, it was not simply the fact that individual folk songs recorded historical events, albeit with considerable variation, that fascinated the early historical scholars such as Liliencron, but rather that folk song could, at all, anchor a series of practices over many centuries in which the same events were narrated again and again. Fundamental to this direction is asking why folk songs pick up and retain some events and not others. The third direction derives from an interest in folk music's potential to historicize, to give an event of the past meanings relevant to the present. The death of a martyr, for example, which entered a corpus of songs several centuries in the past, may again provide an ideological rallying point when recontextualized with ideologies of the present (see, e.g., Peter Assion's study of St. Elizabeth of Thuringia). The historical potential of folk music emerges in the acts of juxtaposing past and present. Finally, methodological consideration of folk music often derives from what is regarded to be its historical character. Processes of change may be internal to style itself, or they may result from the interaction of a repertory with the social conditions or aesthetic structures of time and place; Austrian or Styrian folk music acquires its national or regional character not because it embodies an ossified essence, but rather because musicians have responded to the changing histories of Austria as a nation or Styria as a region.

Historical folk-music research asserts that folk song actually inscribes the past musically. Two further assertions are implicit in this claim for inscription. First, the historical trajectory of folk song resides in the intersection of oral and written traditions. Second, this intersection, the constant exchange between written sources and oral performance, empowers folk music to contain historical texts distinct from, or even hidden from, other forms of narration. It is for such reasons that many of the works annotated here examine the use of music as a medium of social criticism or for the expression of forbidden practices (see, e.g., the works by Brigitte Emmrich and László Tarnói). Folk song often becomes historical the moment its composers and performers make its social text explicit and embed it with the ability to express a resistance that otherwise would not be possible or less effective. Song inscribes the historical moment, which in turn marks the transmission of the song and its record of the past.

The historical nature of European folk song in general and, to some extent, German folk song in particular, distinguishes it from the folk song of other parts of the world. I do not mean to suggest that the narrative properties I have briefly touched upon here are absent in other repertories—they surely are not—but that a predilection, if not an obsession, for history has increasingly preoccupied the ways in which German folk-music scholars have defined their field. In this sense, history has become a means of temporally bounding what folk music is. Through its inscriptive properties, then, Central European folk song reflexively turns upon itself, connecting each performance of a "Steirer"

("Styrian") or a "deutscher Tanz" ("German dance") to the history of places real and imagined. Recognizing this embeddedness of the past in the present, folk-music scholars, as the following works demonstrate, have transformed their subject into a means for writing the history of Central Europe itself.

⋙⋘

333. Antesberger, Günther. "'Honnete Tänz geigen zu därfen...': Thurner und Stadtgeiger zu Klagenfurt—anno 1754." ("'To Gain the Privilege to Play at Respectable Dances...': Turners and City Violinists in Klagenfurt in the Year 1754"). *Jahrbuch des österreichischen Volksliedwerkes* 32/33 (1984): 98–106.

Based on a written appeal by musicians from the turners' (here, referring to building crafts) guild to the city government of Klagenfurt, this article explores the social and public domains of public dancing and music-making in mid-eighteenth century Corinthia, the southern province of Austria. The turners' appeal resulted from their inability to perform at certain types of "respectable" occasions (e.g., some weddings, but many more official occasions of public performance), thereby excluding them from the more lucrative sources of income, which had until that point been the exclusive privilege of the city violinists. The conflict that developed around this privilege yields considerable information about issues of repertory, professionalism, and transformation of the public sphere in eighteenth-century Europe. The repertories of music in the boundary between art music and folk music were numerous and their interrelatedness complex. In the mid-eighteenth century, moreover, new groups of musical professionals and amateurs had mobilized themselves to cross the divide between rural and urban, popular and classical. The conflict examined here, played out in public documents, reveals far more extensive participation in a public musical life than many scholars have previously imagined.

334. Assion, Peter. "Kultzeugnis und Kultintention: Die hl. Elisabeth von Thüringen in Mirakel, Sage und Lied." ("Evidence of Cults and the Construction of Their Meaning: St. Elizabeth of Thuringia According to Miracles, Saga, and Song"). *Jahrbuch für Volksliedforschung* 27/28 (1982/83): 40–61.

An historical assessment of the meaning of St. Elizabeth of Thuringia (1207–31), traced through the evidence of miracles, tales, and songs that recount and represent her life. Assion draws upon examples from diverse sources, both official hagiographic and popular ones, and outlines a history of transmission about St.

Elizabeth. These representations of the saint not only narrate a history of changing religious and cultural attitudes, but they also constantly recontextualize the meanings of her life for successive generations. Songs about St. Elizabeth, therefore, become historical texts about those who sing and transmit them, and about the moments in which performance, transmission, and variation take place. Assion posits that folklore and folk song within it provide powerful and complex texts about the contexts of history, and that interpreting folk-song texts should concern itself less with authentic meaning than with the intent of those who use folk song to voice the meanings of their lives.

335. Braun, Hartmut. "Erwähnungen von Volksmusik im Schrifttum des 17. Jahrhunderts unter besonderer Berücksichtigung der orientalischen Musik am Beispiel Adam Olearius' Beschreibung seiner Reise nach Russland und Persien." ("References to Folk Music in the Writings of the Seventeenth Century, with Special Consideration of Oriental Music in Adam Olearius's Description of His Travels in Russia and Persia"). *Musikethnologische Sammelbände* 7 (1985): 15–31.

Taking the seventeenth-century travel account of Adam Olearius (1599–1671), *Vermehrte Newe Beschreibung der Muskowitischen vnd Persischen Reyse* (1656), as a point of departure, Hartmut Braun argues for the importance of examining early historical sources as a component of folk-music research. Olearius traveled through Russia, the Caucasus, and Persia in order to expand trade routes between northern Germany and Asia. His accounts are replete with musical descriptions, particularly those of instruments, ensembles, ritual, and celebration that accompanied the various activities with which his delegation was associated. These accounts take note of an instrumentarium quite distinct from later observations and those usually described by modern scholars. These seventeenth-century accounts, nevertheless, make it possible to trace a more complete history of musics in the Caucasus, Persia, and modern Iran. Also of particular interest are the accounts of musical practice in religious ritual, not only of Muslim centers but also among Eastern forms of Christianity (e.g., among Armenians). Braun cites many specific examples from Olearius's account and includes several longer passages that afford more detailed descriptions of ritual and ceremony. Braun is particularly concerned with the names used by Olearius and those he encountered, particularly for the genealogical and organological evidence these names provide modern scholarship. A map and six pictures of musical practice from Olearius's account conclude the article.

336. Burmeister, Karl Heinz. "Das Tanzhaus in Vorarlberg." ("The Dance House in Vorarlberg"). In Walter Deutsch and Erich Schneider, eds., *Beiträge zur Volksmusik in Vorarlberg und im Bodenseeraum.* Vienna: A. Schendl, 1983. Pp. 147–63.

Mustering archival evidence and historical descriptions, Burmeister speculates on the social functions of one of the most visible structures of public culture in the Austrian province of Vorarlberg. Visual depictions of dance houses show a structure that was largely open to the public space it occupied, usually in a position contrasting with that of the church. Burmeister argues that the dance house and the church framed a cultural dialectic, the secular and sacred extremes of public life in the Vorarlberg village. The dance house therefore had many functions, ranging from the obviously important role as a setting for dance and musical performance to administrative activities, such as local legal proceedings. The earliest reports of the dance house from the late Middle Ages reveal that it was used by Jews for various activities, dance and music among them. It may well be possible, then, that the dance house provided a site for the performance of cultural difference, even juxtaposing various aspects of difference. The history of the dance house, which stretches into the nineteenth century, offers a lens for the interpretation of the presence of cultural distinctions in the everyday life of Europeans.

337. Danckert, Werner. *Das Volkslied im Abendland.* ("Folk Song in Western Culture"). Bern: Francke, 1966. (Sammlung Dalp, 98).

Both an intellectual history of folk-song research and an examination of the distinctively European qualities of folk song throughout history. Danckert sketches a number of different levels (*Schichten*) in folk song, each of which represents contrasting historical processes and different domains of European culture (e.g., magic or social activities of women). It is clear from the title that Danckert privileges the West as the larger culture area historically definable by folk song. At the deepest level European folk song possesses qualities that existed long before the modern era, qualities usually Germanic and northern. Folk song also embodies its own historical processes, among them the tendency toward polyphony and different forms of dissemination, variation, and disintegration. Many chapters provide surveys of the most significant theories of nineteenth- and twentieth-century scholarship, as well as the primary and secondary literature to which the reader can turn. Of relatively little concern are the modern conditions in which folk song exists. Non-Germanic repertories are surveyed in the book, though primarily those that also existed at a premodern level, for example Finnish, Hungarian, and Celtic music. An excellent introduction to European folk song, though the reader should be aware of the vestiges of earlier fascist notions about Germanic and Nordic layers of European history.

338. Emmrich, Brigitte. "Muth, Muth! Franken... Die kursächsische Liedverbotsliste von 1802: Ein Beitrag zu den Liedverboten nach der Französischen Revolution." ("Courage, Courage! Franconia... The Lists of Forbidden Songs in the Electorate of Saxony in 1802: A Contribution to the Censorship of Songs after the French Revolution"). *Jahrbuch für Volkskunde und Kulturgeschichte* 21 (N.F. 6, 1978): 77–107.

Study of the presence of broadsides in the forbidden song and music culture in the wake of the French Revolution. Emmrich focuses primarily on local printers and the dissemination of broadsides from diverse locations in Saxony. In response to the political repression, new forms and themes for songs arose that expressed the sentiments of social criticism. These songs did not remain connected to the dissemination of broadsides but rather quickly entered the larger repertory of songs sung by workers and others in the laboring classes, whose social life rapidly institutionalized at the beginning of the nineteenth century. A thorough study of song as a medium between politics at the national level and those who responded to politics in their everyday practices.

339. Emmrich, Brigitte. "Zwischen Jakobinerlied und sentimentaler Romanze: Zum Spektrum des Liedguts ländlicher und städtischer Sozialschichten am Ende des 18. und Anfang des 19. Jahrhunderts im ehemaligen Kursachsen." ("Between Jacobite Song and Sentimental Romance: On the Range of the Songs of the Rural and Urban Social Levels at the End of the Eighteenth and the Beginning of the Nineteenth Century in the Former Electorate of Saxony"). *Jahrbuch für Volksliedforschung* 37 (1992): 13–23.

Using extensive archival sources, including printed broadsides, reports of music-making, and collections of song from all parts of Saxon society, this article provides a cross-section of folk-music culture, particularly repertory, in the area of Saxony, now in eastern Germany. Theoretically, the article draws broadly on concepts of folk-music research developed in the German Democratic Republic, especially notions of the ways in which song empowered responses to hegemonic government structures. The extensive notes serve as an excellent introduction to that research. Although songs of opposition and social criticism are among those identified by Emmrich, the overwhelming majority are musical forms of *Trivialliteratur* (popular literature), but more accurately the entertainment culture of the time. These songs were quite different in their production, origin, and function, but remarkably they demonstrated considerable similarity in style and theme. In short, sentimental songs constituted a body of popular literature at the beginning of the nineteenth century, in which Saxons did not openly concern themselves with the politics and power structures of the day. This attitude, Emmrich concludes, reflects the general relation between the working and lower classes and the governments of Germany's states at this point in history.

340. Gansberg, Ingeborg. *Volksliedsammlungen und historischer Kontext: Kontinuität über zwei Jahrhunderte?* ("Folk-Song Collections and Historical Context: Continuity during Two Centuries?"). Frankfurt am Main: Peter Lang, 1986. (Europäische Hochschulschriften, 16; Musikwissenschaft, 17).

A critical assessment of the relation of early and seminal folk-song collections to the cultural worlds they were thought ideally to emulate. Gansberg argues that the tendency to represent early folk-song collections reveals a misapprehension of the meanings such songs might really have held for those who presumably sang them. This misapprehension, so she claims, is no less present in the activities of German publishing houses that reprinted and marketed the early collections as songs of the people, than in the ideologies of folk-song scholars in the German Democratic Republic (e.g., Wolfgang Steinitz and Hermann Strobach), who argued for the social-functional character of historical folk-song collections. The book begins with a comparative analysis of the collections of Johann Gottfried Herder, Arnim and Brentano (*Des Knaben Wunderhorn*), Ludwig Uhland, and Hoffmann von Fallersleben. Gansberg then turns to a close examination of the production of folk song in the anti-nuclear movement in Germany during the 1970s, with special attention to the songs that emerged during the resistance to the building of an atomic reactor in Wyhl in southwestern Germany and the ensuing people's initiatives in Germany, Alsace, and Switzerland. These songs, which Gansberg comparatively analyzes with statistical methods, should have demonstrated exactly the types of conditions idealized by the responses to the early historical collections, but in fact the form of local and regional resistance in the anti-nuclear movement produced repertories and social engagement very different from those constructed for the late eighteenth and early nineteenth century as the canons of German historical folk song.

341. Haefs, Gabriele. *Das Irenbild der Deutschen dargestellt anhand einiger Untersuchungen über die Geschichte der irischen Volksmusik und ihrer Verbreitung in der Bundesrepublik Deutschland.* ("The German Image of the Irish, Based on Investigations into the History of Irish Folk Music and Its Dissemination in the Federal Republic of

Germany"). Frankfurt am Main: Peter Lang, 1983. (Europäische Hochschulschriften, Reihe 19: Volkskunde/Ethnologie, Volkskunde A, 26).

Already in the eighteenth century German folk-music scholars, including Herder, transformed images of the bard's connection to nature into a stereotype of the Irish. Haefs investigates the long history of such images up to the late twentieth century, when they were no less prominent in the German folk scene and were integrated into political movements. Although German images of the Irish often resulted from stereotypes and misreadings of the literature and history of Ireland, they form a complex intellectual history of Ireland as an alternative site of European culture. This site was valued for its connection to nature as well as to politics. In the late twentieth century German folk songs about the Irish focused on these politics as symbolic of the European left, often ignoring their programs of violence. The book examines an enormous wealth of songs and a considerable range of literature, thereby piecing together a very complete historical picture of the Irish. Historically, this study shows that the use of folk song to invent culture is not only local but international, indeed lending the history of nationalism a polyphonic texture.

342. Harms, Wolfgang, ed. *Deutsche illustrierte Flugblätter des 16. und 17. Jahrhunderts.* ("German Illustrated Broadsides in the Sixteenth and Seventeenth Centuries"). Vol. 1: *Die Sammlung der Herzog-August-Bibliothek in Wolfenbüttel*; Part 1: *Ethica, Physica.* ("Vol. 1: The Collection of the Herzog August Library in Wolfenbüttel; Part 1: Ethical Matters, Physical Matters"). Tübingen: Niemeyer, 1985.

The first of a five-volume project to publish broadsides in major German research libraries, this work reprints broadsides with moral and ethical subjects, and those with subjects related to nature, all from the Herzog August Library in Wolfenbüttel. The broadsides appear in large format, so as to be readable and to lend themselves to analysis by readers; facing each broadside is a commentary by an expert scholar, whose analyses often extend also to concise but rich historical essays on genre and forms of popular culture in the print media of the sixteenth and seventeenth centuries. Broadside songs are mixed together with other forms and genres of the broadside, and the interpretations here are broadly interdisciplinary. Broadside songs, therefore, take their place in a larger context of representation and dissemination in early modern Europe (the songs and other broadsides are not limited to German examples, which, nonetheless, predominate). Several of the songs are extensive, with carefully crafted poetic texts, suggesting that they had largely literary functions. Other songs seem to suggest that they appeared as one stage in a process of oral and written interaction. As a whole, the volume suggests that broadside songs developed as components of numerous other phenomena, and their diversity represents complex processes of dissemination, reception, and performance.

343. Klusen, Ernst. *Das Volkslied im niederrheinischen Dorf: Studien zum Lebensbereich des Volksliedes der Gemeinde Hinsbeck im Wandel einer Generation.* ("Folk Song in a Village in the Lower Rhine Region: Studies on the Life of Folk Song in the Town of Hinsbeck during the Course of a Generation"). Bonn-Bad Godesberg: Voggenreiter, 1970.

A comparative study of folk-song practices in a German village. Klusen initially published a monograph devoted to Hinbeck in 1941, and the present volume reassesses the village ca. twenty-five years later, utilizing extensive fieldwork from the mid-1960s. Klusen concerns himself with the "life of folk song," whereby the retention of repertories is only one aspect. This "life" results from the social organization of the town, the ways in which its groups historicize themselves and express their contemporary social cohesiveness through singing practices. Using sociological and statistical research, Klusen distinguishes different generations (e.g., those who would have known the repertories of the late 1930s and those who were in the 1960s first encountering organized folk singing in the schools). Both familial and social genealogies are connected across the generations, thereby providing the basis for statistical comparison. Theoretically, this study is one of the most fully articulated applications of Klusen's concept of *Gruppenlied* ("group song"), which maintains that folk song is a product of social collectives, small and large, to find means of expressing and solidifying their shared activities. The village of Hinbeck, it follows, contains many social groups, and their combined musical activities constitute the folk-music history of the village. Viewed in this way, Hinbeck's musical life, though undergoing substantial internal change, retains an overall unity that has responded to the ways in which the village has been altered or remained the same over the course of a generation that included World War II and the rebuilding of post-war Germany.

344. Lach, Robert. *Eine Tiroler Liederhandschrift aus dem 18. Jahrhundert.* ("An Eighteenth-Century Song Manuscript from Tyrol"). Vienna and Leipzig: Hölder-Pichler-Tempsky. (Sitzungsberichte, 198. Band, 5. Bericht, Philosophisch-historische Klasse, Akademie der Wissenschaften zu Wien).

Assesses the relation of the repertory in an eighteenth-century song manuscript to the various musical traditions it contains, thereby treating it as evidence of the music culture of the Tyrol mountains of Austria. The manuscript, discovered in a farmhouse in 1901, is an anthology containing works in various genres: religious pieces, including extended sections from the mass; works for instrumental ensembles; folk and *volkstümliche* dances; and folk songs in local dialect. Various hands compiled the manuscript, and the errors of several hands made it possible for Robert Lach to unravel the different origins of the manuscript documents. Most significantly, the manuscript reveals that folk, popular, religious, and classical music were woven into the same cultural fabric in eighteenth-century Austria and southern Germany. The rural and bourgeois societies represented by these musical practices were, moreover, in processes of change, for the manuscript included both repertories from the early century and recent popular examples, such as a "Marche Buonebarde" ("March of Napoleon Bonaparte"). The volume concludes with texts of the manuscript's folk songs, in both dialect and High German, and transcriptions of the instrumental sections of the manuscript.

345. Liliencron, Rochus Freiherr von. *Deutsches Leben im Volkslied um 1530.* ("German Life in Folk Song around 1530"). Berlin: W. Spemann, 1884.

A classic study of German folk song in the early Renaissance. Using surviving sources and folk songs that entered oral tradition, Liliencron portrays folk song as a document of the historical and social conditions of the time in which it comes into existence. Significant for this study are the rise of printing technology, the waning of the Middle Ages, with the appearance of folk-music specialists (e.g., minstrels and *Meistersänger*, or "master singers"), and the immediate pre-Reformation period in Germany. The book begins with a critical preface that examines the nature and sources for historical folk-music research. The bulk of the volume consists of folk songs, represented in various forms from the early sixteenth century, for example as tenor lines (i.e., melody) in sacred songs from the period. The "German life" referred to in the title refers to both social function and religious-calendric context. Many of the songs that appeared around 1530 (e.g., "Graf von Rom") entered the canon of German folk ballads, remaining in oral tradition throughout Europe until the present. Of great value for folk-song scholars, folklorists, and historical musicologists, especially medievalists and Renaissance specialists.

346. Liliencron, Rochus Freiherr von. *Die historischen Volkslieder der Deutschen vom 13. bis 16. Jahrhundert.* ("The Historical Folk Songs of the Germans from the Thirteenth to the Sixteenth Centuries"). Leipzig: F.C.W. Vogel, 1865.

Collection, annotation, and analysis of folk songs that narrate specific historical events in the late Middle Ages and early Renaissance. With this volume Liliencron establishes the theory and methods of historical folk-music research, a process of paradigm formulation that he discusses in the book's preface. Liliencron begins by treating texts as a philologist, that is, by determining the relations among various folk songs with similar topics and the manuscripts or printed versions in which they survive. His aim is to use this approach to create a complex of folk-song texts, from which he can extract as much evidence as possible to document an historical event, and then to identify those songs that narrate the event with historical accuracy. The volume contains 124 folk songs, beginning with a song dated 1243, which narrates events attending the relations between Bern (Switzerland) and Freiburg im Breisgau (Germany) at the time of their founding by the Zähringer family in the twelfth and thirteenth centuries. The songs concern battles and individuals, as well as places and events of special significance in late medieval Germany. In his annotation of many songs, moreover, Liliencron describes social conditions and the tensions that characterized the late medieval world. Song 12, "Vom Judenmord zu Deggendorf" ("On the Murder of Jews in Deggendorf"), comes from a 1337 sacred play, in which the massacre of Jews in the Bavarian town of Deggendorf was described (Liliencron, in fact, notes that the song "celebrated" the massacre). In his annotation, however, Liliencron addresses the larger issue of medieval pogroms against Jews in Central Europe, illustrating not only the extent to which pogroms reached epic proportions in the fourteenth century, but documenting the continuation of folk practices that remembered the massacres of Jews well into the eighteenth century, for example, the veneration of massacre sites as important pilgrimage shrines through this period. Accompanying each song is a history of the transmission of the version printed in the volume, with an assessment of its proximity to other sources of historical narration.

347. Litschauer, Walburga, and Walter Deutsch. "'Es reiten drei Schneider' oder: Rossini im Volkslied." ("'Three Tailors Were Riding' or: Rossini in Folk Song"). *Jahrbuch des österreichischen Volksliedwerkes* 41 (1992): 39–48.

Speculates about the origins and transmission of the song "Lamento der Wiener uiber [sic] die Abreise der italienischen Operngesellschaft" ("Lament of the Viennese over the Departure of the Italian Opera Troupe"), in which Italian opera and

Gioacchino Rossini's visit to Vienna in 1822 are parodied. The text of the song, which employs references to departures in both its melody and text, parodies the relation of German to Italian opera, and between Austrian and Italian culture. Variants and fragments of the song were evident in written and oral sources during the next half-century, but most important to the thesis of the article, the song entered a complex tradition of parody songs in Austrian and German folk song, illustrating a process of interaction between folk and popular songs. This interaction exploits the thematic and motivic relations in the variants, in this case folk songs such as the famous "Drei Reiter am Thore" ("Three Knights at the Gate"), which generated new compositions and broadsides, as well as oral variants during the nineteenth century.

348. Meinel, Richard, ed. *Album deutscher Volkslieder.* ("Album of German Folk Songs"). Stuttgart: Flieschhauer und Spohn, 1980.

A nostalgically conceived edition of folk-song postcards, largely from the 1920s. Drawn by the Bavarian artist Paul Hey (1867–1952), these cards are redolent of images of *Heimat*, leading the editor to suggest that the images were largely created for reception away from the homeland, even in German communities abroad. These themes contrast ideologically with the historical period in which they were produced, the Weimar Republic, a time of political ferment and experimentation in the arts. Although the seventy-six folk-song postcards reprinted here seem thematically atavistic, they do illustrate some essential conditions of the phenomenon of musical postcards, historically a widespread Central European tradition. First, *Heimat* in various forms—local, regional, linguistic, national, even racial—dominates folk-song postcards. Second, even though postcards do not lend themselves to performance contexts, they often represent an attempt to draw upon specific musical genealogies to intensify their expressive character; references to earlier folk-song collections (e.g., Herder) are evident in these songs. Third, folk-song postcards not only mediate between oral and written traditions, but they historically document the ways in which oral and written traditions depended upon and influenced one another.

349. Moritz, Marina. "Zur Rezeption volkskultureller Traditionen in der DDR: Der Versuch einer Bilanz." ("On the Reception of Folk-Cultural Traditions in the GDR: Attempt at an Assessment"). *Jahrbuch für Volksliedforschung* 36 (1991): 13–17.

Written immediately after the fall of the Berlin Wall, this article speculates on the historical impact and meaning of the state-sponsored folklore revival in the German Democratic

Republic, which began in the 1970s and accelerated through the 1980s. Fundamental to the revival was the concept of "cultural heritage," whereby GDR residents should witness tradition connected to the history of the state and its ideological meanings. The symbols of tradition were pre-industrial and rural, hence the festival began at the local level and then consolidated at regional and national levels. Folk-cultural tradition should have spread through the cultivation of the revival, which was only possible through performance. Moritz argues that the historical impact of the revival was actually just the opposite of that planned by the state folklore officials. Rather than identifying with the state as the product of folk culture, GDR residents identified with the local traditions and subcultures. Moritz concludes by speculating that folklore in eastern Germany after reunification could become dangerous if it only promoted nationalistic identity.

350. Objartel, Georg. "Studentenlied und Kunstlied im ausgehenden 18. Jahrhundert: Die Liederhandschrift Friedrich August Koehlers (1791)." ("Student Song and Art Song at the End of the Eighteenth Century: The Song Manuscript of Friedrich August Koehler [1791]"). *Jahrbuch für Volksliedforschung* 33 (1988): 19–45.

Examines one of the oldest student-song manuscripts to determine the influence of art songs on student singing on the eve of the major movement of student vocal activity. Collected in Tübingen, the Koehler manuscript contains fifty songs, most of them traditional student songs from the time, but also seven art songs and six songs from *Singspiel.* Part of a larger project devoted to the materials and history of student song, the article provides a detailed discussion of the manuscript's contents and then speculates about the formation of student repertories from the musical contexts of the time. Objartel concludes that it is largely the choice of songs in the manuscript, or any other collection, that bears witness to the uses and aesthetics of the group. The influence of art music on the student singing music, therefore, was determined through performance and the broader functions of singing within the group itself. Objartel also turns to the Koehler manuscript to illustrate the importance of student song in unraveling the broader history of song in Germany from the late seventeenth to the twentieth century and to assert the continued importance of student organizations as sites for music-making. Underscoring this point is the presence of nine songs in the Koehler manuscript that are found in no earlier source.

351. Sachs, Curt. *Musik des Altertums.* ("Music of Antiquity"). Breslau: Ferdinand Hirt, 1924. (Jedermanns Bücherei).

A survey of music in antiquity (Egypt, Syria, Palestine, Mesopotamia, Greece, and Rome) by one of the most distinguished comparative musicologists. Using evidence from iconographic and textual sources, as well as comparison with more recent evidence from the music cultures of the Mediterranean, Sachs presents a model of the evolution of music from simple to complex. The book represents one of the topoi of early German historical musicology *and* comparative musicology, namely, a concept of history based on (1) the increasingly complex forms of music; and (2) the teleological global movement from Asia to Europe. Sachs distinguishes his approach by employing a relativistic framework. For each chapter or culture area, therefore, he seeks to understand music in relation to religious thought, social contexts, relation to nature, or epistemology. He also examines a range of evidence within each culture area (e.g., instruments, scale types, or ensembles), thus recognizing the integrity of each area. The twelve musical examples in the appendix provide early transcriptions of music from Greek artifacts to Abraham Zvi Idelsohn's wax-cylinder recordings in Palestine only a decade earlier (see Idelsohn 1914-1932 in chapter 2), thereby demonstrating a concept allowing one to recognize the music of antiquity in the ethnographic evidence from modernity.

352. Schmidt, Leopold. *Historische Volkslieder aus Österreich vom 15. bis zum 19. Jahrhundert.* ("Historical Folk Songs in Austria, from the Fifteenth to the Nineteenth Century"). Vienna: Österreichischer Bundesverlag, 1971. (Wiener Neudrucke, 1).

A compilation of texts from historical folk songs, beginning with "Des Königs Ladislaus Ermordung" ("The Murder of King Ladislau") from 1457 and concluding with the "Lied von der Ermordung der Kaiserin Elisabeth" ("Song about the Murder of Empress Elisabeth") from 1898. Like these two framing songs in the collection, the historical folk song is topical and specific, created to document a specific event and then disseminated through popular media, usually newspapers and broadsides. Many historical folk songs, especially those surviving in this collection, contain accounts of famous events: battles, murders of important individuals, or disasters of various kinds. Schmidt has also included more localized songs in the collection, for example "Tiroler Auswanderung nach Peru" ("The Emigration from Tyrol to Peru") from 1857, which was probably composed by an emigrant agency to encourage Austrians to colonize an area of the Peruvian Andes. Schmidt's examples come entirely from Austria, or at least from the lands of the Habsburg Monarchy, and they therefore reveal a sort of unity in the documentation and production of Austrian history, suggesting, moreover, that historical folk songs could offer new perspectives on the popular reception of European history. Schmidt provides critical source studies for each song and concludes the volume with a superb essay on the potential for using the historical folk song in the study of national identity and history.

353. Schmidt, Leopold. *Volksmusik: Zeugnisse ländlichen Musizierens.* ("Folk Music: Witnesses to Rural Music-Making"). Salzburg: Residenz Verlag, 1974.

Investigates the relation between folk art and folk music, particularly the way the former witnesses the practices that constitute the latter. The folk art examined here, documented with forty-eight color photographs and detailed descriptions of each, ranges from cowbells and various rural noisemakers to genre pictures and carved figures of musicians. Pictures of musical instruments and their use also trace musical practices of the rural alpine countries, often to show the relation of instruments to other cultural practices, for example, the ways in which Alphorns owe their development to the whips used by cowherders to move their animals to the summer meadows and to create a percussive musical repertory. Rather than arguing for a specific thesis that musical practices are inseparable from other cultural activities in the Alps, Leopold Schmidt allows his evidence, the illustrations from the text and the photographs, to "witness" the complexity of rural music-making. He shows, for example, that cowbells bear witness not simply to local traits, but rather that they reached Austria from many other parts of Europe. The careful decoration of each cowbell also reveals the importance to its role as folk art, not simply a functional object used in locating cattle in the mountains. Rural music-making, as documented in this book, is not isolated, but dependent on the interaction of various craftspeople, diverse customs, and the regional and international relations that together yield European folk-music practices.

354. Sell, Manfred. "Heidjers Tanzmusik: Gedanken zur Sozialgeschichte der Musikanten im Landkreis Harburg." ("Heidjer's Dance Music: Thoughts about the Social History of Musicians in the Harburg Region"). In Jürgen Dittmar, ed., *Dokumentationsprobleme heutiger Volksmusikforschung.* Bern: Peter Lang, 1987. Pp. 123–38.

Speculates on different approaches to documenting music and its social contexts in a region of northern Germany. The Harburg region is south of Hamburg and includes, among other areas, the

Lüneburger Heide. Sell seeks to integrate the social history of music in the region with the documentation methods used for the regional open-air historical museum. Eduard Kück's *Heidjers Tanzmusik*, an overview of regional music-making published in 1911, serves here as a metaphor for the different areas of social history that Sell will investigate. Sell is primarily interested in public music-making. Who made music? Where? Who consumed the music, and why? He focuses therefore on the social processes and transformations in musical life in general, rather than on music as an object, genre, or repertory. During the course of the several centuries he wishes to consider, he observes a growing professionalism in all areas of music-making, from folk music to local music education, and thus a growing division of labor. Documentation of this transformation takes different forms in local literature, newspapers, individual biographies, and interviews with those living in the region. Documention, the author speculates, must ultimately depend on the use of "complexes," in which different social and musical domains intersect.

355. Steinitz, Wolfgang. *Deutsche Volkslieder demokratischen Charakters aus sechs Jahrhunderten.* ("German Folk Songs with Democratic Character, from Six Centuries"). Berlin: Akademie-Verlag, 1978.

An abridged, single-volume edition of the classic two-volume reformulation of German history through consideration of folk song. Folk song figures in this past as one of the active agents for both its creation and its inscription. Fundamental to Steinitz's historical argument is that a broad segment of the folk actively engage in the performance, dissemination, and variation of folk song because it expresses their own relation to their lives as laborers. Collectivity is central to folk song's historical role because folk song provides a rallying point around which working individuals can gather. A democratic folk song should also be "oppositional," which is to say, it should provide a means of voicing criticism against the hegemonic forces of labor and state, and, by extension, it mobilizes a significant population group. Steinitz draws his examples from the most standard German collections, both published (e.g., Erk-Böhme) and archival (e.g., the Deutsches Volksliedarchiv in Freiburg), and therefore his reformulation of history suggests interesting points of intersection for all Germans. His interpretations of the political meaning and the creative potential embedded in song are carefully based on textual and contextual analysis, serving as reinterpretations, not misinterpretations. Even though the history of this book is specific to that of the German Democratic Republic, its rethinking of German history through folk song makes it essential reading. Indeed, German folk-song movements have been connected to workers' culture, and many German folk-song genres (e.g., broadsides) do respond directly to the political issues that have instigated their creation. Hermann Strobach's introduction further situates the volume's relation to Marxist thought in the history of the GDR and to the major themes in folk-music scholarship in general.

356. Stöphl, Susanne, and Maria Walcher. "Beiträge zum musikalischen Leben in Ottakring in der Zwischenkriegszeit." ("Contributions to the Musical Life in Ottakring between the World Wars"). *Jahrbuch des österreichischen Volksliedwerkes* 32/33 (1984): 200–18.

A survey of musical life in the largely blue-collar Ottakring district of Vienna during an historic period of socio-economic and musical change. Ottakring (the sixteenth district) historically formed a boundary region between the inner urban districts and the world beyond the capital city of the Habsburg Monarchy. Musical traditions, such as the popular forms associated with the Schrammel Quartet, developed in the many taverns and wine cellars of Ottakring and emanated outward, marking the urban soundscape and mixing the musical styles of Vienna with those of the different ethnic groups and classes characteristic of the boundary region. Several major events transformed the musical life of Ottakring between the world wars: (1) the dismantling of the Austro-Hungarian Empire; (2) the economic instability caused by unemployment and depression; (3) the rise of new forms and technologies of musical mediation; and (4) the growing conflicts between liberal and conservative political ideologies. Stöphl and Walcher structure the article according to different sites and forms of musical life: musical theater; cinema; radio; street music; house music and dance; music in the public sphere; and musical organizations. On one hand, the changes affecting these sites were historically consistent with Ottakring's boundary position, making the complex musical life of the district even more complex. On the other, the competition between new technologies and diverse forms of live music-making, whether on the street or in the taverns, weakened the financial infrastructure for many musicians. Based on oral-historical interviews and archival research, this study broadens the historical scope for interpreting the role of folk and popular music in the urbanization of Central Europe in the early twentieth century.

357. Tarnói, László. *Verbotene Lieder und ihre Varianten auf fliegenden Blättern um 1800.* ("Forbidden Songs and Their Variants on

Broadsides around 1800"). Budapest: Loránd-Eötvös-University, 1983. (Budapester Beiträge zur Germanistik, 11).

Assesses the processes of censorship revealed in the broadsides published by the "Widow Solbrig" during the first decade of the nineteenth century. Tarnói includes seventy broadsides in the volume, many of them appearing in print for the first time. The volume contains analyses with the broadsides, particularly philological discussion of the history of variation that accompanied different songs and themes. Although the Solbrig collection was examined by several scholars at the beginning of the twentieth century, Tarnói offers new evidence for showing that Solbrig was willing to make changes in the published broadsides in order to make their sale and dissemination possible. Several themes accounted for the forbidden nature of the broadsides. Some songs were partisan, especially in their support of the French Revolution, and others openly criticized social and political conditions at the turn of the nineteenth century. The bulk of the songs, nonetheless, seem to have been forbidden on moral and ethical grounds. The volume makes a valuable contribution to the study of broadside songs because of its documentation of the willingness of a broadside printer to alter and negotiate themes in order to sidestep public censorship.

14

INTELLECTUAL HISTORY

The intellectual history of folk-music research is in many ways inseparable from the history of Central Europe itself during the past two centuries. Beginning with the Enlightenment theories of Herder and intersecting today with the cultural conflicts of German reunification and the growing presence of ethnic groups in Central Europe, the intellectual history of folk-music research provides a rich historical text that makes the past two centuries legible. From a disciplinary standpoint, this intellectual history is one of the most complex areas explored in the chapters of the present book, for it is virtually impossible to separate it from the strands of numerous other intellectual histories. Interwoven into the history of folk-music scholarship are conflicts about nationalism and regionalism, the nature of language, and the relation between art music and popular music. It is in this intellectual history that related disciplines—folkloristics, ethnomusicology, philology, linguistics, historical musicology—converge, sometimes with fruitful results, sometimes only complicating the existing approaches to folk music. A full intellectual history of Central European folk-music research has yet to be written, not least because of the complex fabric it has formed. I intend the works annotated in the present chapter to suggest a broad approach to sketching the outline of such an intellectual history.

The main headings of this outline form from the paradigmatic moments in folk-music research. Distinguishing these moments, causing them to stand out, is their abstract, even artificial, character. The study of folk song began when, simply stated, Herder coined the word *Volkslied*. Subsequent generations of scholars were left with the task of determining what *Volkslied* meant, and when one reflects on the meanings determined in these subsequent generations, one realizes that few agreed with the broad outlines implicit in Herder's publications in the late eighteenth century (cf. the concepts documented in Julian von Pulikowski's anthology). Herder, for example, was not particularly interested in the Germanness of folk song; by the mid-nineteenth century, the term "folk song" rarely appeared without "German" qualifying it. If indeed Herder invented the concept of folk song, nineteenth-century scholars were not content simply to retain it as a mere abstraction. To give it meaning, scholars collected and anthologized; they illustrated by finding examples, thereby justifying the concept and giving it staying power. That staying power has, however, always been fragile, which many of the works annotated below illustrate. The tension between orality and literacy (see, e.g., Waltroud Linder-Beroud) has been one cause for the fragility of concepts. The impact of ideology and politics is further palpable in the identity of folk song (see, e.g., the essays in Helge Gerndt and *"Volksmusik" in der NS-Zeit*).

The intellectual history of folk-music research also results from collective biography. Certain individuals and institutions have dominated that collective biography, and the tensions between and among them have often accounted for the directions of folk-music research. The study of folk songs as texts, for example, has characterized much of the research at the German Folk-Song Archive (DVA) in Freiburg im Breisgau, imprinting on that institution the approaches acquired by John Meier as a folklorist and philologist. The DVA emphasis on texts focused much of the research of scholars associated with it on folk song that exhibited certain traits of Germanness, for example the presence of High German texts in ballads, the genre at the center of DVA research during much of its history. Other individuals and institutions developed different directions (e.g., Josef Pommer's emphasis on the practice and cultivation in Austria, and Eduard Hoffmann-Krayer's approach to Switzerland as a multiregional folk-song landscape).

In addition to the tensions, diverse directions, and theoretical schools that form the many strands of the intellectual history documented in this chapter, there are some noticeable gaps; or rather, there are areas of research that have seemingly exerted little impact on the whole. Collections, for example, were far more influential than the methods used to create them, that is, fieldwork; the end product was more important than the approaches that brought it about. The concern for Germanness, too, has meant that concepts of ethnicity and diversity have played relatively insignificant roles. Still, it is important to regard this intellectual history with enough distance to recognize that, in the past decade, change has begun to take place with much more alacrity, and with multiculturalism and popular music producing multifarious new directions (see, e.g., Holzapfel). These new directions suggest, moreover, that the intellectual history of folk-music research is in a volatile period, and that its individual scholars and institutions are reformulating the ways in which they study folk music in modern and postmodern Europe.

꧁꧂

358. Arnim, L. Achim von, and Clemens Brentano. *Des Knaben Wunderhorn: Alte deutsche Lieder.* ("The Youth's Magic Horn: Old German Songs"). Munich: Windler, 1957. First published in 1806 (part 1) and 1808 (part 2).

The most influential collection of "folk poetry" (*Volksdichtung*) in the nineteenth century, *Des Knaben Wunderhorn* marks the next stage in the intellectual history beyond Herder's *"Stimmen der Völker in Liedern"* and *Volkslieder* (1778–79) because of its focus on German folk-song texts. Arnim and Brentano list various sources for the texts, many of them "oral" and from broadsides, but others from manuscripts in museums and almanacs. There can also be no question that many of these texts were simply written by Arnim and Brentano (e.g., the opening "Das Wunderhorn"). The texts in *Des Knaben Wunderhorn* went through numerous editions during the nineteenth century, with each edition responding to changing attitudes toward folk song. The first edition, nonetheless, clearly establishes a context in which folk song interacts with and influences other types of music, notably art song and folklike compositions. Folk-song collector-composers (e.g., Ludwig Erk and Friedrich Silcher) and art-music composers (e.g., Johannes Brahms and Gustav Mahler) expanded this context by putting it into practice, that is, by creating new repertories based on folk songs, many of them from *Des Knaben Wunderhorn*. In this sense, *Des Knaben Wunderhorn* became canonized and then came to shape the canon of Romanticism and Germanness in music. Folk-song scholars, such as John Meier, later theorized the relation between folk and art music, further qualifying *Des Knaben Wunderhorn* as a paradigmatic collection. The anthology contains only texts, and melody does not appear as a significant consideration. Whereas the texts are published in neat, poetic versions, many are in dialects, which contribute to the larger criteria distinguishing these as German folk songs. A fundamental work for the interpretation of German intellectual history.

359. Bruinier, J.W. *Das deutsche Volkslied: Über Wesen und Werden des deutschen Volksgesanges.* ("The German Folk Song: On the Essence and Development of the German Folk Song"). 7th, improved ed. Leipzig: B.G. Teubner, 1927. (Aus Natur und Geisteswelt, 7).

A volume in a series devoted to the natural and spiritual world, this book ideologically positions German folk song against modernity. Bruinier opens by discussing the places in which one experiences German folk song in the most isolated mountain valleys, through which most people never pass. The rest of the book surveys the diverse contexts in which folk song has come into existence, for example in the songs of medieval minstrels, the groups formed by friends, and in the *Spinnstube* ("spinning room"). The second part of the book is historical, tracing the development of folk song and folk-song collection through different periods. Bruinier emphasizes the ways in which folk song articulates particularly German ways of responding to these historical periods. He concludes by examining specific genres, though he understands these as categories and repertories that embody themes and tropes appropriate to German contexts and cultural practices. Although many of the natural conditions for the German folk song had been supplanted, there remained for Bruinier in 1927 the possibility of recovering those conditions and empowering them to undertake cultural work for modern Germany.

360. Burckhardt-Seebass, Christine. "Archivieren für wen? John Meier, Hoffmann-Krayer und die Frühzeit des Schweizerischen Volksliedarchivs." ("For Whom to Archive? John Meier, Hoffmann-Krayer, and the Early Period of the Swiss Folk-Song Archive"). *Jahrbuch für Volksliedforschung* 35 (1990): 33–43.

A contribution to the commemoration of the seventy-fifth anniversary of the German Folk-Song Archive (DVA) by the director of the Swiss Folk-Song Archive. Cooperation between these institutions has been very close historically, not least because they were founded by the same individual, John Meier. The approaches to archiving, folklore scholarship, and outreach to their respective nations, nonetheless, have historically differed. Burckhardt-Seebass traces some of the different motivations and concepts informing the institutional decisions of the two archives, showing that their directors (Eduard Hoffmann-Krayer assumed the directorship in Basel after John Meier departed for Freiburg im Breisgau) responded to the different national needs of the Swiss and the Germans, as well as to the distinctive historical paths the two nations followed during the twentieth century. Unlike the German Folk-Song Archive, which concerned itself with songs in the German language and, by extension, a European politics of language, the Swiss Folk-Song Archive collected folk songs in a multilingual nation, whose folkloristic politics have persistently remained local and regional rather than international. Burckhardt-Seebass interprets these differences as mutually beneficial when exercised in a spirit of cooperation and exchange.

361. Deutsch, Walter, ed. *Volksmusikforschung in Österreich 1965–1985: Berichte.* ("Folk-Music Research in Austria, 1965–1985: Reports"). Vienna: A. Schendel. (Schriften zur Volksmusik, 10).

Reports commissioned on the occasion of the twentieth anniversary of the Institut für Volksmusikforschung in Vienna.

Submitted by the directors of national and regional, general and specific institutions sponsoring folk-music research—including Walter Deutsch, Gerlinde Haid, Dietrich Schüller, Franz Födermayr, and Rudolf Flotzinger—the reports reveal vastly different approaches to the collection, archiving, and study of folk music, as well as the relation between musicians, scholars, and the government agencies making Austrian folk-music research possible. Each author assumes a different approach to the reports, some describing schematically the activities of an institution, others dealing with scholarly and ideological issues. As an essay in intellectual history, Franz Födermayr's report on folk-music research at the University of Vienna is a thoughtful survey of fundamental concepts of folk music, which he places in the history of the oldest musicology department. The book makes the wide-ranging efforts of Austrian scholars and institutions to investigate and cultivate folk music tangible, not least of all because of the detailed bibliographies it contains.

362. *Deutsche Lieder für Jung und Alt.* ("German Songs for Young and Old"). (Text ed. by Ferdinand August; music ed. by Bernhard Klein and Karl August Groos). Berlin: Realschulbuchhandlung, 1818.

The first general collection of German songs to follow Arnim and Brentano's *Des Knaben Wunderhorn* (1806/1808). Unlike *Des Knaben Wunderhorn*, this volume contains melodies for most of the 120 songs. For the first time in the intellectual history of German folk-song scholarship, then, the music plays an important role in the identity of a song and in the nature of its transmission. (The importance of music to distinguishing German folk-song repertories at this historical moment is further evident in the substantial manuscript bound with a copy of this book in Special Collections of the Joseph Regenstein Library at the University of Chicago, indicating the scope of an expanded second edition, which, however, never materialized.) The title of the collection fails to identify these songs as folk songs, and in fact many of the songs are identified according to the poets who wrote their texts, most of these poets (e.g., Goethe, Friedrich Schlegel, and Ludwig Uhland) living at the time the edition was published. Other songs, however, do not seem to require claims for authorship, and the volume therefore can be understood as representing oral tradition, as well as embodying the interaction of oral and written tradition. The musical transcriptions include only the melody; whereas these are rather simple for the most part, they also do not seem to be stripped of irregularities, suggesting that they do bear witness to common melodies in oral tradition during the early nineteenth century. The songs in the collection demonstrate specific thematic areas (e.g., ballads, national songs, and sacred repertories), which continue to influence the selection of songs and organization of songbooks throughout the subsequent intellectual history of German folk-song scholarship.

363. Flotzinger, Rudolf. "Zwei Kapitel zur Volksmusik in der Musikgeschichte Österreichs." ("Two Chapters on Folk Music in the Music History of Austria"). *Jahrbuch des österreichischen Volksliedwerkes* 29 (1980): 22–33.

Addressing the larger theme of the "Austrian Folk-Song Works in Scholarship and Cultivation," this article argues for the parallel paths of two intellectual histories in Austria. The first grew from the intersection of folk song and the needs of certain social groups, and was largely characterized by the nineteenth-century production of songbooks for choruses, which in turn gave way to the programs in the cultivation (*Pflege*) of folk song proposed and developed by Josef Pommer (see the entries under *Das deutsche Volkslied* in chapter 7). Mobilizing this "chapter" were the practical needs of singing groups and the transformation of the ways in which folk song and folklore could be used to respond to historical changes in Austria. The second "chapter" formed around the persistent presence of folk song in the thinking and institutions of Austrian musicologists. From the earliest scholarly endeavors in the nineteenth century (e.g., those institutionalized by Guido Adler when he established the first chair in musicology at the University of Vienna) folk song was inseparable from the construction of Austrian and European music history. Flotzinger surveys many of the most important works, songbooks in the first chapter, scholarly books in the second, and the paradigmatic moments in his intellectual history of the presence of folk song in Austrian musical scholarship. Although he treats these chapters as separate, he also suggests that their frequent confluence has been one of the most distinctive traits of Austrian music history.

364. Gerndt, Helge, ed. *Volkskunde und Nationalsozialismus.* ("Folklore and National Socialism"). Munich: Münchner Vereinigung für Volkskunde, 1987. (Münchner Beiträge zur Volkskunde, 7).

A congress report from a special conference of the Deutsche Gesellschaft für Volkskunde ("German Folklore Society"), devoted to the ways in which the field of folklore, the institutions of folklore, and folklorists themselves contributed to the ideologies and policies of Nazism and the institutionalization of German intellectual life during the Third Reich. The opening essays investigate the ways in which folkloristic theory allowed itself to be coopted for Nazi policies, for example cultivating local museums and clothing, and the categorization of racial types. The second set of essays examines individuals and institutions that reacted to the ideologies of the Third Reich. Another group of essays treats those affected most directly by German folklore's implication in government activities. Finally, German folkloristics is interrogated in the present to identify those aspects of fascist agenda that survived at the time this book was published, for example, in the German Democratic Republic (see the essay by Wolfgang Jacobeit, pp. 301–18). Not only does folk song serve as a leitmotif throughout the volume, but there are essays by Anka Oesterle (pp. 83–93) and Otto Holzapfel (pp. 95–102) that concern themselves with the Deutsches Volksliedarchiv in Freiburg.

365. Herder, Johann Gottfried. *"Stimmen der Völker in Liedern"* and *Volkslieder.* ("'Voices of the People in Songs' and Folk Songs"). Stuttgart: Reclam, 1975. 1st published in 1778 and 1779.

The publication in which Herder coined the word *Volkslied.* A paradigmatic volume of late-eighteenth century thought, these two works actually constitute two parts of the same publication. The volume serves as a documentary anthology of song texts that Herder uses to illustrate the different traits of folk song. Significantly, none of the nineteenth- and twentieth-century concerns about distinguishing folk song from popular, art, or folk-like songs are present. Quite the contrary, this volume contains poetry by Shakespeare and Goethe, popular and religious songs, songs collected in the New World by missionaries (e.g., Montaigne's commentaries on Jean de Léry's collections from the Bay of Rio de Janeiro), and songs from different national and linguistic areas of Europe. Statistical tables (pp. 475–76) by the modern editor, Heinz Rölleke, show, in fact, that English and Gaelic folk songs (53) outnumber German folk songs (38). Herder shaped his concept of folk song by drawing on diverse sources and genres, thus revealing that these volumes do not canonize a tradition of German folk song, as many presume. For the most part, the songs appear only as texts, but some printed examples are also in the collection. Folk song has considerable literary substance in Herder's estimation, and it is this substance that allows one to trace folk song historically and to study it as a lens on the broader culture itself. Essential to Herder's concept of folk song, therefore, is that it occupies a special position in the culture of which it is a part, and that it maintains historical connections to the past. Close study of the folk songs in this collection, moreover, provides essential evidence for understanding nineteenth-century Romanticism, particularly the ways in which scholars, musicians, and writers shaped their images of folk culture and then reproduced them. Essential reading for any folklorist, ethnomusicologist, or cultural historian.

366. Herder, Johann Gottfried, Johann Wolfgang von Goethe, Paolo Frisi, and Justus Möser. *Von deutscher Art und Kunst: Einige fliegende Blätter.* ("On Germanness and German Art: Some Broadsides"). Ed. and with an afterword by Hans Dietrich Irmscher. Stuttgart: Philipp Reclam jun., 1983. Orig. publ. in 1773.

Responding to a challenge by the Hamburg publisher Johann Joachim Christian Bode to gather a series of essays that would examine the question of Germanness in literature and the arts, Herder published the five essays in this volume. Inspired by the "Sturm und Drang" ("Storm and Stress") movement of the time, the essays examine the roots of Germanness in the past, specifically the canonization of certain traits during the Middle Ages, and in folk song, several sister arts, and history. Herder's essays consider the roles of Ossian and Shakespeare but also make connections to folk song, so that the first essay in the volume is Herder's first contribution to his body of works devoted to folk song. Goethe's essay ponders the characteristics of German architecture ("deutsche Baukunst"), stemming directly from his period as a student in Strasbourg. Paolo Frisi also writes about German architecture, specifically its central role as a Gothic art form. The final essay, by Justus Möser, considers the conditions of German history, taking as a point of departure the local history of Osnabrück. As a whole the essays were extraordinarily important because of their extension of nationalistic thought to the arts at a moment of considerable contestation and historically still a century before the establishment of a single German nation. The anchoring of Germanness in the Middle Ages, moreover, continued to be one of the primary arguments made for German nationalism in the arts and political domination of Central Europe. Herder's essay on folk song, for example, makes it clear even in the title that he is considering the "songs of ancient peoples" ("Lieder alter Völker"). Published as a volume, these essays provide the first major attempt to place folk song in the issues and debates of German nationalism.

367. Holzapfel, Otto. *Spuren der Tradition: Folkloristische Studien.* ("Traces of Tradition: Studies in Folkloristics"). Bern: Peter Lang Verlag, 1991. (Studien zur Volksliedforschung, 6).

A collection of brief, but trenchant, essays that represent the variety and depth of Otto Holzapfel's folk-song and folkloristic scholarship. The essays are grouped thematically around areas on which the author has concentrated: Scandinavian folklore and nationalism, *Formelhaftigkeit*, ballad scholarship, bilingual regions with mixed customs and repertories, the study of prejudice and nationalism, and folk song in modern and changing societies. By "traces of tradition" Holzapfel refers to the persistence of specific symbols and cultural practices through time, though not necessarily or even primarily in an unbroken fashion. Folklore may manifest itself, therefore, in a moment of political crisis, for example, during protests against the building of a nuclear power facility at Wyhl near Freiburg im Breisgau. Such "traces" also characterize the author's most influential theoretical contribution, *Formelhaftigkeit* (the ways in which special meaning and structure are borne by formulas), with which he has offered an alternative to the oral-formulaic concepts of Milman Parry and Albert Lord. Of special interest are the empirical studies of complex mixes of folklore and music along the borders of Germany and Denmark, and Germany and Alsace, as well as in the cross-influences between religious minorities and their surrounding cultures. The book concludes with a bibliography of this important scholar's writings and with a substantial English summary of the contents.

368. Holzapfel, Otto, Eva Bruckner, and Ernst Schusser, eds. *Johann Wolfgang von Goethe (1749–1832): Volksliedaufzeichnungen im Elsaß.* ("Johann Wolfgang von Goethe [1749–1832]: Folk-Song Transcriptions in Alsace"). Bruckmühl: Volksmusikarchiv des Bezirks Oberbayern, 1991). ("Auf den Spuren von...," 6).

By gathering different examples and publications of the folk songs collected by Goethe in Alsace in 1771, this small volume provides a fascinating contribution to the early intellectual history of folk-song research and the way in which fundamental ideas from that history persisted in later approaches. Goethe studied at the University of Strasbourg in 1770–71 and during that time formed a concept of folk song, which later came to shape many of his own concepts of ballad (as a lyrical genre) and creativity in the everyday life of the rural areas of German-speaking Europe. It is from this time that his famous statement that he collected songs *"aus den Kehlen der ältesten Müttergens"* ("from the throats of the oldest mothers") survives. He collected twelve songs and sent these, later with melodies that have since been lost, to Herder, who was influenced by them in the formulation of his volumes on "Volkslieder" which appeared at the end of the 1770s (see Herder 1778/79 in this chapter). Various publications of these songs are compared (e.g., those by the Lorraine collector Louis Pinck at the time of the centennial of Goethe's death in 1932). Analyses and discussions of these songs from recent scholarly publications further illustrate the significance of Goethe's paradigmatic contribution from his student sojourn in Alsace.

369. Lachmann, Robert. *Musik des Orients.* ("Music of the Orient"). Breslau [Wrocław]: Ferdinand Hirt, 1929. (Jedermanns Bücherei: Musik).

One of the fundamental texts of early comparative musicology. Lachmann focuses on "the Orient," whereby he (and other comparativists) meant the so-called high cultures of North Africa, the Middle East, South Asia, Southeast Asia, and East Asia. The "musical systems" of the Orient contrasted sharply with those of the West, and the nature of this contrast provides the basis for organizing this book. Melody in the West (even melody in folk music) naturally leads to harmony, whereas melodic forms in the Orient do not lead to vertical harmonies, even when complex forms of polyphony develop. Indeed, it is the complexity of melody itself, its connection to certain instruments or its propensity to form into complex modal systems, that distinguishes the music of the Orient. It would be too convenient to dismiss the approaches in the book as simple orientalism, thereby failing to learn from its contribution to the intellectual history of modern ethnomusicology and folk-music scholarship. Lachmann develops his concepts of growing complexity systematically, beginning with basic notions of consonance and dissonance, expanding these into scalar and modal structures, then to melodic forms, and finally to rhythmic and polyphonic systems. Many elements of early comparative thought persist at the end of the twentieth century, for example, the privileging of systemeticity as a marker of art music. The volume relies on a selected group of comparative writings on Asian music, making it an excellent guide to the fundamental ideas informing the field during its first half-century of development.

370. Linder-Beroud, Waltraud. *Von der Mündlichkeit zur Schriftlichkeit? Untersuchungen zur Interdependenz von Individualdichtung und Kollectivlied.* ("From Orality to Literacy? Examination of the Interdependence of Individual Creativity and Collective Song"). Frankfurt am Main: Peter Lang, 1989. (Artes populares: Studia ethnographica et folkloristica, 18).

A sweeping historical and historiographical study of the relation between orality and literacy in folk song, ranging from medieval manuscripts to twentieth-century print culture. The point of departure is the reception theory of John Meier (1864–1953), which he articulated in his 1906 *Kunstlied im Volksmunde.* The question posed by Linder-Beroud's title is answered through numerous and convincing case studies, each of which, depending on its moment in history and the folk-music genres involved, provides a different relationship between orality and literacy. These answers stand as alternatives to John Meier's theories that individual and collective processes of creativity in folk song were essentially conflated and therefore different variants of the same process. Linder-Beroud argues, however, that oral transmission of a medieval song, for which we have only surviving manuscript records, was vastly different from a Renaissance song, which is inseparable from a society that was suddenly and profoundly influenced by print culture. The book presents the intellectual history of the orality-literacy paradigms in several distinctive ways. On one hand, intellectual history results from the theories of important collectors and scholars; on the other, individual songs develop their own histories, becoming metaphors for the changing interrelation of orality and literacy. Linder-Beroud is dogmatic about none of this, although the word "interdependence" in her subtitle underscores her belief that one is not possible without the other, thereby making folk song impossible without some form of literary tradition and transmission. A valuable and stimulating introduction to the intellectual tradition of German-language folk-song scholarship.

371. Pulikowski, Julian von. *Geschichte des Begriffes Volkslied im musikalischen Schrifttum: Ein Stück deutscher Geistesgeschichte.* ("History of the Concept Folk Song in Musical Writings: A Case of German Intellectual History"). Heidelberg: Carl Winters Universitätsbuchhandlung, 1933.

Culls commentaries on folk song from various musical writings in German, beginning in 1774 (Christian Friedrich Daniel Schubart) and concluding in 1931 (Otto Eichberg). Pulikowski relies not only on concepts penned by scholars concerning themselves specifically with folk song, but also by musicians and artists, whose approaches are shaped by their understanding of the relation of folk song to art music. The sources upon which Pulikowski relies also span a wide gamut, including journalism and dissertations. It is Pulikowski's thesis that the concept folk song has broadly influenced German music history and the ways in which music in general was conceived and inscribed into various practices. In the second part of the book he suggests categories for the various approaches to the function of folk song in German intellectual history. The variety of these approaches is inclusive and extraordinary, ranging from thinkers who connect folk song to the love of the fatherland to those connecting it to human love, the church, the youth movement, and the renewal of art. Most of the extracts in the book contain both a short statement by a particular writer and a brief commentary by Pulikowski. Frequently, Pulikowski writes with imagination, and even humor, both of which contribute to making this book a good read. The indices and other means of cross-referencing make the volume very accessible, allowing the reader to locate quickly what a given composer might have expressed about folk song, or how the concept of folk song changed when nineteenth-century nationalism gave way to the growing awareness of ethnic groups in Europe. An indispensable and enlightening introduction to the intellectual history of folk song and German social and cultural thought.

372. Schepping, Wilhelm. "Lied- und Musikforschung." ("Song and Music Research"). In Rolf W. Brednich, ed., *Grundriß der Volkskunde: Einführhung in die Forschungsfelder der Europäischen Ethnologie.* Berlin: Dietrich Reimer Verlag, 1988. Pp. 399–422.

In the context of a volume introducing the areas of folklore research, this essay focuses on folk song and folk music, which here means European music, often specifically German. Schepping argues that the specific discipline forms from ethnomusicology and musicology, but that the term best describing the field of study is *musikalische Volkskunde* ("musical folklore"). The study surveys different concepts of folk song, particularly the role of song in society. Although Schepping distinguishes two areas of research (song and instrumental music), he argues strongly for the methodological rethinking required by expanding more traditional philological approaches devoted to song into the cultural contexts of instrumental music. Both historical methods and the new practices characterizing popular-music research are presented systematically. The volume contains almost no account of non-European repertories or ethnomusicological approaches growing from their study.

373. Schneider, Albrecht. *Musikwissenschaft und Kulturkreislehre: Zur Methodik und Geschichte der Vergleichenden Musikwissenschaft.* ("Musicology and the Theory of Culture Areas: On the Methods and History of Comparative Musicology"). Bonn-Bad Godesberg: Verlag für systematische Musikwissenschaft, 1976. (Orpheus, 18).

An interpellation of the relation between musical scholarship and the theory of culture areas, with an intellectual history of the influence of that relation on the development of comparative musicology and ethnomusicology. Schneider begins the book with an extensive look at *Kulturkreislehre* itself, comparing its specific formulation in Central European anthropology with related attempts to situate the development of unified traits with a specific area and the cultural identity of that area. Initially theorized by the Austrian ethnologists, Pater Wilhelm Schmidt and Pater Wilhelm Koppers, the theory of culture areas allowed for cultural distinctiveness as the result of the patterns of development anchored by a centripetalizing identity. This theory was used to argue against a single evolutionary explanation of culture. Instead, the theory of culture areas explained how musical traits formed patterns of relatedness, hence musical areas in which styles, repertories, and systemic properties (e.g., tuning) served to connect music to place. Cultural and musical regions, moreover, lent themselves to comparison, and comparative musicology adapted some of the fundamental tenets of *Kulturkreislehre*, when its advocates (e.g., Werner Danckert in the study of folk music, or Erich M. von Hornbostel in the study of world music) mapped musical systems throughout the world. American cultural anthropology after World War II developed related concepts of culture areas, for example, by instituting area-studies approaches, which were further adapted to American ethnomusicology in the second half of the twentieth century. With its extensive interpretation of literature in several languages, this book remains one of the most complete intellectual histories of comparative musicology and ethnomusicology during the twentieth century.

374. Schüller, Dietrich. "Österreichische Volksmusik im Phonogrammarchiv der Österreichischen Akademie der Wissenschaften." ("Austrian Folk Music in the Sound Archive of the Austrian Academy of Sciences"). In Walter Deutsch, Harald Dreo, Gerlinde Haid, and Karl Horak, eds., *Volksmusik in Österreich*. Vienna: Österreichischer Bundesverlag, 1984. Pp. 106–11.

A brief history of the role of the Phonogrammarchiv of the Austrian Academy of Sciences in the folk-music research of Austria and Austrian scholars. Founded in 1899, the Phonogrammarchiv fostered research activities by providing sound-recording equipment and a center for the research and comparative analysis of music. Schüller traces the development of different types of sound-recording mechanisms, noting the ways in which they permitted or encouraged certain types of research. The article also contributes to a larger understanding of intellectual history because it relates technological advances to the individuals who put them into practice. Of particular interest is the role played by the Phonogrammarchiv in the investigation of Austria's diverse cultural, linguistic, and religious groups. Abraham Zvi Idelsohn, for example, employed equipment from the Phonogrammarchiv during the 1910s while undertaking fieldwork in Palestine for his seminal thesaurus of Jewish music (see Idelsohn 1914-32). Károly Gáal also turned to the Phonogrammarchiv in the 1950s when laying the groundwork for research into the folk music of Austria's diverse ethnic communities. Throughout the article the cooperative work between the Phonogrammarchiv and scholars in other Austrian and European institutions is fully evident.

375. Suppan, Wolfgang. "Zur Konzeption einer 'europäischen' Musikethnologie." ("On the Concept of a 'European' Ethnomusicology"). *Ethnologia Europea: World Review of European Ethnology* 4 (1970): 132–37.

A survey of concepts of Europeanness in music and the methodological approaches to the music of Europe. Suppan posits two different poles, one which takes a genre or type of song and identifies it throughout Europe, the other that views the continent from the perspective of an "astronaut," namely as a unified whole with different regions bordering and interacting with each other. Whereas he finds both approaches wanting for lack of a more consistently European methodology, he concludes that viewing the music of Europe as a whole should be the goal of European ethnology. Central to the thesis of the article is the historical nature of European musics, as well as the ways in which history has been characterized by the change that results from interaction between regions and musical repertories. Attempting to locate a musical field that would parallel European ethnology, as it was being envisioned at the time as a new direction in folkloristics, the article does not propose any real theoretical innovation.

376. Suppan, Wolfgang. *Volkslied: Seine Sammlung und Erforschung.* ("Folk Song: Its Collection and Research"). Stuttgart: J.B. Metzler, 1966.

A survey of folk-song research, broken into numerous brief sections, each devoted to a specific concept or area of research. The organization of the book is historical throughout, with each section including the earliest research and the prevailing tendencies in the mid-1960s. Suppan conceives of folk song as the extension of scholarly traditions rather than focusing on genre and folk-song types. Section 3, therefore, examines sources and classification as processes of intellectual history; practice in section 6 is discussed in relation to the scholarly and other activities devoted to interpeting its impact on the history of folk song. The most valuable aspect of the book is the topical organization of the bibliographies, which provide the reader with easy access to the major works on folk song in the German language. Suppan also relates concepts and approaches to social contexts and to social scientific approaches, which in the 1960s was innovative. Some caution should be exercised with terminology and concepts applied to non-Western music, which is entirely addressed with the names of modern nations rather than indigenous cultures. The disparaging stance vis-à-vis musical practices that do not have the same "value" as folk music, particularly in the final section, is unnecessary and inappropriate.

377. *"Volksmusik" in der NS-Zeit: Zielsetzung, Funktion, Praxis.* ("'Folk Music' during the Nazi Period: Establishment of Goals, Functions, Practice"). Dingolfing: BVS Markmiller, 1992. (Niederbayerische Blätter für musikalische Volkskunde, 13).

Case studies and documentation of the uses of folk music, largely in Bavaria, during the Nazi period from 1933 to 1945. Folk music lent itself to diverse purposes in the propaganda and ideological education of the Nazis. Facsimiles of concert programs, communications, and other documents from the period reveal the conscious attempts of specific individuals to use folk music as a means of inculcating a nationalistic and racist program in the practices of local musical organizations. Choruses and wind ensembles changed their repertories, limiting them increasingly to the lists encouraged by the propaganda officials and ministry. The essays in this book (by Fritz Markmiller, Manfred Seifert, Maximilian Seefelder, Ernst Schusser, and Helmut Wagner) describe an extraordinary level of awareness of the potential folk music to heighten nationalism. While at many levels there may only have been vague knowledge of the larger intent of such efforts, certain individuals (e.g., Josef Eberwein and Hans Baumann) skillfully manipulated musical institutions and publishers alike. This study, though regional in scope, joins a growing body of research in the 1980s and 1990s that addresses the extensive cultivation of folk music to serve the political ends of fascism during the Nazi era.

15

RELIGIOUS AND ETHNIC MINORITIES

The title of this chapter deliberately juxtaposes German and American concepts of ethnicity. German-language literature persists in referring to communities or groups with religious, linguistic, or ethnic practices that differ from those identified as German as *Minderheiten*, "minorities." In Germany, this refers primarily to Turkish and Roma residents, as well as to the growing communities of residents from Africa or Asia. In Austria, minorities have a longer history, one inseparable from the memories of the Habsburg Monarchy. The minorities of Austria, then, include Hungarians in Vienna, Croatians in Burgenland, and Slovenians in Corinthia. The term "minority" ascribes a very distinct type of identity to these communities and groups: an identity of difference, indeed of cultural and musical "otherness."

There is no equivalent for "ethnic minorities" in German—one does not say *ethnische Minderheiten*, for the two words work at odds with each other—and religious minorities simply do not appear in the rhetoric of state religion. Theories of ethnicity, most of which have been slow to influence German-language social theory, imply processes of border crossing and cultural mixture, which, in fact, have largely been absent from the history of Central European folk-music scholarship. In an intellectual history of that scholarship, a chapter devoted to religious and ethnic minorities simply would not be written. The present chapter is a modest attempt to redress the ways in which religious and ethnic groups have been excluded from most Central European folk-music scholarship.

Three ethnic groups dominate this chapter, each of them with very different histories in the musical life of Central Europe. The groups that had until the 1990s received the least attention, Gypsies, to whom I shall refer here as Romas and Sintis, two of the largest groups in Central Europe, nonetheless inspired the most imaginative myths in the history of folk-music scholarship. Romas and Sintis have been both omnipresent and invisible in the musical traditions of Central Europe, contributing to the Romanticism and nationalism of nineteenth-century composers and to the theories of Bartók and Liszt. The "otherness" of Romas and Sintis, however, did little to challenge notions of Germanness or even Europeanness in folk music, for it was an evasive "otherness," one that occupied no land, and seemingly was infinitely adaptable to the musical vocabulary of the majority culture.

Jewish folk music has historically demonstrated yet another kind of "otherness," an orientalism that, at least from the mid-nineteenth century to the Holocaust, contributed to the construction of a largely imaginary folk culture in Central Europe. The studies or collections of Jewish folk music that I annotate in this chapter have largely been the products of revivals, that is, of explicit and conscious attempts to invent a Jewish folk music that was believed not to exist. Folk singers and singer-songwriters in Germany and Austria (e.g., Manfred Lemm or the group, *gojim*) absorbed Yiddish songs into their repertories as if to atone for the destruction of the Holocaust. This borrowing from Eastern European Jews, however, followed a long history of folk-song publication in Central Europe, which is evident already in Gustaf H. Dalman's early study of "German-Jewish" folk songs from Russia and Galicia. The "otherness" of Jewish song remains one of the most important markers of distance and "otherness" in the folk-music practices of modern Germany.

Turkish folk music exists in contemporary scholarship only nervously. Through the efforts of ethnomusicologists in Berlin, especially those associated with Max Peter Baumann, Kurt Reinhard, and Ursula Reinhard, attempts have been made to compare Turkish traditions in Germany with those in Turkey. Turkish residents of Germany have also found it necessary to gather and collect anthologies for choruses and other musical ensembles in Germany, thereby situating Turkish music in the practices of first- and second-generation immigrants. These residents of Germany, however, are not immigrants, because they cannot acquire German citizenship, thus enforcing legally their cultural "otherness." They remain minorities, with minority music cultures, because they must.

I have not abandoned the German "minority" in this chapter in order to call attention to the larger concept of folk music that it symbolizes and enforces. The folk music of Romas, Jews, or Turkish guest workers, as well as the folk music of Sorbian minorities in Saxony, whose musical practices have not found their way into folk-music research, exist in the literature as bounded repertories. Influences between minorities and the mainstream have no theoretical presence, and they remain largely invisible in most schools and methods of folk-music scholarship. Musical hybridity fails to turn up in most literature devoted to non-German folk-music traditions, and in most formuluations of tradition, the categories of genre and social function eschew the possibility of hybridity and exchange. At the end of the twentieth century, however, the situation is changing rapidly, with a new generation of scholars working within the ethnic communities and with the religious groups now inseparable from the modern history of Central Europe.

※※◎※※

378. Adamek, Karl, ed., with Irmgard Merkt et al. *Rüzgargülü— Windrose: Deutsch-türkisches Liederbuch, almanca-türkçe Sarkılar.* ("Wind Rose: German-Turkish Songbook"). Bonn-Bad Godesberg: Voggenreiter, 1989.

A collection of Turkish songs, with German translations, intentionally conceived as a means of strengthening cultural awareness between Germans and Turkish residents in Germany. The musical concept suggests that the songs function as translatable cultural goods (e.g., each song includes both guitar and *baglama* accompaniments). Transcriptions, translations, and information about performance stress the practical applicability of the edition. In addition to the practical uses of the book the editor and other contributors have discussed the origins of Turkish songs and provided information about their meaning and classification, drawing attention also to some of the parallels between Turkish and German folk songs. Although the edition is not scholarly, some of the discussions about interrelations between Turkish and German traditions were not previously well known in the German folk-song literature. Illustrations of various kinds enhance the book and its attractiveness to folk singers throughout Central Europe.

379. Akdemir, Hayrettin. *Die neue türkische Musik, dargestellt an Volksliedbearbeitungen für mehrstimmigen Chor.* ("The New Turkish Music, in Folk-Song Arrangements for Mixed Chorus"). Berlin: Hitit Verlag, 1991.

Both an anthology of choral compositions and an analysis of twentieth-century Turkish folk and national music. The author concerns himself primarily with the work of nine composers, who set folk songs or folklike music for mixed chorus, in some cases reflecting the nationalist ideologies of the modern (post-Atatürk) period. These settings also demonstrate a direct connection to the Westernization that this period ushered in, especially the contact between European and Turkish musicians and musical scholars. The volume also contains a concluding chapter explicating a Turkish harmony system, which admittedly is only realizable as an outcome of the exchange between Europe and Turkey. The users of the edition are therefore of two types: Western, especially, German readers, wishing to familiarize themselves with Turkish music, and Turkish communities in Germany, for which a choral movement has provided a strong sense of identity. The edition, therefore, affords the opportunity to the largest ethnic group in Germany to perform and make public its modern identity, which in turn is inseparable from a century of contact and exchange with modern Europe.

380. Baselgia, Guido. *Galizien.* ("Galicia"). Frankfurt am Main: Jüdischer Verlag, 1993.

A photographic study of the Jewish culture of Galicia, a region including parts of modern Poland, Ukraine, Belarus, and Romania, with an interpretive essay by Verena Dohrn. As a border culture Galicia was multicultural, and its Jewish residents also combined histories from Central and Eastern Europe, cosmopolitan and traditional Jewish pasts. The national boundaries of Galicia have shifted so frequently that its culture mixes various nationalistic imaginations (e.g., of the Habsburg Monarchy, and the aspirations of the Yiddish nationalists of the turn-of-the-century) and an indigenous regionalism in which a juxtaposition of religions, languages, and ethnicities was normative. Music figures into the book only tangentially, still, however, as one of the characteristics in which the qualities of Galician culture are most legible. Synagogue traditions survive that contain elements of these qualities, and the Central European revival of klezmer music recovers a mix of sounds from the Galician past. The photographs record both current musical practices and the historical spaces in which Jewish music would have been heard.

381. Baumann, Max Peter, ed. *Musik der Türken in Deutschland.* ("Music of the Turks in Germany"). Kassel: Verlag Yvonne Landeck, 1985.

Based on a several fieldwork projects initiated by the Free University of Berlin in the late 1970s and early 1980s, this collection of essays presents a comprehensive view of the complex music culture of Turkish residents in West Berlin. Numbering ca. 90,000 at the time of publication, West Berlin's Turkish residents worked largely as *Gastarbeiter* ("guest workers"), laborers in German heavy industry, who were denied the possibility of German citizenship, even when born and educated in the country. The essays here are the result of case studies by Berlin ethnomusicologists, some focusing on individual musical organizations, others on traditional instruments in their Turkish-German functions, and still others on the changes within and challenges to the relations between Turks in Germany and Turkey. Some changes in Turkish musical life are characteristic of many immigrant cultures; members of the same chorus, for example, may come from different parts of Turkey, each with distinctive traditions, but in Germany they share a common repertory. Other changes result from issues unique to Turkish culture in Germany; music, for example, becomes a voice for political criticism outside Turkey, whereas, in contrast, it would have been suppressed in Turkey itself. As a whole, these essays reveal that almost no contact and cross influences between Turkish and German musical life had developed by the early 1980s, even though the increase in violence against foreigners, which reached dramatic proportions in the 1990s, was already observable. Turkish music was thriving in West Berlin, but in a world separate from that known by Germans.

382.   Bohlman, Philip V. "Auf der Bima—Auf der Bühne: Zur Emanzipation der jüdischen Popularmusik im Wien der Jahrhundertwende." ("On the Bima—On the Stage: Toward the Emancipation of Jewish Popular Music in Turn-of-the-Century Vienna"). In Elisabeth Th. Hilscher and Theophil Antonicek, eds., *Vergleichend-systematische Musikwissenschaft: Beiträge zu Methode und Problematik der systematischen, ethnologischen und historischen Musikwissenschaft.* Tutzing: Hans Schneider, 1994. Pp. 417–49.

A comparison of Jewish musical practices in the synagogue and on the theatrical stage during the period of emancipation of Jewish culture in Vienna, from the late nineteenth century to the early twentieth century. The stage in both cases—the Hebrew *bima* means both "stage" and "pulpit"—became a site for intensified exchange between Jewish musicians and audiences that experienced the music of both forms of stage as popular music. The performers on both stages, the cantor in the synagogue and the couplet or cabaret singer on the popular stage, acquired the status of stars with considerable followings. Depictions of cantors and stage singers began to picture them on the stage, framed as a commodity for public consumption. New repertories also emerged, for example, the cantorial compositions of Salomon Sulzer, creator of the so-called "Vienna Rite," and the publication of popular songs about Jewish life in Vienna as broadsides. These various stages, therefore, provided musical means for the transformation of Jewish cultural life from private and strictly religious spheres to public and secular ones. The popularization of Jewish music, moreover, undergirded the growth of the cabaret and other forms of stage entertainment, among them the musical and film, whose twentieth-century histories would be unthinkable without their significant Jewish contributions.

383.   Bohlman, Philip V. "Die Volksmusik und die Verstädterung der deutsch-jüdischen Gemeinde in den Jahrzehnten vor dem Zweiten Weltkrieg." ("Folk Music and the Urbanization of the German-Jewish Community in the Decades before the Second World War"). *Jahrbuch für Volksliedforschung* 34 (1989): 25–40.

Postulates that urbanization provided the primary context for Jewish folk music in Central Europe during the period of socio-economic emancipation and cultural transformation from the

Enlightenment until the Holocaust. With the beginning of the modern era, Jews increasingly settled in cities in the German-speaking countries, and they adapted the institutions of their own communities to the urban environment. That process of adaptation meant, furthermore, that the Jewish community was brought into closer contact with a non-Jewish mainstream, which posed a variety of challenges to modern Jewish identity. Bohlman argues that folk songs articulated the problems of those challenges and mediated responses to them. The production and performance of folk songs had come to depend on urban conditions by the end of the nineteenth century, for example, performance in popular contexts in cities such as Vienna and Berlin and publication as broadsides and sheet music. The songs produced in these ways portrayed the conflicts between urban dwellers and newly arrived migrants from the country or from Eastern Europe, between the religious and secular segments of the community, and between different classes in Jewish society. Both religious and secular musical traditions participated in the urbanization of musical culture, and songbooks for both were increasingly mass produced during the Weimar period. Reproductions of four Jewish broadsides from the turn of the century illustrate the article.

384. Dalman, Gustaf H., ed. *Jüdischdeutsche Volkslieder aus Galizien und Russland*. ("Jewish-German Folk Songs from Galicia and Russia"). 2nd ed. Berlin: Evangelische Vereins-Buchhandlung, 1891. (Schriften des Institutum Judaicum in Berlin, 12).

The first scholarly study of Yiddish ("Jüdischdeutsch" in the author's usage) folk songs, employing the philological methodologies of the nineteenth century. Dalman establishes the historical conditions for understanding Yiddish repertories as representative of Eastern European Jewry, that is, as a distinctive culture marked by its own music history and contemporary reality. Characteristically, only transliterated texts appear in this nineteenth-century anthology, but these are presented with copious footnotes that clarify unknown words, particularly those deriving from Hebrew. Uncharacteristic of this period in the intellectual history of folkloristics, Dalman interprets Yiddish folk songs not as artifacts maintained by an isolated folk group, but rather as evidence of cultural contact and negotiation with other linguistic, religious, and ethnic groups in East Central and Eastern Europe, particularly with Roma and Sinti peoples through a larger shared repertory of instrumental music. Moreover, Dalman places folk music in the larger context of popular music, especially that performed by traveling theatrical groups in the second half of the nineteenth century. The songs, ranging from hassidic to Zionistic texts, are identified together with their authors, thereby connecting oral to written transmission. Dalman was a Protestant theologian, and he therefore couches tradition in religious, at times Christological, meanings.

385. Frankl, Hai, and Topsy Frankl, eds. *Jiddische Lieder: Texte und Noten mit Begleit-Akkorden.* ("Yiddish Songs: Texts and Music, with Chords for Accompaniment"). Frankfurt am Main: Fischer Taschenbuch Verlag, 1981.

A product of one of the first duos in the folk-music revival to sing Yiddish folk songs, this volume itself became the primary source for Yiddish songs in the German folk-music scene of the closing decades of the twentieth century. Hai Frankl and Topsy Frankl developed their repertory of Yiddish folk songs in Sweden, but its potential to remember the destruction of Jewish culture in Europe won it a position in the folk-music revival of Germany in the 1960s and 1970s. This collection combines both popular scholarship and the usability of a songbook directed primarily toward amateur folksingers. The book opens with a series of essays about Yiddish culture, its history, and the musical traditions that it spawned. Whereas this mixture of topics was more eclectic than anything else, it nonetheless provided German readers with a set of terms that substantially increased German awareness of European Jewish culture. The songs themselves appear in transliteration, and they appear on the page so that a folksinger with minimal knowledge of guitar chords can accompany herself or himself. Etchings, photographs, and introductory paragraphs frame most of the songs, enhancing the appeal of the volume itself, if, again, the historical connections between songs and illustrations are often oversimplified. With the appearance of *Jiddische Lieder* a growing interest in Jewish folk music swept over Central Europe, and within a decade Yiddish folk songs had become standards for many folk-music groups; the growth of German ensembles devoted to Jewish folk music, both vocal and the instrumental traditions of klezmer music, stems to large extent from the appearance of this collection and other publications it stimulated.

386. Freund, Florian, Franz Ruttner, and Hans Safrian, eds. *Ess firt kejn weg zurik... Geschichte und Lieder des Ghettos von Wilna 1941–1943.* ("There's No Way Back... History and Songs from the Vilna Ghetto, 1941–1943"). Vienna: Picus Verlag, 1992.

A collection of seven essays on the history of the Jewish ghetto in Vilna and an edition of twenty-seven songs that mirror the cultural life and destruction of this former center of Jewish culture in Lithuania. With a foreword by Simon Wiesenthal, this volume situates itself in Holocaust studies as a documentation of the richness of Jewish culture, particularly folk and popular culture, and as traces of resistance during the total destruction of the ghetto by the Nazis. The critical essays focus on both Jewish and non-Jewish personalities, as well as on historical issues in both German (and Austrian) actions and Jewish responses during World War II. The songs, all in Yiddish, comment on the themes in the essays, some of them specifically as Vilna songs. For the most part, the authors of the essays are members of the Austrian group *gojim* ("Non-Jews"), who have recorded the songs on *Ess firt kejn weg zurik... jiddische Lieder aus dem Ghetto in Wilna 1941–1943* (Extraplatte EX 139). Historical and musical texts, therefore, intersect, producing interesting and sometimes controversial interpretations of Holocaust themes.

387. *Die Gesangbücher der Brüderunität und ihre graphische Gestaltung.* ("The Songbooks of the United Brethren and Their Graphic Formation"). Chosen and annotated by Mirjam Bohatcová. Prague: International Arbeitsgemeinschaft für Hymnologie, 1989.

An anthology of graphic material from roughly the first 150 years of the United Brethren, a German- and Czech-speaking Protestant community, which would have an important impact on German-language hymnody in North America, beginning in the eighteenth century. The United Brethren were the first community efffectively to transform the Latin liturgy and music of the Catholic mass into a printed vernacular, the first example dating from ca. 1501. The transformation to the vernacular also incorporated many aspects of music-making from outside the mass and subsequently contributed to the emergence of new sacred musical practices in oral tradition. These songbooks, furthermore, bear witness to the world around them, depicting musicians and the secular world among their other graphic representations. The fifty-two examples documented here span the period 1531 to 1618, thereby richly recording the emergence of Reformation Europe and some of the most important cultural transformations constituting the early modern period in Central Europe.

388. Gradenwitz, Peter. "'So singet uns von Zijons Sang!'—Jüdische Musik und Musiker in ihrer Umwelt." ("'Thus We Sang the Song of Zion!'—Jewish Music and Musicians in Their Environment"). In Andreas Nachama, Julius H. Schoeps, and Edward van Voolen, eds., *Jüdische Lebenswelten.* Vol. 1: *Essays.* Frankfurt am Main: Jüdischer Verlag, 1991. Pp. 185–202.

An historical sketch of Jewish music and musicians, beginning with the musical practices of the land of Israel, moving through the Diaspora, and culminating with modern Israel. Gradenwitz argues a traditional thesis, namely, that Jewish music is different from other ethnic or national musics because throughout most of their history Jews have enjoyed no homeland whose characteristics they could make their own. Jewish music, therefore, combines many different characteristics, and even in modern Israel, what is Jewish in music depends on the lands from which musicians emigrated. Gradenwitz structures his history around great men, particularly composers and performers of Western art music. He further justifies his central argument by demonstrating the fluency with which Jews who were deprived of opportunities to enter the mainstream nonetheless overcame the odds and excelled in the mainstream. Central European history and musicians lie at the core of this history, not least because this essay appears in a volume that accompanied an exhibit to educate Germans on the nature of the "worlds in which Jews lived." Names and dates occur in quick succession throughout, making the article valuable as a reference source.

389. Heinschink, Mozes, and Christiane Juhasz. "Koti džal o mulo... Lieder österreichischer Sinti." ("There Walks the Spirit... Songs of Austrian Sinti"). *Jahrbuch des österreichischen Volksliedwerkes* 41 (1992): 63–86.

Social historical background of Sinti communities in Austria, particularly in Linz, and survey of their repertory, collected for several decades by Mozes Heinschink for a project coordinated by the Austrian Academy of Sciences. The authors examine cultural distinctiveness of both Roma and Sinti peoples in Austria, arguing for the use of these forms of self-identity employed by Austrian Gypsies. The two groups are distinguished in Austria primarily by separate histories and linguistic differences. Despite the devastation of Austrian Roma and Sinti during the Holocaust (ca. half of the 11,000 living in Austria were murdered in concentration camps), both groups have important communities today, living primarily on the edges of the larger cities. The authors argue that Sinti continue to pursue traditional occupations and their culture is continuous with traditions of the past, including their movement from place to place in order to participate in or take advantage of seasonal jobs. Music-making and the production of musical instruments are important components of these traditions. Contemporary repertories reflect these traditions, not least of all because Sinti musicians have been in contact with different music cultures and absorbed aspects of style and genre. Songs sung in the home or small groups have become less important in the second half of the twentieth century, but the variety of influences from urban popular and mediated music, for example, the widespread "Sinti-Swing" form of jazz, has increased. Transcriptions, with texts in both Sinti and German.

390. Hemetek, Ursula. "Musik als Ausdruck der Identität—Roma und Sinti in Österreich." ("Music as an Expression of Identity—Roma and Sinti in Austria"). *Musik & : Jahrbuch der Hochschule für Musik und Darstellende Kunst in Wien* 1 (1994): 101–32.

An overview of concepts and repertories of Roma and Sinti music in Austria, resulting from the early stages of a multi-year project directed by the author. Hemetek is the leading European ethnomusicologist working on the musics of Gypsies, a term she does not use because it is not used by the Roma and Sinti in Austria, and because it recalls for them a long history of prejudice. There is no single group of Austrian Roma or Sinti, either historically or linguistically, which therefore requires that any study examine them as differentiated and distinct groups. Hemetek establishes two broad criteria for the music of Roma and Sinti, the first applying to music played for non-Roma (i.e., outside the community) and the second to music played for the community itself. The best-known examples of the first category are the "Gypsy musics" played as popular music in Hungary and Austria, the music usually associated with an urban and cosmopolitan setting. "Sinti jazz" (e.g., the sound associated with Django Reinhardt) exemplifies the second. Hemetek concerns herself primarily with the music produced internally, empirically examining several repertories, settings, and functions. She sketches the characteristics, for example, of music of the Roma in the eastern Austrian province of Burgenland, which contains the highest percentage of Roma in any Austrian area. The article contains numerous transcriptions, with texts in Romanes and German translation. Hemetek takes a strong political position in the article, making this an outstanding example of politically engaged folk-music scholarship.

391. Jaldati, Lin, and Eberhard Robling. *Es brennt Brüder, es brennt: Jiddische Lieder.* ("It's Burning, Brother, It's Burning: Yiddish Songs"). Berlin: Rütten & Loening, 1985.

A volume of Yiddish songs representing the revival of and interest in Eastern European Jewish culture within the German Democratic Republic during its last decades. The product of a collaboration between a revivalist and a textual scholar in the GDR, the volume contains some Yiddish songs that are relatively well known (especially those with texts by Yiddish poets), but a few that are less common in Yiddish repertories in North America and Israel. The introductory essay situates Yiddish clearly in the eastern areas of Europe, therefore distancing it from Germany and orientalizing it. Insofar as Yiddish was often the language of the Jews who died in concentration camps, it serves also as an emblem of the historical struggle against fascism. Insofar as Yiddish song was the music of an oppressed working class, it forms a repertory of workers' song. The songs themselves appear in transliterated Yiddish and in a facing German translation that lends itself to being sung. Melodies for each of the songs appear at the end of the book. This format mirrors that of the Yiddish songbooks that were published in the early decades of the twentieth century and between the world wars, when German-Jews also turned toward the repertories of Eastern Europe to invent a Central European Jewish folk music. This volume, nonetheless, represents a significant attempt late in the history of the GDR to address the Jewish presence in Europe and its destruction by Germany during the Holocaust.

392. Kovalcsik, Katalin. "Die Volksmusikdialekte der transdanubischen Zigeuner." ("The Folk-Music Dialects of Trans-Danubian Gypsies"). In Walter Deutsch and Rudolf Pietsch, eds., *Dörfliche Tanzmusik im westpannonischen Raum.* Vienna: A. Schendl, 1990. Pp. 263–74.

Argues that diversity characterizes the different Gypsy communities of Hungary. Gypsies constitute Hungary's largest ethnic group, numbering approximately 400,000. This population divides into three groups, with distinctive histories and connections to other cultures and ethnic groups in the region: Hungarian Gypsies, Wallachian Gypsies, and Romanian Gypsies. Despite the adaptation of the musical styles and repertories of these groups to those of surrounding groups, they retain certain dialects that mark them not only as Gypsy, but also as communities connected to specific areas of Hungary. The folk music of Hungarian Gypsies therefore demonstrates both extraordinary adaptability and extensive ability to employ musical style and language to localize Gypsy history and culture. Kovalcsik suggests that these folk musics must be studied locally in order to determine the different paths along which they have developed. Well documented with individual pieces and numerous transcriptions. Both diachronically and synchronically, Gypsy folk music in Hungary is fundamentally multicultural.

393. Landmann, Salcia. "Das Volkslied der Juden." ("The Folk Song of the Jews"). *Jahrbuch für Volksliedforschung* 30 (1985): 93–98.

Identifies the Jewishness in folk song as its exceptional nature, that is, the ways in which Jewish folk song is unlike the folk song of any other ethnic or linguistic group. Landmann traces this unique character to the period of Talmudic learning, in which all male Jews theoretically became literate, usually using a non-vernacular language (e.g., Aramaic, and later Hebrew). Jewish folk song, according to the author, has been able to depend on a cultural context of literacy, with religious traditions of song often growing from the intensive cultivation of worship and learning. Vernacular folk song, it follows, had different sources in the Jewish community, not least among them women's musical practices. The history of Jewish folk song in the modern era intersects with such practices. Yiddish folk song, for example, grows from life in the home, or it employs the commentary of women about the pressures on Jewish society. The article privileges Yiddish folk song, embracing the categories common to collections from Eastern Europe. Landmann recognizes German influences in text structures, but Eastern European influences in melodic structures. Modern popular traditions, particularly those in North America, are viewed with caution as not always characteristically Jewish.

394. Lemm, Manfred. *Mordechaj Gebirtig: Jiddische Lieder.* ("Mordechai Gebirtig: Yiddish Songs"). Wuppertal: Edition Künstlertreff, 1992.

An edition of poems and songs by the Cracow Yiddish poet and carpenter Mordechai Gebirtig (1877–1942). Gebirtig was a prolific poet, particularly from the end of World War I until the Holocaust. Because he remained in Cracow after the Jewish quarter had been transformed into a ghetto (in fact, he was killed by German soldiers on the ghetto streets), his poetry and songs acquire special significance from the transition to ghetto and Holocaust songs. Gebirtig composed in a style consciously reminiscent of traditional Yiddish folk song. Using symbols and poetic forms common in Yiddish folk song, he created melodies for the songs in improvisatory fashion, many of them written down by his daughters or friends. As with many publications of Yiddish folk song in Germany at the end of the twentieth century, this is the product of revivalism. A folk singer and singer-songwriter, Manfred Lemm has compiled this edition from his own repertory of Gebirtig songs, a staple part of his repertory, which he arranged for different performance ensembles. The edition is also a product of Lemm's research, both into the surviving sources, particularly the collections published in Gebirtig's lifetime or shortly thereafter, and through interviews and other types of investigation in Cracow. Essays about Gebirtig, his songs, Jewish life in Cracow, and other contextual aspects open and close the volume. Most songs appear in Yiddish (with both Hebrew and Roman orthography) and in German translation, with melody and chords suggested for accompaniment. The edition represents two revivals: the revival of Yiddish song in the decades prior to the Holocaust, and the German folk-music revival at the end of the twentieth century, a revival increasingly inseparable from the performance of Jewish folk song in Central Europe.

395. Migdal, Ulrike. *Und die Musik spielt dazu: Chansons und Satiren aus dem KZ Theresienstadt.* ("And Music Was Also Playing: Chansons and Satires from the Concentration Camp Theresienstadt"). Munich: Piper, 1986.

A collection of song texts from stage and cabaret performances in the concentration camp at Theresienstadt (Terezín), in the northwestern part of what is now the Czech Republic. The Nazis created Theresienstadt as a type of "model" camp, in which the residents, almost entirely Jewish, could pursue what would appear to be normal lives to outside observers, for example, from the Red Cross. Accordingly, artistic activity of all kinds was permitted, with composers, writers, and visual artists given limited opportunities to create and to receive performances of their works. This book contains the texts of songs performed in the so-called *Freizeitgestaltung* ("leisure-time structure"), the concerts, theatrical events, and cabaret of the camp. The texts of the songs are deeply ironic, many of them clearly cognizant of the future that lay before those interned in Theresienstadt; most were taken to death camps, especially to Auschwitz, where they were murdered. The cabaret tradition, nonetheless, connects the Jewish musical traditions to the urban musical cultures of the late nineteenth and early twentieth century, in which Jewish contributions substantially transformed and modernized the contexts of popular music. These songs, therefore, are not simply documents representing the final moments before destruction in the Holocaust, but narrations of the ways in which Jews in Central Europe used popular-music traditions to articulate a contested history of interaction with non-Jewish European society. Further contextualizing the song texts are selected reviews and commentaries by critics and musicians in Theresienstadt, such as Gideon Klein and Kurt Singer.

396. Nettl, Paul. *Alte jüdische Spielleute und Musiker.* ("Early Jewish Minstrels and Musicians"). Prague: Josef Flesch, 1923.

A classic early study of Jewish musicians in early modern Europe, which is more often cited than read. Nettl does not concern himself here with klezmer musicians, as many have claimed, but rather (1) with the musical activities of Jewish composers in northern Italy, particularly Salomone de Rossi in Mantua and musicians associated with Venice; and (2) with evidence about secular Jewish music-making in northern Europe, particularly Frankfurt and Prague, during the seventeenth and eighteenth centuries. Published in 1923, the book suggests new possibilities for thinking about the Jewishness in European music by considering the social position of Jews in European society. Nettl integrated new research by Abraham Zvi Idelsohn into his evidence, whereby he made the book important for contemporary research into Jewish music. The musical examples in the text and appendices, as well as the documents concerning Jewish musicians in public ceremony, make the book valuable for modern scholarship on Jewish music in Europe.

397. Olsvanger, Immanuel. *Rosinkess mit Mandlen: Aus der Volksliteratur der Ostjuden.* ("Raisins with Almonds: From the Folk Literature of the Eastern Jews"). 2nd printing. Basel: Verlag der Schweizerischen Gesellschaft für Volkskunde, 1931. 3rd printing (facsimile). Zurich: Verlag der Arche, 1965.

An anthology of folklore from Eastern European, Yiddish-speaking Jews, compiled through a commission from the Swiss Folklore Society. The fieldwork for these collections took place in Switzerland, when Eastern European Jews were in the process of emigrating from Europe, primarily to the United States during the decades after World War I; the collection also drew upon previously published material in Yiddish. The volume opens with an introduction, in which Olsvanger situates Yiddish folk culture in the small city (i.e., *shtetl*), thereby giving it an urban context. This urban context provides the theoretical perspective for the book, as the subtitle with its juxtaposition of folk culture and literacy, clearly makes evident. Most of the volume consists of transliterated stories, legends, and song texts (with two transcribed melodies). To make the Yiddish easier to understand, Olsvanger makes extensive use of footnotes and includes an excellent glossary. Folk songs make up an important component in the collection, the main title for which comes from a well-known lullaby, which, after this publication, would be one of the most important ghetto songs during the Holocaust. The emphasis on urban folklore, moreover, allows this collection to show the ways in which Yiddish culture responded to the world around Eastern European Jewish communities, also by absorbing Slavic folklore and texts. An extremely important case of the growing recognition of the diversity of European Jewish culture in the decades between the world wars.

398. Perez, L. "Judendeutsche Volkslieder aus Russland." ("Jewish-German Folk Songs from Russia"). *Am-Urquell: Eine Monatsschrift für Volkskunde* (New Series 2) (1898): 27–29.

Extensively annotated texts of six Yiddish (still referred to as "Judendeutsch" in German at the end of the nineteenth century) folk songs. *Am-Urquell* was a folklore journal that appeared first in the 1890s, and its contents characterized what today would be called *europäische Ethnologie* ("European ethnology"). There are several articles, therefore, that concern themselves with Jewish folklore and customs, and together these document a moment of growing interest in Jewish culture as a component of a larger European cultural area. The songs in this article appear in transliteration, although some original Yiddish terms in the Hebrew alphabet appear in the annotations. One of the first publications of Yiddish folk song for German-speaking readers, Perez's article became one of the most important sources for later anthologies of Jewish folk song and for the study of European Jewish culture in general.

399. Reinhard, Ursula. "Türkische Musik: Ihre Interpreten in West-Berlin und in der Heimat—Ein Vergleich." ("Turkish Music: Its Interpreters in West Berlin and in the Homeland—A Comparison"). *Jahrbuch für Volksliedforschung* 32 (1987): 81–92.

A comparison of the transformation of music in Turkish guest-worker neighborhoods and social settings in West Berlin and in Turkey, largely in the rural areas research by the author and her husband, Kurt Reinhard. Five areas of change are systematically investigated: musical life; contents of musical ensembles; nature of the musician's activities; music in context; and music itself. In West Berlin music-making in all areas differed substantially from that in Turkey, where many of the repertories, combinations of instruments, and individual pieces themselves would have been unlikely, given the different social contexts. Concerts combined repertories from different regions in Turkey, drew from genres that did not belong together, and took place in social contexts that did not exist prior to immigration. Musical professionalism, relegated to certain social classes and ethnic groups in Turkey, became more widespread and egalitarian in Berlin. Despite such changes, Reinhard asserts that the future of Turkish music in Berlin will be richer for the new possibilities Turkish musicians have created.

400. Salmen, Walter. *"...denn die Fiedel macht das Fest": Jüdische Musikanten und Tänzer vom 13. bis 20. Jahrhundert.* ("'...For the Fiddle Makes the Celebration': Jewish Musicians and Dancers from the Thirteenth to Twentieth Century"). Innsbruck: Edition Helbling, 1991.

An extraordinarily detailed historical account of *klezmer* music in Central and East Central Europe. Mustering remarkable archival accounts and fifty illustrations, Salmen demonstrates that Jewish instrumental musicians were present in Europe at least since the Middle Ages. Not only was their presence in different forms of secular music-making much more complex than previously known, but Jewish instrumental musicians may have contributed substantially to a core of European Jewish culture. A major revision of the book is to illustrate the significance of dance in the Jewish community. Salmen examines documents that reveal the presence of dance halls near the center of Jewish quarters in cities and villages. The book surveys basic concepts of Jewish music and culture, particularly as these are relevant to attitudes toward music. Jewish instrumental musicians and dancers, here, remain anchored to folk traditions, with related popular (e.g., dramatic) or religious (e.g., the role of the cantor) traditions touched upon briefly. Salmen's folk historiography, therefore, relies on a continuity that he endeavors to illustrate by filling in the gaps with details and myriad accounts, and by connecting the history of *klezmer* to modern revivals in North America and Europe. The best single account of Jewish secular music in Europe.

401. Sárosi, Bálint. *Zigeunermusik*. ("Gypsy Music"). Trans. from Hungarian into German by Imre Ormay and Christian Kaden. Zurich: Atlantis, 1977.

A monographic study of Gypsy music from Hungarian perspective and within Hungarian social and historical contexts. Sárosi considers Gypsy music as taking place in many different settings, and it therefore develops the necessary stylistic flexibility to be adapted to those settings. Accordingly, Gypsy music is not one kind or genre of music, but many, thereby making it impossible to designate any one style or repertory as Gypsy. Sárosi surveys musical repertories according to genre and social function, beginning with folk music, then considering different types of nineteenth-century popular music, and concluding with musics that reflect the working conditions to which Gypsy music-making is connected. The methodology is that of Hungarian folk-music scholarship, in which the structure of music expresses ethnic and national identity. The structures examined here, nonetheless, are those used by Hungarian scholarship (e.g., transposition and tempo distinctions), which produces analyses in which Gypsy music is measured by its relation to Hungarian music. Because Sárosi recognizes no unifying style or repertory, identity is also problematic for him; Gypsy music necessarily raises problems of hybridity and "contamination." The book contains excellent documentation and many illustrations; it also makes thorough use of the many transcribed examples, therefore making it an excellent source for comparative study of different styles and genres.

402. Ssabanejew, Leonid. *Die nationale jüdische Schule in der Musik.* ("The National Jewish School in Music"). Vienna: Universal-Edition, 1927.

Published as a translation from Russian in "Collection Jibneh-Juwal," a series devoted entirely to Jewish music, this essay examines the history of a consciously Jewish music in Europe during the late nineteenth and early twentieth century. Ssabanejew establishes several stages in the development of a "national music," whereby he means a composed music, which nonetheless explicitly contains a vocabulary of folk-music traits. The history of a national music begins with a folk-melos, that is, folk melodies that reflect the cultural and historical unity of a people. The folk-melos not only shapes a characteristic body of folk music, hence connecting a people to its distinctive history, but shapes the styles and functions of art music. Ssabanejew argues that a Jewish national music began in late-nineteenth-century Russia as composers responded to the collections of folk songs. The Russian "schools of composition and folk song," then, disseminated their influences throughout Europe, and it was this influence that was particularly palpable in an emerging community of composers in Central Europe and in the international impact of their music in North America and Palestine. Conceived as a manifesto for recognizing Jewish music in Central Europe, this essay was further influential through its historicization in the final years before the Nazi ascension to power in Germany.

INDEX

Accordion, 71, 84-85
Adamek, Karl, 283
Adler, Guido, 270
Adorno, Theodor W., 16, 115, 167-68
Aerophone, 80-81
Aesthetics, 22, 55, 93, 146, 156, 159, 234, 248, 259
Ahrens, Christian, 55, 159
Akdemir, Hayrettin, 283
Alberta, 216
Alpine. *See* Alps
Alps, 6, 10, 13, 15, 25, 38-41, 52, 56, 71, 83, 116-17, 173, 177, 189, 210, 235, 241-42, 261
Alsace-Lorraine, 4, 9, 23, 90, 133, 224, 230, 234, 236-37, 253, 273
"Alten Lieder, die," 196
Altmark, 240
Amish, 25, 202, 213-14, 217, 221
Amman, Jakob, 213
Andersen, Flemming G., 141
Anglo-American folk music, 9; popular music, 17
Ankenbrand, Stephan, 51
Annotated bibliography, xi, xiii-xiv, xxi-xxii, 62, 109
Antesberger, Günther, 249
Anthologies, xix, 11, 16, 22, 33, 38, 41, 53, 135, 188, 210, 223, 237, 255, 265, 267, 271, 282, 286, 294
Anthropology, ix, 107, 114, 122-23, 126, 142, 146-47, 150, 276-77
Antonicek, Theophil, 219, 285
Arbeiterliedarchiv, 22

Armistead, Samuel G., 140
Arnim, Achim von, 33, 50, 87, 253, 267, 269
Art music, xix, 4-6, 11, 27, 61, 64, 66, 69, 72-75, 77-78, 83-84, 99, 124, 129, 137-38, 143-44, 153, 157-58, 168, 175, 178, 184-85, 200, 243, 256, 259, 265, 271, 274-75, 289
Âsik, 98-99
Assafiev, Boris, 114
Assimilation, 202, 211, 220
Assion, Peter, 152, 154, 248-50
Au, Hans von der, 133-34
August, Ferdinand, 269
Auschwitz, 35, 293
Austria, x, xiii, xvii, xviii, xx, 6, 15, 17, 19-20, 23, 25, 29, 34, 38-43, 50, 52, 93-94, 106, 110-13, 116-17, 120, 123, 125-26, 129, 131-33, 135-36, 146, 163, 165, 176-77, 181, 191, 199, 202, 206-7, 220, 224-25, 228, 230, 232, 235, 243, 248-49, 255-56, 260-61, 266, 268, 270, 277, 281-82, 289-90
Austro-Hungarian Empire. *See* Habsburg Monarchy
Authenticity, 50, 72
Azerbaijan, 99

Bach, J.S., 144, 192, 198
Bachmann, Eugen, 214
Bachmann-Geiser, Brigitte, 71, 214
Baden-Württemberg, 84, 180, 190, 238

299

History: field of scholarship, xii-
xiii, xix, 202; past of a nation
or region, xvii, 9, 15, 18, 22,
33, 41, 79, 87-90, 105, 113,
129, 134, 142, 154, 156-57,
165-66, 168-69, 180-82, 188,
192, 195, 201, 207, 209, 211,
213, 216, 223, 227, 229, 235,
237, 242-43, 272, 282, 289,
291, 297; of a piece or
repertory of music, 19-20, 35,
54, 61, 66-67, 71, 73-74, 107,
137, 143-44, 146-47, 163, 168,
193-94, 199, 205-6, 215, 222-
24, 247-64, 287
Hit song. *See Schlager*
Hochdeutsch. See High German
Hoerburger, Felix, 5, 28, 55, 61,
78, 112, 159, 161
Hofer, Gerlinde. *See* Haid,
Gerlinde
Hoffmann, Freia, 178-79
Hoffmann von Fallersleben,
Heinrich, 227, 253
Hoffmann-Krayer, Eduard, 266,
268
Hollós, Ludwig, 205
Holocaust, xiv, 45, 151, 282, 285,
287-89, 291-94
Holzach, Michael, 216
Holzapfel, Otto, 9, 43, 51, 89-90,
109, 134-36, 154, 160, 216-17,
221, 227, 230, 239, 266, 271-
73
Horak, Karl, 133, 136, 140, 146,
160, 184, 220, 225, 229, 234-
35
Hörandner, Edith, 152
Hornbostel, Erich M. von, 69-70,
76, 80-82, 121, 209, 241, 277
"Horst-Wessel-Lied," 228
Hucke, Helmut, 155
Hummer, Hermann, 174, 179
Hungary, xix, 40, 58, 64, 67, 81,
134, 141, 154, 168, 203, 205-7,
212, 215, 224, 290-91
Hurdy-gurdy, 72, 74-75
Hutterites, 25, 202, 215-16, 218,
219
Hymn, 213, 215-16, 218, 238

Hymnbook, 25-26, 213, 215, 218-
19
Hymnody, 216, 222, 288

Idelsohn, A.Z., 44-45, 87, 96, 260,
277, 293
Identity: ascribed through folk
song, xi, xix-xx, xxii, 5, 15, 50-
51, 53-54, 64-65, 107, 129,
142, 168-69, 187, 191, 201-2,
207, 223-24, 227, 237-38, 259-
60, 266, 269, 276, 281, 283,
286, 289, 290, 296
Ideology: in folk-music
scholarship, xii, xiv, xviii, xx-
xxi, 9, 16, 18, 21, 23, 29, 34-
35, 37-38, 42, 46, 48, 65, 85,
95, 125-26, 128-29, 133, 139,
144, 187-89, 194-95, 198-200,
202, 210, 224, 232, 235, 248,
266, 270
Idiophone, 71, 80-81
Immigrant group, 187, 192, 247,
281-97
Immigration, xiv, 27, 201, 217-18,
220-21, 295
Improvisation, 71-72
Indiana, 214
INFOLK, 106, 112-13
Innsbruck, 117
Institute for Folk-Music Research
(Austria), 70, 110, 129, 268
Institutionalization, 29, 37, 42,
84, 128, 187-200, 225, 241
Instrument: folk music, 69-85,
112, 167, 178, 181-82, 241,
250, 260-61, 295
Instrumental music, 69-85, 106,
112, 121, 128, 132, 154, 175,
189-95, 202, 215, 217, 220,
226, 231, 241, 256, 276, 286,
296
Intellectual history, xi, xiv, xviii,
xx-xxii, 17, 21-22, 36, 39, 41,
49, 80, 87, 95, 115-16, 119,
121, 126, 133, 135-37, 139,
149-51, 153, 155-56, 176, 182,
221, 230, 233, 236, 240, 251,
254, 265-79, 281, 286

Political songs, 7, 18-24, 35, 42, 58, 179-80, 182, 196
Politics, xi, xx-xxi, 3-4, 9, 18-20, 22, 26, 85, 124-26, 163, 199, 223, 230, 237, 252-54, 266
Pollack, Martin, 168
Polyphony: in folk song, 39, 41, 43, 56, 62, 66-67, 71, 74, 111, 116, 160, 176, 178, 212, 243, 254, 274
Pomerania, 49, 214
Pommer, Josef, 39, 110, 116, 125-26, 130-32, 135-36, 146, 174-76, 187, 226, 240, 266, 270
Popular music, xix, 4-5, 13-18, 39, 47, 49, 61, 72, 78, 83-84, 94, 110, 119, 121-22, 124, 145, 156, 164, 167-69, 175, 177, 180-81, 183, 185, 200, 211, 217, 220, 231, 239, 244, 256, 263, 265-66, 271, 276, 285-86, 293, 296
Popular song. *See* Popular music
Porter, James, x, 121
Postmodernism, 71-72, 155, 165, 213, 266
Potthoff, Wilfried, 91
Pöttler, Burkhard, 152
Practices: cultural, xiii, 25, 70, 82, 85, 119-20, 166, 206, 211, 242, 261, 268, 272
Prague, 114, 293
Print technology, 15-16, 26, 43, 97, 100, 181, 183, 256, 275
Probst, Guntram, 193
Probst-Effah, Gisela, 117
Professional folk musicians, xvii, 45, 128-29, 160, 175, 180, 182-85, 188, 194, 249, 262, 295
Public sphere, 8, 22, 30, 34, 84-85, 91, 125, 157, 165-66, 169, 182, 225, 263, 285
Puchner, Walter, 88, 92, 98, 118, 140
Pulikowski, Julian von, 265, 275
Purity: in folk music, 16

Quatrain. *See Vierzeiler*
Quellmalz, Fred, 8

Race, xiv, 65
Racism: in folk-music scholarship, xiv, xxi, 65-66, 126, 136, 138, 177-78, 194, 258, 270, 279
Rajeczky, Benjamin, 64
Ramstedt, Martin, 123
Raupp, Jan, 174, 181-82
Reckow, Fritz, 158
Reder, Veronika, 239
Reformation, 8, 25, 41, 183, 215, 218, 256, 288
Regionalism, xiv, xix-xx, 3-4, 7, 9, 12-16, 34, 39, 41, 43, 49, 51, 57-58, 60, 73, 89-90, 121, 131-32, 177, 223-44, 247, 265, 284
Reilig, Renate, 168
Reinhard, Kurt, 5, 28, 55, 61-62, 98-99, 108, 159, 282, 295
Reinhard, Ursula, 98-99, 282, 295
Reinhardt, Django, 290
Reischach, 25
Reiser, Tobi, 111, 176
Reiterits, Anton, 173, 182
Reith, Dirk, 118
Related disciplines: as compared to folk-music research, ix
Religion, xi, 281, 284
Religious folk music, 3, 5, 24-26, 66, 191, 203-4, 207, 213-22, 236, 240, 271, 281-97
Renaissance, 73, 75, 158, 185, 192, 240, 256, 275
Repertory, 3, 6, 12, 27, 29, 36-39, 43, 45-47, 51, 54-55, 57, 59-60, 63-66, 70-71, 75, 77, 82, 88, 91-92, 94, 99-100, 118, 121, 125, 130-32, 142, 144-45, 162, 164, 174-76, 178-79, 181, 185, 188-94, 196, 198, 202, 204, 206-7, 210-11, 213-17, 219-23, 229, 231, 233-34, 237, 239, 241-42, 248-49, 252-53, 255-56, 259, 261, 268-69, 272, 276, 278-79, 282, 285-86, 289-90, 292, 296
Representation, 7, 47-48, 55, 59, 93, 100, 184, 214, 254

Made in the USA
Las Vegas, NV
06 December 2021